Islamic Economics Series – 14

Economic Functions of an Islamic State

(The Early Experience)

S. M. HASANUZ ZAMAN

The Islamic Foundation

First edition, International Islamic Publishers, Karachi, 1981

ISBN 0 86037 201 4 (Hardback)
ISBN 0 86037 202 2 (Paperback)

Cover design: Anwar Cara

Published by
The Islamic Foundation,
Markfield Dawah Centre,
Ratby Lane,
Markfield,
Leicester LE6 0RN
United Kingdom

Quran House,
P.O. Box 30611,
Nairobi,
Kenya

P.M.B. 3193
Kano,
Nigeria

British Library Cataloguing in Publication Data
Hasanuz Zaman, S. M.
Economic functions of an Islamic state: (the early experience). – (Islamic economics series v.14)
1. Islamic economics
I. title II. Series
330917671

ISBN 0–86037–201–4
ISBN 0–86037–202–2 pbk

Contents

Creed and Islamic Economics – The Moral Fibre – The
Concept of Ownership – The Concept of Lawful/Unlawful –
The Concept of *'Adl* and *Iḥsān* – The Concept of Opulence –
The Ethics and Rules of Farming – Trade: Principles and
Practices – Consumption and Savings – The Concept of *Infāq*:
The First Duty, the Last Resort – *Zakāt* – *Ghanīma, Fay'*, *Jizya*
– Interest and Loans – The Functions of an Islamic State – The
Functionaries of the Government – The Attitude Towards
Labour.

Land: The Pre-Islamic Practice – Allotment of Land by the
Prophet – During the Pious Caliphate – The Considerations
and the Terms of Allotment – The Ownership of Conquered
Lands – Limitations to Ownership – Regulation of Other
Economic Activities – Price Controls.

The Concept of the *Bayt al-Māl* – The *Bayt al-Māl* During the
Prophet's Time – The Resources of the Prophet's Madina –
The Role of Voluntary *Ṣadaqa* – Other Sources of Income

During the Prophet's Time – Caliph Abū Bakr's *Bayt al-Māl* – The Early Heads of Expenditure.

– The Person of Muqawqis – The Terms of the Treaty – The Population of Alexandria and Egypt – Pre-Islamic Taxes – Collection of Taxes During the Islamic Period – The Issue of the Non-Muslim Officials – Administrative Set-Up.

PART III: ECONOMIC INDICATORS

ABBREVIATIONS

Abu Daud	Abū Dā'ūd, *Sunan.*
Abu Daud (U)	Urdu Edition of Abū Dā'ūd.
A.C.J.	Johnson, *Egypt & the Roman Empire.*
Ag.	Aghnides, *Muhammedan Theories of Finance.*
Agh.	al-Aṣbahānī, *Kitāb al-Aghānī.*
A.S.	Abū Ṣāliḥ, *Churches and Monasteries of Egypt.*
Athir	Ibn al-Athīr, *Tā'rīkh.*
A.U.	Abū 'Ubayd, *Kitāb al-Amwāl.*
Bal.	al-Balādhurī, *Futūḥ al-Buldān.*
Bukh.	al-Bukhārī, *Ṣaḥīḥ.*
Bukh. (U)	Urdu Edition of al-Bukhārī.
But.	Butler, *The Arab Conquest of Egypt.*
Cheikho	al-Yasū'ī, *Shu'arā' an-Naṣrāniyya.*
—— (Adab)	*an-Naṣrāniyya wa Adabuhā.*
Denn.	Dennett, *Conversion and the Poll-Tax in Early Islam.*
Dh. (Ibar)	adh-Dhahabī, *Al 'Ibar. . .*
Dh. (Ṭar)	adh-Dhahabī, *Tā'rīkh.*
E.I. I	*Encyclopaedia of Islam,* Old edition.
E.I. II	*Encyclopaedia of Islam,* New edition.
Gibbon	Gibbon, *The History of the Decline and Fall of the Roman Empire.*
I.A.H.	Ibn 'Abd al-Ḥakam, *Futūḥ Ifrīqiyya . . .*
I.A.H. (M)	Ibn 'Abd al-Ḥakam, *Futūḥ Miṣr.*
I.A.H. (U)	Ibn 'Abd al-Ḥakam, *Sīra 'Umar b. 'Abd al-'Azīz.*
Ibn Ṭayfur	Ibn Ṭayfūr, *Kitāb Baghdād.*
I.F.	Ibn al-Faqīh, *Kitāb al-Buldān.*
I.H.	Ibn Ḥawqal, *Kitāb al-Masālik wa'l-Mamālik.*
I.K.	Ibn Khurdādhbih, *Kitāb al-Masālik wa'l-Mamālik.*
Ist.	al-Iṣṭakhrī, *Masālik al-Mamālik.*
J.G.M.	Milne, *A History of Egypt.*
J.M.H.	Hussey, ed., *The Cambridge Medieval History.*
J. and W.	Johnson and West, *Byzantine Egypt – Economic Studies.*
Jahs.	al-Jahshiyārī, *Kitāb al-wuzarā' wa'l-Kuttāb.*
Kath.	Ibn Kathīr, *al-Bidāya wa'n-Nihāya.*
Khal.	Ibn Khaldūn, *Ta'rīkh.*
Khalifa	Ibn Khayyāṭ, *Ta'rīkh.*
Kh.	Abū Yūsuf, *Kitāb al-Kharāj.*
Kharbutli	al-Kharbūṭlī, *Ta'rīkh al-'Irāq.*

Kindi	al-Kindī, *Kitāb al-Wulāt wa'l-Quḍāt.*
Lestr.	Le Strange, *Palestine Under the Muslims.*
Lok.	Løkkegaard, *Islamic Taxation in the Classic Period.*
Maj.	Ibn Māja, *Sunan.*
Maj. (U)	Urdu Edition of Ibn Māja.
M.B.Y.	Muḥammad b. Yaḥyā, *at-Tamhīd wa'l-Bayān.*
Maq. (Im)	al-Maqrīzī, *Imtā'al-Asmā'.*
Maq. (Kh)	al-Maqrīzī, *al-Mawā'iẓ wa'l-I'tibār.*
Maq. (Nuqud)	al-Maqrīzī, *ān-Nuqūd al-Islāmiyya.*
Mas.	al-Mas'ūdī, *Murūj adh-Dhahab.*
Maw.	al-Māwardī, *al-Aḥkām as-Sulṭāniyya.*
Muq.	al-Muqaddasī, *Aḥsan at-Taqāsīm.*
Mus.	Muslim, *Ṣaḥīḥ.*
Mus. (U)	Urdu Edition of Muslim.
Naji	Ma'rūf Nājī, *'Urūba al-Mudun al-Islāmiyya.*
Naqsh.	an-Naqshbandī, *ad-Dīnār al-Islāmī.*
Nas.	an-Nasā'ī, *Sunan.*
Nas. (U)	Urdu Edition of Nasā'ī.
Ostr.	Ostrogorsky, *History of the Byzantine State.*
Patr. Or. 8	*Patrologia Orientalis,* Vol. 8.
Patr. Or. 13	*Patrologia Orientalis,* Vol. 13.
Qud.	Qudāma, *Kitāb al-Kharāj.*
Qut.	ad-Dīnawrī, *'Uyūn al-Akhbār.*
S.A.E.	Ṣāleḥ Aḥmad Elali, *History of Baṣra.*
Scr. Ar. VII	Patriarch Sa'īd (Eutychius), *Annales.*
S.L.P.	Stanley Lane-Poole, *History of Egypt.*
S.L.P. (Coins)	Stanley Lane-Poole, *Coins and Medals.*
Sad.	Ibn Sa'd, *aṭ-Ṭabaqāt.*
Severus	Severus b. al-Muqaffa', *Historia Patriarcharum.*
Shafi	ash-Shāfi'ī, *Musnad.*
Sira	Ibn Hishām, *Sīra.*
Sti.	as-Suyūṭī, *Ta'rīkh al-Khulafā.*
Sykes	Sir Percy Sykes, *A History of Persia.*
Tab.	aṭ-Ṭabarī, *Ta'rīkh.*
Tir.	at-Tirmīdhī, *as-Sunan.*
Tir. (U)	Urdu Edition of Tirmīdhī.
Waq.	al-Wāqidī, *Maghāzī.*
Watt (Medina)	W.M. Watt, *Muḥammad at Medina.*
Watt (Prophet)	*Muḥammad, Prophet and Statesman.*
Well.	Wellhausen, *The Arab Kingdom and its Fall.*
Yah.	Yaḥyā b. Ādam, *Kitāb al-Kharāj.*
Yaq.	Ibn Wāḍiḥ, *Ta'rīkh.*
Yaq. (B)	Ibn Wāḍiḥ, *K. al-Buldān.*

MAPS AND TABLES

Maps

Tables

Foreword

If contemporary Islamic resurgence has given to the Muslims a fresh realization of their identity, a sense of pride in their past and a new confidence about their future, it has also generated a host of challenges for the intellectuals and the policy-makers. One such challenge relates to the economic role of the state in a contemporary Muslim society. The question has become all the more challenging in the context of the changing role of the state, both in contemporary capitalist societies where the rise of the welfare state and the mixed economy have transformed beyond recognition the traditional capitalist vision of a *laissez-faire* economy, and the socialist world where structural changes are taking place under the banner of *perestroika* and which, if taken to their logical conclusion, may fundamentally change the role of the state in a socialist society. At a time like this it is instructive for the Muslims to re-examine their own sources, both textual as well as historical, to have a deeper understanding of the golden mean that Islam has tried to strike between individualism and collectivism.

Dr. Hasanuz Zaman has addressed himself to this challenging task, researching and reflecting upon this for the last two decades. He has scanned most of the historical sources to recreate the mosaic of *Bayt al-Māl* in the early Islamic experience: the model Islamic state of Madina, during the time of the Prophet (peace be upon him) and the *Khulafā' al-Rāshidūn,* the Rightly-Guided Caliphate.

Basic research was undertaken in the University of Edinburgh where the author was awarded a Ph.D for this work. He has continued his researches ever since as Head of the Islamic Research Unit of the State Bank of Pakistan and as a member of the Council of Islamic Ideology, a constitutional body to help the Government and Parliament of Pakistan to Islamize the society.

An earlier edition of the book was published from Pakistan in 1981 and had a limited circulation. Now a revised version is being published by the Islamic Foundation in its series on Islamic Economics. Dr. Hasanuz Zaman has thoroughly revised the first part of the book. The first chapter is in fact a fresh contribution delineating the essential features of an Islamic economic system and as such providing a theoretical basis for the historical investigations that form the main part of the book. The work in its present form, represents, in my opinion, a most thorough and systematic exposition on the institution of *Bayt al-Māl* in early Islam, and the role of the state in the economic field.

This study, on the one hand, spells out the theoretical foundations and intellectual and spiritual moorings of the Islamic economic approach, and on the other, reconstructs with meticulous care and scientific rigour the essential institutions and critical elements of the early historical expression of Islam, insofar as it demonstrates the economic role played by the state under the Prophet (peace be upon him) and the Rightly-Guided Caliphate. While the author has not made a direct effort to relate this experience to the working of a contemporary Muslim state, he has provided enough theoretical guidance and historical experience for the present-day Muslim economist and policy-maker to draw upon these rich resources to formulate policy guidelines for the present. This work will be acknowledged as a valuable addition to the literature on Islamic economics currently being produced by Muslim economists. I hope it may provoke others to explore the many challenging areas of the public economies of Islam that call for further research and innovative reflection.

Khurshid Ahmad

Leicester
September, 1990
Safar, 1411

Preface to the Second Edition

The present edition contains a completely revised version of Chapter 1, 'The Economic Teachings of the Qur'ān', and Chapter 2, 'The Economic Teachings of the *Ḥadīth*', now consolidated into a single chapter, 'The Essentials of the Islamic Economic System'. It is now a self-contained and comprehensive paper presenting at a glance the basic concepts and principles of the Islamic Economic System as are derivable from the Qur'ān and the *Sunna*. Readers are reminded that this revised version is confined to the text of the Qur'ān and *Ḥadīth* and does not touch upon the juristic details which were later on worked out by great Muslim thinkers.

The first edition of the book was a reproduction of the original dissertation with only minor changes. This edition has been thoroughly edited incorporating linguistic and stylistic improvements. It also contains a Foreword by Professor Khurshid Ahmad, Chairman of the Islamic Foundation.

The draft of the first edition was prepared at Edinburgh, Scotland with the help of the books in the Edinburgh University Library. The revisions and additions have been made in Pakistan where different editions of the books on *Ḥadīth* had to be relied upon. Thus readers will sometimes find two different abbreviations of the same title. The Bibliography will guide the reader should any problems arise in this respect.

I am very grateful to all those who have kindly made suggestions for improving the work and I welcome further help of this kind. My very special thanks are due to the technical editor Mr. E. R. Fox for a very thorough re-editing of the book. My thanks are also due to my colleague Mr. M. Sharif for his valuable assistance in promptly locating the references in the Pakistani editions of source books which I have used in this edition. My thanks are also due to Mr. Furqan Ali who has taken great pains in typing the manuscript of Chapter 1, cleanly and with diacritical marks on an ordinary typewriter.

August, 1990
Muharram, 1411

S. M. Hasanuz Zaman

Preface to the First Edition

This book is based on my dissertation entitled 'Economic Functions of the Islamic State – To the End of the Umayyad Period' which I submitted to Edinburgh University in 1973 for the degree of Ph.D.

In view of the increasingly widespread interest in the subject, not confined to Pakistan, kindled by the desire of the Muslims in many countries to reconstruct their socio-economic life in light of their heritage, the manuscript is being published. Advantage has been taken of this opportunity to revise and enlarge certain portions of the draft to make it more informative and comprehensive.

Of the numerous difficulties with which one has to contend in the course of working in this field, not least is the paucity of properly constructed and analysed material on the subject. This naturally involves one in going to the original sources for the collection of material and then presenting its analysis in light of the overall system of Islam. As an early attempt on the subject, it will perhaps leave much to be desired yet I hope it may provide the background and material for a more comprehensive subsequent work on the subject.

The focal point of the economic functions of the Islamic State is the institution of the *Bayt al-Māl,* the exchequer, and many of the early writers have discussed all the sources of income and the heads of expenditure under the common title of *amwāl* or *kharāj.* Books on *Ḥadīth* and law have treated the subject of the *Bayt al-Māl* under different headings: *Ghanīma, Khums, Zakāt, Jizya, Kharāj* and extra-religious taxes.

The report that the Prophet (peace be upon him) had a writing prepared on *Zakāt, Kitāb aṣ-Ṣadaqa,* for circulation among the *Zakāt-*collectors and the tribal chiefs suggests that the literature on the subject dates back to the earliest period of Islam, possibly to 8 A.H. Portions of the writing are to be found in compilations on *Ḥadīth* and in books of history. This is in addition to those documents which were reportedly sent by the Prophet (peace be upon him) in the form of letters to different Arab princes and tribal chiefs and which generally discussed their financial obligations to the Islamic State.

Specialized works on the different heads of the *Bayt al-Māl* were written during the period when books on *Ḥadīth* and history were compiled. A. Ben Shamesh, in his introduction to the English translation of Yaḥyā's *Kitāb al-Kharāj* has picked out twenty-one books which are known to have been written on the subject during the first 400 years. But this list is confined to those books which bear the title of *al-Kharāj*. Books on the same subject with other names have not been included in it. Most important of such works are those to be found under the title of *al-Amwāl,* the earliest available being Abū 'Ubayd's (d. 244 A.H.) *Kitāb al-Amwāl.* Material relevant to this study is also to be found in books on geography, politics, administration, literature and, in particular, history. This study is primarily based on the published works of Balādhurī, Ṭabarī, Ya'qūbī, Abū Yūsuf, Abū 'Ubayd and Yaḥyā. Their authenticity can be judged when they are supplemented by other classical sources on early history. The works of some patristic writers serve as complementary material and help in clearing up many confusions. The Greek Papyri, although fragmentary and inconclusive, are by far the best documentary evidence.

Of late some studies have been made by Western scholars with a view to re-examining the validity of terminological interpretations of *Jizya* and *Kharāj.* Among them Frede Løkkegaard's *Islamic Taxation in the Classic Period* is the latest book to suggest this approach while D.C. Dennett, in his *Conversion and the Poll-Tax in Early Islam* does not appear to agree with this point of view. Løkkegaard's temptation to criticize as many points in the different stories and narrations as possible has made his work less useful than it might otherwise have been. Dennett has, on some points at least, over-advocated the early Muslim sources, but on the whole has maintained balance and usefulness.

The subject of this book is historical not theoretical. That is why juristic interpretations of the early institutions which developed later on have not been included. I had to content myself with what the reliable historians have recorded about the period. Though many such early practices would seem to be irreconcilable with the later juristic standards, the fact is that they were practised as they are recorded. Sometimes doubts are raised regarding the validity of some of the practices adopted during the Umayyad period, but it should not be forgotten that this period was distinguished by jurists like Ibn 'Abbās, Ibn 'Umar, Sa'īd b. al-Musayyib, Sulaymān b. Yasār, Abū Bakr b. 'Abd ar-Raḥmān, 'Ikrima, 'Aṭā' b. Abū Ribāḥ, 'Urwa b. Zubayr and Ibn Shihāb az-Zuhrī.

The scope of the present study is to try to discover what was really practised and also what ideas the practice was based upon.

In conclusion I would like to acknowledge my indebtedness to the State Bank of Pakistan for granting me study leave without which this research could not have been undertaken. Though the Bank has financed me it does not necessarily share the views expressed in this study. I must also thank my brother, Dr. Zafar Ishaq Ansari for his useful comments, suggestions and criticism on the manuscript which helped me to significantly improve it. However, he must be absolved of responsibility for any errors in substance, expositions or conclusions; I am solely responsible for everything that is contained in it, and only hope that its utility outweighs its shortcomings. I am also grateful to brother Naeemuddin, Architect, for his work on the maps included in the book.

1 Ramaḍān, 1401 **S. M. Hasanuz Zaman**
July, 1981

PART I

FOUNDATIONS

CHAPTER 1

The Essentials of The Islamic Economic System

No important sphere of human activity can be singled out as exempt from Divine Guidance. What is not hinted at in the Divine Guidance is not essentially important and is left to guided human discretion. Thus the questions as to the means of living, the principles of earning wealth, the heads and the range of expenditure, the limits of satisfying wants, the balancing of the effort of individuals with the community's interest, the regulation of the community's jurisdiction so that it is conducive to healthy development of the individual, are all guided by fundamental injunctions and principles. These principles are laid down in the Qur'ān and in the *Sunna* of the Prophet (peace be upon him) as contained in the *Ḥadīth*[1], and form the basis of the economic life of the individual and the community, even though they are not therein elaborated into a system. It is on these principles, as interpreted by the Prophet's Companions and the later jurists and commentators, that the edifice of the economic life of the individual is built and the economic objectives and functions of an Islamic state determined. Even the injunctions that seem to have a moral as distinct from a legal character have far-reaching economic implications and involve both the individual and the state. For example, the Qur'ānic injunctions prohibiting alcoholic drinks, as interpreted by the Prophet (peace be upon him), make it unlawful for the Muslims to enter into this trade, and for an Islamic state to patronize this industry. This has a significant impact on the industrial and fiscal policies of an Islamic state in the sense that this industry can be monopolized exclusively by the non-Muslims and may, under some situations, enjoy exemption from excise levies.

Creed and Islamic Economics

The basic creed that promotes Islamic economic behaviour evolves from the Islamic concept of God, Allah, with the attributes ascribed to

Him. Thus acknowledging of Him the attribute *Al-Mālik* (the absolute Owner of all) or *Al-Raḥīm* (who gives blessings and prosperity, particularly to those who use these gifts as He has permitted) contributes towards building up a Muslim mind. It is Allah Who watches over and protects all things *(Al-Muhaymin),* Who donates all things to His creatures *(Al-Wahhāb),* even the non-believers (17:20), Who is the Provider of all things that are beneficial to His creatures *(Al-Razzāq),* Who opens the solutions to all problems, and eliminates obstacles *(Al-Fattāḥ),* Who constricts *(Al-Qābiḍ)* and expands *(Al-Bāsiṭ)* and is also the Abaser *(Al-Khāfiḍ),* Who is the Just One *(Al-'Adl),* Who preserves all things in detail and for a time preserves them from misfortune and calamity *(Al-Ḥafīẓ),* Who is Generous *(Al-Karīm),* Who responds to every need *(Al-Mujīb),* Who provides a means to solve the problems in the best way *(Al-Wakīl),* Who is the friend of His righteous servants *(Al-Walī),* Who is the Self-Sufficient *(Al-Ghanī)* and Enricher *(Al-Mughnī),* and Who is in reality the Distresser *(Al-Ḍārr)* and the Propitious *(Al-Nāfi')*. The Divine attributes do not only have metaphysical significance; a firm belief in them acts as a powerful source of inspiration and guidance in economic pursuits and planning.

Along with these Divine attributes a number of Qur'ānic verses and an abundance of the Prophet's sayings (peace be upon him) construct a mind that guides individual behaviour in a direction which truly reflects firm belief in Allah's Unity, *tawḥīd.* Without this firm belief the Islamic economic system and, for that matter, the whole of life, falls prey to inconsistency and discord. It is firm belief in the concept of reward in the Hereafter, not the economic calculation, that induces a man to act upon the injunctions regarding physical and financial sacrifice. It is the concept of punishment in the Hereafter, not the economic calculations that stops one from undesirable consumption and forbidden earnings. The degree of firmness in these beliefs determines the degree of success of the Islamic system. To illustrate more precisely, the Qur'ānic exposition of the attribute *Al-Razzāq,* for example, is given in the Qur'ān itself in the following words:

> Allah's are the treasures of the heavens and the earth (63:7). There is not a beast in the earth but the sustenance thereof dependeth on Allah (11:6). His bounty cannot be walled up (17:20). His provision will never deplete (38:54). He is the best of Sustainers (5:114). Anyhow, everything with Him is measured and He sends them down only in appointed measure (15:21). He enricheth and contenteth (53:48). He enlargeth the provision for whom He will, and straiteneth it for whom He will (2:245; 17:30). He has apportioned among them their livelihood in the life of the world, and raised some of them above others in rank that some of them may take

labour from others (43:32). Whosoever fears Allah,[2] Allah will appoint a way out for him, and will provide for him from (a quarter) whence he has no expectation (65:2, 3). Whosoever disobeys Him will be doomed (19:74, 98; 28:58, 78).

How does belief in this attribute influence economic attitude? A firm belief in the divine attribute of the Provider eliminates insatiable lust for amassing wealth through unlawful means and cools down impatience. It dissuades from unhealthy competition and egotism. It relieves tension and anxiety and unhealthy reaction in the event of poor return for one's effort. A firm belief in the divine assurance: 'Whosoever fears Allah, Allah will appoint a way out for him, and will provide for him from (a quarter) whence he has no expectation' (65:2, 3), not only discourages one from becoming avaricious and resorting to unlawful earning but also plays an important role in guiding policy-makers and planners to cast off the capricious fears of loss due to abolition of unlawful institutions and undesirable policies and programmes. Thus the fear of loss in excise duty anticipated in the case of prohibition, or the fear of the failure of the economic and financial system due to abolition of interest, or the fear of decrease in savings or bank deposits due to the imposition of *Zakāt,* do not present a serious challenge to the true believer in Allah's promise: Allah will appoint a way out for him, and will provide for him from (a quarter) whence he has no expectation.

A firm belief in His attribute, *Al-Razzāq,* as expressed in the verse: 'Slay not your children, fearing a fall to poverty, We shall provide for them and for you. Lo! the slaying of them is a great sin' (17:31),[3] – would inspire the policy-makers to be restrained, barring exceptional cases, in launching on economic grounds a country-wide campaign for birth-control, which often provides a refuge for the morally corrupt. Similarly, belief in the divine Wisdom of unequal distribution of wealth (4:32) shuns class antagonism and persuades the well-to-do to share their fortune with the poor, thus reducing the distance between the haves and have-nots.

The belief that Allah is the owner of all treasures and apportions sustenance for the people according to their requirement (15:20–2) deters one from mindless pessimism and a deprivation complex which has been infused into the thinking of developing nations by those powerful countries, who have themselves witnessed the implication of this divine assurance through a tremendous rate of growth with the same 'measured' resources, but who insist on impressing upon the developing countries a gloomy future for want of necessary resources. The Qur'ān, on the other hand, assures us of a generous creation of resources such that 'there is not a beast in the earth but the sustenance thereof depends on

Allah' (11:6), and that 'in the heavens *(samā')* is your providence in addition to that which you are promised' (51:22). The supply of natural resources is, however, not as generous as its creation. Thus the Qur'ānic approach to the phenomenon of scarce supply of natural resources is expressed in the following verse:

> And if Allah were to enlarge the provision for His slaves they would surely rebel in the earth, but He sendeth down by measure as He willeth. Lo! He is informed, a Seer of His bondmen (42:27).

The fact of scarce supply calls for prudent planning for optimum utilization of the available resources.

To sum up, firm belief in divine attributes not only has a far-reaching influence on the general attitude of the individual, it also touches economic enterprises, policy-making and planning. Without such firm belief practising the Islamic injunctions poses formidable difficulties, and leads one to impracticable compromises which result in dualism and hypocrisy.

Supporting this reform in general disposition, the meaningful emphases in the *Ḥadīth* on the attainment of bliss *(Sa'āda)* and blessing *(baraka)* are powerful agents to close the gaps that sometimes seem to appear in putting firm belief into practice. While the Qur'ānic concept of the achievement of success or salvation *(falāḥ)*[4] in the Hereafter provides a purposeful direction for practising the virtues commended in the Qur'ān, the Prophet's saying 'The world has been created for you but you have been created for the Hereafter' and 'Live in this world as if you are a traveller or a passer-by' provide the individual with the complementary approach towards this material world.

The Moral Fibre

A very important and characteristic feature of the economic teachings of the Qur'ān and the *Ḥadīth* is that they are profoundly infused with the moral concepts which act as an inspiring force. At places an economic principle is given economic rationale. But such cases are few compared with those economic principles which emphasize the moral aspect. It is clearly found that economic considerations are subordinated to moral considerations as, for instance, in the verse prohibiting interest *(ribā)* wherein the practice is treated as injustice (2:279). This indeed seems a possible economic ground for prohibition. But the Qur'ān does not end the matter here. It characterizes this practice as soliciting a declaration of war from Allah and His Messenger (2:279) and likens the devourer of interest to one who will rise (from his grave), as one whom Satan has driven to madness by his touch (2:275). Another economic rationale behind the prohibition of interest as laid down in the Qur'ān is that 'Allah hath blighted interest[5] and made almsgiving fruitful' (2:276). But this too is immediately followed by 'Allah loveth not the impious and the guilty' *(ibid.)*. At another place trustees of a bequest are reminded of the economic rationale behind distribution of inheritance among the beneficiaries, and of their duty to be fair in distribution, in the following way:

> And let those fear (in their behaviour towards orphans) who if they left behind them (economically) weak offspring would be afraid of them. So let them mind their duty to Allah, and speak justly (4:9).

The economic rationale behind the distribution of *Fay'*[6] (sequestrated enemy property) or public properties is declared to be that 'wealth may not make a circuit only between the rich among you' and is immediately followed by the warning to 'take only what the Messenger of Allah gives them and to abstain from whatever he forbids them' (59:7). They are also reminded to 'keep their duty to Allah because He is stern in reprisal' *(ibid.)*. Almsgiving and interest are contrasted in the following words:

> That which ye give in usury in order that it may increase on other people's property hath no increase with Allah; but that which ye give in charity, seeking Allah's countenance hath increase manifold (30:39).

Wealth is recognized as 'an ornament of the life of the world' but the wealthy are reminded that it is good deeds and spending for noble causes which are 'better and long-lasting in the Lord's sight for reward' (18:46). Economic and moral considerations seem to be inseparable in the following verses:

> They question thee about wine and games of chance. Say: In both is great sin, and (some) utility for men; but the sin of them is greater than their usefulness. And they ask thee what they ought to spend. Say: That which is superfluous. Thus Allah maketh plain to you (His) revelation, that haply ye may reflect (2:219).
>
> Give not unto the foolish (what is in) your (keeping of their) wealth, which Allah hath given you to maintain; but feed and clothe them. Prove orphans till they reach the marriageable age; then if ye find them of sound judgement deliver unto them their fortune; and devour it not by squandering and in haste lest they should grow up. Whoso (of the guardians) is rich, let him abstain generously (from taking of the property of the orphans); and whoso is poor let him take thereof in reason (for his guardianship). And when ye deliver

up their fortune unto orphans, have (the transaction) witnessed in their presence. Allah sufficeth as a Reckoner (4:5, 6).

But for these instances, the considerations underlying such injunctions are purely moral and religious. Allah's pleasure is made the goal of spending for noble causes (2:195, 262, 272; 3:92; 35:29, 30), providing subsistence to the have-nots (2:171; 76:8, 9), earning livelihood through lawful means (57:27; 62:10), and abstaining from professions causing obscenity and immorality (2:268). Muslims are threatened with damnation in the Hereafter if they indulge in breach of trust and misappropriation (4:10; 2:283), embezzlement (3:161), niggardliness (3:180; 9:34), immoral and obscene activities (29:28, 29, 30), and business relating to misleading pastimes (31:6). They are advised to spend 'of that which Allah hath bestowed on them as food lawful and good' and are reminded to 'keep their duty to Allah in whom they are believers' (5:88). Spending in a noble cause and, in particular, unseen spending, is regarded as an instrument of purification (2:274; 9:103). Success in the Hereafter is possible to achieve through 'abstaining from miserliness' (64:15, 16), and abstaining from use of wine and games of chance, which are regarded as 'Satan's handiwork' (5:90).

Following the Qur'ān, the *Sunna*[7] of the Prophet (peace be upon him) lays even greater emphasis on the moral discipline of the individual. There are innumerable traditions which seek to reform that instinct of man which directs his economic behaviour. Avarice, greed, selfishness and exploitation are not pronounced as economically harmful; they are declared as sinful. Great emphasis is laid on maintaining a balance between the conflicting interests of individuals and the different sections of the society. For example, pious spending *(infāq)* has been emphasized in order to root out greed and selfishness. It is difficult to judge as to which of the two basic sources lays greater emphasis on pious spending. While the *Ḥadīth* reaches the humanly possible extreme of spending there are also categorical traditions to control and regulate unrealistic over-emphasis on the point. They suggest as to how, among whom, and how much should preferably be spent. 'It is better to leave your heirs well-to-do than to leave them destitute and lead them to beg for charity. Whatever you spend over your family is rewarded.'[8] 'The best dīnār is the one that is spent on one's dependents, on the riding animal which is used in Allah's path and among the fellow-beings (engaged) in Allah's path.'[9] 'One who works in order to (earn and) support a widow and destitute is like a *mujāhid* (warrior) in the path of Allah.'[10] Muslims are encouraged to discharge this obligation hoping for its reward in the Hereafter. This behaviour is so highly esteemed and encouraged that a *Ḥadīth* says: 'Even the cashier of the philanthropist will be rewarded.'[11]

In spite of great emphasis on spending upon the less fortunate, the matter has not been left only to a one-way flow. The less fortunate members of the society are, on the contrary, advised to avoid begging for charity.[12] A *Ḥadīth* says: 'This wealth is fresh and sweet. Whosoever takes from it according to his entitlement will meet with blessing. Many non-deserving receivers will get Fire on doomsday.'[13] It is further said: 'The upper hand (i.e. the giver) is better than the lower hand (i.e. the receiver).'[14] The overall view on the matter, from a study of all relevant traditions, suggests that they do not recognize poverty alone as the justification for begging; it is, rather, urgent pressing need that is treated as the proper ground for seeking help from others. A *Ḥadīth* says: 'Begging is permitted only to one of three classes: (firstly) one who has become a guarantor for a payment, to whom begging is allowed till he gets it, after which he must stop begging; (secondly) a man whose property has been destroyed by a calamity which has smitten him, to whom begging is allowed till he gets what will support his life; and (thirdly) a man who has been smitten by poverty, the genuineness of which is confirmed by three intelligent members of his people to whom begging is allowed till he gets what will support his life. And any other reason for begging is forbidden and one who engages in such consumes it as a thing which is forbidden.'[15] In the above sayings the rich man's greed to save and accumulate to the maximum and the poor man's desire to ask for support when he can avoid it have been equally discouraged. Anyhow, the genuine necessities of neither of the two classes have been ignored. A cultivator may face a calamity, a businessman may incur losses and become liable to heavy debts, and a poor man may be out of a job or under-employed. In all these deserving cases the necessity for asking for support is recognized.

This moral view is the underlying motive for distribution of wealth among the needy and seeks a balance to regulate distribution. This basis in morality has not been neglected in other spheres of economic activity. The act of farming is associated with dispensing *ṣadaqa* (charity). An honest trader is ranked among the martyrs *(shahīd)* in the Hereafter. Earning one's livelihood is esteemed as *jihād* (holy war). Contrarily, those who indulge in undesirable economic activities are denounced and threatened with condign punishment in the Hereafter.[16]

The above discussion should suffice to make it clear that the economic structure envisioned by the Qur'ān and the *Sunna* is thoroughly infused with religious and moral principles. But while the current of morality is made to flow beneath the surface of economic life, a process of moral perfection operates also within the economic life itself. While a man is required to refrain from hoarding wealth and exhorted to spend it for a noble cause, he is advised by the Qur'ān to spend of superior but not inferior things (2:267; 3:92, etc.) and to abstain from capitalizing on his spending through publicizing it (2:264). This attitude to the poor is more significant in the case of one's subordinates. Slaves have generally been treated as a commodity and are placed in the lowest tier of subordination. The number of slaves owned by a man used to be the standard of one's richness because, in medieval society, slaves and not paid employees were generally responsible for maintaining livestock, cultivation, trade and entourage. The Qur'ān only persuades its followers to contract manumission of their slaves on receiving from them a certain sum of money (24:33), but also recommends bestowing 'on them of the wealth of Allah' *(ibid.)* so that the procedure of their freedom is facilitated. This economic uplifting of the poor, and emancipation of slaves, cannot be over-emphasized in the context of pre-Islamic Arab society where selfish motives were strong.[17] These measures could only result in minimizing economic inequalities on the one hand, and creating the maximum possible number of independent economic units on the other. In this way the Qur'ān not only intends to achieve economic objectives through the moral disciplining of its followers, but also intends to achieve moral and social objectives with the operation of its economic principles. As a result, these units could become socially and economically inter-dependent as compared with the earlier situation in which most people depended on a wealthy few. And in practice this system of interdependence pulled down the pillars of the old social and economic order.

Before closing this discussion about the role of moral principles in the economic teachings of Islam, it will not be out of place to emphasize that moral culture is not exclusively a personal affair in Islam. Beliefs are no doubt a personal matter and nobody can ever ascertain the degree of another person's faith in the body of beliefs to which he claims to subscribe. But moral discipline makes possible the expression of that faith in social life and does not remain confined to private life. The Qur'ān prescribes it for an Islamic state that it enjoin *ma'rūf,* known virtues, and forbid *munkar,* inequity. It is made clear in the following verses:

> Those who, if We give them power in the land, establish worship and pay the poor-due and enjoin virtues and forbid inequity. And Allah's is the sequel of events (22:41).

> And there may spring from you a nation who invite to goodness and enjoin right conduct and forbid indecency. Such are they who are successful (3:104).

Apart from these moral principles of Islam which have their bearing on economic life, the entire Islamic order is based on moral discipline which, in turn, derives inspiration from its basic conceptions about Allah, about the purpose of man's life, etc. In this way it is essentially the religious world-view of Islam which motivates the entire Islamic way of life and which provides those sanctions that make its rules of conduct effective. But for the firm belief in the basic religious doctrines of Islam and the observance of its moral principles, the Islamic concept of the ownership of property, its guiding directives bearing on consumption and utilization of economic resources, its injunctions regarding monetary and fiscal matters and its principles regarding the distribution of wealth would have been rendered utterly ineffective and meaningless.

The Concept of Ownership

The basic principle which the Qur'ān and the *Ḥadīth* assert in respect of man's economic behaviour is his position *vis-à-vis* the material resources which are produced by Allah for mankind.[18] Islam recognizes man's right to own property for consumption and for production but does not give him absolute right over it. This is discernible from a study of the Islamic law of inheritance under which a number of near relations are made to share the inheritance in fixed ratios whether or not the testator is agreeable to it during his lifetime. The shares to be distributed among the recipients have been apportioned in the Qur'ān and cannot be altered. The Qur'ān is highly critical of the act of destroying crops, cattle and labour force and regards it as a mischief of opponents (2:205). To emphasize limitations to the absolute right of ownership, the Qur'ān attributes the creation of economic resources to Allah in the following words:[19]

> And He it is Who spread out the earth and placed therein firm hills and flowing streams, and of all fruits He placed therein two spouses (male and female) (13:3).
>
> Allah is He Who created the heavens and the earth and causeth water to descend from the sky, thereby producing fruits as food for you, and maketh the ships to be of service unto you, that they may run upon the sea at His command, and hath made of service unto you the rivers; and maketh the sun and the moon, constant in their courses, to be of service unto you, and hath made of service unto you, the night and the day.
> And He giveth you of all ye ask of Him and if ye would count the bounty of Allah ye cannot reckon it . . . (14:32–4).
>
> He it is Who has made the earth subservient unto you, so walk in the paths thereof and eat of His providence (67:15).

This divine gift is emphasized even in the case of man-made goods. This is derivable from expressions such as: 'Allah's bounty' (3:180), 'Allah hath given you (your resources) to maintain yourself' (4:5); 'We have bestowed on them' (35:29); 'He will increase them of His grace' (35:30); 'and let not those who hoard up that which Allah hath bestowed upon them' (3:180); 'in that which Allah hath given thee' (28:77); 'and whatever ye have been given is but a passing comfort for the life of the world' (42:36). All these references attributing the act of giving to Allah speak essentially of Allah's ultimate ownership.

Side by side with these pronouncements the Qur'ān also recognizes man's *ad interim*[21] ownership of these resources. The frequently used phrases such as, 'his wealth' (2:264); 'their wealth' (2:261, 262; 4:2, 6; 9:103; 51:19; 59:8); 'your wealth' (2:188; 4:2, 24; 61:11); 'property of others' (2:188); 'wealth of orphans' (4:10), suggest the *de facto* ownership of man over anything that forms the definition of economic goods. Similarly, expressions like 'ye have your principal' (2:279); 'unto the man belongeth a share . . . unto the woman a share' (4:7); 'they are their (livestock's) owners' (36:71); 'take alms of their wealth' (9:103); 'ye have given unto one of them a large sum of money' (4:20); 'and for the poor Emigrants who have been driven out of their homes and deprived of their belongings' (59:8) are suggestive of the private ownership of the individuals over capital, livestock, precious metals, large sums of money, dwellings and household goods. At some other places words like 'pledge in hand' (2:283); 'and the wealth ye have acquired and merchandise for which ye fear that there would be no sale, and dwellings ye desire . . . ' (9:24); 'pay the poor due thereof upon the harvest day' (6:141), allude to private ownership over amassed wealth, merchandise, dwellings and crops.

The lines quoted above elucidate the Islamic concept of ownership of articles of consumption and means of production. The relationship is best illustrated by the following verses:

> He it is Who hath placed you as viceroys of the earth and hath exalted some of you in rank above others, that He may try you by (the test of) that which He hath given you . . . (6:165).
>
> Believe in Allah and His Messenger and spend of that whereof He hath made you trustees; and such of you as believe and spend (aright) theirs will be great reward (57:7).

According to the above-quoted verses man is supposed to regard himself as Allah's viceroy on earth and take the economic resources therein as a sacred trust to be used in accordance with His pleasure. This position is repeatedly explained in the Qur'ān, directly and indirectly, and man is persuaded to reconcile himself to His vicegerency and treat the economic resources as a trust. The Qur'ānic phrases such as, 'Allah hath bestowed upon them His bounty' (3:180); 'Allah hath given you to maintain' (4:5); 'by that which He hath given you' (6:165); 'who spend of that which We have bestowed on them' . . . 'He will increase them of His grace' (35:29, 30), again and again infuse the same spirit into the mind of man.

The Ownership of Land

In spite of the above allusions to ownership it is meaningful that the Qur'ān does not make any direct or indirect allusion to private ownership of land. The word signifying land *(arḍ)* appears in the Qur'ān in some 500 places, and is used in the sense of a geographic territory (30:9, 25, 42, etc.), distance (30:3), nationality or society (5:32, 64; 7:56, 74, 85, 127; 17:4), state or government (10:83; 11:85; 12:55; 38:36; 40:29), globe (57:21), home-land (7:109; 14:13, etc.), and mineral properties (11:61), etc. The uses which the Qur'ān indicates for *arḍ,* in addition to the innumerable bounties it supplies, are resting-place (2:22; 43:10), accommodation (2:36; 7:24), store of provisions (2:36; 7:24), habitation and cultivation (11:61), wide expanse (71:19), and abode (27:61). In spite of the occurrence of the word in more than 470 places, *arḍ* is used in the possessive case on only eight occasions and there too does not convey the sense of private ownership. It will, therefore, be worthwhile to reproduce the relevant verses to bring the point home:

> The chiefs of Pharaoh's people said, Lo! This is some knowing wizard, who would expel you from your land *(min arḍikum).* Now what do you advise? (7:109–10).
>
> And those who disbelieved said unto their messengers: Verily we will drive you out from our land *(min arḍinā),* unless ye return to our religion (14:13).
>
> He said: Hast thou come to drive us out from our land *(min arḍinā)* by thy magic, O Moses? (20:57).
>
> They said: Lo! These are two wizards who would drive you out from your land *(min arḍikum)* by their magic, and destroy your best traditions (20:63).
>
> Who would drive you out of your land *(min arḍikum)* by his magic (26:35).
>
> And they say if we were to follow the Guidance with thee we should be torn out of our land *(min arḍinā)* (28:57).

O my bondmen who believe! Lo! My earth *(arḍī)* is spacious. Therefore serve Me only (29:56).

And He caused you to inherit their land *(arḍuhum)* and their houses and their wealth, and land ye have not trodden. Allah is Able to do all things (33:27).

It will be seen in the above verses that, except for *(arḍī)* (My land) where the possessive adjective refers to Allah, the words *arḍikum* (your land), *arḍinā* (our land) and *arḍuhum* (their land) convey the sense of 'homeland' not the privately-owned plots of land. It is also this sense of homeland that the following verse, on the forced migration to Madina of the Prophet (peace be upon him), conveys:

And they indeed wished to scare thee from the land that they might drive thee forth from thence and then they would have stayed (there) but a little after thee (17:76).

Other words that can be misinterpreted to support the sense of private ownership are *wirātha,* inheritance, *khilāfa,* vicegerency, and *tamakkun,* domination. But it will be found that the verses containing the word *wirātha* are used either in the sense of Allah's ultimate ownership and omnipotence (3:180; 9:40), the collective ownership of His virtuous bondsmen (21:105; 39:74), or the suppressed class of the society (7:137). In some other places the preposition ل meaning 'for' or '(belonging) to' is used to express the ownership of Allah *(li'llāh)* (5:17, 19, 40, 120; 7:158; 9:116; 10:66) or the ownership of all creatures *(l'ilanām)* (55:10). Similarly the word *khilāfa* is used in the Qur'ān (2:30; 6:165; 27:61; 35:39; 38:26) in the sense of political authority, as is the word *tamakkun* (6:6; 7:10; 12:21; 18:84; 22:41; 28:6). The same attitude is visible in the Qur'ān in respect of all the free gifts of nature, like rivers, streams, mountains, forests, etc. We find the repeated emphasis that the sun and the moon, the day and the night, the earth and the heavens, and the animals have been made of service unto man *(taskhīr)*. This general attitude has only one exception which occurs in the case of livestock in which case the Qur'ān very explicitly declares: 'And they are their owners' *(fa hum lahā mālikūn)* (36:71).

While the above discussion proves the lack of Qur'ānic approval of private ownership of natural resources, it equally proves the absence of Qur'ānic disapproval. As a result the decisive factor becomes the Prophet's *Sunna.* There are a great many instances to suggest that the Prophet (peace be upon him) allotted large tracts of land to a number of Companions.[23] But the conditions on which these lands were allotted to them have yet to be found out. When the Prophet (peace be upon him) gave an ultimatum to Banū Qurayẓa he is reported to have declared the following principle:

> Understand it clearly that land is for Allah and His Messenger. I mean to exile you from here so if anybody has land, he should sell it out otherwise you should understand that land is for Allah and His Messenger.[24]

On another occasion the Prophet (peace be upon him) is reported to have asserted the same thing more generally: 'Old and fallow lands are for Allah and His Messenger, and then they are for you.'[25]

He is also reported to have said:

> The servants are the servants of Allah *('ibād-Allāh),* the land is the land of Allah and who revives dead land, it is for him.[26]

The above-quoted *Ḥadīth* as narrated by 'Urwa b. Zubayr seems to have become the decisive rule in the later period. All these sayings taken together incline towards absolute right of the state over land. Transferring land to the individuals for productive use and allowing the producer the right to own this produce[27] do not prejudice, in any obvious way, the proprietary claim of the state.

It is worthwhile re-emphasizing that the Qur'ānic approach seems to be different in the case of crops, dwellings and orchards. There are verses to suggest the Qur'ānic recognition of ownership over usufruct of land. Thus the injunction 'And pay the due thereof on the harvest day' (6:142), and the Prophet's hint 'And in the treasure-trove is a fifth',[28] suggest recognition of ownership of the produce of land whether in the form of crop or excavated minerals. Verses like 3:49; 16:80 and 24:27, 61 allude to ownership of houses.[29]

Having in view notions of ownership in line with the spirit of the Qur'ān and *Ḥadīth,* Caliph 'Umar made it a rule to revoke the allocation of land if the owner failed to utilize it for three consecutive years.[30] Ziyād, Caliph 'Alī's governor in Iraq (later on Mu'āwiya's governor too) reduced this period of grace to two years.[31]

To sum up the above discussion, the most significant Islamic principle regarding wealth is the distinction between the nature of ownership of natural resources and of the resources produced by man. The former are regarded as in the ownership of Allah; man is a mere trustee. The latter are an endowment from Allah by virtue of His *faḍl* and *raḥma;* man is the owner of what he has lawfully acquired. The benefit of the former is for humanity as a whole; rights of possession thereof are very much restricted so that their possession does not restrict the general benefit. Ownership of the latter is vested in man but the utilization and disposal thereof is regulated so that this ownership does not harm the interest of the society at large. Thus in the former case it is the ownership that has been restricted; in the latter it is the utilization that has been regulated. This comparative position may be explained in the following form:

Goods/Wealth Created by Allah	*Goods/Wealth Produced or Earned by Man*
★ Allah's ownership, man's possession (as a trust).	★ Man's physical ownership and possession. Allah's discretion (as a lawgiver).
★ Restricted private ownership (to safeguard the interest of humanity at large).	★ Restricted personal consumption (to promote social interest).
★ Revocable possession.	★ Irrevocable ownership.
★ Possession transferable.	★ Ownership and possession transferable.

Earning and the Concept of the Lawful and the Unlawful (*Ḥalāl* and *Ḥarām*)

The most important characteristic of a system based on a divine creed and revealed ethics is the concept of good and bad, virtuous and vicious, and lawful *(ḥalāl)* and unlawful *(ḥarām)* which, as in any other sphere of life, plays a key role in determining the broad contours of an economic system. A study of the Qur'ān and the *Sunna* not only provides us with a list of those commodities/items that are not permissible to use but also of those professions and activities which are unlawful. While these basic sources of law lay down the essential characteristics of lawful and unlawful, they also provide the guidelines to determine the desirability or otherwise of any institution or practice that may be introduced as a result of socio-economic changes and technological improvements. The basic principle the Qur'ān provides is that justice and equity be maintained and injustice and inequity be avoided. The equitable way is regarded as the best way of avoiding doubts and disputes between the concerned parties (2:282). Justice and equity are made operative in economic life just as in any other spheres of activity in Islam.

The scope and interpretation of justice and equity can best be understood if the terms are placed in relation to their opposites. This may be elaborated by comparing two verses of the Qur'ān dealing with the same subject:

> Concerning female orphans unto whom ye give not which is ordained for them though ye desire to marry them, and concerning the weak among children, and that you should deal justly *(bi'l qisṭ)* with the orphans (4:127).

Corresponding to this verse another one reads as follows:

> Those who devour the wealth of orphans unjustly *(ẓulman)* they do but swallow fire into their bellies (4:10).

The two verses suggest that the positive *qist,* i.e. fair dealing, corresponds to the negative *ẓulm,* i.e. injustice and inequity. Such injustice is perpetrated in case respect for somebody's property or wealth is violated. This is also discernible from the broader sense of application of 4:29, 30:

> O ye who believe! Squander not your wealth among yourself in vanity, except it be a trade by mutual consent . . . whoso does that through aggression *('udwān)* and injustice *(ẓulm),* We shall cast him into the Fire . . .

Similar violation occurs in theft and, not surprisingly, theft is also called *ẓulm* (5:39). Verses prohibiting interest describe it as *ẓulm* (2:279). This means that the concept of *ẓulm* in Islam is as broad as that of *'adl* and *qisṭ*.

With this basic consideration a summary of the lawful and unlawful practices can be reproduced for a study of their impact on different aspects of economic life.

All goods belong primarily to Allah and have been created or produced for man who has the right to acquire possession, and to use and dispose of them within certain limits. Private ownership must be respected. Earnings may be acquired through personal effort (9:24; 2:267) or through mutual co-operation (43:32). Man should be honest, just and equitable in earning and in dealing with others. He must abstain from injustice and transgression. Performance of supererogatory obligations and sacrifice for others are extolled as commendable. All the activities which are disapproved by God must be avoided. Everything that is against the principle of justice and equity or is detrimental to the interests of other persons or of human society as a whole is prohibited. These include acquisition through theft (5:39), plunder (5:33), interest (2:275–9) and gambling (2:219; 5:90, 91). Practices which cause indecency and immorality are prohibited. These include earnings through obscene professions (2:268; 7:33; 24:33), wine (2:219; 5:90), misleading pastimes (31:6) and prostitution (24:33). Defrauding others is sinful.

This covers earnings through under-weighing and under-measurement (55:9; 83:3), breach of trust (3:161), misappropriation (2:188), embezzlement (3:161), deluding publicity and advertisement, getting a favourable court decree to obtain other's property wrongfully through bribe (2:188) and tampering with documents of business or debt (2:282).

Similarly it is not lawful to destroy potential human capital or production (2:205) for political reasons or on the pretext of economic rationale (17:31). Earning through business in carrion, blood, swine flesh or soothsaying (5:90–1; 2:173) is also not permissible. A man who avoids unlawful means of earnings is respectable. It is unto Allah to make his effort fruitful as much as He will because 'He enlargeth the provision for whom He will and straiteneth it for whom He will' (17:30). It should not be a point of grudge that 'He hath favoured some men above others in provision' (16:71). 'Unto men a fortune from that which they have earned and unto women a fortune from that which they have earned' (4:32). The just way of obtaining an increase is to make an effort in the right direction and to 'ask Allah of His bounty' (4:32). A *Ḥadīth* summarizes the ethics of earning in the following words:

> Fear Allah, be moderate in earning because no soul perishes unless it acquires its (full share of) livelihood even though it takes time. So fear Allah, earn moderately by choosing the lawful and leaving the unlawful.[32]

In addition to the obviously unlawful professions and pastimes, the *Ḥadīth* literature adds a few more activities to the list, such as earning through trade in drugs, astrology, soothsaying, usurpation, portraying/painting living beings, insemination of animals, magic, and tattooing the skin.[33] This is in addition to a large number of trade practices which were found unjust or doubtful.[34]

Along with the activities listed above the Qur'ān and the *Sunna* list a number of items/commodities that are foul or sinful. These items, according to the Qur'ān, include the use of wine (5:90), carrion, blood, and swine flesh (6:146). The *Ḥadīth* literature adds to this list the use of any intoxicants, fats of carrion, and gold and silver utensils. Silk clothes and gold ornaments are banned only for men.[35]

As a rule, the list of lawful and the unlawful, as ordained by the Qur'ān and the *Sunna* and as explained above, cannot be tampered with. But in a case where the spirit of Islam is intended to be followed in a dynamic society a distinction has been made between two different sets:

(1) items of personal consumption like strong drink, swine flesh, etc. which do not accept of any relaxation irrespective of the rationale of prohibition; and

(2) activities and institutions which have been prohibited or legalized on account of some explicit or invisible cause, *'illa*. It is here that the *fuqahā'* have used analogy to expand or restrict the scope of legality/prohibition.

The Concept of *'Adl* and *Iḥsān*

The concept of *'adl* or (almost interchangeable) *qisṭ* occupies a central place in the economic system of Islam. *'Adl* and *qisṭ*[36] are used in the Qur'ān to mean justice, equity or fair dealing. Truth and justice are regarded as inhering in the Word of Allah.

> Perfected is the Word of Thy Lord in truth and justice (6:115).

The Prophets have been given Allah's Books for the people to establish this value (57:25). It is the virtue of justice that is maintaining the entire creation (3:18), and the same virtue is required in legal (4:58, 135; 5:8, 106; 7:29; 16:90; 49:9), social (2:282; 4:3, 127, 129), moral (4:129; 5:8, 106; 6:153), and economic (4:58, 135; 6:153; 11:85; 16:90; 55:10; 57:25), dealings. It is to be practised with individuals (4:135; 5:8, 106; 65:2), orphans (4:3, 127, 129), wives (4:3), tribes (49:9), communities and nations (5:8, 42; 60:8) and even enemies (60:8). It is applicable to speaking, giving witness, acting as a guardian, scribing an agreement, arbitrating between parties, dealing with other peoples, judging in a court of law and making business transactions.

The imperative of *'adl* and *qisṭ* in the Islamic economic order is expressed in the following verses:

> Lo! Allah commandeth you that ye restore deposits to their owners, and if ye judge between mankind, that ye judge justly . . . (4:58).

> O ye who believe! Be ye staunch in justice, witness of Allah, even though it be against yourself or (your) parents or (your) kindred, whether (the case be of) a rich man or a poor man, for Allah is nearer unto both (than ye are). So follow not passion lest ye lapse (from justice) and if ye lapse or fall away, then lo! Allah is ever Informed of what ye do (4:135).

> And approach not the wealth of the orphan save with that which is better, till he reach maturity. Give full measure and full weight in justice. We task not any soul beyond its scope. And if ye give your word, do justice thereunto, even though it be against a kinsman; and fulfil the covenant of Allah . . . (6:152).

O my people! Give full measure and full weight in justice, and wrong not people in respect of their goods. And do not evil in the earth causing corruption (11:85).

Lo! Allah enjoineth justice and kindness and giving to kinsfolk, and forbiddeth lewdness and abomination and wickedness . . . (16:90).

. . . And He has set the measure. That ye exceed not the measure. But observe the measure strictly, nor fall short thereof. And the earth hath He appointed for (His) creatures (55:7–10).

We verily sent Our messengers with clear proofs, and revealed with them the scripture and the balance, that mankind may observe right measure; and He revealed iron, wherein is mighty power and (many) uses for mankind . . . (57:25).

The above verses stress justice and equity in giving and taking and in general conduct with others. In addition, the concept of *amāna* (trust) cited above in verse 4:58 in the context of the Qur'ānic rejection of personal, family, group and class distinctions in administering justice (4:135), has a great bearing on formulating economic policies and plans. It is generally agreed by exegetes that *amāna* encompasses not only material deposits but also rights, duties and privileges.[37] The phrase 'even though it be against yourself or (your) parents or your kindred, whether (the case be of) a rich man or a poor man, for Allah is nearer unto both' (4:135), argues for absolute justice uninfluenced by personal prejudice, nepotism, sentimentality, regionalism or slogan-mongering. Thus the verse, on the one hand, disapproves economic policies that protect and benefit the rich at the cost of the poor and, on the other hand, it disallows a policy which takes care of only the poor by ignoring the interest of the well-to-do. It should be a well balanced policy to accommodate the interest of all the economic classes of the society. Available material resources are scarce (15:21). It is the principle of justice and equity that must guide the allocation of resources and distribution among competing claimants. This is the Qur'ānic concept of *'adl* and must form the nucleus of all economic policies and planning.

The Prophet (peace be upon him) laid great emphasis on the virtues of justice *('adl)* and fair dealing *(qisṭ)* for policy-makers:

Verily the just persons shall be seated on the radiant pulpits *(manābir min nūr)* on the right side of Allah . . . These (just people) adjudicate justly, are fair to their kinsmen, and do justice to the task assigned to them.[38]

Along with the concept of *'adl* and *qisṭ* the concept of *iḥsān* is also frequently repeated in the Qur'ān and the *Ḥadīth*. *Iḥsān* (root ḥ-s-n) means benevolence, fineness, proficiency, or magnanimity in dealing with others. Absence of *'adl* inflicts harm, disturbs peace and harmony but the absence of *iḥsān* does not harm anybody. It implies a more liberal treatment than what justice requires. It begins where the precincts of *'adl* end. It seems at first sight a supererogatory virtue, but the Qur'ānic injunctions –

> Lo! Allah enjoineth *'adl* and *iḥsān,* and giving to kinsfolk, and forbiddeth lewdness and abomination and wickedness . . . (16:90)

– suggests that the attitude of *iḥsān* enjoys a significant position in the Islamic framework.

> Spend your wealth for the cause of Allah, and be not cast by your own hands to ruin; and do good. Lo! Allah loveth those who behave with *iḥsān* (2:195).

> Those who spend in ease and adversity, those who control their wrath and are forgiving toward mankind; Allah loveth such doers of *iḥsān* (3:134).

How the attitude of *iḥsān* compares with *'adl* can be judged from the following verses:

> O ye who believe! Retaliation is prescribed for you in the matter of the murdered; the freeman for the freeman, and the slave for the slave, and the female for the female. And for him who is forgiven somewhat by his (injured) brother, prosecution according to usage and payment unto him in *iḥsān.* This is an alleviation and mercy from your Lord. He who transgresseth after this will have a painful doom (2:178).

> Divorce must be pronounced twice and then (a woman) must be retained in honour or released with *iḥsān.* And it is not lawful for you that ye take from women aught of that which ye have given them . . . (2:229).

The above verses suggest that absolute justice is a legal requirement and a *must,* but the Qur'ān persuades its followers to be prepared to behave magnanimously in claiming their right and be generous in discharging their duty. In addition to the above verses which define the behaviour of *iḥsān* there are numerous verses that insist on behaving magnanimously with parents (2:83; 6:151; 17:23; 46:15), kinsmen, orphans, the distressed (2:83), as also neighbours, fellow-travellers[39] and journeymen (4:36). It should be noted that none (except parents) has any legal rights over the other's wealth.

The role of *iḥsān* in an Islamic society cannot be over-emphasized. While *'adl* eliminates injustice and exploitation and strikes a real balance between rights and responsibilities in the society, *iḥsān* decorates this society with generosity, kindness, mercy, forgiveness, self-sacrifice, mutual co-operation and affection. The Qur'ān insists that traders give full weight and measure (6:153); the *Ḥadīth* recommend for weighing sparingly *(zin, wa arjiḥ)*.[40] The Qur'ān and the *Ḥadīth* both ordain repayment of debt in full and within the stipulated period. But along with it, the lender is recommended to be lenient in pressing for repayment if the borrower is in distress (2:280). On the other hand, the borrower, for his part, is recommended to repay generously.[41] *'Adl* respects private ownership and protects it; *iḥsān* persuades the owner to share the benefits of this ownership with others. Thus while *'adl* is the primary condition of setting up an Islamic Government, *iḥsān* plays a vital role in building up a truly Islamic society; the former is a legal phenomenon while the latter is moral and religious. All that, in general, an Islamic government can unconditionally enforce is *'adl;* it cannot, under normal conditions, press anyone to be magnanimous and broad-hearted in his dealings with another party. It is for the Muslims themselves to behave with *iḥsān* if they wish to build up a truly Islamic society in letter and in spirit. It is only after this that the excellences of an Islamic system are boldly expressed, the blessings of Islam practically demonstrated, and a powerful, cohesive society comes into existence even though its individuals may be lacking in personal affluence.

The Concept of Opulence

Islam does not castigate worldly wealth nor man's application to economic pursuits; the Qur'ān sometimes terms wealth as *khayr* (virtue), *faḍl* (honour), *raḥma* (blessing)[42] and regards it as Allah's bounty. It not only reminds and recounts Allah's blessing which He has granted to man in terms of rain-water, crops, orchards, fish, livestock, riding animals, food, fodder, minerals, precious stones and every known and unknown[43] thing which He has placed within, upon, or above this planet, but also encourages man to explore the hidden and unexploited resources (16:14; 17:12, 66; 29:17; 62:10).

The ideal economic standard of man that the Qur'ān envisages is a contented life. It recognizes the significance of wealth as an adornment of this worldly life (18:46). Allah recounts His blessings to the Prophet (peace be upon him) in the following words:

> Did He not find thee destitute and enrich (thee) (93:8).

The same tone is reflected in respect of Muslims in general:

> . . . If ye fear poverty (from the loss of merchandise due to economic blockade by pagans) Allah shall preserve you of His bounty if He will. Lo! Allah is Knower, Wise (9:28).

A similar wish is expressed when a man would preserve his chastity until he can afford to marry:

> . . . If they be poor Allah will enrich them of His bounty. Allah is of ample means, Aware (24:32).
>
> . . . Let them preserve their chastity if they cannot marry, until Allah enriches them by His grace (24:33).

All this leads to the conclusion that material prosperity enjoys Allah's blessings and is desirable. Yet this prosperity is not unqualified. It has to be qualified because of the danger in man's natural inclination for material resources when that inclination is undisciplined.

The Qur'ān states that man has a lust for wealth (89:20; 4:128) and is violent in this lust (100:8). When he acquires wealth he devotes himself to multiplying and hoarding it rather than spending it, for fear of poverty (17:100; 70:18; 9:24). This attitude to wealth creates in him a number of vices. He becomes niggardly, and persuades other rich persons to keep from spending wealth and to conceal their possessions (3:36–8). He develops an aversion to appeals for spending (47:36–8) and cavils and scoffs at those who give generously (9:79). He becomes boastful and proud (11:10), and this develops rivalry in him and distracts his mind towards worldly lures (57:23; 102:1). If he spends he does so for his public reputation (2:264).

While the Qur'ān does not disapprove acquiring wealth, it does require that affluence not breed the vices hinted at above. Both Qur'ān and *Ḥadīth* guide towards a particular and distinct approach to acquiring and disposing of wealth and material resources, an approach that derives from the Qur'ān's concept of man's position on earth:

> He it is Who hath placed you as viceroys of the earth and hath exalted some of you in rank above others, that He may try you by (the test of) that which He hath given you. Lo! Thy Lord is swift in persecution, and Lo! He is forgiving, Merciful (6:166).
>
> We destroyed the generations before you when they did wrong; and their messengers (from Allah) came unto them with clear proofs but they would not believe. Thus do We reward the guilty folk.
>
> Then We appointed you viceroys in the earth after them that We might see how ye behave (10:14).

Following the basic concept it recognizes the significance of worldly wealth, but with reservations:

> Lo! We have placed all that is in the earth as an ornament thereof that we may try them; which of them is best in conduct (18:7).
>
> Beautified for mankind is love of the joys (that come) from women and offspring, and stored-up heaps of gold and silver, and horses branded (with their mark) and cattle and land. That is comfort of the life of the world. Allah! with Him is a more excellent abode. Say: Shall I inform you of something better than that? For those who keep from evil, with their Lord are Gardens . . . (3:14, 15).
>
> And know that your possessions and your children are a test, and that with Allah is immense reward (8:28).
>
> Your wealth and your children are only a test, whereas Allah! with Him is an immense reward (64:15).

While opulence is called a trial, scarcity too is no differently regarded:

> And surely We shall try you with something of fear and hunger and loss of wealth and lives and crops; but give glad tidings to the steadfast (2:155).
>
> Lo! Thy Lord is ever watchful. As for man whenever his Lord trieth him by honouring him and is gracious unto him, he saith: My Lord honoureth me. But whenever his Lord trieth him by straitening his means of life, he saith: My Lord despiseth me. Nay, but ye for your part honour not the orphan. And ye urge not on the feeding of the poor. And ye devour heritage with devouring greed. And ye love wealth with abounding love (89:14–20).

The Prophet (peace be upon him), similarly, commented: 'The acid test of this Umma is wealth *(māl)*.'[44] He is reported to have invoked Allah for protection from the test of opulence and for protection from avarice; but also from the burden of debt, from need and poverty, and from scarcity.[45] Yet a careful study of the Qur'ān and the *Sunna* reveals that greater attention has been directed to remedying the evil effects of wealth than planning the elimination of poverty. This is perhaps because of the social, moral and psychological consequences of affluence rather than its economic effects. And this is because of the fact that in Islam moral and social betterment transcends affluence. The Qur'ān states:

> And when We would destroy a township We send commandment to its folk who live in affluence *(mutrafīhā)* and afterwards they commit abominations therein, and so the word of doom hath effect for it, and We annihilate it with complete annihilation (17:16).

In places the Qur'ān points out the negative attitude of the affluent toward its scheme of social and moral reform. They not only resist any such scheme (34:34) but also gather a following to counter it (11:116).

The Prophet (peace be upon him) has even more explicitly hinted at some of the effects of affluence:

> By Allah I am not afraid that you will be poor, but I fear that worldly wealth will be bestowed upon you as it was bestowed upon those who lived before you. So you will compete amongst yourself for it, as they competed for it and it will destroy you as it did them.[46]

> I am not afraid that you will worship others besides Allah, but I am afraid that worldly life *(dunyā)* will tempt you and cause you to compete with each other for it.[47]

The Prophet (peace be upon him) is reported to have warned of wealth on different occasions, sometimes with the remark that 'This will divert your attention (from nobler objectives).'[48]

While it is clear that Islam encourages man to earn as much wealth through lawful means as possible, it does not allow him to hold this wealth to monopolize means of production or to restrict circulation of wealth to a limited class of the society. To remedy the effects of ownership of the means of production and excessive earnings the Prophet (peace be upon him) imposed limits on both ownership/possession and on consumption. As for natural resources, man is not allowed to hold them idle; the state has a right to seize these and allocate them to a person who may use them.[49] In cases where a man can use these resources, concentration of such resources is undesirable. It is reported that the Prophet (peace be upon him) once visited a place where a heap of farming implements was piled up which proved large-scale farming. At this the Prophet (peace be upon him) observed: 'A house which has the abundance of these implements brings about a fall in position.'[50] The *Ḥadīth* discourages individual holding of vast tracts of agricultural land. In order to ensure that wealth does not make a circuit between a small group of owners (59:7), the Prophet (peace be upon him) advised the rich to rear sheep and the poor to engage in poultry-farming.[51] According to a *Ḥadīth,* he observed: 'Allah withdraws His blessings from a community in which the well-to-do engage in poultry-farming too.'[52] The purpose of this and similar sayings seems to be to regulate economic activity in such a way as does not allow a particular class to control the opportunities of earning.

Another powerful instrument of diffusing personal holdings is the Islamic law of inheritance which is effective immediately after the death of the holder, and for the poor as well as the rich. Under this Qur'ānic law personal holdings are distributed among the near relations of the deceased holder in prescribed ratios.[53]

Another way of preventing the evils of affluence is regulating consumption. The *Ḥadīth* 'Simplicity is a part of faith', guides the Muslims to a norm that rejects envy and creates homogeneity and harmony in the society. Envy and jealousy are largely the result of ostentatious living on the part of a wealthy few. The Qur'ān and *Ḥadīth* both condemn demonstration of one's resources through luxurious living (28:79).[54] The Prophet's censure is more severe and pointed.

> Keeping horses may be a source of reward to some (person), a shelter to another or a burden to a third . . . He who keeps horses just out of pride and for showing off and as a means of harming the Muslims, his horses will be a source of sin to him.[55]
>
> One of the portents of the Hour will be when the shepherds of livestock start boasting and competing with each other in the construction of higher buildings.[56]
>
> A woman who wears gold ornaments for showing off in pride will only be punished (in the Hereafter).[57]
>
> The worst of meals is the wedding feast *(walīma)* to which only the rich are invited and the poor are left.[58]
>
> There are camels which belong to devils, and there are houses which belong to devils. As for the camels of the devils, I have seen them. One of you goes out with his side camels (for pomp and show) which he has fattened, neither riding any of them nor giving a lift to a tired brother when he meets him. As regards the houses of the devils . . . They are those which are decorated with brocade.[59]
>
> Verily man will be rewarded for all his expenditure except that on the soil, or, as he said, on house.[60]
>
> The Prophet (peace be upon him) once passed by a circular house and enquired about it. He was informed about the owner of the house. On this he observed: Wealth spent on such (luxurious) items would be noxious on the doomsday.[61]

While the Qur'ān and *Ḥadīth* severely condemn avarice,[62] they equally disfavour prodigality.[63] According to the Qur'ān the best course lies between the two extremes.[64] Defining this *via media* has not been left entirely to the discretion of individuals; the Prophet (peace be upon him) elaborated the concept in specific terms. Avarice does not mean holding money for one's own or family's maintenance. The Prophet (peace be upon him) has said: 'It is better for you to retain something than giving the entire surplus as *ṣadaqa'*,[65] and, 'The best *ṣadaqa* is the one that leaves you well-to-do',[66] and 'it is better to leave your heirs well-to-do rather than leave them denuded; do not behave in a way that leads them to beg for charity'.[67] He has also advised: 'When Allah has given you wealth, the effect of this Allah's wealth and honour on you should be visible (to others).'[68] These sayings, read alongside the Qur'ānic permission to 'take care of your adornment at every place of worship and eat and drink, but be not prodigal' (7:31), partly define the concept of this *via media*. The nature of expenditure that the Prophet (peace be upon him) has rejected is spending on unnecessary household items[69] or on luxurious residential buildings. Normally, one may retain extra items of personal use for carefree, comfortable living but in abnormal conditions Muslims are not allowed to hold in their possession even those items of personal use which are surplus with them but are needed by others. The Prophet (peace be upon him) is reported to have once said (while on a journey): 'If anybody has an extra riding animal he should pass it on to the one who does not have one; if anybody has extra provision he should pass it on to the one who does not have any. (He continued this until we thought that nobody of us had any right over his extra possessions.)[70]

The significance of the Islamic approach lies in its attitude towards possessing wealth. The adornments of the worldly life (7:32; 18:17, 46; 57:20, etc.) are described by the Prophet (peace be upon him) as flourishing and sweet, but with a qualification:

> This worldly wealth is flourishing and sweet but that Muslim owner (of this wealth) is good who acquires it through rightful means and distributes it among *mujāhids,* orphans, widows and travellers.[71]

The Prophet (peace be upon him) once advised one of his great Companions, 'Umar:

> Take it to become wealthy. And (in case it is surplus with you), give it away by way of *ṣadaqa*. If something of this wealth comes to you without your desire and request, take it; if nothing comes to you in this way, do not chase it.[72]

This is exactly in line with the spirit of the Qur'ānic verse 57:23:

> . . . That ye grieve not for the sake of that which hath escaped you, nor ye exult because of that which hath been given. Allah loveth not any pride-filled boaster.

Contentment has been emphasized by the Prophet (peace be upon him) as the proper Muslim attitude:

There is no harm in opulence for the one who fears Allah. And for the God-fearer health is better than wealth. And happiness is also a wealth.[73]

To sum up the above discussion, Islam does not disfavour affluence. Love for wealth and the desire for owning it are natural but this natural inclination should not be allowed to breed vice. All material resources have been created for man but he is not free to do with them whatever he desires. He is created as a vicegerent of Allah on this earth. Allah has endowed these resources upon him to test his performance in the world. But this trial of performance is not left to the discretion of an individual's conscience. Allah and His messenger have laid down the principles of regulating affluence so that it does not breed the vices that otherwise emerge. The remedial measures that Islam has taken to prevent wealth from degenerating into evil comprise of putting restrictions on the ownership and use of resources and of the policy of consumption and investment. It encourages man to earn without being greedy and selfish. It discourages him from hoarding, as well as from prodigality, waste, and showing off which breed ostentation and envy. It urges discharging one's duty to others who fall in need of one's support. In normal conditions Islam relies upon voluntary action but in abnormal situations it resorts to legislation to prevent affluence from breeding evil effects and to make it beneficial for the society.

The Ethics and Rules of Farming

The Qur'ānic approach to agriculture is complementary to its approach to the creation and ownership of land. It is very meaningful that the Qur'ān attributes the act of growth in cultivation to Allah alone.

> Have you seen that which ye cultivate? Is it ye who foster it or are We the Fosterer? (56:63, 64).
> Lo! Allah (it is) who splitteth the grain of corn and the date-stone (for sprouting) (6:95).

This is what the Qur'ān emphasizes in respect of all land produce whether of fields or orchards.[74] The points of instruction in these verses lie in their emphasis on unity of Allah and on the utility of land produce to mankind (and all living beings).

> Is not He (best) Who created the heavens and the earth, and sendeth down for you water from the sky wherewith We cause to spring forth joyous orchards, whose trees it never hath been yours to cause to grow? Is there any God beside Allah? Nay, but they are folk who ascribe equals (unto Him) (27:60).

While a large number of verses count the diverse ways of the consumption of land produce by way of food, fuel, fats, fodder, etc. (6:141–2; 16:67; 20:53–4; 23:19–20; 36:80; 79:31–3; 80:27–32), there are, however, a few verses that emphasize distribution of these God-given gifts:

> He it is Who produceth gardens trellised and untrellised, and the date-palm, and crops of diverse flavours, and the olive and the pomegranate; like and unlike. *Eat ye of the fruit thereof when it fruiteth, and pay the due thereof upon the harvest day, and be not prodigal! Allah loveth not the prodigal* (6:141).

The verse last cited is taken to imply the compulsory alms-tax *(Zakāt);* in another verse voluntary distribution is advised:

> O ye who believe! Spend of the good things which ye have earned, and of that *which We bring forth from the earth* for you (2:267).

While the Qur'ān meaningfully confines itself to the creed and general behaviour towards land produce, the *Ḥadīth* literature guides us towards the ethics and operational guidelines of farming.

The Prophet (peace be upon him) belonged to a city where trade was the mainstay of the economy. Like most Makkans, he himself took part in trade before the commencement of his prophethood. Most of his Makkan followers who joined him in Madina were traders. On the other hand, Madina, where the Prophet (peace be upon him) founded a state, was an agricultural city. The Madinans owned lands and engaged in farming and gardening. This business not only required harder work and more devotion than trade and always stood exposed to natural calamities, it also stood in the way of acquiring the knowledge of religion and participating in *jihād.* It was quite possible that observing the quick turnover in trade and the other benefits that go with it many of the devout land-owners might have been discouraged from sticking to their lands. Agriculture has always been the backbone of a stable, prosperous economy and the freshly-born state would have been seriously hampered in its mission had there been any withdrawals from farming. The Prophet (peace be upon him) is known to have not only encouraged this profession but also provided new impetus for bringing new lands under cultivation.[75] Like all the other activities of life he brought this also into the moral domain as a virtuous act. A *Ḥadīth* says: 'The seed which a Muslim grows and is eaten up is a pious spending *(ṣadaqa),* (even) that which is stolen from it is a pious spending, that which is eaten up by beasts or birds is a pious spending.'[76] The Prophet (peace be upon him) is reported to have confirmed the old practice of recognizing the occupation of un-owned barren land by anyone who reclaims it. A *Ḥadīth* says: 'Of course land is Allah's land, slaves are Allah's slaves *('ibād),* so whoever reclaims a dead land is entitled to it.'[77] Another *Ḥadīth* confirms the same thing in a different way: 'Whoever reclaims a dead land possesses it while the labour of a wrongful occupier has no right.'[78]

While these sayings encourage farming and gardening, and bring new lands under cultivation, they do not imply approval of unlimited right to occupy large tracts of land and use these as a means of exploiting human beings. It is stated that the Prophet (peace be upon him) once looked at a heap of agricultural implements and observed: 'A house which has (the abundance of) these implements brings about a fall in position.'[79] The saying does appear to discourage large holdings. But the actual words of the *Ḥadīth* do not point to any economic reason for this discouragement. This might perhaps be because it was not then practically possible for an individual to cultivate large holdings: he either had to leave most of the land idle or employ a large army of labourers or serfs. Leaving resources idle is against Islamic precept. The rule is that man is allowed to possess only so much of natural resources as he can utilize for himself and for the good of the society. In case he fails to do this, they are to be taken from him and passed on to one who can use them. In no case is one allowed to retain God-given resources idly, just for the sake of ownership. It was because of this principle that the second Caliph fixed a maximum period of three years after which idle land was withdrawn by the Government.[80] As regards the use of an army of labourers it was practically impossible due to the absence of such a class in Arabia. The Bedouin who might have been potential labour were temperamentally unsuited to such work. As regards employment of serfs, this was not possible because of two reasons. Firstly, they were not available in large numbers in Arabia in the very early period – non-Muslims were discouraged from settling in Arabia, while at the same time emancipation of converted slaves was encouraged. Secondly, the owner's frequent participation in *Jihād* forced him to leave the land for long periods during which the employment of a large army of slaves on large tracts of land could have given rise to absentee landlordism and a number of social, economic and political problems.

The benefits of title to land have been subjected to restrictions so that the interest of the cultivator is also safeguarded. A harmful condition that the title-holder imposed on the tiller was the taking of a fixed quantity of the produce whether or not the latter got a sufficient return for his labour and capital. In this way a parasite class could emerge at the expense of the interests of the actual producer. It is perhaps in this context that the Prophet (peace be upon him) is stated to have advised:

'It is better for you to give your land to your brother free rather than charge from him a fixed produce for it.'[81] Another form of the prevalent land tenure which often harmed the interest of the farmer was to lease out land to the cultivator in return for a fixed ratio of crop, plus a fixed quantity grown in certain fixed areas of that piece of land. This again made the return from land certain for the title-holder but uncertain for the farmer. It sometimes happened that a large part of the crop was destroyed and after allowing for the fixed portions which were chargeable by the title-holder the farmer might hardly get any just share. This practice was also disapproved by the Prophet (peace be upon him).[82] The alternatives which, in light of the *Ḥadīth* seem to conform to the Islamic standards of magnanimity *(iḥsān)* are: (1) To allow someone the use of land without levying any charge, and (2) to let it out to him for cultivation at a fixed rent in terms of money but not of produce.[83] In case, for practical reasons, these two standards cannot be observed, positive rules of justice have been laid down to rid farming of all the elements of injustice and exploitation. Chapters of *Muzāra'a* and *Musaqat* in the collections of *Ḥadīth* and the details laid down in books on *fiqh* discuss the rules of title holder-farmer relationship under different conditions.[84]

Trade: Principles and Practices

Contrary to agriculture, trade involves a multiplicity of techniques and transactions and is exposed to many more unjust practices than occur in agriculture. The Qur'ān lays down a few basic principles which govern general economic behaviour and involve the ethics of trade too. But the *Ḥadīth* literature refers pointedly to a number of specific practices which fall below the standard of justice and fair dealing.

The number of *Ḥadīth* on the excellences of trade and which teach its proper conduct, runs, in the most comprehensive collection, *Kanz al-'Ummāl,* into four figures but the *Ṣiḥāḥ Sitta* have reported only a few of them. The Prophet (peace be upon him) himself took part in trade yet we do not find any tradition which justifies its superiority to other lawful pursuits. The *Ḥadīth* literature, as expected, subjects trade to moral principles: 'An honest and righteous Muslim trader will fall in with the martyrs on doomsday';[85] 'Allah shows mercy to a man who is kindly when he sells, when he buys, and when he makes a claim';[86] 'God will neither look at nor talk to a false swearer on doomsday';[87] 'If the seller and the buyer both tell the truth and negotiate frankly, both will be blessed; if they conceal from and mislead each other, blessing *(baraka)* will be withdrawn';[88] 'Allah blesses the person who is lenient in sale, in purchase and in making a claim',[89] are some such traditions which seek to inculcate in the people the true spirit which should inspire a Muslim in his business dealings.

While the Qur'ān prohibits eating one another's property by unlawful means *(bāṭil),* the *Ḥadīth* point out what in practice these unlawful means are. They regulate trade practices in such a way that the legitimate interests of both the distributor and consumer are protected. If any of the practices involves uncertainty or loss to either in trade it is treated as unjust. Similarly those transactions which benefit a few persons at the expense of the common good or which lead to exploitation of either party are forbidden. Thus the *Ḥadīth* ban about twenty forms of trade – transactions which were prevalent in the Prophet's time but which contained something objectionable warranting prohibition. All contracts of sale in which the very existence of the commodity is uncertain are declared null and void. The *Ḥadīth* term them as *gharar.*[90] Examples are the sale of fish in water which is not yet caught or of a bird in the air or of a foetus in the womb *(ḥabl al-ḥabla).*[91] The sale of milk in the udder is also termed as *gharar* and forbidden. On the same ground, sale of fruits in an orchard for many years in advance *(mu'āwama)* is also not permissible.[92] Similarly it is not lawful to sell dates growing upon a tree in exchange for dates which have been picked and which are *conjectured* to be equal in point of measurement to those that are upon the tree. This kind of sale is termed as *muzābana* and forbidden in a *Ḥadīth,*[93] as well as the sale termed as *muḥāqala,*[94] which is the sale of wheat in the ear in exchange for a quantity of wheat conjectured to be equal thereto. The principle is the same with respect to the sale of grapes on the vine in exchange for raisins. Bargains determined by the purchaser by the touching of the goods *(mulāmasa)*[95] or by the throwing up of the goods *(munābadha)*[96] or by the casting of a stone *(ḥuṣāt),*[97] perhaps at a goat in a herd for sale, have been held as unlawful. All these transactions involve either *gharar* or *jahl* (ignorance).

Besides the above unlawful sales there are other forms of sale which the Prophet (peace be upon him) did not like. He prohibited boosting the price of a merchandise by a fictitious tender of a high price *(najash).*[98] This is done even to this day in fairs and auctions by appointed agents with a view to prompting others to make a higher bid without any intention on the part of the agent to purchase the commodity. The Prophet (peace be upon him) also prohibited anticipation of the proper market-price. The practice was that people would meet a trade caravan, at a distance from the city, with a view to purchasing the grain brought by the merchants, and then selling it to the people of the city at an enhanced price.[99]

Of all the above sales, *bay' salam* had been the most prevalent form in Madina. This implied a contract of sale requiring an immediate payment of the price while admitting a delay in the delivery of the wares. As a rule the Prophet (peace be upon him) is reported to have forbidden the sale of what is not in one's actual possession.[100] *Bay' salam* is an exception to the above rule. It is declared as valid subject to the condition that the quality and the nature of the article for sale, and the time and place of delivery and the price are clearly defined at the time of making the contract of such sale.[101]

Another exemption was made in the case of *muzābana* contract under which the prohibition was relaxed up to five *wasqs*[102] of dates. The object of providing this exemption was to provide relief to poor families.[103]

While many early trade practices involving unjust transactions have been forbidden, there are *Ḥadīth* to direct a free operation of the market, unhampered by artificial factors. For example, one of the important factors that affects the operation of a free market is monopoly in which a buyer/seller dictates his terms irrespective of the demand and supply situation. A *Ḥadīth* terms it as *bay' muḍṭar* and disapproves it.[104] This form of sale signifies a position of compulsion on the part of the buyer/seller which leaves him no option but to sell/buy the goods at an unreasonable price. The Qur'ānic provision of trading with mutual consent (4:29) implies free consent as has been elaborated in the following *Ḥadīth:*

> It is not lawful for a person to take another person's property without his free will.
>
> It is not lawful for a Muslim to take (even a valueless) stick of his brother without his voluntary consent *(ṭīb nafsih)* for it[105].

Another such factor is advertisement and publicity which has become a bane as well as a boon of materialistic society. It is a useful way of introducing a product to prospective customers. And yet it also has some defects. Publicity can be intra-mural or extra-mural. Display of goods in an attractive way within the shop or sales centre is known as intra-mural publicity while advertisement and propaganda outside this centre is extra-mural publicity. While the early people used very crude methods for both ways of introducing their goods or prices, the modern techniques achieve this object through hand-bills, hoardings, neon-signs, films, newspapers, radio, and television advertisements. Effective and excessive publicity of a product not only frequently infatuates the customer but many a time misleads him. Constant publicity is, to a large extent, responsible for creating an artificial demand for a product which actually is not genuinely needed by the consumer. In view of the real advantages that publicity brings, it was inexpedient to forbid it. The Prophet (peace be upon him) is reported to have put some moral restrictions on this technique of promoting sale. It is stated that once he examined a heap of corn for sale and found that the quality inside the heap was not as good as was shown on the outside. This technique was aimed at misleading the buyers. The Prophet (peace be upon him) censured the vendor and exclaimed: 'Whosoever misleads (others) is not one of us.'[106] Some other similar *Ḥadīth* put a moral check on the misuse of publicity. 'Taking of frequent oaths for canvassing the customer pays much in the beginning but ultimately causes a diminution in livelihood.'[107] 'Do not mislead others by fictitious tender of high prices or by praises of the commodity.'[108] 'O community of merchants, unprofitable speech and swearing have a place in business dealing, so mix it with *ṣadaqa*.'[109] 'The merchants will be raised on the day of resurrection as evil-doers, except those who fear Allah, are honest, and speak the truth.'[110]

Another factor that disturbs the free operation of the market is the activity of intermediaries. The *Ḥadīth* tend to restrict their role as far as possible. They are not only discouraged as between the village supplier and the city wholesaler, and between the retailer and the consumer, but also within the market itself. The activities of the well-known broker with his under-cover practices, and of the bulls and bears who make money without really participating in practical business, who interrupt a free market and disturb the reaching of a natural equilibrium between the forces of current demand and current supply by merely speculative transactions, were disapproved and prevented. The *Ḥadīth* linked the legal sale of a commodity with the condition of *de facto* transfer of possession. It says: 'Do not sell foodgrains before taking them into possession, it is tantamount to selling dirhams for dirhams (money for money).'[111] According to another *Ḥadīth,* the Prophet (peace be upon him) disallowed the sale of a villager's merchandise by an urban seller. Ibn 'Abbās was asked as to what this sale *(bay' ḥāḍir li ba'd)* meant, to which he answered that it meant becoming a villager's broker *(simsār)*.[112] In some other narrations the last version of the *Ḥadīth* is 'leave them to themselves; God feeds them through each other', and 'A city dweller should not sell for a villager, even though he be his father or son.'[113]

Another factor that disturbs the free interplay of the forces of demand and supply is hoarding. The supplier holds back the stock of a commodity in demand in order to create artificial scarcity and effect a rise in price. When the price thus rises, the hoarder brings out his stock to sell it at the higher price. The Prophet (peace be upon him) discouraged this by exclaiming 'Whosoever hoards is a sinner.'[114] The *Ḥadīth:* 'Do not sell foodgrains before taking them into possession',[115] also discourages speculation and forward-trading which ultimately distort the very concept of total supply and effective demand.

The restrictions on charging monopoly price, on advertisement and publicity, on the role of intermediaries, on hoarding and speculation, and on forward-trading make possible the freer operation of the market. Over and above these general principles on trade there are also *Ḥadīth* to regulate the practices of mortgage, partnership, option *(khayār)*, advance trading *(salam)*, surety, bail, insolvency, loans and credit and option to buy neighbouring estates *(shuf'a)*[116] which ensure justice and fair play.

Consumption and Savings

While the Qur'ānic principles of socio-economic behaviour largely govern distribution, exchange and some aspects of production, the principles of personal economic behaviour go a long way to determining the pattern of consumption, volume of savings and the 'what-to-produce' aspect of production. The Qur'ānic principles relating to consumption have a lot of bearing upon the concept of the standard of living which, in modern civilization, has acquired sacrosanctity. In contemporary thought the ultimate aim of all economic activity is thought to be maximum satisfaction of human wants, and the criterion of economic achievement is judged by the living standard obtaining in a society at a particular period of time. This aim, in societies adhering to materialistic values, has generally led each individual in an unbridled race to grab more and more economic resources and attain a still higher standard of living. This has placed man in a vicious circle which is not easy to break. With the values of morality and religion knocked aside, and urged by purely hedonistic motives, the different classes of human society are now confronting each other in an unrelenting hostile posture. Each is doggedly endeavouring to exploit the other and this struggle in some countries has culminated in a socialism which has made them equal in poverty and denied them their rights to freedom, dignity and self-respect. Under this reactionary system the standard of living of the individual is secondary to social requirements and the mix of consumer goods to be produced is not determined by the demand of individuals or households but by the planning authority. Man has been relegated to a position where socially he never was, and an apparently innocent beginning has led humanity to a tragic end.

The Qur'ān and the *Sunna* take an altogether different approach to the question of standard of living. On the one hand, they give due cognizance to natural urges in man which stimulate work, earning, and spending. On the other, they use the force of their eschatological beliefs and moral discipline to suppress the tendencies which expose man to depravity from within himself and from outside. To achieve this purpose they do not shrink from authorizing the state to resort to legislative measures, government initiative and control. Eschatological beliefs and moral teachings are copiously intertwined throughout the Qur'ān and the *Sunna* and are closely linked with their social and economic teachings. The Qur'ān is alert to the fact that its emphasis on moral concepts might incline man to asceticism, to spurning worldly life. To counterbalance this, it emphasizes the significance of material prosperity and induces man to utilize the 'bounties of Allah'. The Qur'ān tends to respect material and sentimental attachments.[117] It treats livelihood as Allah's bounty and urges man to acquire it. This is reflected in the use of the words which carry this sense. Words like *khayr,* virtue, and *faḍl,*[118] bounty, repeatedly appear in the Qur'ān to signify wealth, livelihood, or trade. The functions of wealth are mentioned as source of livelihood (4:5), as ornament or adornment for this life (18:46), as protection against future odds (4:9), as capital for worldly life (42:36), and trial for the Hereafter (6:165). Along with these incentives to earn it repeatedly asks man[119] to satisfy his wants and declare his prosperity, without going to the extent of ostentatious extravagance. The standard of the satisfaction of wants is the yardstick for setting a standard of living. The Qur'ān has not drawn any line beyond which man must refrain from consuming lawful things. This spirit can be understood from the following verse:

> Say: Who hath forbidden the adornment of Allah which He hath brought forth for His bondmen, and the good things of His providing . . . Say: My Lord forbiddeth only indecencies, such of them as are apparent and such as are within, and sin and wrongful oppression . . . . (7:32, 33).

Along with verses like the above, the way in which the Qur'ān has reiterated spending on one's self and on others raises a problem which has faced the Muslim society till this day and poses a challenge as to how capital formation can be effected with this frame of mind. The verse, 'they ask thee what they ought to spend. Say: That which ye spare'[120] (2:219), accommodates for any reasonable consumption pattern. That pattern is governed by taste, tolerance and convention and is bound to differ from man to man. It covers necessities and comforts. The only line drawn beyond this limit is overspending *(isrāf)* which is not desirable even in spending on others, because this may leave the person concerned denuded, rebuked (17:29). The contrary attitude is niggardliness which, in the context of consumption, implies a condition under which man abstains from spending or, in other words, starts accumulating.[121] There can be a number of justifiable motives for such action beyond the natural tendency to accumulate. An individual may be over-sensitive to unforeseen circumstances in the future, or may wish to bequeath sufficient funds for his family. He may also wish to provide for any probable business requirement in the near future. He may wish to save in order to earn profit through speculative investment, if that is possible. It will be seen that the Qur'ān does not altogether rule against these motives.[122] It simply urges man not to exaggerate these motives lest his act of saving disturb the proper circulation and distribution of wealth. To achieve this object it uses its moral force, on the one hand, and its monetary and taxation policies on the other. These moral injunctions of the Qur'ān strike a balance between saving for different motives and spending on oneself and in a good cause.[123] The relevant Qur'ānic monetary and taxation measures will be discussed in the relevant sections.

The Qur'ān envisages the economic structure of society on the basis of the concepts regarding consumption outlined above. In practice, a well-to-do man who wants to save for the different reasons mentioned without neglecting his obligations to Allah and the society cannot but manage to live a simple life. The Qur'ānic warning neither to be niggardly nor to induce others to be so has both a direct and an indirect bearing. Inducing others to be niggardly indirectly may arise as a result of ostentatious display of idle accumulations. The Qur'ān, on the one hand, warns such people of a 'shameful doom' (4:37) and on the other, asks others not to 'covet the thing in which Allah has made some of them excel others' (4:32). This fact of excelling others, or inequality, after practising economic justice, is attributed to Allah and is declared as a trial.[124]

In addition to these measures the *Ḥadīth* also take a number of other steps which are conducive to saving in order to enhance the supply of investible funds. They pointedly disapprove all those activities which the Qur'ān broadly describes as obscene or sinful. These activities, however pleasing they may be, add nothing to the national product. They corrupt people and ultimately effect an inequitable distribution of wealth. The *Ḥadīth* regarding personal consumption incline towards simplicity.[125] For a government official the maximum standard of living is set down in a *Ḥadīth* in the following words: 'Whosoever is our official may marry if he is unmarried, may have a servant if he does not have one, may build a house if he does not have one; but if someone exceeds this, he commits a breach of trust or is a thief.'[126] This *Ḥadīth* gives an idea of the nature of the maximum facilities which could be granted in the Prophet's time. Over and above these measures, the consumption and the use of certain items other than those banned in the Qur'ān have also been disapproved. The use of expensive luxury clothes and of gold and silver utensils are disliked;[127] the latter even banned. Most important of all, the Prophet (peace be upon him) has forbidden Muslims to squander wealth *(iḍā'at māl),*[128] which is taken to mean that a person is not allowed even to give *ṣadaqa* if he is indebted or himself needful. Thus in this circumstance even *ṣadaqa* is treated as squandering wealth. Islam's concern for protection of wealth is evidenced in a *Ḥadīth* which says that a person who is killed in the cause of protection of his wealth *(māl)* is a martyr *(shahīd).*[129] These and all such *Ḥadīth* dissuade one from frittering away resources on unproductive items and enable one to effect savings. The saving acquired through restraint in consumption is not likely to be recklessly distributed. That 'the best *ṣadaqa* is that which leaves you well-to-do';[130] and, 'it is better to leave your heirs well-to-do rather than leave them denuded. Do not behave in a way that leads them to beg for charity';[131] and, above all: 'a person who sells up his house or orchard but does not re-invest the proceeds in similar assets does not deserve blessing *(baraka)*';[132] – are some of the Prophet's sayings that amplify the Islamic approach to consumption *vis-à-vis* savings.

Thus the philosophic beliefs and economic teachings of the Qur'ān and the *Sunna* build a pattern of consumption, of living standard, and of saving, quite distinct from the present-day capitalist or socialist patterns, and avoid the problem of class-antagonism which has been treated by some economic philosophers as 'the history of all the hitherto existing society'.[133]

The Concept of *Infāq*: The First Duty, The Last Resort

The mechanism of redistribution is introduced in the Qur'ān and the *Sunna* generally with the words *'infāq'* (spending), *'Zakāt'* and *'ṣadaqa'*;[134] the last two sometimes in the sense of compulsory levy too. But the most frequently used word is *infāq* which appears in the Qur'ān in more or less 60 places as against *Zakāt* and *ṣadaqa* which appear in about 30 and 15 places respectively. *Ṣadaqa* and *infāq* are intertwined as interchangeable words in the sense of pious spending in verses 2:261–81. Another word which infrequently appears in the Qur'ān to convey the sense of spending or redistribution is *qarḍ ḥasan* (goodly loan) advanced to Allah (57:11; 64:17).[135] This term also sometimes follows the payment of *Zakāt* or *ṣadaqa* too (5:12; 73:20; 57:18). Although *ṣadaqa* is less frequently used in the Qur'ān than *Zakāt* and *infāq,* the concept of it, read in conjunction with the concept of *infāq,* is of great significance in the financial structuring of an Islamic society.

The technical difference between *infāq* and compulsory *Zakāt* lies in their items of levy and *quid pro quo*. *Infāq* can be made of anything to any extent but *Zakāt* is levied on specified items over a certain minimum limit of possession and at a fixed rate and interval. The payer of compulsory *Zakāt* withdraws himself from deriving any direct moral or material benefit and seeks to win Allah's pleasure. *Infāq,* on the other hand, also implies spending in a 'worldly' sense, often expecting moral, material or social benefit. Thus *infāq,* in a sense, encompasses *ṣadaqa,* and is a broader term. Yet one very important difference between the two lies in the invisible and intangible expressions of *ṣadaqa,* in addition to its tangible expressions. Thus it may be a gesture, a word spoken or a service rendered. The Prophet (peace be upon him) has said:

> After sunrise a *ṣadaqa* becomes due on each joint of man. Adjudicating justly between two persons is a *ṣadaqa.* Helping someone in his riding (his horse) is a *ṣadaqa.* Loading one's luggage on his riding animal is a *ṣadaqa.* Speaking good words to somebody is a *ṣadaqa.* Every step treading for *ṣalāh* (offering prayers) is a *ṣadaqa.* Removing any impeding obstacle from a pathway is also a *ṣadaqa.*[136]

On another occasion the Prophet (peace be upon him) has said:

> Looking upon your (Muslim) brother with a smile is a *ṣadaqa.* Urging good deeds and dissuading from vices is a *ṣadaqa.* Guiding a lost traveller is a *ṣadaqa.* Guiding a blind man is a *ṣadaqa.* Clearing the path of stones, thorns and bones is a *ṣadaqa.* Filling a Muslim brother's bucket with water in your bucket is (also) a *ṣadaqa.*[137]

According to a *Ḥadīth:*

> The best *ṣadaqa* is to learn a point of knowledge *('ilm)* and teach it to your Muslim brother. (Ibn Mājah, Vol. I, H. 215.)

Thus the concept of *ṣadaqa* in spite of its narrowness has a moral superiority over *infāq* inasfar as it involves ethics and courtesies in addition to material giving.

Infāq literally means spending. It signifies any spending whether for good cause or bad. That is why spending by non-believers for opposing the religion (8:36), their spending on their wives (3:117; 60:10–11), spending by hypocrites (9:53, 54, 98), spending by Muslims on their wives by way of dower and sustenance (4:34) are all termed *infāq.* If *infāq* qualifies itself to become a *ṣadaqa* it has to be made for Allah's pleasure (2:195); and has to fulfil certain conditions. It is to be made from own earnings or from natural wealth a man possesses (2:267). It should be done scrupulously, without any desire for publicity (4:37–8). While it is not objectionable to give it to others openly, it is more worthy of reward before Allah to conceal the award (2:274; 13:22; 14:31; 16:75). The act of distribution should be made according to the capacity of the owner (65:6, 7); he should not act miserly, nor should he overspend (25:67) so that he sits down rebuked, denuded (17:29). Nobody, even though poor, is exempt from this act of philanthropy. One should not be over-anxious about facing poverty resulting from generosity; it is a diabolical inspiration (2:268). On the contrary, this distribution introduces overall prosperity and well-being (2:261–2), and is ultimately better also for the giver (2:272, 274; 35:39; 64:15, 16). One should not feel that deprivation and the needs of the poor are mere fate and God-apportioned, and therefore have no justifiable claim on one's wealth. This wealth in the owner's possession is the poor man's right and this right should be given to him (47:36). When once given the giver should not expect any reward from the receiver; such *ṣadaqa* will be regarded as a *qarḍ ḥasan* (goodly loan) advanced to Allah Who will reward the giver (2:245; 64:17). One point to remember is that personal, physical contribution *(Jihād)* does not absolve one of the obligation for material contribution (9:54, 55; 42:38).

While the Qur'ān makes it obligatory on an owner who, though poor, can spare something, to spend in a noble cause, the Prophet (peace be upon him) has not confined such spending only to savings. '*Ṣadaqa* is obligatory on each Muslim' the Prophet (peace be upon him) has said. 'And if somebody has nothing to give?' somebody asked him. His answer was: 'Let him work with his hands (to make an earning) for himself and for giving *ṣadaqa*.'[138] This is confirmed by his Companion Abū Mas'ūd Anṣārī's report, which says: 'Whenever the Prophet (peace be upon him) ordered us to give *ṣadaqa,* some of us would go to the shopping centre to carry loads, earn a *mudd*[139] of grain and give *ṣadaqa* . . . '[140] The Prophet (peace be upon him) used to advise orchard-owners to hang a bunch of dates for the destitute whenever they picked 10 *wasqs* (about 1,900 kilo) loads of dates.[141] On another occasion he said to women thus: 'Spend but do not calculate (hoarded money) because Allah would (also) calculate for you. Do not hold your wealth; Allah would (also) hold from you.'[142]

The above sayings work against the preference for cash and for the expectation of a material reward on parting with cash. This is reinforced by another *Ḥadīth*:

> The Prophet (peace be upon him) was asked as to which *ṣadaqa* was the best. On this he said: That one (is the best) which is made while you are healthy; you hope to live (long); you fear poverty (due to giving *ṣadaqa*), but not that one which is delayed so that death approaches you and then you begin to nominate the beneficiaries although, at that moment, it has already become their property.[143]

The only exception that we find to this is the case of a debtor who may not demonstrate his generosity unless he has discharged his liability.[144]

The argument above should not be taken to mean that everybody should always distribute the entire balance that remains after normal daily expenditure and discharge of loans. The actual policy of distribution claims a portion of funds that are surplus after normal expenditure and after providing for unforeseen events, prospects of profitable transactions and security. 'It is better for you to retain something than giving the entire surplus as *ṣadaqa*',[145] is what the Prophet (peace be upon him) advised one of his Companions. 'The best *ṣadaqa* is the one that leaves you well-to-do'[146] is the determining standard of the extent of religious spending.

The standard outlined above is to be maintained in normal circumstances. In cases of emergencies, however, extraordinary measures are advised. For example the Prophet (peace be upon him), while on a *jihād* expedition advised: 'Anybody who has an extra riding-animal should pass it on to the one who does not have an animal; anybody who has surplus provision should give it to the one who does not have it' . . . and he continued so long in this vein that his Companions thought none had any right over his own surplus belongings.[147]

The beneficiaries of this *infāq* not only include those classes that are included in the list of *Zakāt* recipients but also a number of other classes without necessarily considering their financial standing. The heads in common with the beneficiaries of *Zakāt* are the poor, the needy, the functionaries of charitable funds, the slaves, the debtors, the *mujāhid* and the stranded travellers (9:60). Additional heads of the beneficiaries of *infāq* are parents, other near relations, orphans, neighbours, fellow-workers and travellers (4:36) and beggars[148] (2:177). The Prophet (peace be upon him) has disregarded the scrutiny of financial standing of the beneficiary in these words: 'The beggar has a right even though he visits you on horse-back.'[149] Moreover, there is nothing in the Qur'ān and the *Sunna* to restrict the list of beneficiaries to these heads.

In addition to this undefined quantity of *ṣadaqa* or *infāq* the Qur'ān also imposes *ṣadaqa* with fixed rates which it terms as *kaffāra* or expiation. It is prescribed in case of a particular fault in observance of fast (2:184) or in performing *Ḥajj* (2:196). There is also a compensatory payment in the case of flouting an oath or using some sort of metaphorical language for divorce (5:89; 58:3). The expiations in all these cases differ in value. They call for feeding and clothing one poor man in some cases while providing for sixty poor men in some others.[150]

The above introduction to the concept of *infāq* and *ṣadaqa* and their role in redistributing income and wealth along with their intangible and ethical implications leads us to some most important conclusions that have great bearing on the framing of financial policies. It would be worthwhile to first reflect on a few points relevant to this discussion:

(1) The Qur'ān lays down the basic qualifications of becoming a Muslim and prescribes a list of Do's and Don'ts. Its Do's include the five daily prayers, payment of *Zakāt,* performance of *Ḥajj,* undertaking *Jihād* (physically and financially), in addition to acquisition of knowledge, enforcement of *ḥudūd* and justice, propagation of religion, and moral integrity, etc. Performance of all these Do's is obligatory and disregarding them is treated as sinful. But the point to note is that the injunction of doing *infāq* and paying *ṣadaqa* is repeated more frequently than most other injunctions. For example the injunction to seek enforcement of justice occurs in the Qur'ān in six places; of acquisition of knowledge in two places; of payment of *Zakāt* in eight places; to ordain good deeds and forbid indecencies *(amr bi'l-ma'rūf wa nahy 'an al-munkar)* in two places; and to propagate religion in five places. As compared with this, the injunction to practise *infāq,* excluding the giving of *ṣadaqa,* appears in ten places, directly or indirectly. In nine more places *infāq* has been acclaimed as a virtue of the true believers. In addition, the significance of *infāq* and its terms and conditions are extensively reiterated in a number of other places. Precisely speaking, the Qur'ān gives highest priority to *infāq* after[151] its emphasis on prayers *(ṣalāt).* Thus it occupies first place in the Qur'ān in respect of injunctions concerning the material life of man.

(2) The wording of the injunctions regarding the acts hinted at above appears in the imperative. According to some of the authorities on Islamic jurisprudence, the imperative mood is used in the Qur'ān for mandatory rules, unless there is some sign to prove otherwise in which case the imperative mood stands for desirability or permissibility.[152]

(3) The above point gives rise to the question whether the injunctions regarding *infāq* and *ṣadaqa* should be treated as obligatory or as desirable or permissible. The admonitions on miserliness and non-observance of *infāq* and *ṣadaqa* clearly suggest that the practice of *infāq* and *ṣadaqa* is not merely permissible, for while doing a permissible act is not rewardable, its non-observance is also not punishable. Similarly a desirable act is rewardable but its non-observance is not punishable. The rich reward in the Hereafter that is associated with *infāq* and *ṣadaqa* and the condign punishment that is forewarned on non-observance of these acts[153] suggest that they are more than desirable. Moreover, the expressions in the Qur'ān, such as:

> Spend your wealth for the cause of Allah . . . (2:195);

> O ye who believe! Spend of that wherewith We have provided you ere a day come when . . . (2:254);
>
> Believe in Allah and His messenger, and spend of that whereof He hath made you trustees . . . (57:7);
>
> So keep your duty to Allah as best you can and listen, and obey, and spend . . . (64:16),

and the Prophet's saying '*ṣadaqa* is *obligatory* on each Muslim . . . '; and his Companion's remarks 'Whenever the Prophet of Allah *ordered us* to give *ṣadaqa* . . . '[154] are indisputable evidence as to the obligatory nature of *infāq* and *ṣadaqa.* And yet *infāq* and *ṣadaqa* are not treated as obligatory in the sense *Zakāt* is. This is so because in the case of *Zakāt* the items and rates of levy, the slabs and exemption limits and the heads of expenditure, are prescribed in the Qur'ān and *Ḥadīth.* But no such prescription appears in the case of *infāq* and *ṣadaqa.* This means that both are obligatory but the details of *infāq* and *ṣadaqa* are not fixed like *Zakāt* but vary from person to person according to income, holdings, liabilities, standard of living and professional requirements. The most meaningful hint that is to be found in the Qur'ān in respect of quality and quantity of *infāq* is found in the following verses:

> Ye will not attain unto piety until ye spend of that which ye love (3:92).
>
> And they ask thee what to spend. Say: Whatever remains surplus (2:219).

Here again fixity of the amount or rate has been skipped in favour of honest personal judgement by the individuals.

To sum up, *infāq* and *ṣadaqa* are as much obligatory on Muslims as are the five daily prayers and *Zakāt,* but in spite of setting a maximum limit of surplus *(al-'afw)* and being applicable to all sorts of wealth and service, *infāq* and *ṣadaqa* do not involve any specific rates or amount of spending, exemption limits, slabs of taxation and heads of expenditure nor is there any mention of the amount of service one is supposed to render by way of *ṣadaqa* except that 'a *ṣadaqa* becomes due on each joint of a man'. However, the Qur'ān and the *Ḥadīth* have pointed out the functions which *infāq* and *ṣadaqa* are supposed to discharge. This means that Muslims are duty-bound to spend generously of their physical and material resources to ameliorate the overall condition of the society. This is the real meaning of *infāq* and *ṣadaqa* and their purpose, as derivable from the Qur'ān and the *Ḥadīth.* Their aims include support and uplift of relations, neighbours, and colleagues, the poor, the unemployed, the physically weak, the orphans, the *Mujāhid,* the passers-by, riders, the indebted, as well as the enforcement of justice, spreading virtue and suppressing evil, environmental cleanliness, acquisition and dissemination of knowledge, etc.[155]

The above premise leads us to the most important part of this discussion. At the advent of Islam, compulsory *infāq* with discretionary rates and amounts was largely sufficient to achieve the objectives of *infāq* and *ṣadaqa*. The standard of living of the early Muslim people and the stage of civilization hardly called for anything more than direct financial assistance or moral support to individuals. In case the Prophet (peace be upon him), as a ruler, found it necessary to carry out any job, he would advise the Muslims in general or in some cases nominate some particular person or persons to look after it. And thus the job was carried out. The Prophet's recommendation was regarded as obligatory. Thus the task of removing shortage of water or playing host to some tribal delegations or supporting slaves who deserted enemy ranks or even the financing of the Prophet's biggest campaign of Tabūk were all managed through *ṣadaqa* or *infāq*.[156] It was for this reason that the funds which the *Bayt al-Māl* received in the time of the Prophet (peace be upon him) and the Caliph Abū Bakr were found surplus of government requirement and used for direct distribution. When, during the second Caliph's reign, government incomes witnessed a tremendous increase, the Caliph did not find any other larger head of public expenditure than distribution by way of stipends and rations. Salaries to the newly introduced officials involved only nominal funds. Gradually, however, public spending increased but did not exceed *Kharāj* proceeds which might have forced the government to mobilize its institution of *infāq*. Construction of mosques, government offices and go-downs, setting up of shopping centres and cantonments, new urban settlements, and preparation for *Jihād* etc. were the early heads of public spending which did not require any larger amount of funds than *Kharāj* incomes that poured in from newly conquered regions during the second Caliph's reign. As a result, *infāq* and *ṣadaqa* as a source of income were not resorted to. This leads us to the conclusion that this source follows other sources of public revenues receivable from public properties. If these other resources are sufficient to meet public expenditure, the conditions and method of performing *infāq* and *ṣadaqa* would remain voluntary. But in case government sources fall short of its requirements, it may resort to this source. And if it does decide to do so, it will not be practicable nor advisable to leave the conditions and methods of payment at the discretion of the public. The government must be certain of the proceeds it wants to collect through this source within a given period of time. It also has to ensure that payment through this source is made equitably by all (3:134). Thus the institution of *infāq* shall take the form of a modern tax subject to the condition that it is equitably contributed to by all (3:134); and that it does not exceed the Qur'ānic limits of 'Say: Whatever remains surplus'[157] (2:219).

Zakāt

With a view to suppressing interest-mentality the Qur'ān and the *Sunna* have insisted most emphatically on philanthropy and religious spending *(infāq)*. But they have not left the whole matter to the fine conscience of the well-to-do. They have made a portion of this philanthropy a compulsory levy (*ṣadaqa* or *Zakāt*) to remind the people of their obligation to the needy class of the society. This compulsory levy, as the Qur'ān claims, has been prescribed in all the divine religions.[158]

The Qur'ānic insistence on paying *Zakāt* is evident from the frequent repetition of the relevant injunctions.[159] The view that *Zakāt* was obligatory even in the Makkan period is plausible given that the injunctions regarding *Zakāt* are also found in the Makkan *sūras*. We may presume that the obligation to pay *Zakāt* to the government is a late Madinan development: 'Take *ṣadaqa* from their wealth, wherewith thou mayst purify them and mayst make them grow, and pray for them . . . '[160] The rates of *Zakāt* and exemption limits are not found in the Qur'ān. Rather, the details are found in the instructions which were issued by the Prophet (peace be upon him) to his collectors and to the tribal chiefs.[161] Verse 2:219: 'And they ask thee what they aught to spend. Say: That which is surplus', might be interpreted to suggest that during the early period the government was presumably not the sole recipient of *Zakāt*. In any case, the levy of *Zakāt* was to affect the economy in a variety of ways. Firstly, it discouraged hoarding of wealth and compelled the savers either to invest these idle funds or to spend them. But there has always been a maximum limit of spending on one's self. And in the simple, unsophisticated society of the early Islamic period human needs were limited. As a result, consumption soon reached the maximum level leaving the balance as surplus, *'al-'afw'*. The savings could thus pass on from the savers to the class of consumers who were have-nots. This, in turn, had two inter-related effects. Firstly, it diverted the circulation of wealth from among the rich to the poor; and secondly, as a result of this diversion, it affected the consumption pattern of the society. The economic effects of *Zakāt* could be multiplied when its administration was centralized. The most important function which it was to perform was something like social insurance and not very late in the early period it did this. The establishment of an institution which provides insurance to the poor, commands disposable funds to support all the needy classes including undischarged debtors and insolvent businessmen, *al-ghārimūn,* has a significant bearing on the economic set-up of a state. It converts the money market into a supply market and discourages the supplier from dictating his own terms. It is not surprising that, in the Qur'ān the condemnation and prohibition of *ribā* comes alongside extolling the practice of *ṣadaqa*. The two thus seem to be the positive and negative aspects which complement each other in the achievement of the socio-economic objectives of the Islamic state.

It is pertinent to observe that the disposal of the *Zakāt* revenues, like that of *Ghanīma* and *Fay'*,[162] has been specified in the Qur'ān itself. But while the heads of expenditure in the case of the two latter begin with Allah and His Messenger thereby conferring discretionary powers on the government, the expenditure of *Zakāt* funds has not been left to the government. Instead, all the heads of expenditure are specified clearly and cover mostly the poor and the needy:

> The *Ṣadaqāt* are only for the poor and the needy and those who collect them and those whose hearts are to be reconciled and to free the captives and the debtors and for the cause of Allah and for the wayfarer; a duty imposed by Allah . . . (9:60).

The exegetes have discussed in detail the precise application of these heads which are generally self-evident.[163] While the Qur'ān ordains the payment of *Zakāt* and the different heads on which *Zakāt* income is to be spent, the extent and the scope of *Zakāt,* the items which are subject to *Zakāt,* the exemption limits and the rates of levy on different items are all governed by *Ḥadīth*. These details are mostly to be found in the instructions which the Prophet (peace be upon him) is reported to have sent to different tribes or handed to his officials.[164] A very common word which was used for *Zakāt* as also for voluntary spending *(infāq)* was *ṣadaqa* which, as hinted above, was prescribed even during the Makkan period. At that time, *ṣadaqa* was a payment which called for no central authority to administer it. There were no prescribed rates or rules to govern it. In the second year of *Hijra* (migration to Madina) *ṣadaqa* marking the end of the month of fasting (Ramaḍān) was made compulsory and was termed as *ṣadaqat-al-fiṭr*.[165] *Ṣadaqa* by way of *Zakāt* to be administered by a central authority was levied late in the Prophet's life. It was leviable on cash savings, articles of trade, livestock and land produce. The relevant details are found in all the important books of *Ḥadīth* and history. A consolidated list of the different items with necessary details are given as follows:

Items chargeable at 2 1/2%

	Exemption limit	Other conditions
Gold, Silver [166] Cash[167] Articles of trade[168] Minerals[169]	Subject to a minimum of the value of 200 dirhams or 5 *uqiyya* of silver or 20 dīnārs[170]	Payable after the lapse of one full year of holding the value[171] (not clear in the case of minerals)

*Items chargeable at 5% to 10%**

	Exemption limit	Other conditions
Dates, wheat, barley, corn, grains, grapes, raisins [172]	Subject to a minimum of 5 *wasqs* of the produce[173]	Payable at the time of harvesting[174]
Olive	As above	As above
Honey†	–	On collection

*10% in case the crop does not need artificial irrigation; otherwise 5%.

†*Ḥadīth* for and against the exemption are of equal weight. The benefit of doubt will, however, go to the government which is supposed to look after the interests of the poor (Maj., 1,584; Kh., 31–2). The *aḥādīth* for levy have been criticized by Tir., 3, 123.

Items chargeable at 20%

	Exemption limit	Other conditions
Treasure-troves, buried wealth, any other unclaimed wealth found in a deserted place[175]	Nil	Payable on acquiring the same

Doubtful Items

	Exemption limit	Other conditions
Perishable fruits, Vegetables[176]	Exemption limit not given	If leviable, then on harvesting or collection at 5% to 10%
Cotton*[177]		Not clear

*Whether or not there is *Zakāt* on cotton is uncertain because there are *Ḥadīth* to suggest both. Even if it is established that *Zakāt* is leviable on it there is confusion in respect of its rate. It is reported that the Prophet (peace be upon him) agreed to receive 70 mantles *(Ḥullā)* in lieu of *Zakāt* on cotton (Abu Daud, 3, 223–4). That there is no *Zakāt* on cotton is transmitted by Bal., 85 but the source is 'Ikrama and not the Prophet (peace be upon him).

Zakāt on cattle etc.

	Minimum limit	Rate
Sheep/Goat[178]	40	1
Cow/Ox[179]	30	1-year-old calf
	40	2-year-old calf
Camel[180]	5	1 sheep
	25	1-year-old she camel

It will be seen from the above table that not all goods and wealth are taxable. In most cases, *Zakāt* is leviable only above a minimum level. Cattle which are not used for breeding or trade, but are meant for ploughing, drawing, and transport are also exempt.[181] A *Ḥadīth* says: 'There is no *Zakāt* on your slaves and horses.'[182] Similarly goods meant for personal consumption are exempt.[183] The *Ḥadīth* on exemption from *Zakāt* on horses has been re-interpreted by the Prophet's Companions. For example Abū Ḥanīfa adduces his argument on the basis of a *Ḥadīth* narrated by Companion Zubayr[184] which says: 'For every *sawā'im* horse, one dīnār or ten dirhams and there is nothing on horses stationed in forts.'[185] It qualifies the former *Ḥadīth* relative to the use of horses. Caliph 'Umar's practice of levying *Zakāt* on horses practically confirms what Zubayr has narrated. It is stated that in the time of Marwān a council of Companions was held to discuss the matter and in it Abū Hurayra said: 'There is no *Ṣadaqa* on a man for his horses and slaves.' Marwān then said to Zayd ibn Thābit: 'What do you say, O father of Sa'īd?' and Abū Hurayra wondered at Marwān and said: 'I am relating a *Ḥadīth* of the Prophet and he says: What do you say, O father of

Sa'īd?' Zayd thereupon observed that Abū Hurayra was telling the truth but the Prophet (peace be upon him) only meant the horses of the warriors and that horses kept for their offspring were subject to *Zakāt* . . .'[186]

While there exist some ambiguities on the issue of the levy of *Zakāt* on items not generally produced in Arabia (viz. honey, cotton) the *Ḥadīth* on widely-produced items are very clear. The most popular of such items were camels, the *Ḥadīth* on which have been transmitted by the compilers of *Ṣiḥāḥ Sitta* (except Muslim) in greater detail. And because the *Zakāt* on camels involves more or less eleven limits some of the narrators are confused when reporting some intermediate figures. The following table (page 68) will give an idea of the differences in the narration of limits.

It will be observed that in view of the multiplicity of figures the differences in the narrations are much less than might be expected. In respect of levy, however, the difference becomes all the more immaterial. One sheep on every five camels is payable up to twenty, after which the limits are adjusted to levy a camel for the herd: one-year-old she-camel on a herd of twenty-five; two-year-old on thirty-six, three-year-old on forty-six, and so on; the intervening numbers being always exempt.

The heads of the distribution of *Zakāt* have been laid down in the Qur'ān. The *Ḥadīth* seem to have further elaborated some vague points of interpretation from the point of view of the recipient. It is said that there are five well-to-do persons who are allowed to take from *Zakāt* funds; i.e., a man on war-service *(ghāzī),* the collector of *Zakāt,* the debtor, one who buys a good from a recipient of *Zakāt* and one to whom it has been gifted by the recipient of *Zakāt* goods.[187] The first three have also been mentioned in the Qur'ān but the relevance of the *Ḥadīth* lies in its recognition of the entitlement of the three classes in spite of their affluence. The last two are aimed at removing any misunderstanding about the use of *Zakāt* goods by a genuine beneficiary. In many such *Ḥadīth* the word used for the heads of distribution and for elaborating the entitlement to support is *ṣadaqa* which sometimes signifies compulsory *Zakāt* and sometimes voluntary contribution. It is sometimes difficult to find which of the two is meant.

Ghanīma, Fay', Jizya

The generally known term *Ghanīma* (Booty), is mentioned in the Qur'ān with the word *anfāl* (8:1). Verse 8:41 provides for one fifth of *Ghanīma* to be handed over to the government *(li'llāhi wa li'r rasūl . . .),* while the recipients of the remaining four-fifths are not specified.

Table 1
Limits of *Zakāt* on Camels

Narrator	Number of camels subject to new rates											Reference
Anas b. Mālik	5	10	15	20	25	36	46	61	76	91	121	Bukh. (Zakāt)
”	5	10	15	20	25	36	46	61	76	91	121	Abū Dā'ud, 2/130
”	5	10				36	46	61	76	91	121	Nas., 5/18
Sālim b. 'Abd Allāh b. 'Umar	5	10	15	20	25	36	46	61	76	91	121	Abū Dā'ud, 2/132
”	5	10	15	20	25	36	46	61	76	91	121	Kh., 43
”	5	10	15	20	25	36	46		76	91		Maj., 1/573–4
Abū Sa'īd al-Khudrī	5	10	15	20	25	36	46		76	92		Maj., 1/574
An old document	5	10	15	20	25	36	46	61	76	91	121	Waq., 1084, the document was lying with Abū Ja'far
'Amr b. Ḥazm	5	10	15	20	25	36	46	61	76	91	130*	A.U., para. 933

*The limit continues up to 300 with an addition of 10 camels in each lower limit, for example, 130–40–50 and so on. The rate, however, corresponds to a 2-year-old she-camel for every 40 camels and a 3-year-old for every 50.

The implication of this, according to the scholars, was that it should be distributed among the fighters. The government's portion is to be treated as part of the general revenues. But unlike *Zakāt* this source of income is dependent on successful wars which makes it a temporary and undependable source. However, it should be remembered that the injunctions pertaining to booty were made in a society where there used to be volunteer fighters and not paid armies. These volunteers brought their own arms and riding animals and depended on their self-acquired skill and training. Moreover, killed or invalided fighters had no financial guarantee for themselves or for their surviving dependants. The situation in the later period completely changed in all respects; but in the case of an army it is generally difficult to withdraw a benefit or privilege particularly when the threat of revolt, civil war and general turmoil call for the maintenance of a contented and loyal army.[188] The fact that the Qur'ān does not expressly assign the four-fifths to the fighters makes the distribution of *Ghanīma* discretionary on the government. This is supported by the fact that the person in charge of *Ghanīma* has a right to take out from the spoils the edibles for daily use of the fighters during war;[189] to set aside from the four-fifths a substantial portion (about one-third) for awarding prizes to the fighters *(nafal)*;[190] and to include among the beneficiaries those persons who are not fighters.[191] This is over and above the 'chosen pick', *ṣafī,* which the Prophet (peace be upon him) used to set aside for his own use[192] and the *salab,* the personal belongings of the slain enemy which were held to belong to the slayer.[193]

Another source of income for the government is *fay'*. The word has been derived from the Qur'ānic verse revealed in the context of the properties of Banū Naḍīr which fell to the Prophet (peace be upon him) without active warfare: *'mā afā'Allāhu 'alā rasūlihī'* (59:6). Thus the proceeds accruing to the state by way of *fay'* according to the Qur'ānic injunctions, are to be spent for 'Allah and His Messenger and for the near of kin and the orphans and the needy and the wayfarer . . . and the poor Emigrants *(muhājirūn)* . . . and those who come after them' (59:6–10). This suggests that the government has wide discretionary power in spending the *fay'* income. Moreover, the ownership of *fay'* properties cannot be transferred to individuals because this will deprive posterity of their potential benefits. The rationale behind earmarking *fay'* properties for public welfare is given in the Qur'ān as that 'it become not a commodity between the rich among you' (59:7). This is also suggestive of the simple fact that the common man's welfare does not depend on increase in items of ownership but also on increase in the benefits accruing to him without directly owning many of them. Besides, there are properties whose utility can be retained and protected only under government administration and ownership.

Another source of income hinted at in the Qur'ān is *Jizya* or poll-tax. While *Zakāt* is leviable on the wealth of the Muslims, *Jizya* is imposed on the 'People of the Book',[194] *ahl al-kitāb* (9:29). The method of assessment and the heads of expenditure of poll-tax are not specified in the Qur'ān which allows for the discretion of the government in including it in its general budget. The Qur'ān only says:

> Fight against such of those who have been given the Scripture as believe not in Allah nor the Last Day, and who forbid not that which Allah hath forbidden by His Messenger, and who follow not the religion of truth, until they pay the tribute readily, being brought low (9:29).

In the verse the words 'being brought low' *(wa hum ṣāghirūn)* are self-evident and in a sense reflect the spirit of *Jizya*. There is no difference of opinion among exegetes that the word *ṣāghirūn* means humility or state of submission.[195] Similarly, the paying of *Jizya* 'readily', *('an yadin)* implies the payment to be made submissively or personally without the intermediation of an agent.[196] But how far this theoretical interpretation was adopted in practice will be studied in the relevant chapters.[197]

Interest *(Ribā)* and Loans

Prohibition of interest is perhaps the most important reform that the Qur'ān introduced; the positive one being the compulsory levy of *Zakāt* and voluntary spending for noble causes *(infāq)* and *ṣadaqa*. This reform was as relevant to the socio-economic conditions of the age and society as it is necessary now, in this twentieth century, when some modern economists too are becoming sceptical about the role of interest and the usefulness attributed to it.[198] Some modern Muslim scholars have expressed doubts about the proper interpretation of the term *ribā* (interest) and suggested that the Qur'ānic term applies to some other form of interest than the one practised by modern financial institutions.[199] But the literature on the controversy suggests that there is no justification for such arguments.[200] The arguments for and against this position are not relevant to this study. What is relevant here is the role that the prohibition of interest plays in attracting savings in an Islamic society. In addition to the factor of income a man is tempted to save money if someone offers him a return on his savings. Receiving a fixed sum of money on loan without involving oneself in any risk seems to be a very profitable business. This is a surer way of multiplying one's savings as compared with investment in trade or industry which is not only exposed to losses but also requires labour, skill, opportunity, and enterprising spirit. An abominable aspect of lending at interest is the financer's insistence on his reward without any consideration of the fruitfulness of his funds to the user. The Qur'ān disapproves such an insistence on earning wealth. Interest is one of two offences treated by the Qur'ān as an affront and challenge to the whole community. 'And if you do not (give up interest) then be warned of war against you by Allah and His Messenger' (2:279) is the challenge which is given to the devourers of interest. It should not be surprising to learn that prohibition of interest was finally effected during the last year of the Prophet (peace be upon him),[201] after all attempts had been expended to introduce social, moral, and economic reforms. Like any other sphere, only negative measures of financial reform were not depended upon. As regards interest, even pious persons might regard it as an apparently harmless economic activity.[202] However, the havoc that interest can bring about was imperceptible to the simple society of the middle ages. It was with the advent of the industrial era and the development of modern techniques of analysis that the baneful impact of interest was unfolded.[203] An examination of the verses prohibiting interest suggests that the subject of prohibition are Muslims.[204] Moreover, the words: 'Do not devour interest' *(lā ta'kulū 'r-ribā)* suggests that charging but not paying interest is made the object of prohibition. But a logical analysis of the text of the injunctions, the *Ḥadīth* literature and the practical implications of charging interest admit of no such conclusion. As regards the suggestion that prohibition is confined to the Muslims, this also can be ruled out in view of the practical implications of the injunctions in the early Islamic period. This may lead to one more doubt as to its general application on the basis of the argument that during the early period the non-believers also included the People of the Book whose Scriptures did not approve of interest[205] while other non-Muslims would have been exempted from this prohibition. Although it is off the point to examine the question here and though money business was largely conducted by Jews and Christians in Damascus and Baghdad in the early Islamic period, the challenging words of the Qur'ān are too convincing to admit any such idea.

It will be noted that mention of the word *'ribā'* is made in three *sūras*. Verse 30:39 does not call for abolition of interest; it is suggestive of the comparative excellence of *Zakāt* over *ribā*. Verse 4:161 hints at the Jewish violation of the prohibition of interest in their religion. Verse 3:130 enjoins Muslims to abstain from compound interest and verses 2:275–80 aim at complete abolition of interest. The gradual abolition of interest as discernible from these verses is suggestive of the extent to which the practice permeated the contemporary society, on the one hand, and the extent to which the Qur'ān was concerned to ensure the abolition of interest, on the other. A similar approach is discernible only in the case of prohibition of alcohol to which people were badly addicted. Apparently the ban on interest seems to be aimed at discouraging the profit-motive of saving which was nourished by the practice of interest, and making available funds for satisfying the transactions motive of the saver and of others through trade and investment where return is contingent upon the productivity of investment.

The Qur'ān prohibits interest and treats it as a wrongful act *(ẓulm)* while the *Ḥadīth* ban the different forms of transactions which make the advantage of the transaction secure for one party and uncertain for the other.[206] Similarly it also prohibits those transactions which contain an element of interest or which could provide subterfuges to practising interest in the barter economy of the agricultural communities. In the *Ṣiḥāḥ*[207] alone there are about fifteen Companions on whose authority *Ḥadīth* on such barter transactions are narrated with varying details.

> 'Gold is to be paid for by gold, silver by silver, wheat by wheat, barley by barley, date by date and salt by salt, like for like and equal for equal, payment being made on the spot. If these species differ sell as you wish provided that payment is made on the spot.'[208]
> Abū Sa'īd said that Bilāl brought to the Prophet (peace be upon him) some *barnī* dates and when he asked him where he had got them from he replied, 'I had some inferior dates so I sold two sas for a sa'.' On this the Prophet (peace be upon him) said: 'Ah, the very essence of interest, the very essence of interest! Do not do so but if you wish to buy, sell the dates in a separate transaction, then buy with what you get'.[209]

The *Ḥadīth,* like the Qur'ān, also condemn *ribā* or interest in the strongest possible tone. Caliph 'Alī said, he heard Allah's Messenger curse those who took interest, those who paid it, those who recorded it and those who refused to give *ṣadaqa* . . .[210] According to another version, Allah curses the one who charges interest, the one who pays interest, the one who scribes it and the two witnesses who act as evidence.[211] Another *Ḥadīth* says: 'Interest has seventy parts, the least important being that a man should "marry" his mother.'[212] In spite of the severe terms in which interest transactions have been condemned the scope of the *Ḥadīth* prohibiting interest remains to be interpreted. The *Ḥadīth* generally cover six or seven items, viz. gold, silver, dates, wheat, barley and salt: Gold and silver can be said to have covered all the media of exchange, that is money, while the remaining four items were generally produced in Madina or Khaybar and were also exchanged on barter. The question is whether these are the only items where interest will be involved in case of exchange or credit or they should be taken to cover all the media of exchange, food grains, fruits and spices. It was this ambiguity that Caliph 'Umar had to observe: 'The last verse to be sent down was the one on interest, but the Prophet (peace be upon him) passed away without having elucidated it to us; so leave aside interest and whatever is doubtful.'[213]

In any case the *Ḥadīth* cited above had much bearing on implementing the ban on interest. While advancing a loan a Muslim is led to believe that he is engaged in *ṣadaqa,* a pious act, which is rewardable in the Hereafter. Any reward for loan in this world will injure the spirit of the pious act. Companion Anas reported the Prophet (peace be upon him) as saying: 'When any of you makes a loan and the borrower sends him a present or provides an animal for him to ride, he must not ride the one or accept the other unless it is a practice they followed previously.'[214]

With the Islamic outlook on interest presented in the above lines it is now worthwhile to study how the institution of lending is operated without interest.

Islam treats the act of lending more as a moral phenomenon than a purely economic activity. The well-to-do are repeatedly urged to lend money. While finally prohibiting interest, the Qur'ān asks the lenders not only to give up the amount of interest but also to re-schedule their outstanding loans to the convenience of the debtor, preferably by remission of the balance if he is in distress (2:280).[215]

While the Islamic approach to lending apparently seems to be embarrassing for the lender, the rules laid down for the borrower do not leave the lender in the lurch. The Prophet (peace be upon him) has not only himself prayed for protection from the liability of loan[216] but has also declared his choice to go without a loan rather than taking one unnecessarily. The emphasis on simple living,[217] on continence[218] and on condemnation of ostentatious living and pomp and show which the Prophet (peace be upon him) repeatedly pronounced go a long way toward discouraging unnecessary borrowing. Thus borrowing is to be done only when really necessary. The Prophet (peace be upon him) is reported to have refused to lead the funeral *(janāza)* prayers of an undischarged debtor unless somebody offered to discharge this liability.[219] This moral approach is reinforced with legal provisions which, according to the *Ḥadīth,* provide for some punishment of a debtor who, though having means, evades repayment of loans.[220] According to the Islamic law of inheritance debt supersedes the legal right of beneficiaries.[221] While the lender is made to extend a loan as a moral duty and in religious spirit, the borrower is also required to acknowledge this obligation by prompt repayment and expressing his gratitude.[222] 'The best persons are those who are best in settlement (of loans).'[223]

In spite of the moral and legal safeguards of the lender there may be situations under which a loan becomes a bad debt. A soldier may take a loan to prepare for *Jihād* and be martyred without returning the loan, or a person may incur a heavy business loss and be declared insolvent. Even in such genuine cases the liability of the loan is not altogether condoned; it is simply transferred from the borrower to Allah:

> An undischarged loan, insisted the Prophet (peace be upon him), shall be claimed on Doomsday but for three persons on whose behalf Allah Himself will pay. The one who, in order to strengthen himself more than Allah's enemies do, takes a loan;[224] the other who is compelled to take a loan to perform the funeral rites of his brother; and the third one who is compelled to take a loan for his marriage without which he could be involved in a sinful act.[225]

Another *Ḥadīth* includes in the list the businessman who becomes insolvent because of theft, fire or business loss.[226] Anyhow, in the later period when the state could have sufficient funds the Prophet (peace be upon him) declared: 'If somebody bequeaths property, it is for his heirs, but if he leaves a debt it is upon me.'[227] This perhaps involves those cases in which the deceased leaves no assets to discharge his loan.

The Functions of an Islamic State

It will be found that the heads of income as hinted at in the Qur'ān and the *Ḥadīth* with the exception of *Zakāt,* are not permanent and dependable. Yet the Qur'ān and the *Ḥadīth* assign to the Muslims the responsibilities which require substantial funds to discharge them. The setting up of a social order which is imbued with justice and equity, or an economic order in which people are not frustrated in discharging their obligations to Allah and the society as required in Islam, calls for an efficient machinery for administration of justice and for attaining a reasonable degree of economic growth. Thus the functions which the Qur'ān and the *Ḥadīth* assign to the Muslims and which require an organized and stable government to perform them are policy-making and legislation for enforcement of justice, defence of the state, education and research, socio-moral reform and surveillance, law and order, public welfare and foreign relations.

(A) Policy Making and Legislation

The significance of justice, fair dealing and equilibrium in the society has been discussed in the foregoing pages.[228]

The Qur'ān requires the administration of justice in the following words:

> Lo! Allah commandeth you that ye restore deposits to their owners, and, if ye judge between mankind, that ye judge justly (4:58).
>
> O ye who believe! Be ye staunch in justice, witness for Allah, even though it be against yourself or (your) parents or (your) kindred, whether (the case be of) a rich man or a poor man, for Allah is nearer unto both (than ye are). So follow not passion lest ye lapse (from truth) and if ye lapse or fall away, then lo! Allah is ever informed of what ye do (4:135).

The same sense is again conveyed in 5:8 and 7:29, 181 in the Qur'ān. In 5:42 it urges the Prophet (peace be upon him) to judge between people with equity. In another place, Allah ordains the Prophet (peace be upon him) to 'Say: My Lord enjoineth justice' (7:29).

The Islamic approach to justice, equity and balance *('adl, qisṭ)* encompasses all human behaviour in individual as well as in social life. While the basic norm of *'adl* and *qisṭ* is hinted at in the Qur'ān and *Sunna,* the details need to be continuously worked out, keeping in view the institutional changes due to social, economic, political and technological developments. It calls for laying down a strategy that gives equal opportunities to all citizens for their spiritual and moral refinement, social emancipation and economic progress. It calls for discouraging the factors that lead to deprivation and discrimination. This strategy is determined by policy-makers and introduced through comprehensive legislation and judicious planning.

(B) Defence

Islam, as the very word suggests, is a religion of peace and seeks to restore peace for all time. While demonstrating patience against injustice and forgiving the oppressor is regarded as a high degree of moral excellence *(iḥsān)* for individuals, Islam is intolerant to social and political injustice and communal oppression *(ẓulm)*: 'And fight them until persecution is no more, and religion is for Allah. But if they desist, then let there be no hostility except against wrong-doers' (2:193). Thus the war recommended by the Qur'ān does not aim at grabbing land or robbing wealth of the enemy; it is for Allah's pleasure (4:74, 76, 84; 5:35, etc.) and in accordance with the rules of war which the Qur'ān and the Prophet (peace be upon him) lay down. The Qur'ān says: 'Fight in the way of Allah against those who fight against you, but begin not hostilities. Lo! Allah loveth not the aggressor' (2:190, 191). Similarly, war is waged against those who are not willing to make a peace treaty, or who violate the terms of the treaty (8:56, 57, 58). It continues until the belligerent nation again agrees to make a truce (8:61). War can also be declared for self-defence (2:217; 22:40) or for the protection of houses of worship (22:39, 40) or for suppression of resistance to the performance of Islamic norms and rites (48:25). Rebellion against the state also permits war (5:33; 42:39).

It is in view of the above considerations that the Islamic State is supposed to be always prepared for any armed confrontation:

> Make ready for them all thou canst of (armed) force and of horses tethered, that thereby ye may dismay the enemy of Allah and your enemy, and others beside them whom ye know not. Allah knoweth them. Whatsoever ye spend in the way of Allah it will be repaid to you in full, and ye will not be wronged (8:60).

In line with the Qur'ānic spirit, the Prophet (peace be upon him) has also advised the Muslims to wish for peace and not for confrontation. Anyway, if the inevitable has come they are advised to persist.[229] That is why the Prophet (peace be upon him) has declared it obligatory for Muslims to take part in *Jihād* whenever they are called upon to do so.[230] 'Who are the best of the people?' somebody asked him. 'The believer who does *Jihād* with his person and his wealth',[231] was his answer. Ordinarily, an indebted person is not forgiven even in the Hereafter. But the Prophet (peace be upon him) has assured the exemption from the accountability of loan taken for preparing for *Jihād*.[232] Guarding the frontiers of the Islamic state is held an equally admirable job which is rewarded in the Hereafter.[233] 'Keeping watch and vigilance for the sake of Allah for a single day is better than the wealth of the whole world.'[234] While Allah has attributed to Himself instructing David the making of coats-of-mail (21:80), the Prophet (peace be upon him) has encouraged for preparing arms in these words: 'There are three persons who will be rewarded with paradise because of an arrow: (1) the manufacturer, (2) the archer, and (3) the supplier of arrows to the archer.'[235] 'Keep ready for war! Beware! archery is power.' This, the Prophet (peace be upon him) repeated thrice.[236] It is not irrelevant to recall that the Prophet (peace be upon him) took a personal interest in training horse-riding and organizing horse races.[237]

(C) Education and Research

There are numerous verses in the Qur'ān that emphasize acquiring sound knowledge of the Qur'ān (38:29), applying intellectual faculties to religion (9:122), journeying across the land, taking lessons from and disclosing the events of early history (7:176; 29:33–5), concentrating and pondering over physical and metaphysical laws (2:164; 3:190–1; 16:10–15), finding out the wisdom of *ḥalāl* (lawful) and *ḥarām (unlawful)*

(2:219), studying social laws (2:221; 30:28), pondering over the Qur'ānic policy of spending (distribution of) wealth (2:219), studying anatomy and physiology (16:4; 30:8; 40:67), cosmology (2:164; 3:190–1; 16:10–15), the phenomenon of moral and physiological changes (16:4; 30:8; 40:67), exploring the benefits and uses of natural resources (16:65–9), and studying the process of evolution and growth (30:19–28, 50). All these requirements call for an elaborate and well-planned organization of educational and research institutions, observatories and laboratories, etc. Even the Prophet (peace be upon him) has been advised to implore for increase in his knowledge (20:114).

The words that the Qur'ān uses to emphasize the point are *'aql, 'ilm, naẓar, tafaqquh, tafakkur* and *tadabbur,* meaning thereby the use of intellect, prudence, vision, understanding, meditation and deliberation. The point to note is its use of the derivatives of *'aql* (discernment or application of reason) in respect of some of the basic Islamic laws involving the oneness of Allah, kindness in behaviour, birth-control, obscenity, murder and capital punishment (6:151), relationship with profane communities (3:118), and the significance of wealth and worldly lures *vis-à-vis* the Hereafter (28:60).

All this is in addition to the Qur'ānic emphasis on exploration, discovering and using wisdom *(ḥikma)* (2:231; 16:125; 33:34) etc., in the understanding and propagation of religion and on the superiority of the men of learning and wisdom (58:11; 39:9) over those who are not knowledgeable. It is no wonder, therefore, that the Qur'ān confirms that those who have sound knowledge, *al-rāsikhūn fi'l-'ilm,* would have a firmer belief in the Book than others who are sceptical (3:7). The Qur'ānic warning in this respect is very significant:

> Follow not that whereof thou hast no knowledge. Lo! the hearing and the sight and the heart – of each of these it will be asked (17:36).

Knowledge and wisdom are prophetic qualities. Lot, David and Soloman are described in the Qur'ān as having been endowed with knowledge and wisdom (21:74, 79, 80). Joseph claimed to have mastered knowledge and guardianship which qualified him for the office he held. The Prophet (peace be upon him) claimed that he was deputed as a teacher *(mu'allim)*.[239] He is reported to have emphasized: 'Acquiring knowledge is a duty on each Muslim.'[240] 'Useful knowledge *('ilm nāfi')* is one of the three things which survive even after the possessor's death.'[241] Acquiring knowledge and disseminating it to others are regarded as the best *ṣadaqa*.[242] 'People would come to you for acquiring knowledge; welcome them on the Prophet's advice and teach them.'[243] The Prophet (peace be upon him) was so much concerned with acquiring knowledge that he held a quack liable in case he practised medicine without (proper) knowledge.[244] On his part he used to invoke Allah to protect him from behaving as an ignorant person and falling a victim to ignorance.[245]

The evidence cited above amply proves the significance which the Qur'ān and the Prophet (peace be upon him) attach to education. It should also be remembered that the rules involving *ḥudūd* punishments, compensation *(diyat)*, and inheritance, as prescribed by the Prophet (peace be upon him), are very comprehensive and require a high degree of juristic sense and mathematical skill to apply in the administration of justice.

(D) Socio-Moral Reform and Surveillance

This function of the government is derivable from the following verses of the Qur'ān:

> And there may spring from you a nation who invite to goodness, and enjoin right conduct *(ma'rūf)* and forbid indecency *(munkar)*. Such are they who are successful (3:104).

> And the believers, men and women are the protecting friends one of another. They enjoin the right conduct and forbid the wrong, and they establish worship and pay the poor due, and they obey Allah and His Messenger . . . (9:71).

It will be found that the purpose of the above verses can be realized only when the function of 'enjoining and forbidding' is performed under government authority because the coverage of virtues and vices is all-embracing. The performance of this function requires a large army of preachers and overseers who may be appointed to persuade citizens to abide by religious and civic laws and social and moral duties and to dissuade them from violating these laws. It is in fact this function of the state which facilitates the setting up of a truly Islamic society motivated by moral force.

As a natural corollary to this function it is necessary to organize an institution to look after the results of the reform. This surveillance is performed by the institution of *ḥisba* whose job it is to ensure that the man in the street and in the market discharges his duties in accordance with the moral norms of the *Sharī'a.* There are reports that the Prophet (peace be upon him) used to depute some persons to monitor the operation of the market.[246] Ibn 'Umar has reported: 'When we bought food-grain from the riders, the Prophet of Allah sent somebody to us to stop us from reselling the commodity in the place of purchase unless the same was transferred to its place of sale.'[247] According to another report, the sale of food-grain by conjecture was punishable during the Prophet's time as it involved the sale of goods without transferring the same to the market place.[248]

(E) Maintenance of Law and Order and Enforcement of Ḥudūd

While the act of surveillance is supposed to be the duty of every Muslim, this cannot be left as a totally voluntary duty. It is for the government to ensure that a group of persons is effectively engaged in this task on a full-time basis. In either case the government must take a hortatory role and act as a moral force. It is equally the duty of the government to use its force in order to maintain law and order in the country. The Divine scheme of life as enunciated in the Qur'ān and *Ḥadīth* hates *fasād* (corruption) and *ẓulm* (injustice)[249] in the society. The frequent mention in the Qur'ān that 'Allah does not like *fasād*' and that Allah does not like *ẓulm* and the severe admonitions which the Qur'ān associates with these vices make it obligatory for an Islamic state not only to suppress these vices but also to plug all the loopholes that lead one to indulge in them. The term *fasād* is used in the Qur'ān to convey the following meanings:

(1) Creating chaos and confusion (2:11, 27, 30, 205; 17:4; etc.).
(2) Violating moral limits (26:151, 152).
(3) Under-weighing and under-measurement (11:85–6).
(4) Harming unity and co-operation among Muslims (8:73).
(5) Disintegrating the nation into classes and discriminating against the down-trodden (28:4).
(6) Disturbing the social, religious or political set-up (7:74, 85, 86).
(7) Murder (5:32), burglary (12:70), dacoity or banditry (5:33), and homosexuality (29:30).
(8) Egotism (23:71) and violation of divine law (89:11, 12).
(9) Misuse of wealth and neglecting others' rights in one's wealth (28:76, 77).
(10) Forbidding others from following the divine path (16:88).

The word *ẓulm* is used in the Qur'ān in the following connotations:

(1) Disobedience to the dictates of Allah (2:35; 6:23; 11:37; 17:59), His Messenger (6:136), and following one's own desires (30:29).
(2) Depriving others of their rights (2:272, 281; 4:10, 30; 10:54; 16:111; 20:112).
(3) Disregarding fair family relationship as visualized in the Qur'ān (2:229–31).

(4) Practising interest (2:279).
(5) Concealment of evidence (2:140).
(6) Stopping others from prayers and destroying worship houses (2:114).
(7) Laying false charges for punishment (12:79; 17:33).
(8) Oppression of the weaker class of the society (16:41).
(9) Indulging in vices (6:83).

The *Ḥadīth* literature encompasses such a large number of acts which the Prophet (peace be upon him) has treated as *fasād* or *ẓulm* that a volume would be needed to list them. To cite one example, a *Ḥadīth* warns parents against refusing to marry their daughters if a man of acceptable religious and moral integrity proposes; the refusal would bring about *fasād* in the society.[250] Another *Ḥadīth* terms procrastination by a resourceful man (from repayment of debt) as *ẓulm*. 'Fear the curse of the oppressed'[251] warned the Prophet (peace be upon him). The Prophet himself (peace be upon him) invoked Allah to protect him from doing injustice and from being the victim of injustice.[252]

While the function of surveillance is to ensure that *fasād* and *ẓulm* are discouraged in the society, the violations are strictly dealt with through its machinery of law and order and judiciary. There are some offences whose punishments have been laid down in the Qur'ān (2:178; 5:32, 33, 38, 45; 24:2, 4) or *Ḥadīth*[253] and are called *ḥudūd*. The *Sunna* also lays down elaborate rules of *diyat* (blood money) and compensation for injuries. In addition there are some other offences whose punishments have not been prescribed and these can be brought under statutory law along with those offences which have not been specified in the Qur'ān.

The above requirement calls for setting up a judicial system that ensures that *ẓulm* and *fasād* are eliminated from the society, that law and order prevail and justice is made available to all the citizens. It is interesting to note that a large number of the Prophet's sayings lay down the qualifications of a judge and the rules of procedure for administration of justice.

(F) Public Welfare

As stated earlier the Qur'ān repeatedly emphasizes that everything in the universe has been made for the benefit of mankind. It also emphasizes the use of knowledge and research in exploring and exploiting natural resources. The advice not to neglect one's portion in the world's bounties (28:77) also intends maximizing the benefit of natural resources. The verse legalizing the use of material resources to the extent of adornment of worldly life points to the limit of utilization. As the achievement made out of this exploitation and exploration is gradual and measured by Allah (13:8; 15:21) the government has to set the priorities in the availability of benefits and opportunities. As a result it has to begin with those heads which are hinted at in the Qur'ān and which naturally enjoy basic importance.

Among the list of priorities, food *(rizq)* ranks top. The word *rizq* appears in the Qur'ān in various connotations but the most popular sense of the term is food (and fodder) which is to be found in land and water (2:22; 7:10; 10:59; 16:14; 30:40; 50:9–11; 80:27, 32, etc.). Another source of food is livestock which also provides clothing, shelter and transport in addition to satisfying aesthetic sense (16:5–7, 66, 80; 36:72; 43:12, 13, etc.). Another facility which the Qur'ān hints at is shelter which may be natural or man-made (7:74; 16:80; 21:81). Several *Ḥadīth* dislike disease and emphasize good health. One among Allah's blessings for the Prophet (peace be upon him) is the restoration of his health when he falls ill (26:80). The Qur'ān regards honey as Allah's blessing due to its remedial property (16:69). This is in addition to other items which the Prophet (peace be upon him) has recommended for their curative function, and to actions which advance hygiene.[254] All these together point to the significance of protecting life (5:32), and restoring and maintaining good health.

To sum up, the Qur'ān and the *Sunna* give priority to food, clothing, shelter, transport, life-saving and health; the provision of all of which come under the heading of public welfare. It is thus the bounden duty of the government to ensure that these basic necessities are easily available to the people. This calls for well-organized departments of agriculture, industry, construction, transport, communications, health and employment. This is in addition to attaining peace and consolation through conjugal life. It hardly needs emphasizing that, in the Islamic scheme of life, protection of chastity through happy married life occupies a very important place. A *Ḥadīth* says: 'An unmarried person's loan for marriage with a view to protecting his chastity will not be accountable on Doomsday.'[255] The Prophet (peace be upon him) has warned guardians to marry their daughters in case a man of acceptable religious and moral standard proposes. 'If you fail to do so it will multiply scandals *(fitna)* and corruption on earth.' Somebody inquired: 'Even if the proposer lacks financial and social status?'; on this the Prophet (peace be upon him) repeated the same advice twice.[256] In view of the importance of marriage it is no wonder that the Prophet (peace be upon him) has treated it as a government responsibility to facilitate marriage of government officials. 'Whoso works under us has a right to take a wife if he does not have one, take a dwelling if . . . '[257] A man who does not have these basic requirements of life is really needy. It is the responsibility of the government to create favourable conditions to ensure the availability of these basic requirements. The Prophet (peace be upon him) has warned: 'If Allah places anyone in charge of some tasks for the Muslims but he neglects their need and misery, Allah would neglect his need on doomsday.'[258] In addition to their emphasis on facilitating the supply of food, clothing, shelter, medical care, transport, clean environment and happy conjugal life, the Qur'ān and the *Ḥadīth* lead us to provide for a better quality of social and civic life. The nucleus of social life in Islam is the mosque. The Prophet (peace be upon him) has made it obligatory to set up this social centre and to keep it clean.[259] 'Moving aside the obstructions in the common passage is a *ṣadaqa*.'[260] 'Removing a thorny bush (from a public place) is an act of piety.'[261] The matter of providing facilities does not end here. The Prophet (peace be upon him) has warned the people to fear Allah in respect of animals: 'Ride on them properly, and feed them properly.'[262] This behaviour is not prescribed only for domestic animals but is extended to cover all living beings.[263]

(G) Foreign Relations

The Qur'ānic provisions of war and treaties with other nations and countries allude to the necessity of organizing not only an army, as mentioned above, but also foreign missions, to look after the interest of the Islamic state in foreign lands and to ensure that the terms of treaty and other agreements that are made with alien nations are faithfully observed and peaceful co-existence is made possible. Islam, as the very word implies, aims at bringing about peace. In order to ensure that conditions of peace, internally as well as externally are fully met, it has to engage an efficient and effective corps of diplomats in its foreign missions, not only to maintain friendly relations with other nations but also be watchful over any possible signs of betrayal or conspiracy against the Islamic state. Such diplomatic missions have been known to the Muslims ever since the earliest days of Islam. The Prophet (peace be upon him) not only received foreign missions[264] but also sent his own missions to foreign princes with his message of peace and in some cases with gifts.[265] In some cases he would also send teachers and preachers.

The Functionaries of the Government

The principles explained above and the institutions held responsible for implementing these principles can function efficiently only when there is a competent administrative machinery to apply them. Such administrative machinery requires two things in order to function properly: knowledge of the rules and regulations, and a strong moral discipline and sense of responsibility. Many of the best economic policies and plans are doomed to failure for want of these two qualities in administrators. This is also true in the case of the economic principles of Islam which are inspired by moral force.

While the teaching of Islamic principles attained great significance in the Arab society, the moral training of the Muslims with a view to entrusting them administrative jobs was also not neglected. A *Ḥadīth* generalizes this situation in the following words:

> Each of you is a shepherd and each of you is responsible for his flock. The man who rules over the people is a shepherd and is responsible for his flock; a man is a shepherd in charge of the inhabitants of his household and he is responsible for his flock; a woman is a shepherdess in charge of her husband's house and children and she is responsible for them; and a man's slave is a shepherd in charge of his master's property and he is responsible for it. So each of you is a shepherd and each of you is responsible for his flock.[266]

The following *Ḥadīth* directly touch upon this question:

> An office is a trust; it is a humiliation *('ār)* except for those who rise equal to the task and pay to each his due.[267]

> Whosoever keeps himself engaged in satisfying the requirements of his brother, Allah also cares to satisfy his requirement.[268]

> Allah does not take pity on those who do not take pity on the people.[269]

> Beware of the curse of the oppressed.[270]

> If Allah places anyone in charge of his people but he fails to protect their interest and to wish well for them, he will not smell the fragrance of paradise.[271]

> What else than the sin that a man stops the food of the one who is under his charge.[272]

> The worst of the officers are those who are harsh and unkind. Beware! Do not be among them.[273]

The Prophet (peace be upon him) has enjoined upon rulers to be just and honest:

> On doomsday Allah will overshadow the just ruler.[274]

> The just rulers will be seated on the illuminated pulpit on the right side of Allah. They adjudicate justly in respect of their family and subordinates.[275]

Serious notice has been taken of corruption and misuse of authority. Breach of trust and embezzlement are severely condemned. 'On doomsday I shall not intercede for him who is involved in breach of trust.'[276] The Prophet (peace be upon him) is said to have been so sensitive to financial irregularities that he did not hesitate to condemn one of his officials in public who informed him that he (the official) had accepted gifts from the Muslims. Apparently this was not so serious a matter as to be impeached in a public gathering. Ibn al-Lutbiyya, the officer concerned, was appointed as a collector of *Zakāt.* He was the Prophet's agent, and the people, out of their love for the Prophet (peace be upon him) and their sense of gratitude to the officer might have willingly offered him the gifts. But, if once allowed, it could bind the people to offer presents to officers and open the door of corruption. The Prophet (peace be upon him), in order to nip this evil in the bud, condemned the practice in the strongest possible tone:

> What an officer! I send him and then on his return he says: This is for you and this has been presented to me. Why did he not sit in his father's house or in his mother's house to see if he is still offered presents. By Him in Whose control is Muhammad's life! everyone of you who gets anything in this way shall be brought on doomsday with his (gift of) camel, cow or sheep, loaded on his neck and making noise.[277]

On another occasion the Prophet (peace be upon him) is said to have observed: 'Whosoever we appoint an officer and he misappropriates a needle or even a less expensive thing will be required to come with it on doomsday.'[278] When the Prophet (peace be upon him) appointed Mu'ādh a collector of *Zakāt* (or a *Qāḍī*) in Yemen he warned him not to accept anything without his permission because, as the *Ḥadīth* says, 'it is a breach of trust and whosoever commits it, will be required to produce it on doomsday.'[279] Another *Ḥadīth* curses the giver and the receiver of bribes.[280] It is reported that the Prophet (peace be upon him) followed a policy of not appointing as his officials those who wished to be appointed.[281] Another *Ḥadīth* says: 'If we appoint anybody to a job and pay him his subsistence and then he takes anything in addition to it, this is embezzlement.'[282]

All the *Ḥadīth* quoted above base the training of the officials on morals. The underlying force is the sense of answerability to God. It is this sense of answerability that protects the functionaries of the government from corruption, indiscipline and irresponsible behaviour even though they may be underpaid and over-loaded with work. This approach discards the offensive theory that underpayment leads to corruption. 'Whosoever works for us may marry if he is unmarried; may employ an attendant if he has none; may take a house if he does not have one; but if he takes anything over and above these he is a usurper and a robber.'[283] Another *Ḥadīth* restricts this facility to attendant and riding animal, not marriage or house, perhaps because the Companion addressed was already married and had his own house.[284] These facilities may or may not be over and above the payment for meals because, in the Prophet's early period, most official functions were performed voluntarily. In either case what is pertinent to note is that this remuneration did not cover all the necessities that could be faced in the Madinan civilization of that period. It did not provide anything for necessities like clothes, shoes, household goods and social requirements. This was so perhaps because the government itself had limited resources. Anyway, it was the moral training of the functionaries of government that restrained them from indulging in malpractices to satisfy their basic requirements.

While moral training of the functionaries of the state was of basic importance, the matter was not left entirely to personal correctness. Since the time of the Prophet (peace be upon him) strict vigilance was exercised over the performance of the officer appointed for a particular job.[285] Caliph 'Umar and his followers used to specify in clear terms the duties, powers and the functions of these functionaries.[286] Circulars were also sent to these officers reminding them of their duties and reiterating the importance of leniency, good behaviour, justice and benevolence.[287] Caliph 'Umar, being very rigid in discipline, also bound the appointed officer not to ride a decorated animal, wear fine clothes, eat sifted flour and appoint a durwan at the gate of his residence.[288] He also used to prepare a statement of the assets of his officers to check the rate of increase during the tenure of their office. The story of confiscation of half of the properties of more than a hundred officers is well known.[289]

The People Vis-à-vis the Functionaries

While the Prophet (peace be upon him) has laid emphasis on the moral training of his officials he has also advised the people not to be impatient or misled by emotions in case they find some weakness among officials.

> When a *Zakāt* collector reaches you for collecting *Zakāt* he should leave you only fully satisfied.[290]

The Prophet (peace be upon him) has warned that if anybody witnesses any untowardly thing in his ruler he should tolerate it because the one who breaks away from the body politic *(sulṭān)* by an inch dies the death of *jāhiliyya.*[291]

It is said that once the Prophet's commander, Khālid refused to allow the belongings of a slain enemy to the slayer because they were very precious. The person complained about him to the Prophet (peace be upon him) who advised Khālid to hand over the property to the complainant. On this the complainant humiliated Khālid which offended him. The Prophet (peace be upon him) advised Khālid to endure it but criticized the people for disregarding the officials:

> Do you want to leave my officials to me; enjoying yourself the benefit of their good deeds and leaving them alone in their trouble.[292]

While the rulers and the functionaries of the state have been urged to fear Allah in discharging their duty, be just, honest and well-wishers of the people, the people for their part have been advised to be tolerant of their rulers' human errors and even their excesses. They are advised to comply with them unless they order a sinful act.[293]

The Prophet's emphasis on moral training of government functionaries can be viewed from two related perspectives. Firstly, it is the moral element that is primarily responsible for successful and effective functioning of any system; and, secondly, the Islamic system as a whole disfavours chaos, confusion and anarchy in the society that erupt because of political instability or social disturbance. Islamic institutions prosper only in a peaceful atmosphere which is created through close co-operation and understanding between the government and the people and an atmosphere of respect and tolerance for each other. Thus while the Prophet (peace be upon him) has emphasized the moral uplift of officials, he has also advised the people to respect law and endure the hardship that is caused sometimes because of unsound decisions and erroneous policies of the officials.

> It is your duty to listen to and obey your rulers in your easy time and hard time, in your joy and misfortune, and in case they (unjustifiably) prefer others to you.[294]

> It is the duty of a Muslim to listen to and obey whether he likes it or dislikes, unless the rulers order him to do a sinful act in which case there is no listening and obedience.[295]

> The best of your rulers are those whom you love and who love you, whom you pray for and who pray for you; and the worst of your rulers are those whom you hate and who hate you, whom you curse

and who curse you. On this the people asked: 'Should we not dismiss them with our swords?' The Prophet (peace be upon him) retorted: 'No! not while they continue establishing *ṣalāh* (prayers) among you. And whenever you witness among your rulers anything that is abominable, hate it but do not disobey them.[296]

After me you shall witness (among rulers) favouritism and undesirable acts, said the Prophet (peace be upon him) to a delegation of Helpers *(anṣār)*. On enquiring as to what he advised them in such a situation the Prophet (peace be upon him) said: 'Give them their due and invoke Allah for yours'.[297]

On another occasion the Prophet (peace be upon him) advised the Helpers to endure the injustices of the succeeding rulers.[298]

The above *Ḥadīth* sufficiently amplify the Qur'ānic provision to 'obey Allah, His Messenger and those of you who are in authority' (4:59) and elaborate the conditions and the extent of such obedience. What transpires from the above discussion is that while moral reform of the functionaries of the government occupies a key place in state-craft the possibility of misjudgement, miscalculation or of administrative or moral lapses by human beings is fully anticipated and allowed for. This allowance provides them a respite to correct themselves and compensate for their wrongs before the people lose their self-restraint.

The Attitude Towards Labour

Labour problems as known today could not be conceived of anywhere in the Medieval Ages. Slaves formed the largest bulk of labour. Yet there are instances to suggest that slaves were not the only labour force. Free persons also worked for wages. The Prophet himself (peace be upon him) is reported to have worked as a labourer before the commencement of his prophetic ministry. A free man would be willing to work as an ordinary labourer for anyone only when he was very poor and thus the employer was placed in a position to exploit him. Yet it is found that a large part of *Ḥadīth* literature on the subject makes direct reference to conduct with slaves and a small part of it to free labour. A *Ḥadīth* says: 'Feed your slaves whatever you yourself eat and clothe them whatever you yourself wear and if he has a toilsome job to do then help him.'[299] Another *Ḥadīth* suggests: 'Slaves are your brothers whom God has placed at your disposal. So feed them whatever you eat, clothe them with whatever you wear and remember, do not entrust them with troublesome work; but if you must have it done then help them.'[300] This attitude has ultimately turned into a direction which discourages the very institution of serfdom.[301] 'If anybody frees a slave, it will become for him a ransom from the Fire.' This approach to slaves is suggestive of a much better behaviour with free labour.

A number of sayings of the Prophet (peace be upon him) attach great dignity to personal labour:

> If any person among you acquires a cord to tie a pack of charcoal wood for carrying it for sale and thus Allah protects his honour; that is better than begging from people who may or may not give him.[302]

> The best of the meals is the one which one eats through (earning from) his personal effort.[303]

> The best earning is the one which a man acquires through his own labour; and a man's son is also his earning.[304]

As a result the Prophet (peace be upon him) took special care to ensure that a worker is not maltreated.

'Pay the employee his wage before his sweat dries'[305] is the *Ḥadīth* that indicates the spirit of the employer's behaviour with his labourer.

Another *Ḥadīth* warns about the same point in a more forceful tone:

> On the day of resurrection Allah will be adversary of three persons: the last among them is the person who hired a worker, took full labour from him but did not pay him (accordingly).[306]

This attitude to labour is not only the natural result of the sense of justice and benevolence which Islam inculcates in its followers but has also its socio-economic rationale:

> You are provided with assistance and sustenance because of your weak.[307]

> Seek me among your weak; of course you are helped and catered for by your weak.[308]

These and other such *Ḥadīth* aim at smooth and effective functioning of the different income groups and professions as envisioned in the Qur'ān, thus:

> We have apportioned among them their livelihood in the life of the world, and raised some of them above others in rank that some of them may take labour from others; and the mercy of thy Lord is better than (the wealth) that they amass. (43:32).

Notes and References

1. While preparing this note the following commentaries of the Qur'ān have been utilized:

   1. Ṭabarī: *Tafsīr*
   2. Qurṭubī: *al-Jāmi' li-aḥkām al-Qur'ān*
   3. Ibn al-'Arabī: *Aḥkām al-Qur'ān*
   4. Jaṣṣāṣ: *Aḥkām al-Qur'ān*
   5. Bayḍāwī: *Anwār at-Tanzīl wa asrār at-Ta'wīl.*

In the *Ḥadīth* literature the *Ṣiḥāḥ Sitta* (the six most sound compilations) have been generally relied upon.

2. Pickthall, keepeth his duty to Allah for the word 'fears'. Throughout this book M. Pickthall's English Translation of the Qur'ān has been used unless otherwise mentioned in the note.

3. The Prophet (peace be upon him) is reported to have said: 'It is a great sin to "kill" your child for fear of his sharing in your meal.'

4. 3:104, 130; 23:1–11; 59:9; 64:16; 87:14, etc.

5. Pickthall, usury.

6. For an explanation of the term see below; also Chapter 5.

7. The *Sunna* of the Prophet (peace be upon him) in the context of this study has been divided into two parts. Firstly, the behavioural teachings of the Prophet (peace be upon him) which inspire and guide general attitude; and secondly, his own practices as a ruler, policy-maker and administrator. The first part of the *Sunna* will be discussed in this chapter while the second part will be spread over the following chapters according to the matter under discussion.

It should be kept in mind that the teachings and principles as reported to have been laid down in the *Sunna* are not abstract theories; they are meant for ordinary human beings, are capable of being understood by people of all mental levels and are capable of being put into practice. The *Ḥadīth* literature mostly defines, reasserts, or elaborates the basic principles as laid down in the Qur'ān. The language of the *Ḥadīth* on economic questions is only as technical as could be understood by the Arab society of the Prophet's time.

8. Bukh. (U), 2, 40.

9. Tir., 8, 144 (parenthesis ours).

10. Tir., 8, 146.

11. Mus., 7, 111.

12. Mus., 7, 126.

13. Tir., 9, 222.

14. Mus., 7, 124–5.

15. Mus., 7, 133.

16. See below.

17. Prof. W.M. Watt: *Islam and the Integration of Society,* London, 1970 (chapter on The Place of Economic and Social Change).

18. And We have given you power in the earth and appointed for you therein a livelihood . . . (7:10)

Say: Who hath forbidden the adornment of Allah which He hath brought forth for His bondmen, and the good things of His providing . . . ? (7:32)

He it is Who created for you all that is in the earth. (2:29)

19. Here and hereafter M.M. Pickthall's translation of the Qur'ān has been reproduced, unless otherwise stated.

21. *Ad interim* in the sense that the Qur'ān terms all these possessions as *matā'* (provision) only for a while. This was according to the Qur'ān made clear to Adam when he was deported to this planet:

> Go down (from hence), one of you a foe unto the other. There will be for you on earth a habitation and a provision for a while. (7:24)

23. For a list of such persons and the particulars of land see chapter on Land Ownership and Controls.

24. Bukh., (Jizya), 9; Mus., 12, 90.

25. A.U., 674. Here and hereafter the numbers against A.U. refer to paragraph rather than page numbers.

26. Yah., 289. Here and hereafter the numbers against Yaḥyā refer to paragraph numbers.

27. For further discussion on the subject refer to chapter on Land Ownership and Controls.

28. Nas. (U), 2, 107.

29. For further discussion see chapter on Land Ownership and Controls.

30. Yah., 247, 287, 294.

31. Bal., 356.

32. Maj. (U), 1, 608 (parenthesis mine).

33. Bukh. (U), 1, 733, 770–3, 788, 789; 2, 653; 3, 346, 893; Mus. (U), 4, 303; Nas. (U), 3, 276, 402–8, 445, 571.

34. For a full discussion see below, s.v. 'Trade'.

35. Nas. (U), 3, 402, 408, 511; Bukh. (U), 1, 770, 773; 2, 653; 3, 189; Mus. (U), 5, 282, 283.

36. According to a saying, *qisṭ* is a Greek word and means *'adl* (Bukh. (U), 3, 928).

37. It is reported in Mus. (U), 5, 115 that when pious Abū Dharr requested the Prophet (peace be upon him) to appoint him to an office the latter refused him with the remark: 'O Abū Dharr, you are weak but that (office) is an *amāna* (trust). It is (a source of) disgrace and repentance on the day of resurrection except for those who took it on merit and discharged (properly) whatever it requires.' According to Bukh. (U), 3, 525 the Prophet (peace be upon him) is reported to have said: 'Wait for the day of judgement when *amāna* is being misused.' Somebody enquired, how is it misused? On this he said: 'When the affair is entrusted to an incompetent person . . . '

38. Mus. (U), 5, 116.

39. The Qur'ānic expression *al-jār dhi'l janb* (4:36) has been interpreted by Bukhārī to mean strangers who travel together (Bukh. (U), 1, 876).

40. Abu Daud (U), 2, 620–1, 'K-al-buyū''.

41. Bukh. (U), 2, 825, Chapter *'ḥusn qaḍā''*.

42. For the term *faḍl* see 2:198, 268; 3:170, 173, 179; 4:32, 54; 5:2; 9:28, 59, 74, 75, 76, etc. For the term *khayr* see 2:180, 215, 272, 273, etc. For the term *raḥma* see 17:100; 18:16, etc.

43. The Qur'ān says: 'And in the sky is your provision, *rizq,* in addition to what has been promised to you.' (51:22)

44. Nas. (U), 3, 488.

45. Bukh. (U), 3, 483; Nas. (U), 3, 486 *et sqq.*; Abu Daud (U), 1, 341 *et sqq.*

46. Bukh. (U), 2, 519.

47. Bukh. (U), 2, 534.

48. Bukh. (U), 3, 502.

49. See above, for a maximum of grace period of three years fixed by Caliph 'Umar and two years fixed by Ziyād.

50. Bukh. (Muzāra'a), 2.

51. Maj. (U), 2, 39–40.

52. *Ibid.* However, according to Ibn al-Jawzī the authenticity of the *ḥadīth* is doubtful.

53. Qur'ān: 4:7, 11, 12, 176.

54. Mus. (U), 6, 523–4.

55. Bukh. (U), 1, 819.

56. Bukh. (U), 3, 462.

57. Nas. (U), 3, 400.

58. Mus. (U), 4, 65.

59. Abu Daud (U), 2, 314–15.

60. Maj. (U), 2, 256.

61. *Ibid.* (parenthesis mine).

62. Qur'ān, 3:179; 4:37; 9:35; 47:38; 57:27; 70:17, 18, 21; 89:19; 92:8–11; 100:8; 103:1–3.

63. Qur'ān, 4:6; 6:142; 7:31; 17:26–7.

64. Qur'ān, 17:29; 25:67.

65. Bukh. (U), 2, 248.

66. Abu Daud (U), 1, 366–7.

67. Bukh. (U), 2, 40.

68. Nas. (U), 3, 417.

69. A *Ḥadīth* says: 'The Prophet (peace be upon him) has said: A bedding for the man, one for his wife, one for his guest; a fourth one would become for Satan.' (Mus. (U), 5, 290)

70. Abu Daud (U), 1, 366.

71. Bukh. (U), 2, 77.

72. 'Without desire' has been freely translated for *ghayr mushrif* as no appropriate word is available. 'Do not chase it' has been translated for *fa lā tutbi'hu nafsak.* (Bukh. (U), 3, 767)

73. Maj. (U), 1, 608.

74. For example, refer to 2:22; 6:142; 7:57; 16:5, 11–14; 32:27; 35:27; 36:33; 39:21; 42:11; 50:9; 55:10; 80:27–32.

75. The curious fact is that although there are no indications in the Qur'ān justifying or disapproving the private ownership of land, there is not a single *Ḥadīth* to suggest that the Prophet (peace be upon him) disapproved private occupation of land during his ten-year rule in Madina.

76. Mus., 10, 213–14.

77. Bukh. (Muzāra'a); *cf.* Qasṭalānī, Shihāb ad-Dīn: *Irshād as-Sārī,* Cairo, 1905–9, Vol.4, p.184.

78. Tir., 6, 147. This obviously means that if a person begins to till another person's land he will have no right to it even if he has reclaimed it. This is further confirmed by another *Ḥadīth* transmitted by Tirmidhī, 6, 148.

79. Bukh. (Muzāra'a), 2.

80. Yah., 247, 287, 294. For more details see chapter on Land Ownership and Controls.

81. Mus., 10, 207.

82. Mus., 10, 196.

83. The *Ḥadīth* narrated by Rāfi' has greatly confused the issue of *muzāra'a.* He was of the view that the Prophet (peace be upon him) had disapproved giving of lands in consideration of any sort of payment. But taken on the whole it seems that the Prophet (peace be upon him) did not mean total abolition of this practice. That is why the other two senior Companions, Ibn 'Umar and Zayd b. Thābit differed with Rāfi'. Ibn 'Umar's argument was the wide prevalence of the practice during the time of the Prophet (peace be upon him) and of the Pious Caliphs without censure. On the other hand, Zayd's argument was the context of the *Ḥadīth* which, according to him, Rāfi' did not pick up (Abu Daud 3, 350–5). Zayd narrated that two persons who had a quarrel called on the Prophet (peace be upon him) for judgement, who, knowing about their dispute, observed: 'If this is your condition then do not let out your land.' Rāfi' picked up only the last portion of (the Prophet's) speech (but missed the earlier) (Nas., 7, 50).

84. For example, Bukh. (U), 1, 805–14; Abu Daud (U), 2, 638–40.

85. Maj., 2, 724.

86. Maj., 2, 742.

87. Nas., 5, 81.

88. Bukh. (U), 1, 731.

89. Bukh. (U), 1, 730.

90. Mus., 10, 156–7.

91. *Ibid.*, Bukh. (Buyū'), 92.

92. Abu Daud (U), 2, 232–3.

93. Bukh. (Buyū‘), 128; Tir., 6, 52–3; Mus., 10, 183–8.

94. *Ibid.*

95. Bukh. (Buyū‘), 94; Mus., 10, 154.

96. *Ibid.*

97. Mus., 10, 156–7.

98. Bukh. (Buyū‘), 89; Tir., 6, 38.

99. Mus., 10, 160.

100. Bukh. (U), 1, 747.

101. Bukh. (Salam), 3.

102. For weights and measures see Appendix.

103. Mus., 10, 182–9.

104. Abu Daud (U), 2, 635.

105. For the former *Ḥadīth* see Khaṭīb Tabrīzī, *Mishkāt al-Maṣābīḥ,* Karachi, 1368 A.H., p. 255; for the latter, Aḥmad b. Ḥanbal, *Musnad,* n.p., n.d., Vol. 5, p. 425. (parenthesis mine).

106. Tir., 6, 55.

107. Mus., 11, 43.

108. Tir., 6, 38.

109. Maj., 2, 726.

110. *Ibid.*

111. Bukh. (Buyū‘); (Mus., 10, 168–9). According to another *Ḥadīth,* Ibn ‘Abbās is reported to have observed that they did not confine this *Ḥadīth* to food-grain only.

112. Maj., 2, 734–5.

113. Maj., 2, 734; Mus., 10, 165.

114. Mus., 11, 33; Maj., 7, 728.

115. See above.

116. See relevant chapters in *Ḥadīth* literature.

117. 5:96; 16:5–18; 18:7, 46; 28:77.

118. For *khayr* see 2:180, 215, 272, 273; 100:8, etc. For *faḍl* see 62:10; 73:20; 2:198; 4:32, 73, etc.

119. 4:37; 82:20.

120. Pickthall, ‘superfluous’ for ‘you spare’; the original word being *al-‘afw.*

121. For unjustifiable motives and refrains from reasonable expenditure. This is termed *bukhl* and regarded as undesirable.

122. 4:8, 9; 17:26, 29.

123. 3:180; 4:36, 39, 128; 9:34.

124. 6:166.

125. The Prophet (peace be upon him) has said: 'Simplicity is (a part) of faith' (Maj. (U), 2, 543).

126. Abu Daud (U), 3, 185.

127. Nas., 8, 199.

128. Bukh. (U), 1, 535.

129. Bukh. (U), 1, 856.

130. Bukh. (U), 1, 535.

131. Bukh. (U), 2, 40.

132. Maj. (U), 2, 89.

133. Karl Marx and F. Engels, *The Incipit of the Communist Manifesto.*

134. For example, 2:2, 195, 254, 265–8, 270, 271, 274; 3:134; 9:35, 54, 55, 99; 13:27; 14:31; 16:75; 30:39, etc.

135. This should not be confused with *qarḍ ḥasan* or ordinary loan that is advanced by one person to another. It is also known as *qarḍ ḥasan* because it must be free of interest. According to popular belief *qarḍ ḥasan* signifies a loan that is repayable at the convenience of the borrower or that may be written off in case the borrower fails to repay it even though he may be in a position to do so. The *shar'ī* concept of this loan is, however, different from the popular belief. It is a contractual obligation and must be discharged. Its non-payment within a stipulated period may invite legal action against the defaulter. It is called *qarḍ ḥasan* because it involves a number of virtues on the part of the lender, namely:

(a) The lender sacrifices his present satisfaction for the sake of his brother's.
(b) The lender exposes his own savings/resources to the uncertainties in the future that are associated with lending.
(c) The lender willingly deprives himself of the potential productivity of his savings.
(d) The lender advances his money/resources without expecting any return or reward from the borrower. He expects a better reward from Allah.

It is because of these factors that a *qarḍ* is treated to be a *qarḍ ḥasan,* virtuous loan.

The *Sharī'a* recommends registering a contract of loan duly witnessed by two men, and, if necessary, backed by a pledge, mortgage or sureties. The lender is not allowed to claim anything over and above the amount of loan advanced by him. The borrower is urged to repay the loan within time. In case the borrower is overtaken by misfortune the lender is advised to grant a respite to the borrower. In case the borrower has the capacity to repay the loan but fails to do so in time the lender has a right to bring him to book. The defaulter may be humiliated and punished. A court of law may declare a debtor insolvent and may seize his properties and assets to dispose of the liability of debt. The debtor's house, utensils, clothes and tools of earning cannot, however, be seized. In the event of the death of an undischarged debtor, the debt is the first claim on the bequest followed by the will. A will or commitment to donate or gift something, made on the death-bed, is binding up to one-third only. But the borrower is not absolved of the entire liability of the loan that he has borrowed during his life.

136. Bukh. (U), 2:124; Mus. (U), 3, 33, 35 with minor difference in words.

137. Tir. (U), 2, 41.

138. Bukh. (U), 1, 540.

139. A measure. For weights and measures see Appendix.

140. Bukh. (U), 1, 785.

141. Abu Daud (U), 1, 366. It should be kept in mind that *Zakāt* is leviable if the produce exceeds 5 *wasqs*. Obviously the act of sparing a bunch of dates if the pick exceeds 10 *wasqs* is over and above the prescribed *Zakāt.*

142. Bukh. (U), 1, 892.

143. Abu Daud (U), 2, 432.

144. Bukh. (U), 1, 832.

145. *Ibid.,* 2, 48.

146. Abu Daud (U), 1, 369; Bukh. (U), 3, 166.

147. Abu Daud (U), 1, 366–7.

148. *Cf.* Bukh. (U), 2, 77; Mus. (U), 3, 27.

149. Abu Daud (U), 1, 367.

150. Details of some such expiations are also to be found in *Ḥadīth* literature, s.v. *Kaffārāt* and *K-al-aymān wa'l nudhūr.*

151. The emphasis on doing *infāq* sometimes precedes *ṣalāh* and compulsory *Zakāt,* see for example 2:177.

152. See Shaykh Aḥmad, alias Mullā Jīwan: *Nūr al-Anwār,* gloss: Muhammad 'Abd al-Ḥalīm al-Rājī: *Qamar al-Aqmār,* Lahore, 1957, pp. 25–6.

153. For example:

> Who hoard their wealth and enjoin avarice on others . . . We prepare a shameful doom. (4:37)
>
> They who hoard up gold and silver and spend it not in the way of Allah, unto them give tidings of a painful doom. On the day when it will (all) be heated in the fire of hell and their foreheads and their flanks and their backs will be branded therewith . . . (9:34, 35)
>
> But nay! for Lo! it is the fire of hell eager to roast. It calleth him who turned and fled, and hoarded wealth and withheld. (70:15–18)

154. Bukh. (U), 1, 785.

155. Q.v. note on 'the functions of the state' for a detailed discussion.

156. For details see pp. 141–2 s.v. The Role of Voluntary *Ṣadaqa.*

157. In cases where public spending increases tremendously due to an explosion in population or changes in civilization leading to the emergence of numerous social wants, where individual preference cannot be recognized or, where the market fails to determine these wants or where private enterprise cannot be relied upon, the task of allocation of funds for satisfaction of such wants is to be undertaken by the government. Similarly, in a situation when citizens have refused to sacrifice personal gains in favour of social benefits it becomes impossible to rely upon voluntary contributions. Even if a large number of people agree to contribute, equity in sacrifice cannot be ensured. It is the government that can determine the standard of equity and the method of enforcing it. Moreover it is this factor of individualism that poses a problem of equitable distribution of benefit of

public goods to all the people. Combined with this factor is the policy of allocating funds in such a way as to ensure minimum instability in price levels. All these factors call for a major role of the government in organizing its public expenditure programme and in imposing direct and indirect taxes.

158. For a detailed discussion see the chapter on *Zakāt*.

159. 2:3, 43, 83, 110, 177, 277; 4:77; 9:5, 11, 18, 71; 27:37, 56; 73:20; 98:5, etc.

160. 9:103.

161. See Chapter 6.

162. See below for details.

163. See below.

164. For details, see Chapter 6.

165. Mus., 7, 57–8. It is a per-head flat rate payable by the guardian of the household.

166. Nas., 5, 23, 37.

167. Abu Daud, 2, 129–30.

168. Abu Daud, 2, 128.

169. A.U., para. 863. Hereafter the number after A.U. indicates the paragraph.

170. Bukh. (Zakāt), 85; Nas., 5, 23; Abu Daud, 2, 129–30.

171. Tir., 3, 125; Abu Daud, 2, 129–30.

172. Yah., 382, 509–11, 514–15, 532–4, 535. Here and hereafter the number after Yah. indicates the paragraph.

173. Kh., 31; Mus., 7, 50–3; Nas., 5, 39–40.

174. Qur'ān, 6:141.

175. Nas., 5, 44; Abu Daud, 3, 244; A.U., 856–7.

176. Kh., 31–2. Although the *isnād* of the *Ḥadīth* is criticized (Tir., 3, 132), there is nothing to suggest that it was imposed by the Prophet (peace be upon him) or the Pious Caliphs.

177. Bal., 85; Abu Daud, 3, 323–4.

178. Bukh. (Zakāt), 57.

179. Nas., 5, 26.

180. Bukh. (Zakāt), 85.

181. A.U., 1006.

182. Mus., 7, 55; Tir., 3, 101–2; Nas., 5, 35–6.

183. Tir., 3, 125.

184. This *Ḥadīth* is not transmitted by any of the *Ṣiḥāḥ* works.

185. Ag., 257.

186. Ag., 258.

187. Abu Daud, 2, 160.

188. For terminological sense and other discussion, see Chapters 5 and 7.

189. Abu Daud (U), 2, 367.

190. Abu Daud (U), 2, 381–6; Tir. (U), 1, 494.

191. Abu Daud (U), 2, 379; Bukh. (U), 2, 177, 180; 2, 614.

192. Abu Daud (U), 2, 474, 491, 492.

193. Mus. (U), 5, 13; Bukh. (U), 2, 184; Abu Daud (U), 2, 375.

194. See also Chapter 7.

195. Bayḍāwī, 1, 383; Ṭabarī, *Ṭafsīr*, 14, 200; Jaṣṣāṣ, 3, 125.

196. *Ibid.*, for all sources; also Qurṭubī, 8, 115.

197. See Chapter 7.

198. For example, J.M. Keynes: *A Treatise on Money,* London, 1971, and *General Theory on Employment, Interest and Money,* London, 1963; Roy Harrod: *On Dynamic Economics,* London, 1948; article 'Is Interest Obsolete?', E.V. Bohm-Bawerk: *Capital and Interest,* London, 1890; Karl Marx: *Das Capital,* Moscow, 1969.

199. Iqbal Suhayl: *Taḥqīq-e-Ribā* (Urdu), Azamgarh, 1933; Jafar Shah Nadvi: *Commercial interest kī fiqhī haysiyat,* (Urdu), Lahore, Fazlurrahman: *Ribā and Profit,* Eng. tr. *Umma,* March 1965, etc.

200. Abu'l Ā'lā Maudūdī: *Sūd,* Lahore; Abū Zahra: *Buḥūth fi'r-Ribā,* Beirut, 1970; S.H. Zaman: 'Islam vis-à-vis Interest Rate', *Islamic Culture,* January 1966; Muhammad 'Abd-Allah al-'Arabī: 'Banking in Islam', *Majjallat al-Azhar,* May (1965); Nejatullah Siddiqi: *Some Aspects of the Islamic Economy,* Lahore, 1970; *Some Economic Aspects of Islam,* ed. Motamar 'Ālam al-Islāmī, Karachi, 1965; M. Umer Chapra: *Towards a Just Monetary System,* The Islamic Foundation, Leicester, 1985; Ziauddin Ahmad: 'Some Misgivings About Interest', *Interest-free Banking in Pakistan,* Institute of Bankers in Pakistan, Karachi, n.d.; Report of the Council of Islamic Ideology on the Elimination of Interest from the Economy, Islamabad, 1980.

201. All works on exegesis.

202. 'O ye who believe! Observe your duty to Allah, and give up what remaineth from *ribā* if ye are believers.' (2:278)

An earlier verse reads: O ye who believe! Devour not *ribā* doubling and quadrupling . . . (3:130)

M. Pickthall, 'usury' for interest.

203. See n. above.

204. See above.

205. The provisions regarding interest and many other provisions in favour of debtors are made to apply only to the Israelites: 'If thou lend money to any of my people that is poor by thee thou shalt not be to him as a usurer neither shalt thou lay upon him usury.' In the Talmud there is no question of loans at interest so the subject is hardly touched upon. A loan was a debt and, therefore, was annulled by the sabbatical year, like other debts. It could avoid the provisions of the sabbatical year by the use of Prosbul. According to the Talmud: 'Interest is like the bite of a snake, one feels only when it begins to swell.' And: 'Gamblers and usurers are not trustworthy witness.'

The words of Jesus contain allusions to borrowing and lending but, as we should expect of one who refused to be a judge and divider (Luke 14:12), there are no direct precepts to guide the Christian conscience. Nevertheless, the early fathers looked upon usury with severe disapproval. They may have been influenced in certain cases by the classical moralists, but the determining standard for them was the Old Testament legislation and the general principle of the New Testament, more especially a standard interpretation of Luke 6:35. Some of them accepted till recently as still binding on Christians the Old Testament precepts (Ex. 22:25; Dt. 23:19; Ps. 15:5; Ezk 18:8) regarding the prohibition of interest as only a preparation for the higher demand of the Gospel to forego even the capital. (*E.R.E.* and *Dictionary of the Bible:* s.v., 'Usury' and 'Interest')

206. See above.

207. The six most sound compilations on *Ḥadīth*.

208. Mus., 11, 13.

209. Mus., 11, 22.

210. *Mishkāt,* tr. Robson, 2, 605, with almost similar sense; *cf.* Abu Daud, 3, 333.

211. Mus. (U), 4, 327.

212. Maj., 2, 39.

213. *Ibid.*

214. Maj., *cf. Mishkāt* (Robson), 2, 605.

215. The Prophet (peace be upon him) in one case ordered his Companion to forego a portion of his claim while in another case (an insolvent debtor, perhaps) he appealed to the Muslims to donate towards the settlement of a claim; the amount falling short of the claim was written off (Bukh. (U), 1, 939; Mus. (U), 4, 275; Nas. (U), 3, 485, 487; Bukh. (U), 3, 483).

216. Bukh. (U), 3, 483; Nas. (U), 3, 485, 487.

217. Maj. (U), 2, 543.

218. *Passim.*

219. Bukh. (U), 1, 790.

220. *Ibid.,* 1, 827.

221. Qur'ān, 4:11, 12 as interpreted by all exegetes.

222. Nas. (U), 3, 280.

223. Nas. (U), 3, 283.

224. This is in respect of a loan for *Jihād.* In cases where the *mujāhid* has borrowed for a non-*Jihād* purpose the Prophet (peace be upon him) has warned: 'If anybody dies a martyr's death but is indebted, he will not go to paradise without paying off his debt.' (Nas., 7, 315)

225. Maj. (U), 2, 74.

226. Al-Mundharī, 'Abd-al-Aẓīm b. 'Abd-al-Qawī; *Al-Targhīb wa'l Tarhīb,* Cairo, 1954, Vol. 2, p. 602.

227. Tir. (U), 2, 72.

228. S.v. The Concept of *'Adl* and *Iḥsān.*

229. Bukh. (U), 2, 135–6; 3, 795–6.

230. Bukh. (U), 2, 76; 2, 59; 72.

231. *Ibid.*, 2, 59–60.

232. Maj. (U), 2, 74.

233. Abu Daud (U), 1, 524–5.

234. Bukh. (U), 2, 90.

235. Abu Daud (U), 1, 528–9.

236. *Ibid.*

237. Bukh. (U), 2, 84.

239. Darimi (U), *K-al-'Ilm*.

240. Maj. (U), 1, 107.

241. Abu Daud (U), 2, 439.

242. Maj. (U), 1, 107.

243. *Ibid.*, 1, 114.

244. *Ibid.*, 2, 352.

245. Nas. (U), 3, 490.

246. Bukh. (U), 1, 744.

247. *Ibid.*

248. Bukh. (U), 1, 748.

249. Qur'ān, 2:205; 3:57; 5:64; 28:77; etc.

250. Tir. (U), 1, 331. According to another version *(ibid.)*, *fitna* (scandal) for *fasād*.

251. Bukh. (U), 1, 844.

252. Nas. (U), 3, 485.

253. The punishments *(ḥadd)* for drinking and debauchery are laid down in the *Ḥadīth*, *cf.* Mus. (U), *Kitāb al-Ḥudūd*, chapters on drinking and debauchery, Vol. 4, 496 *et seq*.

254. It is not possible here to detail the great importance that the Prophet (peace be upon him) attached to health and hygiene: 'There is not a single disease which is not curable. Allah gives relief when (proper) medicine is used', and, 'A quack is liable if he practises medicine without knowledge', are two of the many sayings which not only persuade people to use medicines but also to learn medical science. While the Prophet's mention of items like milk, honey, bran, vinegar, mushrooms, antimony, negella indica (seed), cassia senna, myrtle, etc. as medicines for certain diseases might be popularly-known remedies, his emphasis on the principles of hygiene was his unique contribution to healthy living and the prevention of diseases. His instructions on cleanliness of body and use of clean water for drinking and for ablution are really surprising, keeping in view the desert peninsula he belonged to. (For some of the references see Bukh. (U), 2, 238; 3:198, 268–81, 333, 334, 338, 340, 696; Maj. (U), 2, 352, 356, 360; Tir. (U), 2, 61–70; Mus. (U), 1, 478; 4, 298; 5, 264, 360–6; Abu Daud (U), 1, 42–53, etc.) This is in addition to the Qur'ānic hints at hygienic living through its emphasis on cleanliness of body, clothes (2:222; 8:11; 74:4, 5; 4:32; 22:29) and place of worship (2:125).

255. Maj. (U), 2, 74.

256. Tir. (U), 1, 331.

257. Abu Daud (U), 3, 185.

258. Abu Daud (U), 2, 465.

259. *Ibid.*, 1, 369, 387, 397.

260. Bukh. (U), 1, 850.

261. *Ibid.*, 1, 854.

262. Abu Daud (U), 1, 538.

263. *Ibid.*

264. It is reported by Bukh. (U), 2, 198 that the Prophet (peace be upon him) was so concerned about this that he insisted on this aspect even on his death-bed: 'And welcome foreign delegations and present them with gifts as I used to do.'

265. Bukh. (U), 2, 105, 693.

266. Bukh., (Jumu'a), 18.

267. Mus., 12, 209.

268. Bukh. (U), 3, 687.

269. Bukh. (U), 3, 848.

270. Bukh. (U), 2, 654.

271. Bukh. (U), 3, 760.

272. Mus., 7, 82.

273. Mus., 12, 213.

274. Nas. (U), 3, 451.

275. Nas. (U), 3, 450.

276. Mus., 12, 216–17.

277. Mus., 12, 218–22.

278. Mus., 12, 222.

279. Tir., 6, 79.

280. Maj., 2, 775.

281. Bukh. (Ijārāt).

282. Abu Daud, 3, 185.

283. Abu Daud (U), 2, 464.

284. Maj. (U), 2, 538; Nas. (U), 3, 448–9.

285. For a number of examples see: A.U., 956, 1052, 1081–92; Kh., 47, 72.

286. Kh., 67 and chapter for 'Umar, 'Alī and 'Umar II.

287. Sa'd., III, 1, 201; Tab., 1, 2802; Tab., 2, 1366–7.

288. Ad-Dinawrī, Qut. ('Uyūn), 73.

289. Sad., III, 1, 203, 221.

290. Tir. (U), 1, 201.

291. Bukh. (U), 3, 730.

292. Abu Daud (U), 2, 374–5.

293. Mus. (U), 124–7.

294. Mus. (U), 5, 125.

295. Mus. (U), 5, 126. It is beyond the scope of this study to dilate upon the issue of rising up against the ruler *(khurūj)* as discussed by the early thinkers in the light of this and other *Ḥadīth*.

296. Mus. (U), 5, 138.

297. Bukh. (U), 3, 730.

298. Mus. (U), 5, 132.

299. Tir., 8, 126–7.

300. Maj. (U), 2, 405.

301. Also see n. 1, Chapter 8.

302. Bukh. (U), 1, 551.

303. Bukh. (U), 1, 729.

304. Nas. (U), 3, 220.

305. Bukh. (U), 1, 867–8.

306. Bukh. (U), 1, 783.

307. Bukh. (U), 2, 92.

308. Nas. (U), 2, 339–40; also Bukh. (U), 2, 92 with different wording.

CHAPTER 2

The Moral Foundations of Economic Life

In the first book of the Bible the Arab nomad is summed up in the person of Ishmael: 'He will be a wild man; his hand will be against every man and every man's hand against him.'[1] It was the Arab of such stock before whom lay his country, 'bleeding and torn by fratricidal war and inter-tribal dissension, his people sunk in ignorance, addicted to obscene rites and superstitions, and with all their desert virtues, lawless and cruel.'[2] These Arabs were wild nomadic people who, surrounded by hardships, had to display endurance and fortitude and, pressed by hunger develop qualities of aggression and ferocity. Fierce individualism and all-embracing distrust was their chief characteristic.[3] The settled man regarded the nomad as a natural enemy and the nomad regarded the settled man as a legitimate prey.[4]

What these people could be supposed to do is indicated by Ibn Khaldūn in the following words:

> The Bedouins are a savage nation, fully accustomed to savagery and the things that cause it. Savagery has become their character and nature. They enjoy it because it means freedom from authority and no subservience to leadership . . .
>
> . . . The very nature of their existence is the negation of the building which is the basis of civilization. This is the case with them quite generally.
>
> Furthermore, it is their nature to plunder whatever other people possess. Their sustenance lies wherever the shadow of their lances falls. They recognize no limit in taking the possessions of other people. Whenever their eyes fall upon some property, furnishings or utensils they take them. When they acquire superiority or royal authority they have complete power to plunder (as they please). There no longer exists any political (power) to protect property, and civilization is ruined . . .

> Furthermore, the Bedouins are not concerned with laws, or with deterring people from misdeeds or with protecting some against others. They care only for the property that they might take away from people through looting and imposts. When they have obtained that, they have no interest in anything further, such as taking care of people, looking after their interests, or forcing them not to commit misdeeds.[5]

The character of the Bedouins portrayed above should have been conducive to winning a battle but not conquering a land or a nation. And retaining the conquered land should have been all the more difficult for them. What could be expected of these unsophisticated illiterate people was the storming of a tribe or a nation, to perpetrate mass killings and plunder, and then return to their abodes; or settling in the fertile lands by killing or driving away the defeated people. They showed no mercy to their enemy; their lust for immediate material gains would not allow them to plan their economy, wait for yearly returns to the subjects, and leave with them sufficient resources for a comfortable living. But, practically this did not happen. Under the leadership of the Arab townsmen they fought against much larger enemies patiently and with perseverance, routed them, subdued them; and having annihilated the armies, they came to generous terms with the subjects and spared them to live safely, peacefully, and honourably as a tributary nation, under their protection.

When the Arab tribes emerged as a rising power, united under the banner of Islam, they faced great and powerful rivals. At first they were no match for the Persian and Byzantine empires, who had at their disposal a unique administration with a highly differentiated and well-trained civil service. Their military techniques were superb and they – mainly the Byzantians – possessed an excellent legal frame-work and a highly-developed economic and financial system.

It was in this perspective that the Muslim society had to make its way. With a limited knowledge of their surroundings, some experience of trade and the simple practice of the administration of tribal institutions they had to rely upon two factors: their ideology and their moral discipline, inspired partly by their ideology and partly by their group feeling, *aṣabiyya.* These two factors helped them become a world power of the first order. A careful analysis of the early history makes it abundantly clear that it was this moral discipline that enabled them to overcome a number of technical, administrative and legal obstacles. These two factors formed the basis of their life and their economic principles. The relevance of this basis to the economic life of the Muslim society has been partly discussed in Chapter 1. This chapter is intended as an inquiry into these principles as adhered to by the Muslim officials during the period under study.

During the Prophet's time the Muslims followed what was ordained in the Qur'ān and what the Prophet (peace be upon him) directed them to do. The Prophet himself was treated as a legislative authority and an ideal. As he was directly engaged in training his followers, he immediately stopped them in the event of a breach of moral discipline. After the conquest of Khaybar, when cultivated land was divided among groups of Muslims and passed on to the local Jews on condition of share-cropping, the Muslims treated the land as their own property and began to use its produce without the Jews' permission. On knowing of this the Prophet (peace be upon him) assembled the Muslims and observed: 'We have given protection to the lives and properties of these Jews and appointed them as our workers. They are now in a treaty relation with us. Eating out of their property without fair return for it is unlawful.' After these instructions there arose no further complaints against them.[6] This instruction laid down the basic principle of non-exploitation of a weaker party. It was this sense of justice that the custodian of the Khaybar properties, 'Abd Allāh b. Rawāḥa, displayed when he went to share the crop with the Jews. He piled up the total produce in two equal heaps and gave them the option to take either[7] lest they should have a feeling of injustice or exploitation. When the Prophet (peace be upon him) deputed Mu'ādh as a collector of *Zakāt* and taxes in Yemen, he advised him not to take 'the nicer parts of property' by way of *Zakāt* and warned him to 'beware of the curse of the wronged'.[8] The spirit of this advice was also to check any possibility of injustice. This emphasis on the moral fibre was also obvious when the Makkan Muslims migrated to Madina as destitutes and the Madinan Muslims, without any feeling of constraint, offered to share with them half of their properties so as to facilitate their rehabilitation.[9]

The inspiring force behind this sense of justice, fair play and fellow-feeling was the fear of God and the desire to seek His pleasure. This required no administrative delicacies or service regulations. There are numerous stories in books of Islamic history which show this basic fibre woven in the different spheres of the Muslims' activities. These early historians are generally responsible and trustworthy and only a few of their narrations require scrutiny. They reflect the norm which, according to the historians, was taken for granted during the early period.

It has been reported above how Mu'ādh was advised when he was sent to Yemen as collector of *Zakāt* and taxes. When he returned from there and Caliph Abū Bakr asked him to furnish the account, he retorted: 'Shall I have to keep two accounts: one to please Allah and the other to satisfy you? By God! I shall never work for you again.'[10] Though this behaviour smacked of indiscipline from a purely administrative point of view, it also reflected a sense of answerability to God. It was the accomplishment of this training that 'Umar, as a *Qāḍī* (judge) under Caliph Abū Bakr was kept idle for months because no dispute was referred to him.[11] When Caliph Abū Bakr went to Makka and assembled the people to inquire if they had any grievances against the government or its officials, there was no report against either.[12] The *Bayt al-Māl* during Abū Bakr's time was left without a guard.[13]

This was the debut of the nascent society which had no administrative machinery or traditions worth the name. The rights and duties of the civil servants and of the general public were not clearly defined. The new principles for a dynamic, expanding society were not yet applied. To Caliph 'Umar was to be attributed the thrilling take-off of the Islamic society by his creation of precedents which were to form an ideal for a long time to come.

Caliph 'Umar, firm in principles and strong in disposition, demonstrated moral discipline in his own person and thus set an example for his subordinate officers. He treated the government funds exclusively for public welfare, renouncing all financial privileges that were taken for granted by rulers in other contemporary societies. Also, his council of advisers would not allow him any privileged position distinguishable from that of the general Muslims. This asceticism might have been unenviable to many other officers who had a better financial background[14] but was, nonetheless, a source of inspiration to them. Caliph 'Umar, when given by the Prophet (peace be upon him) a very fertile piece of land at Khaybar which could provide for his comfort, made it an endowment for the poor, kinsmen, slaves, travellers and guests.[15] 'Amr, the conqueror of Egypt, earmarked for him a plot of land for his house like that given to thousands of other Muslim soldiers in Egypt. Caliph 'Umar ordered him to convert it into a shopping centre and allot the shops to traders.[16] Caliph 'Umar continued with his own trade during the early days of his caliphate. When once he needed money to finance his share in the business he requested the Companion 'Abd ar-Raḥmān ibn 'Awf to lend him the required amount. 'Abd ar-Raḥmān was surprised at this request because one of the functions of the *Bayt al-Māl* was to advance loans to individuals. He retorted: 'Why don't you borrow it from the *Bayt al-Māl*?' 'No!' remarked 'Umar, 'I won't do that because if I die before repayment, you will propose to write it off as a bad debt and the *Bayt al-Māl* will suffer; but if I borrow it from you, you will not spare it and will arrange to receive it from my bequest.'[17] He was once advised by a physician to use honey which, at that time was available only in the *Bayt al-Māl*. He stood up in public and sought permission to use honey for which ordinarily he was not supposed to be eligible.[18] When he entered Jerusalem as a conqueror, the bishop was moved to see him in untidy and rough clothes and presented him with a suit. Caliph ‘Umar refused to accept the suit, but when the bishop insisted, he agreed to borrow it only for as long as his own clothes were cleaned. And he accepted and returned the borrowed suit accordingly.[19]

Caliph ‘Umar, meticulous in his own dealings, also expected his officers to behave in a dignified manner. He reacted immediately if any of his officers, who were generally the Prophet’s Companions, fell short of his exacting standards. His confiscation of half of the properties of his officers is perhaps highly instructive and is found with varying details in all the histories of that period. It is stated that he used to prepare a list of the properties which a person owned before he was assigned a government office.[20] When ‘Umar came to know of a poem in which the poet spoke of the riches which had been accumulated by Nu‘mān, the officer of Emessa and two other officials,[21] even though there was no proof against them, ‘Umar responded quickly and appointed Maslama as inspector and magistrate and advised him to take away half of each officer’s property.[22] Maslama left Madina with a letter of authority mentioning the purpose of his appointment but without any police or guards. It was taken for granted that he would not be harmed by any of the officers in the remote provinces. It was also taken for granted that in case Maslama wanted these governors to forego half of their property, the governors would not resort to deception for the sake of saving face and defending their position. Caliph ‘Umar also instituted a public inquiry against Sa‘d, the governor of Kūfa on reports of leniency in the sale of *Khums,* the fifth of booty.[23] Companion Abū Hurayra, the collector of *Zakāt* in ‘Umān, received a salary for his office. He also received his pension from the *Bayt al-Māl* as was payable to all the early Muslims. However he also engaged in horse-trading and added to his savings.[24] Caliph ‘Umar accused him of being a thief of God’s property and took away all his savings.[25] He not only impeached the officials but also ensured that their kinsmen did not take any undue advantage of their office. He took away a portion of the earnings of the brother of the collector at Ubulla because this officer used to lend his brother public money which he invested in profitable business.[26] Caliph ‘Umar did not even spare his own sons. They were once given public money in Iraq to be deposited in the central *Bayt al-Māl* at Madina. The funds were given as a loan to be repaid in full at the destination. However, they traded with it *en route* and returned the principal to the caliph who, knowing of this, immediately took away a portion of their profit.[27] Such supererogatory standards of moral behaviour, as inspired by the personal example of the caliph, helped greatly towards the general training of the Muslims. The more firm the caliph, the more cautious were his subordinate officials. When Ḥīra was conquered in A.H. 12, Khālid, the commander of the Muslim army was honoured with presents which were despatched by him to the caliph who advised his commander to adjust their value against the stipulated *Jizya* (poll-tax)[28] because taking anything more than this fixed tax was unjust. Following this ideal the governor of Kūfa, when he used the material of the palace of Ḥīra adjusted the value of the material against *Jizya*-money.[29] Another example of this sense of justice was evident in the case of the conquered people of Syrian cities, who paid tribute to the Muslim general Abū 'Ubayda. The tribute was treated as a tax in lieu of the protection provided to the tributaries by the Muslim government. When the Muslim army had to concentrate on some other front, the general returned the amount because he had to leave these cities unprotected.[30]

To cite another example, 'Utba b. Ghazwān, another general, once sent some sweets to the caliph who returned them with the remark that he would not eat a thing which was not available to all the Muslims.[31] The same answer was given by Abū 'Ubayda when he was invited to a meal by the subjugated citizens.[32] The spirit of submission to the requirements of extraordinary moral discipline can be found in a thrilling example set by the most popular and invincible general, Khālid, half of whose wealth was to be taken over. When Abū 'Ubayda executed the orders of the caliph, Khālid even took off one of his shoes. Abū 'Ubayda did not see any sense in separating the pair of shoes; yet Khālid retorted: 'The orders of the *Amīr al-Mu'minīn* must be fully carried out.'[33]

It is not possible to cite examples of the moral level of the ordinary Muslim. Instances of a high degree of moral accomplishment are recorded only when the event is extraordinary. However, an estimate of this level by the rather implacable 'Umar is worthy of note. When he received in *Khums* (a fifth of booty) the property of the Persian emperor, studded with precious stones and gold and silver pieces, and, finding these articles intact, he admitted: 'Highly honest indeed is the nation which has sent these articles!'[34]

Although the history books are replete with instances of the high moral conduct of the people of the early Islamic era, this chapter has mostly been confined to a few examples which have a bearing on the subject-matter of this book. In a nutshell, the instances speak of a great sense of justice, strict observance of trust, honesty, and integrity, and of the concept of equality in rights and privileges – a metamorphosis of the Bedouin character. Though the law, traditions and common sense allowed them more than what they enjoyed, they set for themselves a standard which even after allowing for concessions and relaxations could not infringe a just degree and matched any other moral system. An embarrassing situation sometimes arose when an officer challenged the validity of the caliph's insistence on moral scrupulousness. On such occasions the caliph did not behave like a dictator; he rather resorted to law or convincing argument. When 'Umar deputed Maslama to take over half of the property of each officer, one of them refused to surrender his.[35] 'Umar did not take any further action against him, perhaps because he knew there was no legal justification for doing so. When Abū Hurayra protested at Caliph 'Umar's action and refused to work under him, the latter could not convince him of his stand.[36] Caliph 'Umar was also in a quandary when his decision to keep the Sawād lands undistributed was challenged. He and his supporters got out of it only when, after three days of unnerving and harsh exchanges, Caliph 'Umar cited in his support a verse of the Qur'ān.[37] When Caliph 'Umar advised the governor of Madā'in, Ḥudhayfa, to divorce his Christian wife, the latter found no legal justification for this directive in regard to this purely personal matter and refused to comply with it. He posed a counter-question as to whether the caliph regarded it to be *ḥarām* (unlawful) and what was the rationale behind the demand. Caliph 'Umar, rather than taking disciplinary action against Ḥudhayfa, admitted that his marriage was lawful, but pointed out that the Christian women of Madā'in were so enamouring that if the Arabs were freely allowed to marry them they would neglect Arab women. On this point only, Ḥudhayfa was convinced.[38] When Caliph 'Umar wrote to 'Uthmān b. Ḥunayf ordering him to allot a stretch of land to a particular applicant, he found it an unusual practice. Rather than promptly complying with his order, he wrote to Caliph 'Umar to confirm it.[39]

The above instances suggest an emphasis on morality and the supremacy of law. In fact it was this emphasis on morality that made the supremacy of law possible. Though this state of affairs did not end with Caliph 'Umar, the full demonstration of this quality could not be effectively made during the following period of political confusion and chaos. Caliph 'Uthmān was not so strict as his predecessor and a small group of unscrupulous persons confused the entire situation. Caliphs 'Uthmān and 'Alī had no less a brilliant record of service to Islam for thirty-five and forty-five years respectively. They can rightly be regarded as the heroes of Islam like their predecessors. Caliph 'Uthmān was one of the richest Companions of the Prophet (peace be upon him) and his wealth served the cause of Islam at some of the most critical junctures of its history. He refused to draw a salary for his office because he had his own resources.[40] He was equally anxious to see that his officers were more concerned with discharging their duties to the people and giving them their due than in securing the rights of the government. 'Become the supporters and protectors of the people rather than collectors of taxes', thus he addressed his first letter to his officers.[41] But by this time the resources of the *Bayt al-Māl* had been expanded enormously and he did not need to exercise the same austerity as Caliph 'Umar. He hardly infringed the supremacy of law but on some points his own interpretation of it was different from that of his predecessors.[42] He was as competent to interpret any ambiguity in law as Caliph 'Umar was. However, Caliph 'Alī, rather than reinterpreting the law adhered strictly to what was practised by the Prophet (peace be upon him) and his two successors. On some points, however, he exercised his personal judgement without offending the senior Companions.[43] Apart from political chaos in the last few years, the situation was almost the same with Caliph 'Uthmān although there were some differences during the caliphate of 'Alī. When 'Uthmān relieved Abū Mūsā of the governorship of Baṣra, he sanctioned for him sufficient money for his later life. Abū Mūsā, although penniless and hard-pressed at the time, did not find any justification in Caliph 'Uthmān's granting him this *ex-gratia* payment.[44] The same amount was offered by 'Uthmān to 'Abd Allāh b. Arqam in charge of the *Bayt al-Māl* at Madina, who refused this amount on the plea that he had been working for the sake of God and not for monetary benefit.[45]

Caliph 'Alī's asceticism in his personal expenditure excelled that of his three predecessors. He was not unaware of the Caliph's right to subsistence from the *Bayt al-Māl* but he voluntarily deprived himself of it. He took his sword to the market to sell it because he needed money to buy a shirt.[46] When some of his friends found him shivering in the cold they advised him to get himself a woollen mantle from the *Bayt al-Māl,* but he chose to forego the right.[47] Caliph 'Alī's respect for law can be summarized in an interesting observation reportedly made by his angry brother 'Aqīl in the presence of Caliph 'Alī's rival Mu'āwiya, in the context of a story which requires more than existing evidence to be fully acceptable, but which portrays 'Alī's character more than Mu'āwiya's. It runs thus: 'Aqīl called on 'Alī for financial help. 'Alī presumably did not think it right to assist him from the *Bayt al-Māl* and, therefore, refused, saying that he would not like to be arraigned (before God) as a thief of public money. 'Aqīl went to Mu'āwiya who was ruling in Damascus and Mu'āwiya awarded him a large amount and, hoping to receive the compliments of 'Alī's brother, requested 'Aqīl to address the public. 'Aqīl thus acknowledged the favour: 'Brothers, 'Alī preferred his religion to me while Mu'āwiya preferred me to his religion.'[48] Whether or not the story is true it does point to a situation which would shelter elements seeking to defeat the supremacy of law. There are reports to suggest that this trend had set in not long after the death of Caliph 'Uthmān when Ibn 'Āmir, the governor of Baṣra took all the assets of the provincial *Bayt al-Māl* and joined the rebels.[49] Caliph 'Alī imprisoned the governor of Ray who embezzled the land-tax funds, but he managed to escape to Mu'āwiya.[50] Cases of fraud were also reported in Caliph 'Umar's time,[51] but such criminals had no protection. Cases of undeserved favour and immunity from the law began to appear by the end of 'Alī's caliphate, and with his death began another period in which the ruler was not very keen to suppress the forces of evil.

The early caliphs set an example of clean personal records in regard to financial interests. Abū Bakr and 'Umar took from the *Bayt al-Māl* only as much as enabled them to make both ends meet, and on their death-bed they wished to reimburse their receipts from their bequest.[52] 'Alī did not take even that much. 'Uthmān, on the contrary, supported the *Bayt al-Māl* itself and relieved the government of serious strain on many occasions. It should be no surprise, therefore, that he did not bequeath a large fortune.[53] In spite of his enormous wealth, and the resentment of some people against him, one could not accuse Caliph 'Uthmān of any undesirable practice of multiplying wealth. These earlier caliphs had a very clear concept of the *Bayt al-Māl*. After 'Alī, however, the position changed. Many of the actions and policies of these caliphs were justifiable only on the grounds of later juristic opinions but the surviving Companions of the Prophet (peace be upon him) generally had a different standard of judgement. Mu'āwiya asked Ibn 'Umar as to the constructions he had put up. Ibn 'Umar observed: 'If this is from God's wealth *(māl Allāh)* then you have committed a breach of trust; but if it is from your own wealth, you are a spendthrift.'[54] It was this sort of rigid critical judgement of the senior members of society that frequently stopped the later rulers from riding roughshod over Islamic principles. However there was a dual standard: publicly they had to heed moral principles and could not be seen to violate the law, while internally they did not or could not control their misbehaving officials.

In the situation outlined above, the first blow was to the concept of justice. Formerly, it was regarded as an obligation of justice to receive only as much from the *dhimmīs* (the protected citizens) as was mutually agreed upon, or pre-assessed. Any other payments were adjusted against the amount of tribute.[55] Now, the rulers did not hesitate to claim more than what was due. The revenue officers of Iraq demanded of the people of Sawād all the presents on the festivals of Nawroz and Mehrjān which were presented to the authorities in the pre-Islamic period. It is stated that the total value of these presents amounted to ten million dirhams.[56] There is reason to believe that the caliphs were not unaware of this excess. The same practice was later on adopted in Khurāsān.[57] These presents were claimed as a right. The central mosque of Wāsiṭ was built with material brought from other cities. Though the people there protested, that did not move the rulers to pay for the material as was done in Caliph 'Umar's time.[58]

While appropriation of the funds of the *Bayt al-Māl* continued as previously, this misappropriation was now allowed as a matter of right, or by way of leniency. The ruling family was given special grants, and endowed with large plots of agricultural land.[59] A ruler could now endow any amount to poets in appreciation of their panegyrics,[60] or to his own son to appease him.[61] The governor of Baṣra, at the time of his dismissal requested the Umayyad caliph not to check his accounts of the *Bayt al-Māl*. His request was acceded to.[62] When the governor of Khurāsān called on the ruler he was asked about the amount of revenues he had brought with him. He reported it to be twenty million. He was then given the option either to submit the accounts and money for audit or take away the amount and resign. He chose the latter course and got off.[63] Many governors were near relatives of the rulers, and were exempt from submitting accounts or sending any portion of revenues to the *Bayt al-Māl*.[64] Large amounts could be granted by way of political bribes[65] or written-off by way of friendship.[66]

Another deviation from the examples and precedents set by the Pious Caliphs was the generous concept of the chosen property *(amwāl ṣafiyya)* which was now revived for the first time since the Prophet's death. The Pious Caliphs had treated it as the privilege of the Prophet (peace be upon him), but now the Umayyad ruler could pick any public property as his own. Even private properties were not safe from this 'pious choice' for they could form a part of the ruler's personal wealth. He could pick any private house,[67] even the lands of Fadak,[68] the personal properties of a governor under punishment[69] or any other properties which, in the earlier days, formed part of public wealth.[70] It was presumably through these acquisitions and misappropriations that the ruling class became the richest class. And it is presumably because of this tendency that subordinate officers also amassed as much money as possible as quickly as possible. Though sometimes these officers got away with their ill-gotten gains, very often they were brought to book and were made to relinquish more than they had acquired.

Some of the specific cases cited above may be defended on grounds of the reinterpretation of the law which was then practised, while a few others might have been given the benefit of the doubt on the ground of historians' alleged prejudices. But the evidence of such infringements is so plentiful in many spheres that any attempt at defending the positions of these rulers in many cases would sound unconvincing. The justification of some others, in the face of growing political anarchy and confusion, may be understandable but with many qualifications.

In spite of all the instances of malpractice as mentioned above, it should not be taken to mean that justice, law and morality were absolutely discarded. The concept of justice was still there, but with many a loophole. Supremacy of the law was recognized, but with reservations. The rulers were still aware of their duty to the public, but themselves enjoyed more privileges and immunities than were conceivable in the time of the Pious Caliphs.

The revolutionary changes that were brought in by ‘Umar II were an extraordinary endeavour to revive the early traditions.[71] Nonetheless the deviating rulers also had at least something to their credit. When Mu‘āwiya was approaching his death he offered half of his property to the *Bayt al-Māl.*[72] Earlier he had wanted to extend the central mosque in Damascus which was proving too small, owing to ever larger congregations. It was possible only if a portion of the courtyard of the church of St. John was included in it. And, justice required that the bishop should freely agree to forego or sell this portion. However the bishop refused to do so and Mu‘āwiya was not able to extend the mosque. Later on, ‘Abd al-Malik also offered a lucrative amount but he also met with a discouraging response.[73] ‘Abd al-Malik dismissed one of his officers on the report that he had received presents from the people.[74]

An artisan of ‘Akka had some flour-mills and other revenue-earning items which Caliph Hishām offered to buy. When the owner refused to sell them Caliph Hishām did not try to misuse his authority.[75] These rulers, whatever their own behaviour did try to see that their subordinate officers were not violating the limits of the law. ‘Abd al-Malik wrote to Ḥajjāj: ‘In my capacity of Amīr al-Mu’minīn, I am God’s trust *(amīn).* Refusing anybody his right or giving anybody without his right are like evils before me.’[76] Sulaymān b. ‘Abd al-Malik advised all his kinsmen and courtiers to listen to, obey and fear God.[77] When Marwān appointed his son ‘Abd al-‘Azīz, as governor of Egypt, he advised him to do justice and good to everybody.[78] When ‘Abd al-Malik was informed that Ḥajjāj had perpetrated some excesses in suppressing the rebellion of Ibn al-Ash‘ath he wrote to him: ‘I order you to pay blood-money to the survivors of those who have been killed by mistake; and compensation be given in cases where they have been knowingly killed. Confiscated properties and lands be returned to their owners.’[79]

Up to Mu‘āwiya’s time, the officers themselves could defy the orders of the caliph if they judged that the caliph was violating the law. When Mu‘āwiya advised his officers to raise the rate of tax in some parts of Egypt, the officers refused to obey the order because they thought it was a violation of the treaty with the Copts.[80] The governor of Iraq asked his deputy in Khurāsān to send to the caliph the entire quantity of gold and silver which had been taken as booty. The deputy refused to do so because, according to him, this contravened the Qur’ānic provision of the distribution of booty.[81] The caliph wrote to the governor of Egypt asking him to allot a spacious plot of land to somebody. The governor did not comply with the request because, according to him, the land in question could not be given to anybody under the terms of the treaty.[82] But by the time of Muʿāwiya's death most of the senior Companions had passed away and the resistance against unlawful actions had weakened. Yet, even in the later period, there are instances to suggest that violation of the rules of justice was kept within certain limits. In the case of major policy issues, and legal disputes, resort was made to the Qur'ān. If there was any ambiguity in the Qur'ān, reference was made to *Ḥadīth* as quoted by a reliable person.[83]

We have presented above the bright as well as the dark side of the rulers. But for successful functioning of an economic institution based on ethics it is not the rulers alone, but the entire society, that count. And thus the maladministration of some economic institutions at certain times cannot be blamed entirely on the later rulers. Their irresponsibility, no doubt, lay in ignoring the moral training of their officials, particularly that of the newly converted Muslims. The decline in moral values of the officials that started under Muʿāwiya might have been arrested by another equally noble prince, ʿAbd al-Malik, who ruled for a fairly long period. But unfortunately he became involved in the chaotic political situation. His frequent attempts to improve the situation were frustrated and he had no alternative but to support his officials' ruthlessness when the divisive forces grew. He seems to have diverted himself from negative activities to positive work after suppressing Ibn Ashʿath's revolt (A.H. 82), although the Khārijites were still at large. But this left only a short period of peaceful rule before his death in A.H. 86. Thus the ills of the body politic spread gradually and imperceptibly in many directions. However, before the first century of Islam which had begun so gloriously ended on a tragic note, ʿUmar II addressed himself to the task of putting things on an even keel. His reforms[84] began at home, then reached the government officials. The last stage of his reforms should have involved the public at large, had he had sufficient time to do so. Unfortunately his successor, rather than continuing the reforms hastened to undo them, mainly because they involved some loss to the economy and of royal privileges. But ʿUmar II's approach had become so popular with the public that the rebel Yazīd b. al-Muhallab gathered around himself large crowds in the name of ʿUmar II's *Sunna*.[85] When things seemed to be out of control in Iraq after Hishām, the ruler appointed ʿUmar II's son as governor[86] and he succeeded in slowing down the turmoil, at least for a time. ʿUmar II had said: 'The spirit of economic laws is justice *(ʿadl)* and generosity *(iḥsān)*.'[87] The history of the Pious Caliphs reflects the truth of this observation. The ruler, on the eve of the end of the Umayyad dynasty, at last admitted:

We committed injustice to our subjects and they became disappointed with our justice. They wished to get rid of us. Our tax-payers were overburdened so they deserted us, destroyed our estates and emptied our treasuries.[88]

But by then it was already too late!

Notes and References

1. Gen. 16:12.

2. Syed Ameer Ali: *The Spirit of Islam,* London, 1923, p. 15.

3. Bertram Thomas, *The Arabs,* London, 1937, p. 13.

4. *Ibid.,* p. 15.

5. Ibn Khaldūn, 'Abd al-Rahmān Ibn Muḥammad: *Muqaddima* (Prolegomena), Cairo, 1904, pp. 118–20. (English rendering by Rosenthal.)

6. Maq. (Im), 328.

7. Bal., 41.

8. Bal., 83.

9. Sad., III, 2, 77.

10. Qut., 80–1.

11. Sad., III, 1, 130.

12. *Ibid.,* 133.

13. *Ibid.,* 151.

14. It is narrated (Sad., III, 1, 201) that one of his officers, Ḥafṣ, once called on Caliph 'Umar. When it was lunch time 'Umar invited him to join him. Ḥafṣ refused, saying: 'Your food is coarse and rough. I have better meals ready for me at home.'

15. Bukh., Shurūṭ, 10.

16. I.A.H. (M), 92.

17. Sad., III, 1, 199.

18. *Ibid.,* 198.

19. Patr. Or., 476.

20. Sad., III, 1, 203.

21. I.A.H. (M), 147.

22. *Ibid.,* Bal., (377) has given the names of nine officers half of whose property was taken over. Ibn Sa'd, (III, 1, 203) has reported that 100 officials were affected.

23. Sad., 5, 44.

24. Bal., 93 and Maq, 2, 259 (*cf.* 'Umar Abū 'n-Naṣr, *'Umar,* 187) report that Caliph 'Umar, while he fixed salaries for his officials, advised them not to hoard wealth or invest their incomes in immovable properties or in farming.

25. Bal., 93.

26. Bal., 377.

27. Mālik Ibn Anas, *Muwaṭṭa'* (narration, Yaḥyā), chapter on *Qarḍ* (loan).

28. Tab., 1, 2042.

29. Bal., 284.

30. Kharaj, 80–1; *Chronicum Anonymum ad annum Christi* 1234, pertinens, ed. J.B. Chabot CSCO, *Scriptones Syri,* III, Series XIV, 1937, p. 195. *Cf.* Denn. 57. See the former sources for Emessa; the latter for Damascus. Kh., 80–1 for all cities.

31. Bal., 323–4. The presumable reason why he did not distribute the sweets in Madina seems to be his emphasis on training his officers.

32. Tab., 1, 2171.

33. Tab., 1, 2149, 2527.

34. Tab., 1, 2450.

35. It was Abū Bakr who said: 'By God, if this is from God's property I have taken, it is not permissible for you to take some and leave the remaining; but if it is our property it is not (lawful) for you to snatch it away.' Yaq., 2, 147.

36. *Ibid.*

37. Kh., 13 *et seq.*

38. Tab., 1, 2375.

39. Maq. (Kh.), 1, 97.

40. M.B.Y., 98, 99.

41. Tab., 1, 2802.

42. An example of this is the Qur'ānic injunction on distributing the one-fifth booty under different heads of expenditure. Caliph 'Uthmān believed that the Qur'ānic words 'God and His Apostle' signify the ruling authority, after the Prophet's death and, therefore, the kinsmen of the caliph also had a share in the 'fifth' as the kinsmen of the Prophet (peace be upon him) had while he was alive. For more discussion see the chapter on '*Ghanīma* and *Khums* (Booty and the fifth)'.

43. See chapters on '*Ghanīma* and *Khums*' and '*Zakāt*'.

44. Sad., 5, 32.

45. Dh. (Tar), 2, 299. The number of officers who were reluctant to accept a salary was much greater in Caliph 'Umar's time.

46. Kath., 8, 3.

47. *Ibid.*

48. Dh. (Tar), 2, 234.

49. Sad., 5, 34.

50. Bal., 315.

51. Bal., 449. A man misrepresented himself as a collector of taxes and took away the public funds.

52. Sad., III, 1, 137.

53. Mas., 3, 76. The other version is that he had distributed among the poor and the kinsmen all his cash and livestock. It is reported (Tab., 1, 2952) that Caliph 'Uthmān himself admitted: 'When I became caliph I had the largest herd of camels and sheep. Now all that I have is two camels . . . '

54. Yaq., 2, 221.

55. Tab., 2042.

56. Jahs., 24.

57. Tab., 2, 1635.

58. Bal., 2, 288, 299.

59. Bal., 284.

60. Sad., 5, 275.

61. Tab., 2, 96.

62. Kath., 8, 28; Tab., 2, 69.

63. Kath., 8, 94; Jahs., 29. Even the rebel Ibn Zubayr refused to call to account his governor at Kūfa which led to the rising of Mukhtār against him. Mas., 3, 272.

64. Tab., 2, 1167; Yaq., 2, 210–11; Kindi, 31, 55.

65. Kindi, 31; Khal., 2, 186 Supp.

66. Bal., 333; Tab., 2, 189.

67. Bal., 281.

68. Sad., 5, 286. Fadak was a stretch of land at Khaybar which was chosen by the Prophet (peace be upon him) after whose demise it could either be used for certain specific purposes or passed on to his kinsmen. In neither case was it to become the personal property of the ruler nor could it be passed on into the ownership of a third party.

69. Tab., 2, 164.

70. Yaq., 2, 222.

71. Discussed in the following chapters.

72. Tab., 2, 202.

73. Bal., 131. Walīd, after the bishop's refusal to accept a much larger amount, however, seized it and effected the expansion. 'Umar II, in order to make up for this injustice, reached a compromise with the priest: church for a church *(Ibid.)*.

74. Mas., 3, 321; Jahs., 43–4.

75. Bal., 124–5.

76. Mas., 3, 34.

77. Yaq., 3, 46.

78. Kindi, 47.

79. Mas., 3, 341.

80. Bal., 219.

81. Kath., 8, 29.

82. I.A.H. (M), 85.

83. Mas., 2, 49; Yah., 289; Qut., 83; Ag., 258.

84. For his reforms see chapters below, *passim*.

85. Tab., 2, 1392.

86. Tab., 2, 1854.

87. A.U., 120.

88. Mas., Cairo, 3, 159. *Cf.* Kharbutli, 391.

CHAPTER 3

Land Ownership and Controls

Land: The Pre-Islamic Practice

In pre-Islamic times, too, land was owned by individuals, by the community, and by the 'state'. All three forms of ownership were known to the Arabs at the advent of the Prophet (peace be upon him). Some wealthy Makkans possessed land in fertile towns. 'Utba and Shayba had their gardens in Ṭā'if.[1] 'Amr also had a valuable stretch of land there.[2] Abū Sufyān had landed property at Balqā' in Syria.[3] Pastures used for grazing livestock were treated as community land. What the tribal chief reserved for his own cattle or for any other purpose was in the tribal sense a royal possession. Pre-Islamic Arabic literature frequently hints at such lands.[4] The Egyptian lands were considered to be the property of the Roman emperor, and a substantial portion of these lands was considered to be so even during the Byzantine period.[5] Caliph 'Umar took over as state properties all land which, in the pre-Islamic days was owned by the emperor of Persia or his family.[6]

Allotment of Land by the Prophet

When the Prophet (peace be upon him) migrated to Madina, many Madinan Muslims had their own agricultural land. The Prophet (peace be upon him) not only confirmed their ownership, but himself set a positive precedent by allowing land to individuals. The land thus allotted by him falls into two categories: (i) land for housing, and (ii) land for farming or gardening. History books record a number of names of important persons to whom plots for housing were allotted. A list of names falling under the latter category of land is given below.

Table 2. Agricultural Lands Distributed by the Prophet

	Name of allottee	Location with particulars of land, if available
1.	Abū Bakr	Banū Naḍīr (Al-'Āliya) and somewhere else.[7]
2.	'Umar	Khaybar[8]
3.	'Alī	Bi'r Qays, Shajara, Faqīrayn[9]
4.	Zubayr	Khaybar (oasis), land at Banū Naḍīr (oasis) at or 30 miles from Madina[10]
5.	Bilāl b. Ḥārith	Land with mineral deposits at 'Aqīq valley[11]
6.	Miqdād	Banū Jadīla[12]
7.	Ḥamza b. Nu'mān	Wādī'l Qurā[13]
8.	Fūrāt b. Ḥayyān	Wādī'l Qurā[14]
9.	Ḥassān b. Thābit	The garden of Bayruḥā'[15]
10.	Mujjā'a	Ghūra, Gharāba, Ḥabal[16]
11.	Zayd al-Ṭā'ī	Exact location not given; may be his own region[17]
12.	Ṣafwān b. Umayya	Valley between Ḥunayn and Makka[18]
13.	Abyaḍ b. Ḥammāl	Salt mines of the hilly land at Ma'rib (later withdrawn)[19]
14.	Name not given (probably Salma b. Akwa')	Around his brother's grave, probably at Khaybar[20]
15.	Sulayṭ Anṣārī	(Later surrendered by him)[21]
16.	People of Juhayna (or Muzayna)	Location not given[22]
17.	*Anṣār* (Helpers) as individuals	The Prophet (peace be upon him) intended to distribute Bahrayn among them but they preferred to do without[23]
18.	'Alqama's father	Ḥaḍramawt[24]
19.	Nephew of a non-Muslim	Yanbu' during his return from Badr[25]
20.	'Abd ar-Raḥmān b. 'Awf	Banū Naḍīr[26]

This list, though by no means comprehensive, gives an idea about the Prophet's policy in respect of the allotment of land on the basis of private ownership.

During the Pious Caliphate

This policy was also followed by the Prophet's caliphs. The Pious Caliphs are reported to have allotted land to individuals.[27] Caliph 'Umar transferred all the lands of Khaybar[28] and Fadak to hundreds of allottees after he exiled the Jews from there. He distributed Ra's al-'Ayn among a number of Muslims.[29] He also directed his governors in Iraq and Syria to allot large tracts of land to the exiled non-Muslims of Najrān.[30] In the very early stages of the conquest of Sawād he intended to distribute them among the fighters but later on refrained from doing so.[31] Historians have given the names of a number of persons to whom he gave land.[32] It is, however, reported that he was not in favour of allotting land in Egypt, Iraq and Syria, to individuals although some exceptions in this regard have been recorded.[33]

Caliph 'Umar's policy was also followed by his successor, Caliph 'Uthmān. By his time the Arab conquests had widely expanded the available land. Moreover, unlike Caliph 'Umar, who had taken over vast lands of the Persian royal family and kept them as unallotted state lands, Caliph 'Uthmān found it more in the interest of the state to give them to individuals for reclamation and for contributing a portion of their proceeds to the state coffers.[34]

The process of distributing cultivable land was, thus, accelerated in his reign. Many of the newly-conquered lands were also distributed by him in order to encourage the Muslims to dwell there so that these areas were not left at the mercy of the subjugated population.[35] Balādhurī and Maqrīzī have mentioned a number of persons to whom Caliph 'Uthmān allotted land in different regions.[36] In the later period, for some reason, he also exchanged the title of the lands in Iraq with those in the Ḥijāz and Yemen.[37] Caliph 'Alī intended to distribute the lands of Sawād but refrained from doing so for social considerations.[38] Records suggest that he was as generous as his predecessors in giving away land.[39]

The Considerations and the Terms of Allotment

It is clear, therefore, that the Prophet (peace be upon him) and the Pious Caliphs did allot land to individuals. The nature and the terms and conditions on which this land was allotted is yet to be examined.

Firstly, curiously enough, the early sources also give the names of persons like Companions 'Uthmān and 'Abd ar-Raḥmān b. 'Awf, who were among the wealthiest Muslims of Madina, as the owners or the allottees of land. 'Uthmān had land at Wādī'l Qurā and Ḥunayn[40] and 'Abd ar-Raḥmān was given a stretch of land at Banū Naḍīr[41] Curiously, the same person is sometimes seen to have been given land by the Prophet (peace be upon him) and the caliphs. The Prophet (peace be upon him) awarded Al-Zubayr a stretch of land in Khaybar,[42] Caliph Abū Bakr gave him land at al-Jurf, Caliph ‘Umar bestowed on him land in Al-‘Aqīq, and Caliph ‘Uthmān gave him a plot of land somewhere else.[43] Mujjā‘a was also allotted land by the Prophet (peace be upon him) as well as by the first three caliphs.[44] Secondly, during the early period the caliphs did not reserve any land for themselves, or even for their sons. Thirdly, during the reign of the Pious Caliphs loyalty to the caliph was no consideration in the granting of land which was granted either in appreciation of services in the cause of Islam or to consolidate the loyalty of the converts to their new faith and community.[45] Fourthly, these lands do not seem to have been occupied by anybody because there are hardly any reports of legal proceedings or disputes on the issue, even after the death of the caliphs concerned.[46] The fifth point pertains to the nature of the land allotted them. Even later geographers do not sufficiently indicate whether these lands were barren at the time of allotment. In the context of a large part of Arabia, it is understandable that due to scarcity of water, cultivable land was scarce. Yet there seems no point in awarding such barren land to people who have no easy prospects of reclamation or rehabilitation. It is, therefore, probable that most of the land in Arabia allotted to them was marginal land and required some additional inputs to give a satisfactory yield by way of a farm or garden. Had it not been so the Madinans would not have been prepared to exchange their lands in Iraq for those in the Ḥijāz and Yemen during ‘Uthmān’s caliphate.[47] There was such a rush for land in the Ḥijāz that, fifty years after Caliph ‘Uthmān, there was hardly an unoccupied plot left for Caliph ‘Abd al-Malik.[48] The sixth point that requires study pertains to the terms of allotment. Historians clearly speak of allottees’ ownership rights over these lands. It is reported by Wāqidī (Table 2) that a man requested the Prophet (peace be upon him) to allot him a stretch of land around his brother’s grave. The Prophet (peace be upon him) awarded him a big tract of land and promised an equal area of land if he worked it. Thus the first award was unconditional; the second was subject to the condition that the man worked the first piece of land – an incentive to work. Throughout the early period, there are numerous instances of transfer of land through purchase, sale and gift. Caliph Abū Bakr himself offered his land for clearing his debt to the *Bayt al-Māl.*[49] This adjustment was possible only because he had ownership rights over the land. Historians have reported a number of transactions involving transfer of land by different ways.[50] Such transfers continued throughout the later period and no ruler, scholar, or jurist ever objected to the practice.[51]

In pre-Islamic days one of the ways of acquiring ownership was to bring unoccupied and uncultivated land under the plough. This was confirmed in Islam as an entitlement to occupation. The *Ḥadīth* narrated by 'Urwa in the context of a suit supports this practice.[52]

The Ownership of Conquered Lands

In the early period of conquests, agricultural land was not allotted in the conquered territories. Cantonments were, however, built for the army, and soldiers were allotted land for housing. Caliph 'Uthmān, and after him the Umayyad rulers, started giving away land in these regions. The land in the subjugated territories consisted of two broad categories: (i) treaty land conquered without war, and (ii) land conquered by force. The first category was governed by the terms of treaty and regarded as the common property of the Muslims *(Fay')* and hence inalienable, while the second category was treated as state owned. It included land under cultivation, arable, waste or barren. Of these the latter was unoccupied and was generously allotted. The land of the protected people was generally treated as landlord's and was not re-allotted to anybody. Caliph 'Umar made the *Fay'* land inalienable.[53] Caliph 'Uthmān allotted state-owned land.[54] But later on this distinction was often not adhered to.

The practice of generous allotment of land began with Mu'āwiya, whose name appears most frequently in this respect. This was the first time that the ruler himself became interested in adding extensively to his fiefs in all his dominions. First of all he took over Fadak as his chosen property *(ṣafī)* and bestowed it upon Marwān, the Governor of Madina,[55] and land in al-Ghūṭa which belonged to one Ibn Fūqā who was heirless.[56] He also added to his properties by purchase, sale and gifts.[57] Many of the big tracts of land he owned in Wāsiṭ were barren and water-logged and areas of dense forests[58] which could be reclaimed only at the expense of the public exchequer. Such tracts of land were spread throughout Iraq, particularly those owned by the emperor and the royal family of Persia, and were chosen by the Umayyad rulers for themselves and their kinsmen, and allotted to their officials, favourites and the general public. The provincial governors were also at liberty to give fiefs to whosoever they wished. Land was also allotted in appreciation of meritorious service to the government or on humanitarian grounds. The number of such awards had assumed abnormal proportions by the end of the Umayyad rule.[59]

Limitations to Ownership

Regarding the Islamic approach to the question of the ownership of land and the role of the government in this respect, the details that are available do not categorically confirm the terms of allotment. Whether these allotments awarded ownership, possession or permanent right to the use of the land is not clear. But the fact that this land, in most cases, could be sold or gifted, and could also be taken back by the government, suggests that the allottees were given permanent but revokable rights to the land. Land is a free gift of nature, and when the private ownership of land is regarded as permissible in Islam, the permissibility of the private ownership of man-made means of production is beyond doubt. But this should not be taken to mean that ownership of land in the early Islamic period was treated as an absolute right. The Prophet (peace be upon him) is said to have rejected interdiction of salt and water.[60] By these two things he seems to have meant the natural resources which have great value for the general public. That is why he is reported to have cancelled the allotment of a salt mine which had earlier been bestowed upon Abyaḍ b. Ḥammāl.[61] He also prohibited the cutting and burning of bushes by the public within twelve miles, and hunting within four miles, of Madina, with a view to safeguarding the livestock wealth of the community.[62] There are valid reasons to believe that this prohibited area also included privately-owned land. Caliph 'Umar appointed a guard to stop and punish anybody pulling or cutting off branches of trees in or around Madina.[63] Over and above such protective measures the government had the right to reserve for state purposes any suitable plot of land or take away from people their land or houses in the public interest. Caliphs 'Umar and 'Uthmān, and some later rulers, wanted to extend the Prophet's mosque in Madina and they took over and demolished the adjacent houses. The owners were forced to surrender their houses and compensation was paid to them.[64] The people of Fadak were exiled from their land after they had been paid compensation for their respective shares in the land.[65] Reservation of land for state purposes began in the Prophet's time. The authority for any such reservation, as explained in the *Ḥadīth,* is vested in the state only. The *Ḥadīth* reads: 'The authority to reserve a pasture *(Ḥimā)* rests in God and His Prophet'.[66] Here again the words 'God and His Prophet' refer to the authority of the state. The Prophet (peace be upon him) reserved Baqī' as a grazing farm for the state-owned camels and horses.[67] The principle underlying this reservation was occupation of a part of land which was generally inaccessible to private grazing cattle, although open to the cattle of the poor.[68] There was already a protected area in Ṭā'if and the Prophet (peace be upon him) had appointed Sa'd as administrator of that *'Ḥimā'*.[69]

A protected area was also declared in Yemen for the horses, camels and other livestock of the people of that region,[70] and Caliph Abū Bakr extended the protected area by adding Rabdha.[71]

The policy of discriminating between small and big herds continued.

Caliph ‘Umar expressly advised officials in charge of these areas to drive away the cattle of the rich owners like ‘Uthmān and ‘Abd ar-Raḥmān, but allow those of the poor.[72] Although there is no mention of the practice of protecting land in the later period, yet because of the expansion in armies and increased government interest in maintaining its armed strength, the practice can be presumed to have grown.[73] This assumption is also supported by the fact that ‘Umar II ordered all protected land to be thrown open to the general public.[74]

There are many more instances of the government taking over land which was the rightful property of individuals than of lands converted into protected areas. Caliph ‘Umar withdrew the land of Sawād from Bajīla who had been, according to agreement, given a quarter of the area.[75] Historians have described the land which was taken over by the government and treated as state property in Iraq as:[76]

1. Forests.
2. Ponds and pools.
3. The land of the Persian emperor and his kinsmen and courtiers.
4. The whole of Dayr Yazīd.
5. The land of Persian soldiers who were killed.
6. The land of fugitives, etc., etc.

As a matter of precedent the lands of Sawād and Egypt should have gone to the soldiers who had conquered them, but Caliph ‘Umar, instead of so distributing them, brought them into the collective ownership of the Muslims and took over their management.[77] In addition to this forced collectivization of some lands, conditions were imposed to ensure the proper use of land. While the conventional law of the ownership of dead land was practically recognized,[78] Caliph ‘Umar made it a condition that land should be used within three years of taking possession, failing which it was left open for anybody else who could revive it.[79] Ziyād, the governor of Iraq (under Caliph ‘Alī and later under Mu‘āwiya), who normally gave not more than sixty *jarībs*[80] of land, reduced this period to two years,[81] presumably because of the increased government interest in providing development facilities. But whether or not the allotted land was actually confiscated on account of its non-revival during the later period is not known.

To sum up, private ownership of land was practised throughout this period. Land was given by the Prophet (peace be upon him) and his successors with the right to use or to transfer the title. At times the absolute right of ownership was taken away by the government and conditions and restrictions on its use or transfer were imposed in the larger interest of the community. Land was also collectivized and nationalized. The government alone had the right to reserve any stretch of land as a protected area for government purposes. Private ownership of public utility land was in no case recognized.

An analysis of the cases of seized and taken-over land suggests that such measures were taken:

(i) if the allotment was temporary or for a stipulated period as happened in the case of as-Sundar *(sic)* who alone was allotted a tract of land in Egypt by Caliph 'Umar, the land having been restored to the state after the allottee's death;[82]

(ii) if the government enacted an amendment in the rules of allotment of land in some area, as was done in the case of Banū Bajīla;[83]

(iii) if the land was not used by the occupant within the prescribed period.[84] Specific cases are not reported;

(iv) if the allottee failed to pay the revenue due from him, as happened in the case of Hilāl of Banū Muta'ān who was allotted a hilly tract by the Prophet (peace be upon him) on some payment converted into a regular condition for continued occupation;

(v) if the interest of the state so demanded, as was done by Caliph 'Umar in the case of the people of Najrān and Fadak;[85] and

(vi) if the good of the community so required, as frequently happened, such as over the expansion of the Prophet's mosque in Madina.[86]

Though the government took over the land, it paid compensation only in the last two cases – in one the government had a commitment to the protected citizens under a treaty, and in the other it seems that the investment of labour and capital in the building of houses was also involved.[87] In none of the other four cases does compensation appear to have been involved.[88]

Regulation of Other Economic Activities

The curtailment of absolute rights in respect of property was not only practised in the case of land, it was practised in other areas of ownership as well. The difference is that in the latter case, rights of ownership, once given, were not withdrawn. The government controlled and regulated economic activity in such a way as to achieve the object of setting up a just socio-economic order free of exploitation. As a result, trade and commerce were subjected to the principles of the Qur'ān and the *Ḥadīth*. Trades which are unlawful in Islam[89] were banned. The Prophet's treaties with the Thaqīf, Hawāzin and the people of Najrān required a ban on transactions involving interest.[90] Use of or trade in wine was declared unlawful for the Muslims, and the Prophet (peace be upon him) was not ready to relax this law even in the case of derelict orphans who possessed no other property.[91] Transactions involving uncertainty and any possibility of dispute, as were banned in the *Ḥadīth,* were also banned. The Prophet (peace be upon him) appointed an inspector to ensure that unlawful transactions were avoided,[92] and himself visited the market, advising the traders to observe moral principles in trade.[93] Sometimes, he would thrust his hand into a heap of corn that was for sale to check if the quality of the corn deep inside was the same as outside. He would take serious notice of any fraudulent practice in transactions.[94] His successors were also active in controlling trade and commerce. Caliph 'Umar not only refused to accept wine by way of *jizya*[95] and to levy excise duty on the same; he went so far as to burn the house of a Muslim who used it as a wine shop and exiled another Muslim who sold wine.[96] Caliph 'Alī once set a whole village on fire after receiving reports that it had become a den of drunkards.[97] 'Umar II prohibited the transporting of wine from one town to another.[98] The government was also vigilant in stopping adulteration. Caliph 'Umar prohibited adding water to milk.[99] Interest was prohibited not only for the Muslims but also for the non-Muslims. Violation of this law is stated to be one of the reasons for the exile of the people of Najrān.[100] Curiously, there are no reports of 'Umar imposing a ban on the sale of ration cards which he had issued and which were an entitlement to receiving a certain quantity of provisions. The objectionable aspect of this transaction was the sale of a commodity before actual possession of the same. Some individuals are reported to have withdrawn from the sale proceeds of these cards when they came to know of their unlawfulness.[101] The practice was, however, strictly banned by Marwān who deputed policemen to seize such cards and hand them back to the owners.[102] Caliph 'Umar, in the national interest, forbade the Arab Muslims to till the soil because he wished to prevent their adoption of a settled life with a view to retaining them as soldiers.[103]

Coinage was not the concern of the early Islamic state. Later on, however, when coins were minted the state took steps to control their quality. The minters were generally authorized dealers and money changers,[104] and serious action was taken on detecting any dishonesty or fraud in this business.[105] Ḥajjāj nationalized this trade in Iraq and, perhaps, this was also the case in Syria; but it is not clear if private minting was abolished throughout the empire. 'Umar II is reported to have punished an unauthorized minter and to have burnt his die.[106]

Price Controls

While the Prophet (peace be upon him) did not like the imposition of any controls on prices, the later rulers did not leave the consumers at the mercy of businessmen. Caliph ʻUmar kept himself informed of the price situation even in the remote parts of his dominion.[107] Caliph ʻUthmān used to discuss the price situation at the time of congregation.[108] Caliph ʻAlī used to visit the market personally and enjoin fair dealing on the traders.[109] Ziyād, the governor of Iraq, was vigilant about the price situation and punished severely those who unjustifiably increased prices.[110] A similar policy was generally adopted by the Umayyad rulers.[111] Walīd also visited the market but whenever he found that prices were unreasonably low he advised the traders to increase them.[112] In this respect ʻUmar II was an exception in that he would leave the prices of agricultural goods to the free operation of the forces of supply and demand. He adopted the same policy in regard to trade when he wrote to his governor: 'God has made land and waters for seeking His bounties. So let traders travel without any intervention. How can you intervene between them and their livelihood!'[113] Anyhow, he disfavoured trading by the ruler. He wrote to one of his governors: 'I am of the view that the ruler should not trade. It is (also) not lawful for the officer to trade in the area of his office *(fī sulṭānihī . . .),* because when he involves himself in trade he inadvertently misuses his office in his interest and to the detriment of others, even if he does not like to do so.'[114] ʻUmar II also disallowed people employing others in risky jobs. He wrote to his governor about mines: 'As I considered it I found that gain in mining was but particular *(khāṣṣ)* but its harm was general *(ʻām)* so stop people from working in mines.'[115] He wished to standardize the weights and measures throughout his dominion *(yakūn wāḥidan fī jamīʻ al-arḍ kullihā)*[116] but he perhaps could not do so. However, there are reports to suggest the appointment of inspectors *(nāqid)* at different places who checked the weight of the coins.[117] He advised his governor of Egypt to ensure that a camel was not overloaded.[118] The report that the Prophet (peace be upon him) forced the Muslim soldiers to return the captives of Hawāzin[119] illustrates the power of the state to use even compulsion in certain circumstances.

The restrictions on different trades and activities gave rise to the institution of *ḥisba* (inspection) and the *muḥtasib* (inspector) enjoyed wide powers to intervene in situations which were found injurious to public interest.

The above discussion gives an idea of the government's role in the field of economic activity and suggests that Islam, from the very beginning, did not leave the various economic factors to operate absolutely freely. It exercised effective control to ensure their operation within the limits prescribed and for the maximum benefit of the community.

Notes and References

1. Tab., 1, 1200.

2. I.F., 22.

3. Bal., 135.

4. Cheikho, 153, 157. Kulayb Wā'il b. Rabī'a, for example, reserved a pasture for his camels, an area for hunting and for water. To quote some verses:

انک فی حمی کلیب الازهر   حمية' من مذحج و حمير
سيعلم آل مرة حيث كانوا   بان حماى ليس بمستباح

5. J.G.M., 126–7.

6. A.U., 694.

7. Sad., III, 1, 132, 138; Kh., 34.

8. Mus., 11, 86; Kh., 34.

9. Bal., 27; Yah., 245.

10. A.U., 676, 690; Bal., 34; Bukh. (Khums) 58; Sad., III, 1, 72.

11. Bal., 27; A.U., 677.

12. Sad., III, 1, 114.

13. Bal., 84; Sad., IV, 2, 74.

14. Bal., 103.

15. Bukh. (Waṣīyya), 17.

16. Bal., 102.

17. Tab., 1, 1748; Sira, 2, 373.

18. Waq., 946.

19. A.U., 683; Bal., 84; Yah., 346.

20. Waq., 658.

21. A.U., 675.

22. Yah., 287; Kh., 34.

23. Bukh. (Musāqāt), 24.

24. Bal., 84; Tir., 6, 149–50.

25. Waq., 20.

26. Bal., 31.

27. Kh., 35; Sad., III, 1, 72, 75, 89; Yah., 242, 244, 248; Bal., 26, 34; Waq., 721; Maq. (Kh.), I, 97.

28. These lands were distributed by the Prophet (peace be upon him) collectively, the crop of a tract of land to be shared by one hundred persons. Caliph 'Umar perhaps distributed the share in crop except in some specific cases. He did not generally allow their transfer by way of inheritance. It is curious to note that in the beginning Caliph 'Umar did not seem to be in favour of allotting large pieces of land to individuals. He is reported to have refused to grant to 'Abbās the land at Baḥrayn which was reportedly allotted to him by the Prophet (peace be upon him) (Sa'd., IV, 1, 12, 14). Caliph Abū Bakr allotted land to Ṭalḥa but his adviser 'Umar refused to sign the transfer deed as witness (A.U., 685). But after the extensive conquests in Iraq and Syria, he seems to have changed his mind.

29. Bal., 181.

30. A.U., 503; Bal., 77.

31. Yah., 103.

32. Bal., 26; Yah., 184, 248; Maq. (Kh.), 1, 97; Kh., 35.

33. Bal., 346, 360; I.A.M. (M), 137, 138; A.U., 687–8; Yah., 246; Maq. (Kh.), 1, 96.

34. It is reported that these lands in Caliph 'Umar's time earned 9 million dirhams while the revenues in Caliph 'Uthmān's time rose to 50 million dirhams, after they had been allotted by him. Maq. (Kh.), 1, 96. According to Kh. (32), 4 or 7 million dirhams in 'Umar's time. According to Bal., (272), 700,000 dirhams.

35. For example, the lands of Antioch (Bal., 153).

36. Bal., 272, 273, 353–4; Maq. (Kh.), 1, 96.

37. Bal., 346, 356; Tab., 1, 2854; Athir, 3, 52.

38. Kh., 21.

39. Maq. (Kh.), 1, 97, has given the names of two persons only to whom 'Alī gave land. A big courtyard or a farm to Kardūs and a stretch of land for raising livestock, to Suwayd.

40. Mas., 3, 76.

41. Bal., 31.

42. A.U., 676.

43. Sad., III, 1, 72; Bal., 272–3.

44. Bal., 102.

45. Caliph 'Uthmān has been made a point of polemics on the issue of giving lands to his kinsmen, but the list of allottees does not justify any such view. (see nn. 35 and 36).

46. During Caliph 'Umar's time, one such dispute arose when Sa'd gave the land of one Banū Rufayl to Sa'īd. The original occupant who had a treaty complained to Caliph 'Umar and got back his land (Yah., 184).

47. Bal., 359, 360.

48. Bal., 359.

49. Sad., III, 1, 132.

50. Waq., 690, 694, 719, 720; Bal., 26 etc.

51. It is interesting to note that when Ibn Hubayra tried to pick out in Ḥijāz a piece of unallotted land for the caliph, he came across a tract which was not allotted under any

registered (or recorded) deed and asked to whom it belonged. A man came forward and claimed ownership over it. 'How did you get it? Ibn Hubayra asked the man. The man recited a couplet:

ورثناهن عن آباء صدق   و يورثها اذا متنا بنينا

(We have inherited these lands from our forefathers and our children will inherit them after we die.) (Bal., 359–60). Ibn Hubayra was so disgusted with this that he withdrew from his effort.

52. Yah., 289. For other *Ḥadīth* on the subject see p. 65.

53. Yah., 136–8, 156–7, 168.

54. See p. 313.

55. Bal., 46.

56. Sh., 13.

57. Bal., 48, 49, 68; Bukh. (Waṣiyya), 17; I.A.H. (M), 132–3; Dh. (Tar.), 2, 289; Kathir, 8, 28.

58. Bal., 288.

59. Bal., 153, 185, 209, 280, 355–62; A.U., 693; Tab., 2, 843, 1641.

60. Yah., 345.

61. Yah., 346; Tir., 6, 149–50.

62. Kh., 59.

63. Bal., 22.

64. Tab., 1, 2011; Bukh. (Khuṣūmāt), 7.

65. A.U., 24; Waq., 707.

66. Bukh. (Musāqāt), 18; A.U., 727.

67. Bukh. (Musāqāt), 18; Waq., 425; Bal., 23; Ibn S'ad has given the name of the place as Qubā (II, 1, 68).

68. Waq., 425.

69. Waq., 973.

70. Tab., 1, 1879; Sad., III, 1, 220; 5, 6.

71. Bukh. (U), (Musāqāt), 1, 819.

72. Kh., 60. He also added Sharaf as a protected area for camels (Sad., III, 1, 220).

73. Literary works seem to be the alternative source of finding the details of this practice. Aghānī, for example, writes about an official who was in charge of Ḥimā in Kūfa, 5, 137.

74. Sad., 5, 281.

75. Kh., 18; Bal., 267.

76. Bal., 272.

77. Tab., 1, 2468; Bal., 265; Yah., 49; I.A.H. (M), 82; Maq. (Kh.), 1, 166.

78. See pp. 122–3.

79. Yah., 247, 287, 294.

80. Bal., 357.

81. Bal., 356.

82. I.A.H. (M), 138.

83. See p. 125.

84. *Ibid.*

85. Abu Daud, 2, 146, 147; Tir., 3, 124.

86. See pp. 124–5.

87. *Ibid.*

88. When Bajīla surrendered land Caliph 'Umar advanced him eighty dīnārs and fixed pensions for the people of his tribe (Kh., 18, Bal., 268).

Eighty dīnārs cannot be regarded as compensation even for a quarter of the area of Sawād. As regards pensions, all the soldiers were entitled to it and after Bajīla's people joined other Muslims in war they automatically became eligible for pensions. Therefore pensions also could not be treated as compensation for land. The story of an old lady of Bajīla's people who refused to surrender her portion of land unless Caliph 'Umar gave her an expensive camel and a handful of dīnārs (A.U., 155), is an exceptional case and only reflects 'Umar's leniency to the lady. It should not, however, be ignored that there was a long time-lag between the withdrawal of land and the beginning of pensions.

89. For this discussion see Chapter 1.

90. A.U., 469, 506; Bal., 67. The first two tribes wanted the Prophet (peace be upon him) to permit it for them after they embraced Islam.

91. A.U., 281; Bal., 67.

92. A.U., 184–7; Mus., 10, 169.

93. Tir., 6, 39.

94. Tir., 6, 35.

95. A.U., 128.

96. Sad., III, 1, 202.

97. A.U., 268, 279, 280.

98. *Ibid.*

99. I.A.H. (U), 22.

100. Bal., 77.

101. I.A.H. (M), 166.

102. *Ibid.* Possibly during Marwān's governorate of Madina.

103. I.A.H. (M), 162.

104. Bal., 455.

105. See Note on Coinage for full discussion.

106. Bal., 455.

107. Tab., 1, 2718.

108. Sad., III, 1, 40.

109. Sad., III, 1, 18; Bal., 257.

110. Kharbutli, 366.

111. *Ibid.*

112. Tab., 1, 1271. We find a similar report about Caliph 'Umar who once advised a seller either to increase the price of raisins or to move away from the market place to his house. He did so when fresh stock was reportedly reaching Madina. However, he reviewed his decision and allowed the seller to continue. Bayhiqī, Abū Bakr Aḥmad, *Al-Sunan al-Kubrā,* Hyderabad (India) 1352 A.H., Vol. 6, p. 29.

113. I.A.H. (U), 98 (pertains to lawful trades only).

114. *Ibid.,* 98–9.

115. Sad., 5, 281.

116. I.A.H. (U), 98.

117. Karmalī: *Nuqūd,* p. 12. *Cf.* Kharbutlī, 374.

118. I.A.H. (U), 160.

119. See Chapter 5 for a full discussion.

PART II

THE *BAYT AL-MĀL*

CHAPTER 4

The Concept and the Early History

The concept of public finance as a separate subject of study in modern economics is not very old. But in Islam the concept occupies a very important position, and it is because of this that the books on this subject are some of the earliest ones written in Islam.[1] They discuss the subject as copiously as can be conceived of a scholar of that age. This concept is signified by the term *Bayt al-Māl* which is not only the nomenclature of a treasury but practically of the entire fiscal system of the state.

The Concept of the *Bayt al-Māl*

The question as to whether the *Bayt al-Māl* was set up by the Prophet (peace be upon him) is generally discussed by historians and scholars in terms of premises where large quantities of goods and incomes were dumped and taken out. But the question of premises in deciding about the history of its inception seems to be irrelevant. The more important question is to examine if the concept of the *Bayt al-Māl,* its items of income, its heads of expenditure, its rules of operation were known to and practised by the Prophet (peace be upon him) or not. If it was so the institution of the *Bayt al-Māl* was initiated by him whether or not he had set apart any premises for it. The concept of the *Bayt al-Māl* and the major items of its income and expenditure were all provided in the Qur'ān and the Prophet (peace be upon him) practised on those lines with the scanty funds that were made available to him. Moreover, when the Prophet (peace be upon him) is reported to have asked his personal attendant Bilāl to take with him Jābir and pay him the price for his camel[2] which the Prophet (peace be upon him) had bought; or when he called for Maḥmiyya, who was in charge of his *Khums* property to advise him to pay the dowry money *(Mahr)* on behalf of two of his relations,[3] he seems to have had some place other than his own house in which to keep money and *Khums* property.

Since the occupation of Banū Naḍīr the Prophet (peace be upon him) had a regular income. But this income can be treated as negligible in view of the requirements of the simply-run city state of Madina which was surrounded by bloodthirsty neighbouring tribes. As a result of this, *ad hoc* funds were raised in the event of an emergency. In the case of income by way of *fay'* and *khums,* the requirements of their distribution were too pressing to leave any balance. In spite of this unenviable financial situation the Prophet (peace be upon him) implanted in the minds of his followers a concept which could not be obliterated till the end of the period under study. This was the concept of trust; the wealth of the *Bayt al-Māl* to be treated as God's wealth, *māl-Allāh* or the Muslims' wealth, *māl-al-Muslimīn* as against the imperial treasury or the emperor's wealth. This concept implied that the monies paid into the treasury were God's trust and the common property of the Muslims and that the ruler was only a trustee, whose duty was to expend them on the common concerns of the Muslims while allowing for himself nothing more than a fixed stipend. This concept was practically adhered to by the Pious Caliphs but accepted only in theory by the later rulers.

The concept attributed a unique position to the *Bayt al-Māl* which was treated as a separate entity from the ruler. This entity was not a physical person, yet, as a financial institution, it was subjected to the principle of prohibition of interest that could occur in sale or exchange of its properties or in lending and borrowing. This prohibition was strictly enforced by the Prophet (peace be upon him) and his successors in their position of custodian of the *Bayt al-Māl.*[4]

The concept seems to have attained an emotional sanctity in the early days. Caliph 'Umar tried to explain the different aspects of this concept on several occasions. For example, he is reported to have observed:

> There is no Muslim who has no right in this *Fay'* (public wealth) except what your right hand possesses.[5]
>
> It is my endeavour to satisfy all the requirements of the Muslims as far as possible. But if we fail to do so we shall try to practise austerity in our life so that we all may have a similar standard of living.[6]
>
> I did not find the betterment of this *māl* (wealth) except in three ways:
>
> (i) it is received by right, (ii) it is given by right, and (iii) it is stopped from wrong. As regards my own position *vis-à-vis* this wealth of yours; it is like that of a guardian of an orphan. If I am well-off, I shall leave it, but if I am hard-pressed I shall take from it as is genuinely permissible.[7]

> I have become an obstruction between you and your sources of earning. Whosoever among you has any wealth he has it at our disposal. So nobody should treat a saddle or a rope or a string as a valueless thing. It is the wealth of the general Muslims. There is not a single Muslim who does not have a share in it. When these goods are in individual ownership they are valued; but when they become the common property of the Muslims they are treated as valueless, being Allah's wealth.[8]

With this concept in mind, when Caliph 'Umar found that Abū Hurayra, his collector of *Zakāt,* had also invested his personal earnings in business and added to his wealth he chided him for being a *thief of Allah's wealth.*[9] Caliph 'Alī was more firm in his behaviour with the *Bayt al-Māl.* He is frequently found quoting a *Ḥadīth* that it was not permissible for the Caliph to take *from Allah's wealth* except two portions: the one which he and his family would eat and the other which he laid before the people.[10] The concept of the right of the entire Muslim community to the *Bayt al-Māl* was so emphasized that on this point Abū's Sawdā succeeded in cajoling Abū Dharr to rise up against Mu'āwiya, the Governor of Syria under Caliph 'Uthmān. Abū's Sawdā' whispered, 'Mu'āwiya calls this wealth *Allah's wealth,* which means he does not think the Muslims have any right to it.' Abū Dharr called on Mu'āwiya and criticized him on this point. Mu'āwiya said: 'I shall not accept that it is not Allah's wealth but, anyhow, I shall now call it *the Muslims' wealth.*[11] Ibn 'Umar once called on Caliph Mu'āwiya who asked him about his impressions of the constructions he (Mu'āwiya) had made in Damascus. Ibn 'Umar's prompt reaction was: 'If you have spent it from Allah's wealth you have committed a breach of trust, but if it is from your personal resources even then you are a spendthrift.'[12] 'Abd al-Malik criticized his rebel Ibn Zubayr in these words: 'He was not competent to be a politician while he spent *Allah's wealth* as if it was his father's bequest.'[13] By this 'Abd al-Malik meant Ibn Zubayr's niggardliness in spending among the Muslims. When Ḥajjāj, the governor of Iraq, reported against Muhallab he wrote to the caliph: 'Muhallab has embezzled *Allah's wealth.*'[14] When Yazīd was made governor of Khurāsān, he asked his predecessor to furnish the accounts of *Allah's wealth.*[15]

It seems that the Muslim community throughout this period was very sensitive to this concept. It was treated to be a justifiable point of rallying against any ruler. During the battle of Ṣiffīn a man came forward to address the opponents of Caliph 'Alī and inquired in a tone of astonishment if 'Alī had misused *Fay',* the *public wealth.*[16] One of the points emphasized by the Khārijites as an argument in support of their rebellion was the rulers' misuse of public funds.[17] The public could not be pacified even if the misuse of funds was made for the sake of an apparently good cause. For example, when they came to know that Walīd had spent a large amount on the reconstruction of the mosque of Damascus they criticized it as unjustifiable expenditure. Walīd was not able to silence them by arguing that there was sufficient surplus in the *Bayt al-Māl* for the next three years and that he had spent this amount out of his personal property.[18] The unjustifiable use of public wealth seems to be one of the factors responsible for the overthrow of the Umayyad dynasty.

It was this concept which permeated the Muslim society and formed the basis of its behaviour and determined its reaction to any ruler. The more the concept with all its ensuing details was adhered to by a ruler, the more popular he was and vice versa. Yazīd III became conscious of the fact and announced a number of revolutionary changes in his government's attitude to the *Bayt al-Māl* which is suggestive of the causes underlying the dissatisfaction of the people with the Umayyad rulers. Yazīd said:

> . . . I shall neither construct a palace, nor a house, nor a canal. I shall neither amass wealth nor give (special) allowances to my wife or children. I shall also not transfer money from one place to another unless the place has been well-protected and its people have been provided sufficient funds to strengthen themselves. If, then, there is a surplus, it will be transferred to the nearest city which is more needful of money. There will be no toll tax along the border of your respective towns that may put you in hardship. I shall also not levy *Jizya* on your protected natives which compels them to leave you and destroy their race. I shall give you your annual pension and monthly rations so that the entire wealth is distributed among all the Muslims equally and so that the farthest from me among you may become like the nearest to me among you . . .[19]

But unfortunately Yazīd III was too late to calm the people.

The *Bayt al-Māl* During the Prophet's Time

The 'Constitution of Madina' had put the financial responsibility of the different communities respectively on themselves during peace-time. 'It is for the Jews to bear their expenses',[20] was one of the conditions that were laid down in the charter of the early state. In the case of war, however, the situation was different. 'The Jews shall bear expenses along with the believers so long as they continue at war.'[21] Anyhow, the Jews were, perhaps, not supposed to help finance the expeditions which the

Prophet (peace be upon him) continued with a view to effecting an economic blockade of the Quraysh.

But the problem of the Jews was relatively short-lived. For as long as they had been in Madina they seem to have been reluctant to contribute their share. The Muslims, on the other hand, were generally too poor to finance an expanding government. It was against this background that the government endeavoured to organize itself. An appraisal of the early resources can be made by a study of the quantity of equipment on the expeditions which the Prophet (peace be upon him) sent or led.

The Resources of the Prophet's Madina

On the eve of the Muslims' first encounter with the Quraysh at Badr, the Muslim army of 317 persons had only two horses.[22] Not all the fighting men had the use of camels to ride to the battlefield. Though they had some camels taken from the Quraysh by way of booty, these were not enough to ensure that the whole army was kept ready for any possible threat of retaliation from the enemy. That is why in 3 A.H. many of the wounded Muslims had no riding animals on which to return from Uḥud.[23] When the Prophet (peace be upon him) besieged Banū Qurayẓa, the Muslim army had thirty-six horses. Later, in 6 A.H., the 1,500 fighters at Ḥudaybiya had only 200 horses.[24] The persecution and exile of the Jews of Madina and the conquest of Khaybar and Fadak had greatly reduced the immediate demand for army equipment and riding-animals although the supply was still insufficient for the large army deployed at Tabūk.

As regards the finances for extra-military purposes, the situation was even more discouraging. Many zealous Muslims could not accompany the Prophet (peace be upon him) on his journey for *umrat al-qaḍā* simply for want of resources.[25] In 8 A.H. a man is reported to have requested from the Prophet (peace be upon him) just 200 dirhams, which he was committed to pay as dower; but the Prophet (peace be upon him) could not afford even that much for him.[26]

The Role of Voluntary *Ṣadaqa*

The major source of finance during the early years of Islam was voluntary contribution to *ad hoc* funds. This was a well-known way of financing social requirements. Even before Islam, the Makkans provided free meals to pilgrims by pooling donations from their community; and the institution was called *Rifāda.*[27] They even financed the Battle of the Ditch by raising contributions from all the tribes[28] who wished to wipe out Islam and the Muslims. There are stories which suggest that the Prophet (peace be upon him) too used to raise funds by a general appeal to the audience, or any particular group among them.[29] Also he would send his deputies to appeal to the absent Muslims. At other times he would assign a specific purpose and ask the Muslims to donate for it. When there was a general shortage of water, he asked of his audience who would buy such-and-such a well. When a gentleman offered to do so[30] the purpose was achieved. When the people of Muḍar called on the Prophet (peace be upon him), he appealed to the Muslims to help them and they were given help.[31] The Prophet himself went to Banū Naḍīr to collect funds for the blood-money of protected persons.[32] While he was besieging Ṭā'if he promised freedom for those enemy slaves who would join him. A number of slaves came but the government had no means to support them. The Prophet (peace be upon him), therefore, distributed them among the well-to-do Muslims as their guests.[33] The expedition to Tabūk was perhaps the most important one which the Prophet (peace be upon him) led. It was probably aimed at demonstrating the Muslim strength to the adventurers in the north, and as a test of the loyalty of the newly-converted tribes. No single Muslim was allowed to stay at home. All were required to donate as much as possible to finance the expedition. It is reported by historians that 'Umar brought literally half of his belongings, while Abū Bakr gave everything in his house. Wealthy 'Uthmān also proved equal to expectations.[34] There were such large-scale donations that an army of 30,000 men and 10,000 horses was fully equipped.

Other Sources of Income During the Prophet's Time

Although they were an important source of finance, voluntary donations were by no means a regular and certain source of income. Banū Naḍīr, and a portion of Khaybar and Fadak, were regular sources of income although they were considered as the Prophet's personal share.[35] During the last years of his life the Prophet (peace be upon him) also appointed collectors of *Zakāt* who were sent to different tribes to collect *Zakāt* from the Muslims and *Jizya* (poll-tax) from non-Muslims. Generally *Zakāt* was distributed where it was collected and was hardly a source of income worthy of mention. *Jizya* was received in cash and in kind.[36] The importance of these sources can be recognized in the light of the report that the largest amount that the Prophet (peace be upon him) received under this head was 80,000 dirhams from Baḥrayn.[37]

One of the less important sources of income was the ransom of enemy captives. While some of the poor captives of Badr were set free without ransom, others had to pay from 1,000 to 4,000 dirhams.[38] The Prophet (peace be upon him) required Nawfal to give 1,000 lances by way of ransom.[39] There is no mention in early Muslim history of any other reasonable captives than at Badr. The captives of Ḥunayn were set free without ransom.[40]

After the conquest of Makka, the Prophet (peace be upon him) had to distribute some money among the poor soldiers, send blood-money to the Muslims of Jadhīma, and further equip his army for an operation against Hawāzin. He borrowed from Ṣafwān, Ḥuwayṭab and Ibn Rabī'a. He also borrowed some coats-of-mail and riding-animals.[41] One of the conditions of the treaty with the people of Najrān, was that they should advance a loan of war equipment and horses in the event of trouble from Yemen.[42]

Caliph Abū Bakr's *Bayt al-Māl*

Abū Bakr was unfortunate to inaugurate his caliphate with a series of wars against the apostates, some of whom refused to pay *Zakāt* to the central government. Details of any source of income during his period are lacking, except for a quantity of *Khums* (fifth) of the booty in Iraq and Syria. Voluntary contributions were not asked for. The *Bayt al-Māl* was now moved to the neighbourhood of the caliph and in it was placed everything that was received by way of *Zakāt, Jizya, Khums* or land-tax. It is stated that during his short period Abū Bakr received about 200,000 dirhams.[43] This probably did not include the goods received by way of *Jizya, Khums* or land-tax. Not long after the beginning of 'Umar's rule, the situation changed.

To sum up the above discussion, *Ṣadaqa* was an important source of finance in the Prophet's time. Other sources of income were *Zakāt, Fay' Khums* or a fifth of booty, and *Jizya* or poll-tax.[44] Of these sources *ṣadaqa,* though mostly depended upon, was an irregular and uncertain source while the income from *Khums* depended on the nature of the expedition and the value of the booty. The other sources were regular and increased with the increase in personal wealth and conquests. Loans and ransom may also be included as additional sources but their role was negligible.

The Early Heads of Expenditure

The expenditure of the funds raised in the early period was confined to limited heads. The Prophet (peace be upon him) used to defray from Banū Naḍīr's properties his annual expenses and spent the remainder on emergencies, supplies, horses and arms.[45] The income from Fadak was reserved for wayfarers while that of Khaybar he divided into three parts: two parts among the Muslims and one part for the expenses of his household. He returned whatever remained after defraying these expenses to the paupers among the emigrants.[46] But the expenditure of the *Fay'* property on all the kinsmen and similar other expenditure was regarded by some as strictly restricted to the Prophet (peace be upon him) but not to his successors who were supposed to take for their family only, but not for all their relations *(dhawi'l qurbā)*. That is why the portion which he used under this head was, after his death, transferred to them, but the other portions were managed by his successors for those purposes which the Prophet (peace be upon him) used them.[47]

While the Prophet's *fay'* was spent for a few main heads, other incomes were spent for all the other requirements. The Prophet (peace be upon him) used the income from the captives of Banū Qurayẓa to buy war material.[48] Another expenditure was the payment of wages of officials, although regular salaries were not paid to anybody.[49] It was the responsibility of the government to pay blood-money to those who were wrongfully killed by the Muslim army, or in a case where the culprit could not be caught. Examples of the former are Khālid's onslaught on the people of Jadhīma[50] and the killing of two persons of Banū 'Āmir,[51] and of the latter is the payment of blood-money on the murder of 'Abd Allah b. Sahl, whose murderer could not be legally traced.[52] Payment of money to visiting delegations and to newly-converted influential persons was an additional head of expenditure.[53] Many newly converted Muslims, and non-Muslims, were also given money mainly with a view to reconciling their hearts *(ta'līf al-qulūb)* or attracting them to Islam.[54] In the later days when the position of the *Bayt al-Māl* became relatively sound the government took upon itself the repayment of loans due from poor deceased persons. The Prophet (peace be upon him) promised: 'If anybody leaves a bequest, it is for his relations; if anyone bequeathes a loan it will be on me.'[55] One of the functions of the *Bayt al-Māl* was to buy the freedom of Muslim slaves. Salmān's manumission money was paid by the Prophet (peace be upon him) from the funds of the *Bayt al-Māl.*[56] The *Khums* (fifth) money was also used as dower money by the Prophet's relations.[57]

Caliph Abū Bakr used the funds of the *Bayt al-Māl* for the same purposes as was done during the Prophet's time. He was paid some salary from the *Bayt al-Māl,* although he later on advised his relations to reimburse the *Bayt al-Māl* from his property.[58]

The most popular way of spending government incomes in these early days was their prompt distribution among the Muslims. People used to assemble whenever the government received anything in cash or kind and were given equal shares.[59] This method practically left no balance for emergency expenditure. That is why the *Bayt al-Māl* was found empty on the deaths of the Prophet (peace be upon him) and Abū Bakr. They only left their successor a number of riding animals for fighting.

Notes and References

1. See Introduction.

2. Bukh., (Buyu'), 1957.

3. Sad., IV, 1, 40–1.

4. Al-Sarakhsī, Shamsuddin, in his *K-al-Mabsūṭ* has reported a number of instances of the Prophet's and his successors' rejection of such transactions as involved *ribā*. (Vol. XIV, Cairo, n.d., pp. 4–8.)

5. Yah., 15. 'What your right hand possesses' means slaves.

6. Tab., 1, 2368.

7. Qut., 75.

8. A.U., 663.

9. A.U., 665.

10. Kath., 8, 3.

11. Tab., 1, 2859. That Mu'āwiya called it God's wealth is evident from Abū 'Ubayd's statement (A.U., 620) that when Mu'āwiya distributed some residual funds he said: 'It is not my property; it is God's *Fay*' which He sends for you'. For greater details of the story, see p. 302.

12. Yaq., 2, 221.

13. Yaq., 3, 20.

14. Tab., 2, 1213.

15. Bal., 414.

16. Tab., 1, 3128.

17. Tab., 2, 984.

18. Kath., 9, 149.

19. Tab., 2, 1834–5.

20. Sira, 1, 303.

21. Sira, 1, 302; A.U., 517.

22. Waq., 27.

23. Tab., 1, 1428.

24. Watt, Medina, 46.

25. Maq. ('Ilm), 1, 336.

26. Tab., 1, 1607–8.

27. Tab., 1, 1099.

28. Waq., 1, 389.

29. Bukh. ('Ilm), 41.

30. M.B.Y., 156.

31. Mus., 7, 102–4.

32. Tab., 1, 1448.

33. Sad., II, 1, 114.

34. Sad., II, 1, 114–19; Abu Daud, 2, 174; M.B.Y., 170.

35. Mus., 12, 70; Yah., 79, 81, 87; Bal., 33; Waq., 377–8.

36. Bukh. (Zakāt), 34.

37. Sad., IV, 1, 9.

38. Waq., 129; Sira, 1, 402–3; Sad., II, 11.

39. Sad., IV, 1, 31.

40. Tab., 1, 1674 *et sqq.*

41. Tab., 1, 1650–1, 1659; Waq., 1, 882, 889, 890; Sad., II, 108; Maq. ('Ilm), 1, 395.

42. Bal., 75, 76.

43. Sad., III, 1, 152.

44. For the meanings and interpretations of these terms refer to Chapters 1, 5, 6 and 7.

45. Yah., 86–7; Waq., 377–8; Mus., 12, 70. The property was also distributed among a few persons (Bal., 33; Tab., 1, 1453).

46. Yah., 86, 87; Waq., 377–8.

47. Mus., 12, 76–81.

48. Tab., 1, 1497.

49. Mus., 7, 137.

50. Waq., 882.

51. Tab., 1, 1650–1; also 1, 1448.

52. Tab., 1, 1448.

53. Bukh. (Jizya), 9; Waq., 715.

54. Waq., 959, 980; Watt, 348 *et sqq.*

55. A.U., 540; Bukh (Kifālāt), 7.

56. Sad., IV, 1, 56, 57.

57. Sad., IV, 1, 40–1.

58. Sad., III, 1, 137.

59. Even the slave Muslims received an equal share with the free Muslims, A.U., 599, 603, 645, 646; Sad., III, 1, 129, 137, 151.

CHAPTER 5

Ghanīma and *Khums*
(Booty and Fifth)

Ghanīma (booty), like *Zakāt,* is to be distributed in the manner laid down in the Qur'ān. In light of the Qur'ānic teaching, the function of the government in respect of both these incomes is merely that of a dispenser. Four-fifths of the *Ghanīma* is supposed to be the share of the fighters, while the remaining one-fifth is to be retained by the government to be spent for the purposes mentioned in the Qur'ān (8:41).

The Role of the *Bayt al-Māl*

That the *Bayt al-Māl* at the centre is not involved in the collection and distribution of most of the *Ghanīma,* does not seem to justify its inclusion under the heading of the *Bayt al-Māl.* But in spite of this, the government has been invested with wide powers in deciding about the method and the quality and quantity of distribution; and the fact that the Prophet (peace be upon him) sometimes distributed on a selective basis; that land was not always distributed; that *'Ṣafī',*[1] *'Nafal',* and *'Salab'* were often taken out of the *Ghanīma;* that entitlement to the *Ghanīma* was decided by the government, leading some of the later jurists to believe that distribution of the *Ghanīma* was discretionary and not binding on the government, suggest that the government was not only an intermediary in distribution, but it exercised its function as a distributor of the funds which otherwise would be its property. *Zakāt* is also a fund in respect of which the role of the government is that of an intermediary – money and goods taken from a few are distributed among a few others, sometimes within the same community and sometimes outside. Yet it forms a source of income for the *Bayt al-Māl.* The difference between the two is that *Zakāt* is first transferred to the *Bayt al-Māl* while the *Ghanīma* is disposed of without involving any official or functionary of the *Bayt al-Māl.* In any case this brings the subject of *Ghanīma* under the economic functions of the state. It is included, however, under the *Bayt al-Māl,* firstly because in the early days of Islam the *Ghanīma* and the *Khums* had much bearing on relieving the burden of the *Bayt al-Māl* and thus indirectly supporting it, and secondly, because a fifth of *Ghanīma* had always been treated as the right of the *Bayt al-Māl* exclusive to the Muslim fighters. It is also discussed here in order to avoid meaningless repetition of events and statistics under two different headings.

The Pre-Islamic Practice

While the *Ghanīma* share of fighters was a well-known and recognized fact in Arabia,[2] the Prophet (peace be upon him) did not relate it to the old Arab custom. He, like many other things, related it to the universal tradition. 'God did not legalize the *Ghanīma* for any *Umma* except for mine.'[3] This *Ḥadīth* suggests that the Prophet (peace be upon him) did not express his willingness to legalize it simply because it was an Arab practice, but because God had specially favoured him as against the other Scripturaries (and probably non-Scripturaries).

It is reported that when 'Adī visited the Prophet (peace be upon him), the latter asked him if he received the one-fourth portion *(al-arbā')* of the *Ghanīma* from his tribe. When 'Adī confirmed it, the Prophet (peace be upon him) said: 'Don't you know that it is not permissible in the religion of the Rukūs'[4] – an intermediate religion between Christianity and the Church of Saint John, professed by 'Adī.

The Arabs were not generally followers of any Scriptures. They had their own standards and values based on tribal tradition rather than on revelation. It seems that some of them were also professional '*Ghanīma*-hunters' who took part in third-party wars with the object of seizing the *Ghanīma.* Wāqidī has reported about two such persons who wished to join the Muslims for this purpose when they were marching towards Badr.[5]

Despite the fact that the basic motivation of *Jihād* (holy war) comes from somewhere else, the economic element of *Ghanīma* as a motivating force has not been absolutely neglected. This element was not without justification for the people of a nascent state, who were surrounded by sanguinary, bellicose tribes, and who were long since used to acting on this motivation.

It was this element that the Prophet (peace be upon him), while on the expedition to Khaybar, clearly warned:

> Only those persons should accompany me who desire *Jihād.* As regards *Ghanīma;* no![6]

The expedition to Tabūk also required substantial physical and monetary sacrifice without any prospect of *Ghanīma*.[7] But on other occasions this element was not altogether ruled out.[8]

The concept of the *Ghanīma* and the *Khums* as a permanent source of income to the *Bayt al-Māl* presupposes a state of perpetuity in successful *Jihād* operations. Should the whole world profess Islam or the enemy be too strong to be fought, or is inaccessible, *Jihād* will not be possible and *Ghanīma* will cease to exist. It is not, therefore, a permanent source of income like *Zakāt*.

Terminological Interpretation

In the Qur'ān there occur different words to signify the different categories of booty. *Fay'* signifies the wealth which is captured by the Muslim without having to engage in active warfare. *Khums* is that one-fifth portion of *Nafal* (booty) which is apportioned for the *Bayt al-Māl* before distributing anything among the fighters. After the *Khums* is apportioned for the *Bayt al-Māl,* booty is distributed among the fighters as against *Fay'* which the Prophet (peace be upon him) used for the benefit of the whole community. But it seems that in spite of this distinction, the Muslim historians have used the word *Fay'* to indicate both. For example, Ibn Hishām's heading about the *'Ghanīma'* of Badr reads thus: 'A description of *Fay'* at Badr and of the captives.'[9] Similarly, when Ibn Hishām says: 'So Khaybar became a *Fay'* between the Muslims while Fadak was exclusively for the Prophet (peace be upon him) because they did not tread over (this land) with their horses and riding animals',[10] it clearly means that in the former case he is using the word *Fay'* which should have been used in the latter case. On another page Ibn Hishām says: 'The Muslim women accompanied the Prophet (peace be upon him) to Khaybar and the Prophet (peace be upon him) gave something for them from the *Fay'* but did not give them a usual share in it.'[11] Wāqidī also uses the word *Fay'* in the same sense when he reports: 'A man asked the Prophet (peace be upon him) for something from the *Fay'*. The Prophet (peace be upon him) said: I am not permitted to dispose of even a needle or thread from *Fay';* I shall neither take nor give it. Then a man asked for a fetter-lock *('iqāl);* the Prophet (peace be upon him) said: It will be given when the *Ghanīma* is distributed.'[12] Khalīfa b. Khayyāṭ also uses the two terms interchangeably when he describes the *Ghanīma* acquired at Jalūla.[13] Ṭabarī reports that 'Ḥakam sent an elephant to Caliph 'Umar who returned it with the remark that the price (of this animal) should be distributed among those whom God has given it as *Fay'*.'[14] It seems that some of the reports made on the authority of the Prophet (peace be upon him) have given sanction to use the word *Fay'* in a wider sense.

It will be noted that the Qur'ān (8:1) uses the word *anfāl* (sing. *nafal*) for the *Ghanīma* as a noun while the verbal form of *gh-n-m* is used to indicate the same thing (8:41, 68). But later on the word *nafal* in the context of *Ghanīma* was used in a different technical meaning. The derivative of *gh-n-m* as a noun in the technical sense of the *Ghanīma* is used only in the form of *maghānim,* (4:94; 48:15, 19, 20) with its singular as *maghnam,* not *Ghanīma.* Similarly the word *Fay'* in the Qur'ān is used only in the verbal form, *'mimmā afā' Allāhu 'alayka'* (whatever Allah has brought to your possession, 33:50), and *'afā' Allāhu alā rasūlihī'* (Allah brought in possession of His messenger, 59:67). Later on the jurists made a distinction between the different forms of the distribution of this *nafal.* Therefore, in order to avoid confusion in the use of the language of history and the application of the terms, the following terminological sense, developed in the books of law, will be used. The term *Ghanīma* will mean moveable property sequestrated by the Muslim army, for distribution. *Khums* will signify the fifth which is to be transferred to the *Bayt al-Māl. Fay'* is that enemy property which is retained and administered by the government. *Nafal* is that award which is made by the caliph or the commander over and above the share of the *Ghanīma* whether or not it was promised in advance. *Salab* signifies the personal items of the slain enemy, taken over by the slayer. *Ṣafī* means what the ruler picks out, generally from the *Ghanīma,* for himself.

Ghanīma During the Prophet's Time

It is reported by the historians that the first *Ghanīma* was seized by 'Abd Allāh b. Jaḥsh during his expedition against the Quraysh before the event of Badr.[15] It was natural for him to treat the *Ghanīma* according to the old Arab custom and a report suggests that he did so. But another report suggests that he put off the distribution until he had received the Prophet's approval[16] because, in the pre-Islamic days also, the chief of the tribe was supposed to distribute the *Ghanīma* and retain a portion of it for himself. The pre-Islamic couplet:[17]

لک المرباع منها و الصفایا   و حکمک و النشیطه و الفضول

sheds ample light on the different portions which the chief of the tribe conventionally retained. But before the event of Badr there was no Islamic principle as to the use of the *Ghanīma.* When they seized the *Ghanīma* at Badr, they did not hesitate to use it, but this soon led to controversy[18] which was decided by the Qur'ānic verses which in the first stage (8:1) seized it from the Muslims and placed it at the disposal of the Prophet (peace be upon him) while shortly afterwards they were made entitled to it after 'one-fifth' share *(Khums)* was passed on to the Prophet (peace be upon him) for 'Allah and His messenger' (8:41). It was the first *Ghanīma* which, according to their standards, appeared to be 'substantial'. According to Wāqidī, 'all the Muslims on their return had a ride, clothing and food, while at Badr they had only seventy camels and two horses'.[19] The total value of the *Ghanīma* or the *Khums* has not been given by early historians but Maqrīzī reports 'that it included 150 camels, 10 horses, weapons and hides. Over and above the fifth portion taken out as *Khums,* the Prophet (peace be upon him) also apportioned for himself a share equal to others.'[20]

The total number of military expeditions which the Prophet (peace be upon him) despatched is reported to be about sixty-five, of which twenty-seven were led by him. But most of these wars were of typical Arab fashion which proved to be decisive after a few skirmishes. Only in a few cases did the enemy take refuge in forts. Wars fought on enemy land also involved occupation of the land after conquest. The significance of the economic return from the thirty-eight expeditions which were not led by the Prophet (peace be upon him) can be appraised from the fact that the cumulative figures of the number of camels seized by way of *Ghanīma* does not exceed 3,000. The value of other goods and properties seized during these expeditions is even less impressive. The effect of the *Ghanīma* was not, however, insignificant in providing support to enterprising individuals. The *Ghanīma* alone on a few expeditions attracted these individuals and this provided a stimulus to continue them. The *Khums* of the expedition of the Qarda is said to have amounted to 20,000 dirhams; the remaining 80,000 dirhams were distributed among 100 fighters at a rate of 800 dirhams per head[21] – quite a boon! But such cases were few and far between. Anything was, however, better than nothing. Compared with these, the expeditions led by the Prophet (peace be upon him) were of more benefit politically and economically, and their additional significance lay in setting precedents which formed the basis of a number of laws. The expedition against Banū Qaynuqā' not only brought rich *Ghanīma* but also increased trade opportunities for the emigrant traders because the former were traders or dyers.[22] Their properties were distributed among the Muslims and the *Khums* thereof was passed on to the Prophet (peace be upon him). Before the distribution of the *Ghanīma* the Prophet (peace be upon him) chose a few weapons for himself. This choice of the Prophet (peace be upon him) was treated as *'ṣafī',* chosen. Later on the conquests of Banū Qurayẓa and Khaybar added considerable resources to the *Bayt al-Māl* and provided relief to the Muslims. The *Ghanīma* from Ḥunayn was the last rich addition to the properties of the Muslims and the *Bayt al-Mal* during the Prophet's time, although the earlier *Ghanīmas* included houses, estates and agricultural lands.

Apart from expeditions where the army was involved in fighting, there were also instances when the enemy surrendered without any fighting or offered to conclude a treaty before an army action was planned. In these cases the land and properties were treated as *Fay'* and passed on to the government *in toto*. Examples of such lands are those of Banū Naḍīr, Fadak and a portion of Khaybar. Communities in treaty relationships saved their properties from becoming *Ghanīma* or *Fay'* and were governed by the terms of the treaty.

The Exceptions

As a general rule, four-fifths of the *Ghanīma* was distributed among the fighters, but there were exceptions to the rule, such as the following:

(i) Makka was conquered by force, but it was not treated as *Ghanīma* or *Fay';* it was accorded special treatment.[23]
(ii) Women are reported to have taken part in most of the wars and helped the fighters in nursing, cooking and, in certain cases, defence as well, but they were not given a fighter's share of the booty.[24] They were, however, paid something by way of gift or remuneration.
(iii) Slaves of the fighters took part in active war and received remuneration but not a share.[25]

The following categories of persons were also entitled to a share in the *Ghanīma*:

(i) Non-Muslim allies if they took part in war. Wāqidī has reported about ten Jews who fought with the Prophet (peace be upon him) against the people of Khaybar and who were given a share in the *Ghanīma.*[26] Ṣafwān b. Umayya, still an unbeliever at Ḥunayn, was among those who received a lion's share, perhaps by virtue of being the leader of an allied contingent.[27]
(ii) Fighters who were exempted from taking part in the fighting due to illness or injury during wartime.[28]
(iii) The man who negotiated a peace treaty with the people of Fadak.[29]
(iv) Fighters killed during war operations.[30]

In this connection the case of Badr is unique insofar as the *Ghanīma* was also distributed among persons who were not present on the occasion. Wāqidī has mentioned four such persons:

1. The person who persuaded others to go to Badr;
2. The person who was prepared to go but fell ill and died at the eleventh hour;
3. Two *Anṣār,* (Helpers)[31]. No reason has been given but Ibn Sa'd has provided some details about such persons. He lists the following eight persons who were given a share in the *Ghanīma:*

(1) 'Uthmān, whom the Prophet (peace be upon him) left behind in Madina to nurse his ('Uthmān's) wife.

(2, 3) Two persons who were tipped for espionage.

(4, 5) Two deputies of the Prophet (peace be upon him): one of whom was appointed over Madina and the other over Upper Madina, 'Āliya.

(6, 7) Two persons who were suffering from fatigue and so returned.

(8) One whom the Prophet (peace be upon him) stopped for an unknown reason.[32]

Each of the above-mentioned persons was given an equal share in the *Ghanīma.* The captives of war were distributed by lot. Most reports suggest that a horseman was given three times as much as a foot-soldier.[33] The total amount of the *Khums* that was transferred to the *Bayt al-Māl* has not been mentioned by the early historians. But, if we accept Maqrīzī's statement about the quantity of the *Ghanīma,*[34] the *Khums* amounted to thirty camels, two horses, and some weapons, over and above a share in the captives.

The above principles as to who is and who is not entitled to a share in the *Ghanīma* were also observed later on.

Ghanīma Properties and the Method of Distribution

While above are listed those entitled to a share in the *Ghanīma,* the following elucidates the categories of things which were distributed and the method of distribution which was followed during the Prophet's time:

(1) As already stated, land was involved only in the case of a few expeditions. The properties of Banū Naḍīr, Banū Qurayẓa, Ghaṭafān, Banū Tamīm and the lands of Wādi'l Qurā, Baḥrayn, Yamāma, and Khaybar were taken over either as *Ghanīma* or as *Fay'.* But land was distributed among the fighters only in the case of Khaybar.[35]

(2) All moveable properties of the enemy were distributed.

(3) It was prohibited to sell, remove, or use the properties of the *Ghanīma* before distribution. Food and fodder were the only exceptions.[36] According to Wāqidī, food, fodder and hides were also not subjected to the *Khums.*[37]

(4) The *Ghanīma* arms could be borrowed before taking out the

Khums and before distribution. They were, however, returnable when the war was over.[38]

(5) The *Ghanīma* properties were generally collected at one place. The Prophet (peace be upon him), if he liked, would take any select article for his personal use *(Ṣafī)* or for awarding it to anybody *(Nafal)* or for both. Then the *Khums* was set aside for the *Bayt al-Māl.*

(6) The remaining portion was then distributed among those entitled to it. Sometimes the properties were auctioned and sold to the highest bidders who could pay the price out of their share of the *Ghanīma.* This meant that each share of the *Ghanīma* was, in such cases, determined and calculated in terms of its monetary value. This technique is reported to have been adopted in respect of the household goods of Banū Muṣṭaliq, Banū Qurayẓa and at Khaybar.[39]

(7) Distribution was generally made by giving cash or properties to individuals or by organizing them into pools and giving a share of a pool for mutual adjustment into smaller units. This practice is reported to have been adopted in the case of the properties of Banū Qurayẓa and those of Khaybar.[40]

(8) The *Ghanīma* lands of Khaybar were divided into eighteen portions and each portion was collectively allotted to a group of 100 fighters. One person from each group was made responsible for the distribution of its income and produce among the members of his group.[41]

(9) While there was usually equal distribution of the *Ghanīma,* there were instances of favoured treatment.[42]

(10) If the Prophet (peace be upon him) wished to distribute something only among a limited group of persons, he used to get the approval of the group to be deprived. This he did in the case of the property of Banū Naḍīr, which he distributed only among the Emigrants, and in the case of Khaybar where he also included in the *Ghanīma* some late-comers.[43]

The *Ghanīma* of Ḥunayn

The distribution of the *Ghanīma* of Ḥunayn among the Quraysh by way of reconciliation of hearts *(ta'līf al-qulūb)* has involved controversy as to whether it was made from the *Ghanīma* or from the *Khums.* The reason for the controversy is the report that the *Anṣār* were aggrieved over it. Whether reconciliation of hearts is also a head of *Khums* expenditure has not been pointedly discussed by jurists. The Qur'ān specifically gives only five heads of expenditure of the *Khums* property. Yet the Prophet's example suggests that the ruler had the authority to spend it for other purposes as well, one instance of which is that he bought war materials from the *Khums* income. But if the distribution among the Quraysh was made out of the *Khums* while the *Ghanīma* was distributed among all other fighters and also among the *Anṣār,* this could account for the grievance of the *Anṣār.* However, a proper interpretation of the stories is possible only if the facts are critically examined because it is the reporting of details that is responsible for the confusion.

It is reported that Banū Hawāzin and their allies, some 20,000 fighters, advanced along with their belongings and families against the Muslims. After a couple of skirmishes they took to their heels and the Muslims seized large quantities of the *Ghanīma* which they had left – valuables, camels, livestock and captives. According to Wāqidī and Ibn Sa'd,[44] the Muslims seized the following:

1. Captives 6,000
2. Camels 24,000
3. Sheep/goats 40,000 or more
4. Silver 4,000 *Ūqiyya*

The Prophet (peace be upon him) distributed large amounts of *ex gratia* per head to many newly-converted Muslims of Makka (perhaps also to some unbelievers). Ṭabarī has given a list of eighteen persons,[45] most of whom have also been listed by Ibn Sa'd.[46] Ibn Hishām, citing different authorities has given a total of thirty-eight names.[47] Almost all these sources inform that the Prophet (peace be upon him) awarded 100 camels each to most of them. Other Muslims got four camels or forty sheep/goats each. Captives were also distributed among the fighters. A horseman was awarded three times the share of a footman.[48] These facts, along with some calculations can be rearranged and verified:

1. 12,000 persons including 2,000 Quraysh took part in the expedition against Hawāzin, etc.
2. They seized 24,000 camels and more than 40,000 sheep.
3. *Khums* was taken out of this *Ghanīma.*
4. The Prophet (peace be upon him) distributed about 100 camels each to about forty Qurayshites, etc.
5. There were 2,000 horsemen in the expedition and their share was three times the ordinary share.[49]
6. The portion of the *Ghanīma* was to be distributed as 10,000 shares to footmen and 6,000 shares to horsemen, a total of 16,000 shares.
7. Allowing some margin for the number of sheep but supposing there were 60,000, equal to 6,000 camels, plus the 24,000 camels in stock, would make a total of 30,000 camels.
8. Deduct the *Khums,* viz, 30,000 minus 6,000 = 24,000 camels.

9. Divide the 24,000 camels into 16,000 shares and the answer is 1.5 camels per share and not 4 camels as given by the historians.

It is assumed that the Quraysh were awarded from the *Khums* and not from the *Ghanīma*[50] because in the latter case the number of camels per share would have been reduced further. But if the calculation is reversed on the basis of four camels each the total number of camels seized comes to 16,000 × 4 = 64,000, being the four-fifths of total *Ghanīma* or 80,000 camels including sheep equalling one tenth of a camel.

In any case, the different sets of figures do not reconcile with each other if it is assumed that all the fighters including the *Anṣār* were given four camels each. What appeals to common sense is that the possibility of misreporting the small, single digit, per-head share is less than the multiple aggregate figures of camels, sheep, silver, captives, etc. But this does not seem to solve the problem. If a share of four camels each was not satisfactory for any reason, the sense of deprivation should have been widespread mainly among the poorly trained, newly converted Muslim tribes rather than among the *Anṣār* alone as has been reported by the historians. Before suggesting any solution the following facts might be noted.

According to Wāqidī, the Prophet (peace be upon him) advised Zayd to count the number of people and the quantity of *Ghanīma* and then distribute it at a rate of four camels or forty sheep each.

The remaining properties of the *Ghanīma* were sent to Madina.

The *Anṣār* complained that the Prophet (peace be upon him) gave the *Ghanīma* to his tribe *(qawm)* and also gave *large quantities* to other tribes but neglected the *Anṣār*.[51]

These, along with the facts mentioned above, suggest the possibility of the following situation:

1. *Khums* of 24,000 camels and 40 or 60 thousand sheep was set aside to be transported to Madina.[52]
2. Out of the remaining stock more than 3,500 camels were given to the Quraysh and other tribal chiefs.
3. The remaining, about 20,000 camels, were distributed among 5,000 fighters at a rate of four camels each. This cross-section of recipients was sufficient to satisfy most of the tribes.
4. Although there is no report to suggest that the Emigrants *(Muhājirūn)* were also given any camels, the fact was that their tribe *(qawm)*, Quraysh, did receive some.
5. The *Anṣār* perhaps did not get anything, and this aggrieved them because of their superior position in Islam as compared to the still uncommitted Quraysh of Makka.

6. It is easy to see why the Prophet (peace be upon him) did not try to console them by giving them something from the *Khums* which was transported to Madina. Firstly, because he had promised to pay many Muslims compensation for the captives of Hawāzin which were compulsorily taken away from them. And secondly, the Prophet (peace be upon him) was planning to lead the largest-ever expedition to Tabūk, for which not only the reconciling of hearts at Ja'irrāna was necessary but also a great quantity of arms and a large herd of riding animals. It was soon proved that he harvested a rich crop of what he had sown at Ja'irrāna.

Now as regards Wāqidī's report about the share of four camels to each *('fa kānat sihāmuhum li kulli rajulin arba' min al-ibil aw . . .')*, it can be suggested that he did not mean four camels to each of the 12,000 Muslims; he meant each of the Muslims who it was decided should be given a share – perhaps the later accessions to Islam – by totally neglecting the *Anṣār,* the *Muhājirūn,* and some others. What grieved the *Anṣār* was not that they alone were neglected; it was their position of seniority which they thought was not considered. They had willingly sacrificed their economic interests for the sake of the poor Emigrants whom they had treated as senior to themselves. But they were not willing to make sacrifice for the sake of those wealthy newcomers who, until the last week, were staunch enemies of the Prophet (peace be upon him) and of Islam. That is why when the Prophet (peace be upon him) reassured them that their position of seniority was secure, they were consoled and did not worry about his offer to allot them lands at Baḥrayn.[53]

The *Khums*

While the government apportions four-fifths of the *Ghanīma* to the fighters, the *Khums* (one-fifth) is retained by it for specific purposes: 'For God, and for His Messenger and for the kinsmen, and for the orphans, paupers *(masākīn)* and the wayfarers.' The words 'God and His Messenger' are taken to mean the government but during the Prophet's time the Prophet himself (peace be upon him) was 'the government'. The term 'kinsmen' *(dhawi'l qurbā),* during his life was taken to mean the kinsmen of the Prophet (peace be upon him) who, according to Sa'īd Ibn Jubayr, were the children of Hāshim and Muṭṭalib.[54] It can be assumed that each of the five heads would not have been met every time that the Prophet (peace be upon him) received the *Khums.* As a result the expenditure of the *Khums* depended on the urgency of a particular head of expenditure. In the early Madinan period of the Prophet (peace be upon him), the *Khums* receipts were very meagre and the personal requirements of the Prophet's own family were quite pressing. The gradual increase in the *Khums* property eased the personal financial stringency of the Prophet (peace be upon him) and the situation was further relieved by the addition of the *Fay'* receipts. Now the *Khums* receipts could also meet other heads of expenditure. Orphans, paupers and wayfarers were also now financed.[55] The Prophet (peace be upon him) also utilized these funds in providing arms and riding animals for *Jihād*.[56] He used his discretion to dispose of the *Khums* receipts as he thought fit. In the case of the *Khums* of Banū Qurayẓa, for example, Ibn Sa'd reports: 'The Prophet freed some of the captives, gifted some to others while he put into service whom he liked. Similarly, he did with the goods whatever he thought fit.'[57] It is also reported that he exchanged some of the goods and slaves of Banū Qurayẓa for war equipment.[58] The *Khums* of Khaybar was quite substantial as compared with any other so far. This was the first *Khums* income which was certain and regular. The Prophet (peace be upon him) first of all apportioned the produce of the land among his kinsmen in a quantity which sufficed for their annual food requirements. Historians have given details of the quantities of food-grain and dates that were apportioned for his wives and kinsmen.[59] Apart from meeting his food requirements, the Prophet (peace be upon him) also spent the *Khums* income on financing some other requirements of his kinsmen. For example, he arranged for the marriage of his two cousins from the *Khums* money.[60] Expenses incurred on the marriage of the widows of Banū Hāshim were also met from the same source.[61]

It seems that at a later stage the proportion of expenditure on heads other than kinsmen substantially increased. That is why the Prophet (peace be upon him), before distributing the *Ghanīma* of Ḥunayn said: 'Nothing except the *Khums* of the properties God has bestowed on you, will remain with me and even that much will (ultimately) be returned to you.'[62] This apparently meant that apart from a portion for meeting the basic requirements of the Prophet's family, the entire expenditure of the *Khums* would be spent on the general welfare of the Muslims.

The person in charge of the *Khums* properties during the Prophet's time was Maḥmiyya b. Jaz'.[63] According to Abū Yūsuf, 'Alī looked after the supervision of that portion of the *Khums* which was exclusively for the Prophet's kinsmen,[64] but other reports contradict this statement.

Ghanīma and *Khums* During the Pious Caliphate

The institutions of the *Ghanīma*, the *Khums* and minor items like *Ṣafī*, *Salab*, and *Nafal*, remained almost unchanged during the period under study. The changes that took place after the Prophet's demise were in respect of *Ṣafī* and the kinsmen's share of the *Khums*. The first four caliphs refrained from taking any *Ṣafī,* but later rulers did so. The head of expenditure of *Khums* entitled the kinsmen *(dhawi'l qurbā)* was reviewed and reinterpreted.

The conquests of the rich territories of Persia, Syria, North Africa, Spain, and Asia Minor, within the period under study, brought large quantities of *Ghanīma* into the hands of the Muslim army and enriched the *Bayt al-Māl*. These conquests started immediately after the Prophet's demise, and within a few years goods and valuables were pouring in from all sides. At this stage less than 100,000 men were deployed on different fronts, and the amount of *Ghanīma* that they might have acquired can be conceived by the fact that Khālid, who took part in various expeditions for about five years, collected goods and cash valued at 160,000 dirhams.[65] Even so this would seem to be a modest figure if the picturesque accounts of the *Ghanīma* accruing from Madā'in, Bukhārā, Ifrīqiyya, and Andalus, as reported by the historians, are correct.[66]

While Caliph 'Umar decreed that a person should be entitled to a share in the *Ghanīma* who had witnessed the event, or who, as a helper, had participated before the burial of the dead,[67] 'Umar II included the messengers, postmen, and the agents *(wakīl)* who were sent from the army.[68] All other beneficiaries remained the same as in the Prophet's time.

Expeditions which brought smaller quantities of *Ghanīma* were numerous and much more regular. While moveable properties were distributed by way of *Ghanīma* and the *Khums* was transferred to the government, land conquered in these areas was not distributed; it was converted into *Fay'*. The same policy was pursued throughout the Umayyad period, and perhaps became a precedent for all time. Within a hundred years the Muslims had occupied territories stretching from the Punjab in the east and North Africa and Spain in the west, but the land was left untouched.

The quantity of *Ghanīma* received can be judged from the value of the *Khums* collections. It was the *Khums* property of Madā'in and then of Jarmūk that led Caliph 'Umar to distribute annual stipends to all the Muslims who had, or were taking part, in wars.[69] There is reason to believe that the Pious Caliphs were careful to spend the *Khums* collections properly. But unfortunately later stories raised some controversy about Caliph 'Uthmān in this regard. The first allegation concerned his awarding of the *Khums* receipts to his kinsmen, the second about giving the *Khums* to 'Abd Allāh b. Sa'd b. Abī Sarḥ, commander of the expedition to Ifrīqiyya, and the third about selling the *Khums* property to Marwān at a much lower rate than the free market price.

As regards the first point, it is reported that after the Prophet's death, people were divided on the share of the *Khums* payable to the Prophet (peace be upon him) and his kinsmen. One group was of the view that the Prophet's share should be taken by his caliph. Another group was of the opinion that the share of the kinsmen should be passed on to the Prophet's kinsmen. A small group believed that the share of the kinsmen should be passed on to the kinsmen of the caliph. Then all of them agreed that both shares should be utilized for providing arms and riding animals,[70] and this was done by Abū Bakr and 'Umar. But it seems that 'Uthmān believed that the share of the Prophet's kinsmen should be transferred to the caliph's kinsmen while 'Alī (and Ibn 'Abbās) believed in the continuation of the old practice of distributing it among the Prophet's kinsmen. It should be observed that Caliph 'Uthmān's interpretation of the Qur'ānic phrase *'dhawi'l qurbā'* (kinsmen) was as valid as that of Caliphs Abū Bakr, 'Umar and 'Alī. 'Alī would have been justified in restoring their share to the Prophet's kinsmen during his rule but he refrained from doing so, perhaps on political grounds.

As regards Caliph 'Uthmān giving the *Khums* to 'Abd Allāh b. Sa'd b. Abī Sarḥ, it should be noted that he was not an innovator of this practice. Caliph 'Umar had already offered Jarīr of Bajīla a quarter of the *Khums* of Sawād if he, along with his tribe, would join the Muslim army in Iraq.[71] Caliph 'Uthmān offered the same inducement but with a more convincing justification. The event requires a peep into the earlier history of the expedition to Ifrīqiyya.

When 'Amr sought Caliph 'Umar's permission to overrun Ifrīqiyya, 'Umar refused on an apparently superstitious ground. He is reported to have written to 'Amr: 'Don't go there, it is "Mufarriqa" not Ifrīqiyya. It betrays others and they betray it.'[72] Whether or not this convinced 'Amr, he stopped his advance. It is quite natural to believe that the contents of the letter would have been known to other generals and soldiers. Caliph 'Umar's action was a demonstration of the old Arab method of depending on prognostic interpretations of things and events. But if such a situation had been allowed to prevail it could have led in wrong directions. Caliph 'Uthmān therefore acted wisely when he advised his general to advance this feared 'Mufarriqa' and, in order to boost his morale, promised him a portion of the *Khums.*[73] Had Caliph 'Uthmān not taken this action, many Muslims could have begun thinking in these prognostic terms, and might have stopped their advance at the point where Caliph 'Umar had left them. There were many cities obstructing their advance which, without any literal connotation, conveyed a bad sense. For example, Kush in Persian means 'kill', Makrān in Arabic means 'double deceit', Munqalaba means the 'over-turned', and so on. In fact it is very difficult now to estimate the great wisdom of Caliph 'Uthmān's decision in relation to the future course of Islamic history. He at least set the wheel of history to rotate with the same force and in the same direction as before.

As regards the allegation of selling the *Khums* to Marwān, it should be remembered that the *Ghanīma* and the *Khums* could both be sold and their price used for specific purposes. The Prophet (peace be upon him) did it.[74] It is reported that Sa'd, the governor of Kūfa also did so[75] and sent the sale proceeds to Caliph 'Umar. A more interesting report is found about the governor of Syria selling *Khums* property to 'Umar's son 'Abd-Allāh. When Caliph 'Umar came to know of this transaction he annulled the transaction, sold the property at a much higher price and after giving a portion of the profit to 'Abd-Allāh deposited the remainder in the *Bayt al-Māl*.[76] There is no report of Caliph 'Umar taking any action against his governor. In the case of Sa'd, however, Caliph 'Umar appointed a committee to enquire into the reports against Sa'd, one of many being that he was lenient in the sale of *Khums*.[77] Caliph 'Uthmān's 'fault' in this respect was that throughout his life, he was generous and lenient.

Apart from the above arguments one point should be made very clear. To err is human and 'Uthmān was a human being. But the genuineness of any allegations against any reputed person must be judged against the background of his temperament and past performances, and any allegations against 'Uthmān would require much stronger evidence than has been reported by some historians.

During the Umayyad Period

While the *Ghanīma* continued to be distributed among the soldiers, even after the Pious Caliphs, the collection of the *Khums* seems to have been an arbitrary choice sometimes in the caliph's name and sometimes at the discretion of the army commander who wanted to please his governor or caliph. Governor Ziyād advised his commander in Khurāsān to pick out all gold and silver from the *Ghanīma,* in compliance with the wish of the caliph.[78] Mūsā b. Nuṣayr is reported to have brought back large quantities of *Ghanīma* to please the caliph instead of distributing it among the deserving soldiers.[79]

Distribution of the *Khums* which, after the Pious Caliphs had been treated carelessly, was set right by 'Umar II. He advised his officials to distribute the *Khums* only among the deserving persons.[80] He also restored the payment of the amount of the *Khums* to Banū Hāshim which, according to Ibn Sa'd, was stopped by Mu'āwiya.[81]

Salab and *Nafal*

The practice of awarding *Salab* and *Nafal* after the Prophet (peace be upon him) is generally not recorded by historians. But because they did not involve large amounts, had become a convention, and did not deprive the government of anything, it can be presumed that they continued. A strong factor that supports this presumption is that the soldiers now needed more material incentive than before. Examples of Caliph 'Umar's granting of large *Nafal* to Jarīr and Caliph 'Uthmān's awarding of a fabulous *Nafal*[82] to 'Abd-Allāh b. Sa'd have already been discussed. Local commanders also granted *Nafal* to encourage their soldiers. Khālid, Sa'd, and Muthannā, for example, used to give special awards to their soldiers and these were given from the *Khums.*[83] While the Prophet (peace be upon him) did not take away any *Khums* out of the *Salab* even though it was valuable,[84] Caliph 'Umar, admitting that it was never done before him, levied the *Khums* on a *Salab* valued at some 30 to 40 thousand dirhams.[85]

Misuse of the *Ghanīma*

If the *Ghanīma* is seized by the fighters themselves, it is difficult for the commander or the person in charge of the *Ghanīma* to embezzle anything from it. It is, however, easier for the soldiers to dupe their commanders while they are collecting it from the enemy camps. Reports suggest a high degree of moral responsibility among the soldiers in this respect. While these reports can be believed in view of the emotional fervour at the time of victory and collection of valuable *Ghanīma,* it does not mean that all the soldiers possessed a similar sense of responsibility. Incidents of dishonesty are not recorded by the historians, perhaps because it is something which no one but the thief knows about. In the case of officials, however, Ṭabarī mentions two incidents of misappropriation in the *Ghanīma* properties: the first was in 77 A.H. by Bukayr b. Wishāḥ and the second and more serious one in 104 A.H. by Ḥarashī in the *Ghanīma* of Sughd.[86]

Notes and References

1. For explanation of *Ṣafī* and the following terms, see p. 150.

2. For example, some of the pre-Islamic poets describe the practice in the following words:

Burrāq:

تولت رجالى بالغنائم و الغنى   مزجين لـلا جمال من دكلان

Saffāḥ:

ملا وا من الاقطا نتين ركيه ٭ منا وآ بوا سالمين و اغنموا

Bishr:

الا لاتد اعوا انها خيل وائل ٭ عليها رجال يطلبون الغنائما

Zuhayr:

وشب له فيها بنون وتوبعت ٭ سلامه اعوام له و غنائم

Cheikho, pp. 146, 183, 322, 567.

3. With a similar sense: Bukh. (Ṣalāt), 84; Mus., 12, 53; Tir., 7, 42.

4. Sira, 2, 375.

5. Waq., 47.

6. Waq., 634.

7. Waq., 991.

8. For example, for the expedition to Badr, see Waq., 1, 20; Sad., II, 1, p. 6; Tab., 1, 1285; Abū Bakr's call, Bal., 115; for 'Umar's, Tab., 1, 2160, 2188; Bal., 253; for 'Uthmān's, Bal., 201; for Khalid's, Tab., 1, 2031; for 'Amr's, 1 AH(M), 56; Kindi, 7, etc.

9. 1, 391.

10. 2, 229.

11. 2, 232. For other examples, see 2, 173, 225, 241, 320, 324; 1, 402.

12. Waq., 681.

13. Khalifa, 128.

14. Tab., 1, 2708.

15. *Passim.*

16. Sira, 1, 367–8; Sad., II, 1, 5; I, 2, 119.

17. Cited in as-Sarakhsī: *Sharḥ as-Siyar al-Kabīr.* Hyderabad, 1335 A.H., 2, 12. Mirbā', one fourth; Ṣafāyā, chosen 'pick'; Nashīṭa, a valuable 'catch' in the way; Fuḍūl, residual.

18. Sira, 2, 2. According to Ṭabarī, 1, 1334, the controversy arose as to the entitlement to the *Ghanīma.* Muslims were divided into three groups. The first was chasing the fleeing enemy. The second was collecting the *Ghanīma* and captives. The third was guarding the Prophet (peace be upon him). Each group was pleading for its service to be recognized as the most significant one.

19. Waq., 1, 26.

20. It is possible that Maqrīzī (Maq. (Im), 1, 94,), might have come across a reliable source of information which is now extinct. But it is equally possible that he might have worked out an arithmetic calculation on the basis of Wāqidī's report, thus: Wāqidī says there was nobody who did not have a ride on his return while before it they had only seventy camels and two horses. Now supposing that the number of Muslims at Badr was not more than 340, and that the seventy persons already having a camel returned on their camels 1:1, 250 persons would be left without a ride. Leaving some margin for a few horses let us suppose 240 persons required a ride, 2:1. It means that they should have at least 120 camels, and eight horses for the remaining ten persons, two of whom already

had their own. This number should be arrived at after the *Khums* is taken away which means (120 × 5/4) + (8 × 5/4) or 150 camels and ten horses. If the report is really based on arithmetic calculation, many other variables may be possible with change in some hypotheses. For example, 100 camels plus 25 horses if all the Muslims would go 2:1 as usual; or 200 camels plus 25 horses if the 70 camel owners would like to return in doubles as before, and so on.

21. Waq., 198.

22. *Ibid.*, 178–9.

23. A.U., 157–9; Sad., II, 1, 99; Bal., 51, and *passim.*

24. Tab., 1, 1586; Sira, 2, 232; Mus., 2, 190–2; Waq., 686–7.

25. A.U., 881; Sad., II, 1, 83, III, 1, 34; Waq., 104–5, 684.

26. Waq., 684. Wāqidī has also quoted another opinion that they were given something by way of remuneration but not a share, but Abū 'Ubayd (A.U. 518) supports only the former view.

27. Waq., 943.

28. *Ibid.*, 684.

29. *Ibid.*

30. *Ibid.*, 102, 522, 684.

31. *Ibid.*, 101.

32. Sad., II, 1, 6.

33. Sira, 2, 173; Tab., 1, 1497; Kh., 10.

34. See note 20.

35. Kh., 38.

36. Sad., II, 83; Sira, 2, 230; Waq., 664.

37. Waq., 665, 680.

38. Waq., *Ibid.*

39. Sad., II, 46, 56, 78; Waq., 521, 665.

40. Waq., 521, 665; Sad., II, 82–3; Bal., 38.

41. Waq., 689–90.

42. Sad., II, 61, 83, 85.

43. Yah., 92; Sad., IV, 2, 54.

44. Sad., II, 110; Waq., 949.

45. Tab., 1, 1679 *et sqq.*

46. Sad., II, 110.

47. Sira, 2, 320–2.

48. Waq., 949.

49. *Ibid.*

50. This is suggested by Mus., 7, 150; Waq., 948.

51. Waq., 947 *et seq.*

52. Tab., 1, 1685.

53. Chapter 3. Throughout this discussion we have completely neglected the figures reported by Ṭabarī on the authority of Ibn Isḥāq (1, 1674). According to this report the total number of camels was 6,000. If this figure is accepted then most of the statements of all the other historians will have to be rejected. The interesting thing is that in *Sīra Ibn Hishām* this number is given for the captives, on the same authority. He quotes: 'And there were, with the Prophet (peace be upon him), 6 thousand of the dependents and women of Hawāzin and the camels and the sheep whose number cannot be counted.' In the face of this difference in figures Ṭabarī seems to have relied on Wāqidī's statement of per-head distribution of four camels (1, 1685).

54. Kh., 11.

55. *Ibid.*

56. A.U., 821.

57. II, 54.

58. Tab., 1, 1497.

59. Bal., 38, 41; Bukh. (Muzāra'a) 9; Sad., III, 1, 124; IV, 1, 11.

60. Sad., IV, 1, 40–1.

61. Waq., 381.

62. A.U., 765, 810.

63. Mus., 7, 179.

64. Kh., 11, 12.

65. When Khālid returned to Madina his earnings were halved by Caliph 'Umar. Khālid, nevertheless, possessed goods and cash valued at 80,000 dirhams.

66. Tab., 1, 2444 *et sqq;* Khalifa, 1, 397; I.A.H., 86; I.A.H. (M), 210.

67. Bal., 257; Khalifa, 1, 148.

68. Sad., V, 260.

69. Tab., 2411–18.

70. Kh., 11, 12.

71. Tab., 1, 2186. The reports by Bal. (267), A.U. (156), and Kh. (18), may lead to the conclusion that Caliph 'Umar promised this *Nafal* from *Ghanīma* because the fighters of this tribe formed one-fourth of the whole army. But this opinion makes no sense. Sawād had not been conquered at that time and Caliph 'Umar's policy regarding the distribution of conquered lands was not known. Therefore, it was taken for granted that in case Sawād was conquered and the lands were distributed like the lands of Khaybar, Jarīr would naturally take a one-fourth portion of Sawād lands by virtue of his numerical strength and not by the grace of Caliph 'Umar. This offer of one-fourth would make sense only if it was something more than the right of Jarīr, and this is possible only if the one-fourth portion of the *Khums* as reported by Ṭabarī is treated as correct.

72. Bal., 227.

73. Tab., 1, 2814.

74. Sad., II, 46, 56, 78; Waq., 521, 665; Sarakhsī; *Al-Mabsūṭ*, Cairo, n.d., Vol. 14, pp. 6, 7.

75. Sad., 5, 44.

76. Chapter 2, supra, p. 107.

77. Sad., 5, 44.

78. Kath., 8, 29.

79. Khalifa, 1, 408; I.A.H. (M), 210.

80. Sad., V, 257–8.

81. *Ibid.*, 287–8.

82. The extent of this *Nafal* can be conceived by the fact that according to Ya'qūbī (II, 155) the value of *Ghanīma* amounted to 25 million dīnārs. This means that one-fifth of the *Khums* payable to 'Abd-Allāh amounted to 1 million dīnārs. Many historians agree that the per-head distribution of *Ghanīma* of Ifrīqiyya stood at 1,000 dīnārs for a footman and 3,000 for a horseman. (Khalifa, 165; I.A.H., 44; I.A.H. (M), 184; Kindi, 12).

83. Tab., 1, 2027, 2028, 2233.

84. Mus., 12, 64; Abu Daud, 3, 97.

85. A.U., 780; Ṭabarī, Abū Ja'far Muḥammad b. Jarīr; *Kitāb Ikhtilāf al-Fuqahā'*, ed. J. Schacht, Leiden, 1933, p. 117.

86. Tab., 2, 1024, 1446.

CHAPTER 6

Zakāt
(The Poor-Tax)

The Qur'ān ordains the payment of *Zakāt* or the inter-changeable word *as-Ṣadaqa* on wealth *(māl)* and crops, and lays down the heads on which *Zakāt* proceeds are to be spent.[1] The rates of payment, the nature and quantities of wealth and crops on which it is to be charged, and the rules of exemption from *Zakāt* are not found in the Qur'ān. However it stands to reason that these necessary details should have been explicitly laid down for without that the Qur'ānic emphasis on paying *Zakāt* would have been rendered meaningless. This has been done by the Prophet (peace be upon him) who laid down these rules quite elaborately.[2]

The Pre-Islamic Levy

The concept of charging a religious tax is not a Qur'ānic innovation. In ancient Babylonia 'the revenues of the temples and priesthood were derived also from compulsory offering which included the *esria* or tithes. These had to be paid by all classes of population from the king downwards, either in grain or its equivalent in money'[3]. The Old Testament also provides for the payment of tithes:

> And all the tithe of the land, whether of the seed of the land, or of the fruit of the tree, is the Lord's: it is holy unto the Lord (Lev. 27:30).
>
> Thou shalt truly tithe all the increase of thy seed, that the field bringeth forth year by year (Deut. 14:22).
>
> And, behold, I have given the children of Levi all the tenth in Israel for an inheritance, for their service which they serve, even the service of the tabernacle of the congregation (Num. 18:21).
>
> And that we should bring the first fruits of dough, and our offerings, and the fruit of all manner of trees, of wine and of oil, unto the

priests, to the chambers of the house of our God; and the tithes of our ground unto the Levites, that the same Levites might have the tithes in all the cities of our tillage (Neh. 11:37).

But there seems to be a world of difference between the Qur'ānic concept of *Zakāt* and the earlier concept in respect of object, scope and applicability. The ancient and Biblical tithes were meant for purely religious institutions while the Qur'ānic 'tithe' is meant for giving economic support to the society and not to any religious hierarchy, so

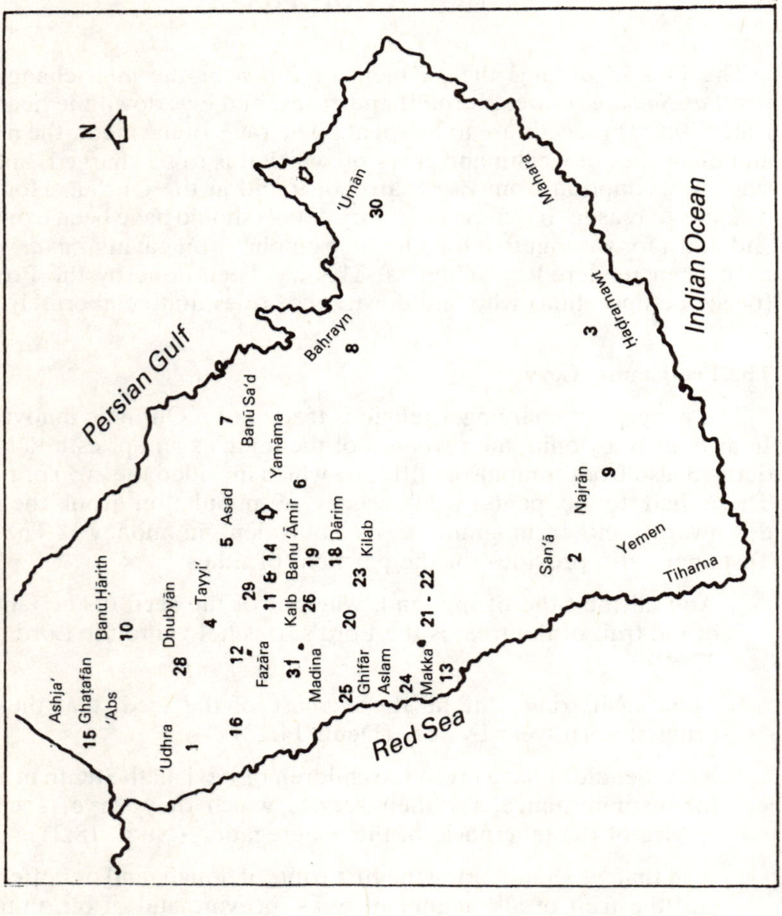

Map 1. Places where *Zakāt* Collectors were sent by the Prophet

much so that its use was made unlawful for the Prophet (peace be upon him), his kinsmen and posterity. The Prophet (peace be upon him) is reported to have written: 'The Apostle of God is the supporter of your rich and the poor, and *Ṣadaqa (Zakāt)* is unlawful to Muḥammad or the members of his household; it is only a means of purification, given to the needy and the wayfarer.'[4] Similarly, *esria* or tithe was collected from all the classes of society and passed on to the religious institutions while *Zakāt* is collected only from the rich and passed on only to the poor and is applicable to items of wealth. These points suggest that there is no affinity between the earlier concept of *esria* or tithe and the Islamic concept of *Zakāt* except on one minor point: the rate of ten per cent. But even in this respect the affinity is very limited because the rates of *Zakāt* vary from two and a half per cent to ten per cent.

Zakāt During the Prophet's Time

The history of the role of the government in collecting and distributing *Zakāt* begins very late in the Prophet's Madina. Although the covenant with the *Anṣār* at al-'Aqaba required them to pay *Zakāt,*[5] it seems to have been prescribed as a voluntary personal obligation and can be termed as pious spending *(infāq),* without any specific rules and legal requirements. *Zakāt* as a compulsory levy with its set of rules was introduced by the Prophet (peace be upon him), probably when he sent his collectors to different tribes. These collectors were required to collect *Zakāt* from the well-to-do and distribute the same among the poor.[6] Balādhurī has suggested two different dates when the Prophet (peace be upon him) sent 'Alā b. al-Ḥaḍramī to Baḥrayn to collect *Zakāt,* etc. – the years 6 and 8 A.H.[7] But there must be some doubt whether by 6 A.H. *Zakāt* had become a compulsory levy by the government. If so there should have been a mention of collectors sent out to the converted Muslims in other tribes. It is therefore probably safer to presume that in 6 A.H. 'Alā was sent to preach or to deliver the Prophet's letter to the prince of Baḥrayn, and in 8 A.H., when his preaching had induced many to embrace Islam, he was entrusted also with the collection of *Zakāt.* Ṭabarī not only confirms 8 A.H. as the time of deputing 'Alā as a tax collector[8] but also mentions that 'Amr was sent to 'Umān the same year to collect *Zakāt.*[9] It is almost certain that most of the collectors were sent about 9 A.H. Historians mention the names of a number of persons who were despatched to different tribes. The following list, and the map on page 168, give an idea of the places and names of the tribes where these collectors were sent.

The dashes against the place/tribe represent a positive mention by the historian given at the head of the column.

Table 3
Places/Tribes where *Zakāt*-Collectors were sent by the Prophet

		Sīra[10]	Tab.[11]	Wāq.[12]	Khal.[13]	Sa'd[14]
1.	'Udhra (came on their own)					
2.	San'ā	–	–			
3.	Ḥaḍramawt	–	–		–	
4.	Ṭayyi'					
5.	Asad	[–]	–		–	
6.	Banū Ḥanẓala	–	–		–	[–]
7.	Banū Sa'd b. Bakr	–		–		
8.	Baḥrayn	–	–			
9.	Najrān	–	–			
10.	Banū Ḥārith	–				
11.	Kalb				–	–
12.	Fazāra			–	–	
13.	Banū Muṣṭaliq				–	–
14.	Banū Murra				–	
15.	Ashja', Ghaṭafān 'Abs				–	
16.	'Udhra, Salamān Balī			–	–	–
17.	'Awdh/al-Anbā'				–	
18.	Dārim				–	
19.	Banū 'Āmir				–	
20.	Banū Sulaym			–	–	–
21.	Hawāzin, Jashm, Naḍar				–	
22.	Thaqīf				–	
23.	Kalb			–	–	–
24.	Aslam					
25.	Ghifār			[–]		–
26.	Muzayna			–		–
27.	Ka'b			–		–
28.	Dhubyan			–		–
29.	Sa'd Hudhaym					–
30.	'Umān		–			
31.	Madīna			–		–
		8	8	10	16	12

Although the items on which *Zakāt* was levied were not too many, the different rates, mainly in the case of livestock, were rather complicated. Because of this the collectors were specially trained for the job. There are several reports that the Prophet (peace be upon him), before sending his officials, not only informed them of the rates, etc., but advised them about the method of assessment and collection, and also the kind of moral conduct which they should demonstrate.[15] Yet it seems that some of the collectors ignored these instructions and gave cause for complaint.[16] This is also discernible from some of the clauses provided in the documents which the Prophet (peace be upon him) is reported to have sent to different tribal chiefs.[17] The collector is sometimes stated to have reported that he had forgotten the details of the *Zakāt* levy.[18] This perhaps made it necessary to write down the relevant details and send them to the officials in order that there should be no further grievances among the *Zakāt*-payers. This was ultimately done and a document *(Kitāb aṣ-Ṣadaqa)* circulated as a basic set of rules for future practice.[19]

Historians have also reproduced a number of letters which are said to have been written by the Prophet (peace be upon him) to different tribal chiefs and princes. Many of these contain the rates of *Zakāt* on different items. Some of the relevant particulars of such documents[20] are reproduced below:

1. To the princes of Ḥimyar:

   Perform prayers, pay the *Zakāt* and submit the fifth for God from the booty and the share of the Messenger and his chosen part.

   What is laid down on believers in the matter of tax from land a tithe of what the springs and rain-water irrigate and half a tithe on what is watered by the irrigating bucket.

   For every 40 camels a two-year-old milk-camel and for every 30 camels a 2-year-old male camel and for every 5 camels a sheep and for every ten camels two sheep. For every 40 cattle one cow and for every thirty cattle a bull or a cow-calf.

   For every forty sheep pasturing freely, one sheep. This is what God laid upon believers in the matter of *Ṣadaqa*. Who gives more, it is to his merit.[21]

2. To Banū Kalb:

   In the case of flocks pasturing on their own a suckling she- camel free from defect should be paid on every fifty camels. Camels employed in carrying provisions are exempted from taxation. On well-fed sheep they have to pay a three-year-old goat whether pregnant or full of milk.

On what is watered by a channel from a permanent spring they have to pay a tithe of the produce yielded by the land and on the *idhī* palms, half of it is paid according to assessment of the collector. *The tax rate on them should neither increase nor be exacted in parts.*[22]

To Khath'am:

They have to pay the tithe on what is irrigated by water flowing on the surface of the earth and half the tithe on what is irrigated by bucket.[23]

To Bāhila:

Whoever brings into cultivation an ownerless barren land and from which no advantage is derived and it contains places where cattle lie and spend the night; to him it shall belong.

(After laying down the rates of *Zakāt* on animal heads): 'the tax collector *has no right to collect taxes on these animals except in their pasturing grounds.*'[24]

To the deputation of Thumāla and al-Ḥuḍḍān:

They shall not have the palm trees assessed or the dates measured until these are placed in the drying yard. They have to pay one wasq for every ten wasqs.[25]

The Share of the Centre

The provisions italicized in the text suggest the possibility of their inclusion as a result of some complaints about the behaviour of the officials. 'Alā ibn al-Ḥaḍramī was withdrawn as a collector in Baḥrayn because of a complaint by the *Zakāt*-payers.[26] Along with these safeguards, *Zakāt*-payers were also advised to be tolerant to, and co-operate with these officials.[27]

The tradition that *Zakāt* is to be collected from 'their rich' and distributed among 'their poor' may infer that the role of the *Bayt al-Māl* is only nominal in respect of *Zakāt,* and that it would ultimately be entitled to only that which was collected in the capital city *(dār al-khilāfa)*. Certain reports seem to confirm this inference. It is said that the Prophet (peace be upon him) sent 'Amr to collect *Zakāt* at 'Umān.

He took it from the rich and disbursed it among the poor.[28] A later report states that Mu'ādh used to spend the *Zakāt* collections in Yemen but when in Caliph 'Umar's time he sent some of the residual *Zakāt* funds, 'Umar criticized it.[29] Ziyād deputed one of the Prophet's Companions to collect *Zakāt* from a city in Iraq. When he returned and Ziyād enquired about the funds, he replied: 'Oh you mean the *Zakāt* funds. Well, I took it in the way I used to do in the Prophet's time and disposed of it in the way I used to do in his time.'[30]

However there are also reports that suggest that the Prophet (peace be upon him) used to receive funds from outside Madina as well. In some cases there is confusion as to the nature of these funds: whether they were *Zakāt* or *Jizya,* which was also collected by the *Zakāt* collectors. There are also clear cases which prove that the Prophet (peace be upon him) received *Zakāt* from the remote regions. Balādhurī reports that Ḥamza b. Nu'mān, a chief of Banū 'Udhra, was the first to bring the *Ṣadaqa* of his tribe to the Prophet (peace be upon him).[31] It is also possible that the collector would have carried to the Prophet (peace be upon him) a portion of *Zakāt* or in some cases the *Zakāt* funds which remained undistributed. The most relevant argument in support of the central government share in *Zakāt* can be adduced in the context of Abū Bakr's war against apostates.

From the above arguments it appears that *Zakāt* was sometimes paid by the tribes directly to the *Bayt al-Māl.* On other occasions the collectors did not necessarily distribute among the paying community all that they had collected. Distribution might depend on the requirements of a particular tribe, perhaps to be decided by the collector. The distribution to relatively well-off tribes might leave a credit balance for transfer to the *Bayt al-Māl.* Moreover, there could also be situations where there were fewer Muslims than non-Muslims and the Muslims were mostly the payers but not the claimants of *Zakāt.* In such cases also *Zakāt* funds would be transferred to the *Bayt al-Māl.*

Zakāt **Receipts in the Prophet's Time**

Details of the amount of *Zakāt* received by the Prophet (peace be upon him) are not found anywhere. There appear to be many reasons for this. Firstly, a large portion of *Zakāt* was distributed by the collectors locally and the accounts were not generally kept in writing, nor any registers maintained. Secondly, the proceeds of *Zakāt* received by the Prophet (peace be upon him) were distributed forthwith. Thirdly, counting of funds was not a popular method of distribution; it was often effected by handfuls of coins. In the cases of dates or food-grain too, measures were more popular than weights. And, because it was distributed gratuitously no standard measure was necessary. However in the matter of livestock and riding animals a count was kept. It is reported that there were 40,000 camels in the *Bayt al-Māl* when the Prophet (peace be upon him) passed away.[32] But this figure can hardly be accepted as reliable. The Prophet (peace be upon him) died about eighteen months after the expedition to Tabūk and the story of 'seven weepers'[33] suggests that the resources of the *Bayt al-Māl* had been exhausted without providing riding animals to the last seven fighters. It seems implausible that within a period of eighteen months, during which no important war was fought, that the *Bayt al-Māl* would have acquired 40,000 camels by way of *Zakāt.* Moreover, this number of camels would require a cumulative total of about two million camels owned by the Muslims, and provided that the entire *Zakāt* of camels was passed on to the *Bayt al-Māl* without distributing any portion of it locally. What can safely be believed is that the Prophet (peace be upon him) bequeathed a large number of camels in the *Bayt al-Māl.*

The report that the tax collector of Baḥrayn sent 80,000 dirhams to the Prophet (peace be upon him), the largest amount he ever received,[34] also does not give us an accurate idea about *Zakāt* receipts because this included receipts by way of *Jizya* too. This is supported by the fact that, according to the same report, the Prophet (peace be upon him) gave to 'Abbās out of this income.[35] Had it been *Ṣadaqa* only, the Prophet (peace be upon him) would not have granted this income to his uncle. He was so strict about this principle that he would not allow his relatives or *mawlā* to act as collectors or their assistants.[36] The only way of calculating the receipts of *Zakāt* in cases where the figures for *Zakāt* and *Jizya* are mixed up is to deduct the amount of *Jizya* (which is recorded in most cases) from the total and the remainder will be *Zakāt.* But unfortunately, in the case of Baḥrayn neither is the total amount of *Jizya* given nor the total number of persons who were liable to *Jizya* known. Only the rate of *Jizya* per head is given and this does not give any idea about the total *Jizya.*

If accurate information about the total volume of *Zakāt* collection in the time of the Prophet (peace be upon him) is scarce, a great amount of material is available in our sources as to how the collection of *Zakāt* was organized. In some cases, like that of Banū 'Udhra, the payers voluntarily brought their *Zakāt* to Madina.[37] Some reports suggest that *Zakāt* on rare procurements was collected by the Prophet himself (peace be upon him) whenever any such case was reported to him. It is said that once a man informed the Prophet (peace be upon him) that he had acquired some money from ownerless ruins outside Madina. The Prophet (peace be upon him) deducted *Zakāt* at a rate of twenty per cent *(khums)* and returned the remainder to the man.[38] Apart from such unusual cases the general practice was to appoint *Zakāt* collectors. Even the capital city had one. These collectors were first trained in the law of *Zakāt* and the ethics of tax collection. The story of one such trainee has been briefly mentioned above. The story goes like this:

> A man from Banū Taghlib narrated: I called on the Prophet (peace be upon him) and embraced Islam. Then he taught me Islam and taught me the way to take *Ṣadaqa* from my tribe *(qawm)* which had embraced Islam. Then I came back to the Prophet (peace be upon him) again and said: O Messenger of God! I still remember everything you taught me but *Ṣadaqa*. So may I work as an *'āshir* (general tax collector)? The Prophet (peace be upon him) said: No, the taxes *('Ushūr)* are on Christians and Jews.[39]

Some reports indicate that these collectors were given written instructions.[40] In most cases the collectors belonged to the tribe where they were deputed, but not always.[41]

In the Prophet's time the collectors were not salaried officials. They were, however, paid something from *Zakāt* funds. This head of *Zakāt* expenditure is derived from the Qur'ānic phrase *'wa'l 'āmilīn 'alayha'* (the officials of *Zakāt*). This is also confirmed by the stories narrated by the historians. 'Umar, the Prophet's collector in Madina,[42] said that the Prophet (peace be upon him) assigned him some work and paid for it.[43] According to Ibn Sa'd, two of the Prophet's kinsmen, 'Abd al-Muṭṭalib b. Rabī'a and Faḍl b. 'Abbās, requested the Prophet (peace be upon him) to assign them to collect *Zakāt* in order that this might become a source of earning for them. The Prophet (peace be upon him) refused on the ground that they were his kinsmen for whom earnings from *Zakāt* funds were undesirable.[44] The Prophet (peace be upon him) did not allow even his *mawlā,* Abū Rāfi', to act as assistant to a collector on the same ground, arguing that a *mawlā* is treated as belonging to his master's tribe.[45]

The public response to the collectors varied. In some cases people willingly offered more and better quality than they were required to do.[46] On the other hand there are reports of complaints and grievances lodged by the *Zakāt*-payers, which were sometimes remedied by the Prophet (peace be upon him) and sometimes rejected, which meant that the reports were not realistic.[47]

The assessment of *Zakāt* in the case of animals, cash, gold and silver was a simple matter. However in the case of food-grain and dates, it must have been cumbersome as it involved a metric system of weights and measures. It is not certain why this metric system had gained sanctity since ancient times. Divisions and sub-divisions in geometric ratio (1/2, 1/4, 1/8, 1/16) would be easier in the absence of large weighing scales than the metric system (100, 50, 25, 10, 5, 2 1/2). For instance, four sub-divisions of a quarter gives the quotient 1/16 while to obtain 1/10 the division is relatively difficult and cumbersome: divide unto halves; then sub-divide one half into five equal parts to give the quotient 1/10, a seventh sub-division of a part gives 1/20 and an eighth one, 1/40. It is not known how this difficulty was resolved in the case of food-grain. But in the case of dates and grapes, experts were sent to estimate the *expected* total produce and *Zakāt* was then assessed on the basis of this conjecture and not the exact quantity of the crop.[48] To eliminate any possibility of injustice, a third or sometimes a quarter of the estimated quantity was first exempted from assessment.[49] *Zakāt* was collected only when the crop was picked out and became ready for use. Bukhārī has narrated on the authority of Yaḥyā b. Ādam about the practice of receiving an equivalent substitute for *Zakāt* on food-grain. Yaḥyā has reported on the authority of Ṭā'ūs that Mu'ādh said in Yemen: 'Bring me cloth or garments, which I shall accept in place of *Ṣadaqa* (on food-grain) as it is easier for you and better for the Emigrants.' But Qasṭalānī has expressed doubts about Ṭā'ūs's direct hearing from Mu'ādh. According to him another source, Bayhaqī, has narrated the story with another chain of narrators *(isnād)* and it suggests the substitution for *Jizya* but not *Zakāt*. This has further confused the issue because the levy of *Jizya* in Yemen was already stipulated in the form of money or garments. The '*Jizya* on land' could be in the form of food-grain but some reports suggest that land in Arabia was charged *Ṣadaqa ('Ushr)*. And it might have been that *Ṣadaqa* which Mu'ādh had offered to substitute. In any case it was later on believed on the basis of such reports that *Zakāt* on a commodity could be paid in the form of its equivalent value and that it could be transferred from one place to another.[50] The conclusion drawn from the report does not seem to be far-fetched because in the case of *Zakāt* on camels, the difference in the age of the camel, or the levy in the form of sheep/goats was substituted by the Prophet (peace be upon him) for dirhams – a goat commutable at ten dirhams, a two-year-old she-camel plus two goats or plus twenty dirhams was held as a substitute for a three-year-old camel.[51]

Zakāt payment was required after the lapse of one full year or on harvest. There is evidence to show that advance payment was also made.[52] Payment of *Zakāt* did not absolve all the financial liability of the Muslims towards the society or the state, for the Prophet (peace be upon him) not only made it voluntary to pay *Zakāt* even on exempted amounts and items[53] but also encouraged people to pay voluntarily more than was legally due as *Ṣadaqa*. He is reported to have said: 'It is a duty from God which is incumbent upon Muslims. It is better for him who increases in the amount of its payment.'[54]

The *Zakāt* collectors did not have a free hand in collecting *Zakāt* or distributing it or remitting any balance to the Prophet (peace be upon him). Many of them were required to produce accounts. When Ibn al-Lutbiyya submitted his accounts he set aside the articles which he had received by way of gifts and this was taken very seriously by the Prophet (peace be upon him).[55]

Distribution of *Zakāt* Funds

Zakāt receipts, like any other income, were not retained by the Prophet (peace be upon him) even for a few days. He distributed them as soon as they were received. Camels were an exception to this practice because they were generally retained for distribution among the fighters. Outstanding claims and requests were also accommodated.[56] It is believed that these funds must have been spent on the beneficiaries specified in the Qur'ān because no evidence to the contrary is available.

Bukhārī has narrated that the Prophet (peace be upon him) once branded camels with his own hands.[57] There must have been others to do this time-consuming job but the Prophet's precedent inspired the early caliphs, as rulers, to exert personal care in discharging their duties towards the people.

Caliph Abū Bakr's War on Apostates

The institution of *Zakāt* continued after the Prophet's demise without any considerable change. The beginning of Abū Bakr's reign was marked by an immediate challenge to it, but the situation was soon brought under control and the threat averted. The historians have unfortunately mixed up the issue of apostasy and of the non-payment of *Zakāt* in such a way as to give a dreadful picture of the revolt against paying *Zakāt*. But an analysis of the different aspects involved in the issue does not support that impression.

Before the Prophet's death, some claimants to the prophethood had already appeared. Aswad al-'Anasī who had gathered much support had been killed the day before the Prophet's death, yet he left an obstinate contingent of followers who continued to operate in and around Yemen. The Prophet's death encouraged many other ambitious persons to stake their claim to the prophethood. Musaylima again became active and was now joined by a 'prophetess', Sajāḥ and her followers. Their field of operation was the tribes of Tamīm with a foothold in Banū Ḥanīfa. Ṭulayḥa sought support in the near north of Madina and got some following. Dhū't-Tāj, though not prominent, became active in some areas of Baḥrayn.[58]

Besides these claimants to prophethood and their followers, there were a few tribes who, although they did not follow any of them, refused to pay *Zakāt.* Examples are Banū Kalb, Ṭayyi' and Dhubyān.

A third group consisted of those tribes which did not believe in these Prophets. Though they did not press their refusal to pay *Zakāt,* they perhaps had serious doubts about the future of the Muslims and Islam. They did not like to take sides at this indecisive stage of the struggle and were, therefore, reluctant to pay *Zakāt* to the central government collectors. Examples are Sulaym,[59] Hawāzin and 'Āmir.

Believing in the prophethood of the above-mentioned claimants was, in Islamic law, tantamount to apostasy; but refusal to pay *Zakāt* could be termed apostasy when it was established that a person disbelieved in the obligatory nature of *Zakāt.* And this seems to be a doubtful claim. Caliph Abū Bakr is nowhere stated to have adjudged that the persons refusing only *Zakāt* were apostates. His line of approach was that he was not agreeable to their making any distinction between the prayers *(Ṣalāt)* and *Zakāt*[60] and that he would not spare anybody who did not pay his *Zakāt* to the central government – as was done during the Prophet's time.[61] While his first condition can be interpreted in a variety of ways, the second condition possibly implies that the problem was not that of paying *Zakāt* as such – it was that of paying *Zakāt* to the government at the centre. That is why there are reports to suggest that during this period of turmoil most of these tribes generally paid their *Zakāt* to other people. According to Ṭabarī for example, 'Qays revolted (against the provincial government of Ṣan'ā) and exacted taxes from the neighbouring areas. But he was indifferent as to whether he should follow Abū Bakr or (the followers of) al-Aswad.'[62] Whatever his own attitude might have been, the report clearly shows that people were already paying *Zakāt.* In the same way, when Zibriqān and Aqra' called on Abū Bakr (perhaps to pay their collections of *Zakāt*) they requested him 'to write for them the *Kharāj* (incomes) of Baḥrayn and promised that none of their community will desert Islam'.[63] This story, produced by Ṭabarī, supports the same point. Similarly, the collectors who were sent to the tribes of Tamīm had already collected the *Zakāt* and were now waiting for each other's action in regard to sending the *Zakāt* collections to the government or spending it within their own tribes or clans.[64] The full story of these collectors, as reported by Ṭabarī, makes the point more clearly understandable:

'The Prophet (peace be upon him) had already sent out his collectors to Banū Tamīm before he died.

Zibriqān b. Badr was the collector in (the clans of) Rabāb 'Awf and Abnā'.

Qays b. 'Āṣim was the collector in Muqā'is and the attached clans.

Ṣafwān b. Ṣafwān and Sabra b. 'Amr were the collectors in Banū 'Amr; the latter was at Bahda while the former was at Khadm. Both (Bahda and Khadm) are the clans of Tamīm.

Wakī' b. Mālik and Mālik b. Nawīra were the collectors in Banū Ḥanẓala: one for Banū Mālik the other for Banū Yarbū'. When Ṣafwān got the news of the Prophet's death he packed up the collections of his own region and those of Sabra's region and joined Abū Bakr. Sabra stayed in his place because of the nuisance of Rabāb.

Qays waited quietly to watch what Zibriqān was doing because Zibriqān was angry with Qays and had always frustrated his attempts to improve his relations with Zibriqān. Now Qays waited for Zibriqān's move so that he could go against him. When he found that Zibriqān had not given any indication as to what he was planning, he said: "Woe to Ibn al-'Ukliyya! He has frustrated all my plans. I fail to understand what to do. If I follow Abū Bakr and give him the *Zakāt* collections, he might spend them among Banū Sa'd and Zibriqān will let me down in those clans. On the other hand, if I spend these collections among Banū Sa'd he will let me down before Abū Bakr." Qays at last decided to distribute those funds among Muqā'is and other clans and acted upon this plan. Zibriqān remained faithful and followed Ṣafwān to Madina with his collections from Rabāb, 'Awf and Abnā. After his return there was everywhere a general turmoil and apostasy and everybody began to think of his own self. But Qays regretted what he had done and when 'Alā al-Ḥaḍramī came to him, he collected the *Ṣadaqāt* of his region and went to 'Alā on his own, to follow him in *Jihād*.'[65]

The story speaks for itself. There is nothing in it to suggest that most of the clans refused to pay *Zakāt*. On the contrary, there is surprising evidence in the story of the willingness of some clans even to pay their *Zakāt* twice. This, and all the other stories of this kind as reported by Ṭabarī also suggest that the outstanding *Zakāt* for the year had already been paid out in most of the places. Therefore, there was now no question of paying the *Zakāt* again the same year. The funds were now lying with the collectors. Therefore, the question of refusal to pay *Zakāt* was not very relevant in the case of the general public; it was mostly relevant in the case of tribal collectors. And for those collectors who refused only to deposit *Zakāt* with the centre, the issue was whether a central, or in other words, an extra-tribal authority had any right to levy any taxes on them. The problem of Tamīm and the surrounding tribes took a serious turn only when Musaylima, joined by Sajāh, resorted to violence.

Further proof of the assertion can be found in the nature of Caliph Abū Bakr's operations against the revolting groups. Ṭabarī mentions eleven different expeditions which Abū Bakr sent out to suppress the revolts.[66] Map 2 shows how most of these expeditions were directed against those areas which were occupied by the claimants of 'prophethood' with the exception of a few tribes in the north (see no. 5 on the map) or some indifferent tribes in the near south of Madina (no. 8), but even there the possibility of indirect influence of Ṭulayḥa cannot be ruled out. This is further supported by the report, if accepted to be equally plausible, that within three months of the beginning of his reign, Caliph Abū Bakr received 'such large amounts of *Ṣadaqa* as to exceed the requirements of the Muslims (of Madina).'[67]

Along with this small group of non-payers of *Zakāt,* mention may also be made of the tribes of Ḥaḍramawt who were willing to pay *Zakāt* but, because of mishandling by the collector, matters took a different turn. The Prophet (peace be upon him) is reported to have warned the collectors not to take nice properties in *Zakāt.*[68] The collector in one of the cases looked at an excellent young camel, he felt tempted towards it and marked it for collection as *Zakāt.* Another technical flaw in this respect, as pointed out by the assessee, was that it did not belong to him. This led to a heated exchange of words and the collector, unmindful of the general situation throughout the country, unjustifiably resorted to force. This worsened the situation and gradually a general revolt spread.[69] As a result Abū Bakr had to despatch a contingent to suppress the revolt.

The question still remains as to why these few tribes refused to pay *Zakāt* and why the apostates mixed up the issue with their alliance with the new 'prophets'? It is hardly credible that those tribes also primarily wished to avoid the payment of *Zakāt* and, in order to cope with any threatened action against them, took refuge with the claimants of prophethood. It cannot be denied that for a long time it had been against Arab traditions to pay any tribute to any government (and there was also no organized government in Arabia except in the far south). While the early Greek historian, Herodotus, mentions the payment of tribute by the subordinate princes to the emperor of Persia, he makes a mention of the Arab exemption from paying these taxes.[70] This fact dates this Arab tradition centuries back. It is also reported by Ṭabarī that Qurra who was backed by a large army of Banū 'Āmir said to 'Amr: 'Arabs will not willingly pay tax on their incomes. But if you condone it, they will listen to you. If you disagree I doubt they will support you.'[71]

These arguments have been partly examined in the preceding discussion and a further examination of the situation will make it clear. The presumption of the general refusal on this ground would imply that they were observing all other basic obligations of Islam. But it seems it was not so. The first test of their loyalty to Islam which Abū Bakr suggested to Khālid was to see if they also offered their prayers with and like the

Map. 2. Arabia During Apostasy

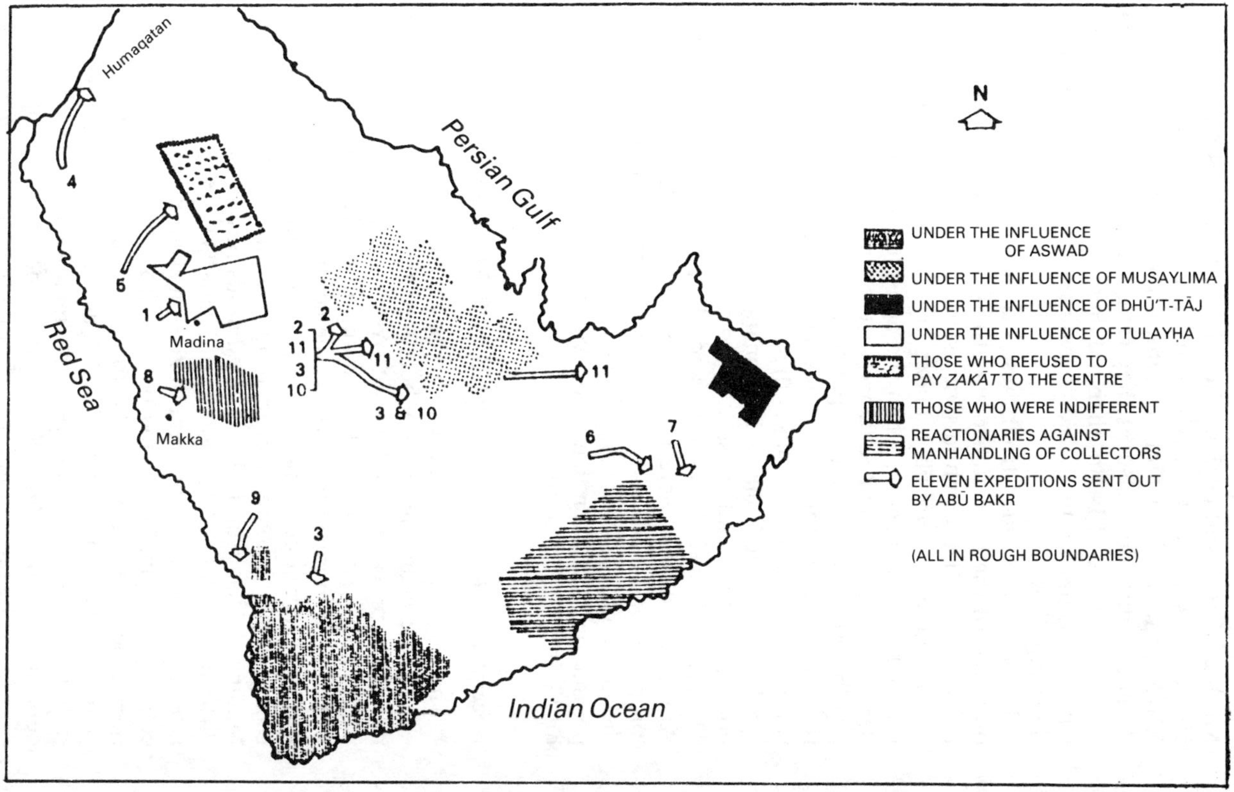

Humaqatan
Persian Gulf
Red Sea
Indian Ocean
Madina
Makka
N
UNDER THE INFLUENCE OF ASWAD
UNDER THE INFLUENCE OF MUSAYLIMA
UNDER THE INFLUENCE OF DHŪ'T-TĀJ
UNDER THE INFLUENCE OF TULAYḤA
THOSE WHO REFUSED TO PAY ZAKĀT TO THE CENTRE
THOSE WHO WERE INDIFFERENT
REACTIONARIES AGAINST MANHANDLING OF COLLECTORS
ELEVEN EXPEDITIONS SENT OUT BY ABŪ BAKR
(ALL IN ROUGH BOUNDARIES)

Muslims.[72] It was after this 'acid test' that the question of their conduct about *Zakāt* arose. Similarly Abū Bakr wrote to all his commanders: 'Give them an opportunity to reform themselves. If they accept, then do not disturb them. But if they refuse, then attack them unless they re-enter the fold of Islam, then tell them their rights and duties. Collect whatever is due on them and pay whatever is due to them. Do not give them any time . . . '[73]

It can be concluded from these instructions that the matter was not only that of their reluctance about paying *Zakāt,* but also that of their attitude to other essentials of Islam. This situation seems to have developed most probably under the influence of the claimants of prophethood. Secondly, when the apostates turned against Islam, the demonstration of their defiance of the central authority of Islam was possible only by refusing the payment of *Zakāt* – the only expression of the supremacy of the central government. If *Zakāt* was withdrawn the centre's interest in controlling these regions automatically weakened. It would, then, need only a little manoeuvring to finally throw out the non-tribal Muslim administrator and replace him by a 'brother apostate'. Thirdly, as Map 2 shows, it was not the general thinking of most of the Arabs. Those who were under the influence (free or coercive) of the 'prophets' and made it a pretext for non-payment of *Zakāt* belonged to the group of Ṭulayḥa which formed a very small segment of the Arab population. And even that group was the first to re-embrace Islam when hit by the Muslim army.

Receipt of *Zakāt* During Caliph Abū Bakr's Time

Thanks to the firm and swift action by Abū Bakr and the lack of unity among the claimants of prophethood, the revolt was suppressed and normalcy prevailed throughout Arabia within a few months. The institution of *Zakāt* began functioning as it did during the Prophet's time with the difference that perhaps the centre's share in *Zakāt* collections was now increased. That is why, within three months of Abū Bakr's reign, *Zakāt* income exceeded the requirements of the people of Madina.[74] That Abū Bakr received in his *Bayt al-Māl* a total of 200,000 dirhams (excluding commodities) during his entire period of caliphate is a figure that does not seem to give an accurate idea of the total *Zakāt* collections during his period because from Baḥrayn alone the Prophet (peace be upon him) is stated to have received 80,000 dirhams in one year.[75] This amount included *Zakāt* as well as *Jizya.* What Abū Bakr is stated to have received perhaps mentions that amount which he deposited in the *Bayt al-Māl,* but not those receipts which were distributed by him without transferring them to the *Bayt al-Māl.* For no period under study are the figures for the collection of *Zakāt* available, nor can they be worked out.

The Use of Analogy in *Zakāt*

The beginning of the era after the Prophet (peace be upon him) brought with it new problems and challenges in respect of the institution of *Zakāt* too. The conquests of the new territories added new lands with new owners, new products and new sources of income. The rates of *Zakāt* which were fixed in the less wealthy Arab society could now be seen to be incommensurate with rising levels of income, fixed salaries to all the army personnel, and addition of much more fertile tracts of land with enormous potentials of yield. It will be recalled that some of the letters that are said to have been written by the Prophet (peace be upon him) contained two claims – payment of *Jizya* at a fixed rate per head and payment of *Zakāt* at a fixed rate of the value of the item in question. In other words, it was the established practice of the Prophet – the *Sunna* – to charge *Jizya* and *Zakāt* at particular rates . But since the very early days after the Prophet (peace be upon him) a part of this *Sunna* was subjected to major changes but the other part was left untouched and later on it was taken to enjoy the sanctity by way of *Ijmā',* consensus. An example of tampering with the terms of *Jizya* is the one levied on the non-Muslims of Najrān who, like the non-Muslims of Ḥimyar, Ayla, or Baḥrayn were levied at a rate of one dīnār per head or in the case of Najrān, 2,000 *ḥullas ad-valorem.* It was reduced and revised by the later rulers so much so that Umar II refixed it at 200. The rationale was that because *Jizya* in this case was levied on heads and the number of heads of *Jizya*-paying persons had declined, the total should have been reviewed but not the rate per head. But firstly, in the case of the per-head levy too the rate of one dīnār was not followed in newly conquered territories and, secondly, in *Zakāt* also the subject of levy – land produce or the level of opulence – had undergone considerable change, and thus the paying capacity.

Another point that the early caliphs and the later rulers had to face was their behaviour towards new items of wealth which were vaguely mentioned in *Ḥadīth* or altogether omitted. In this respect the early caliphs and Umayyad rulers exercised their independent judgement on the basis of analogy. Although the report that Caliph Abū Bakr started to deduct the amount of outstanding *Zakāt* from pensions or salaries[76] *(Waẓīfa)* cannot be reliable without a clear explanation of the sense of pension, because in his reign, as the historians report, neither were pensions fixed nor any salaries distributed, yet a similar report about Caliph 'Uthmān[77] can be treated as plausible and seems to have been an effective means of deducting outstanding *Zakāt* at source. Mu'āwiya is also reported to have followed the same practice.[78]

While analogy was being used to expand the application of *Zakāt* to new items of wealth, Caliph 'Uthmān's decision to withdraw from collecting *Zakāt* on non-apparent wealth, *māl bāṭin*[79] had far-reaching effects. Other decisions that were taken by the caliphs, on the basis of analogy were the inclusion of new items of wealth for the purpose of the levy of *Zakāt* and the use of analogy in determining the rates of *Zakāt* on and exemption limits for these newly introduced items. The number of these items was limited to only those which were mentioned by the Prophet (peace be upon him). The list of such items was gradually expanded. Caliph Abū Bakr levied *Zakāt* on *vars*.[80] *Zakāt* on honey was a disputed issue but Caliph 'Umar was in favour of levying *Zakāt* on it.[81] He introduced another innovation to distinguish between honey collected in the mountains and that obtained in the plains and fixed a rate of one-twentieth for the former and one-tenth for the latter,[82] perhaps because more labour was involved in the former case. He also levied *Zakāt* on *sawā'im* horses[83] (pastured horses reared for multiplying) and a fifth on the produce of waters.[84] Ibn 'Abbās, the governor of 'Alī in Kūfa, levied *Zakāt* on *dasātij al-kurāth*[85] (a vegetable, presumably non-perishable, and used as spice). Mu'āwiya's innovation was to revise the rate of *ṣadaqat al-fiṭr* in terms of wheat and reduce it to half the quantity of barley[86] fixed by the Prophet (peace be upon him). He did it perhaps because of their relative difference in quality and price. Ḥajjāj advised that *Zakāt* be levied on pearls[87] at the rate of twenty per cent. He also levied *Zakāt* on vegetables,[88] but it seems that the defiance of the levy by a Prophet's Companion on the authority of a *Ḥadīth* made him withdraw.[89] 'Umar II changed 'Umar I's policy of levying *Zakāt* on horses and honey[90] and reduced 'Umar I's rate on fish from 20 per cent (tech. *Khums*) to two and a half per cent, subject to an exemption limit up to the value of 200 dirhams.[91] He also levied *Zakāt* on minerals at a rate of two and a half per cent and added lentils and pulses to be charged like wheat, etc. viz., 5 per cent to 10 per cent.[92]

Caliph 'Umar took a very important decision of changing the rates of *Ṣadaqa* as a substitute for *Jizya* leviable on the non-Muslims of Banū Taghlib.[93] The reports recorded by most historians are almost alike. Yaḥyā reports that 'Ubāda b. an-Nu'mān said to 'Umar: 'O commander of the faithful! You know the might of the Banū Taghlib when they are facing the enemy and should they assist the enemy against you, it would be a burdensome affair. Therefore if you decide to give them something, do so.' Thereupon he made a treaty with them, stipulating that they should not baptize their children as Christians and that the *Ṣadaqa* should be doubled on them.[94] According to this treaty Banū Taghlib paid double the *Ṣadaqa* that was imposed on Muslims from everything on which Muslims paid the *Zakāt,* such as camels, cows, sheep, grains, and fruits. But nothing will be taken from anything which falls below the exemption limits.[95] Caliph 'Umar took this decision when, in the case of another Arab Christian tribe, Ghassān, he had refused such conditions and as a result, the latter – 30,000 strong – reportedly migrated and joined the Byzantine ruler. Caliph 'Umar was made to realize the disadvantages of his political decision. It is reported that he later on offered the same conditions to Jabala, the Ghassanid chief, but he refused to accept the offer.[96] Later on Mu'āwiya is reported to have succeeded in bringing him round, but Jabala died before he could return. Aghnides has recorded two more cases of the same nature during the Umayyad period: those of Balkh and Sughd – both were exempted from *Jizya* and levied *Ṣadaqa.*[97]

Along with these new levies, decisions were taken about giving exemption to some new items. Caliph 'Umar exempted pomegranates and apricots from *Zakāt,* because 'they were of the thorny trees', although their yield was many times more valuable than that of vineyards.[98]

There was a precedent that the Prophet (peace be upon him) received advance payment of *Zakāt,* but there was no precedent of putting it off. Caliph 'Umar, at the time of famine in and around Madina *('ām-ar-ramāda)* put off the *Zakāt* collections for a year perhaps in Arabia only and then collected the outstanding claims the next year.[99] Caliph 'Alī exempted apples and similar fruits. There is also a report that the provincial government of Iraq exempted mineral produce like oil, and mica *(ze'baq)* in order to boost their production.[100] 'Umar II, contrary to the decision of Caliph 'Umar, exempted *sawā'im* horses and honey.[101]

In respect of land, Caliph 'Umar decided that if the owners of agricultural land in Iraq embraced Islam before their conquest, their land would be treated as *Zakāt ('Ushr)* land but not *Kharāj* land. Balādhurī reports of some such lands at 'Uyūn aṭ-Ṭuf (the springs of aṭ-Ṭuf).[102] Similar was the case with many lands along the Euphrates.[103] Ḥajjāj converted all such lands into *Kharāj* lands. 'Umar II again converted them into *'Ushr* land. The Governor, 'Umar b. Hubayra, again levied *Kharāj* on them. But Hishām reconverted many of them into *'Ushr* lands. At last the 'Abbāsid Caliph al-Mahdī restored them according to 'Umar II's decision.[104] The border belt of Syria which was allotted to Muslims also paid *'Ushr.*[105]

Collection and Distribution of *Zakāt*

The total collections of *Zakāt* cannot be determined for any period up to the end of the Umayyad rule. The historians and geographers have given many valuable statistical details about the later period but they cannot be made a point of analogy, interpolation or extrapolation for want of information about as many factors as the changes in population, religion, land tenancy system, and other sources of income and the per-head average holding of wealth liable to *Zakāt.* While income by way of *Zakāt* and *Jizya* from Baḥrayn in the Prophet's time is claimed to be 80,000 dirhams, it rose to 500,000 dirhams in Caliph 'Umar's time.[106] This ratio of increase within a few years suggests the irrelevance of any guesswork in respect of a whole province, let alone the whole of the empire.

The policy of local distribution of *Zakāt* continued at many places during Caliph 'Umar's reign. According to a report by Sa'īd b. al-Musayyib, Mu'ādh was appointed as collector in Banū Sa'd or Banū Dhubyān. He collected their *Zakāt,* distributed it locally, and returned empty-handed.[107] Sa'd (b. Abī Waqqāṣ) who was a collector with Ya'lā b. Umayya reported: 'We used to go out for collecting *Zakāt* and had nothing with us on our return except our lashes.'[108] The situation changed only with the change in the level of incomes brought about, *inter alia,* by the distribution of *Zakāt.* This policy continued at least for about a century in some districts. This was perhaps one of the factors that made it difficult to record the figures of *Zakāt.* It might, however, be conceived that *Zakāt* proceeds should have gradually increased with the increase in opulence and fresh conversions to Islam. During Caliph 'Umar's time the converted Muslims in far-off districts like Barqa and Zawīla are reported to have started paying their *Zakāt* (and *'Ushr*).[109] That Caliph 'Umar had to add new grazing fields as *ḥimā* and Caliph 'Uthmān made further additions to them suggest the ever-increasing number of *Zakāt*-camels and livestock. Caliphs 'Umar and 'Alī are reported to have pressed that a person receiving pension must pay *Zakāt.*[110] It has already been recorded that in many a case it was deducted at the time of the payment of these pensions.[111] In the later period when chaos set in and when the confidence of the Muslims in the integrity of their rulers was shaken, the attitude of many people might have been affected and they might have wanted to stop paying *Zakāt* to the government. But it seems that the Companions of the Prophet (peace be upon him) not only continued to pay *Zakāt* to the government but also persuaded other Muslims to do the same. They included persons like mother 'Ā'isha, Ibn 'Umar, Sa'd, Abū Hurayra, and Abū Sa'īd al-Khudrī.[112]

There are no reports of any change brought about in the mode of assessment of *Zakāt.* The probable reason could be that the early caliphs' faithful following of the Prophet's system made it a matter of convention and any deviation from it would be tantamount to offending the *Zakāt*-payers – the Muslims.

The Policy and the Heads of Distribution

The policy of distribution was affected by many considerations generally without prejudice to the Qur'ānic heads of expenditure. Local distribution was preferred but it seems that the requirements of the central or provincial *Bayt al-Māl* were also not neglected. The practices during the early caliphate have already been discussed in the preceding pages. It is reported that 'Umar II wrote to his collectors to send half the *Zakāt* to the centre and distribute the other half locally. But the next year he wrote to them to retain all the *Zakāt* collections[113] and distribute them locally presumably because the centre did not need it. Caliph 'Umar I seemed to have been very particular about spending the *Zakāt* collections among the Arab villagers. This is evident from the report that on his death-bed, he advised his successors to return to them whatever was received so much so that each of the village men should become the (prospective) owner of a hundred camels.[114] In his later period Caliph 'Umar is also reported to have made a change in the general policy of distribution. Formerly he was convinced about the soundness of discriminating between people on the basis of their services to Islam but later on he seems to have become inclined towards equal distribution.[115] He is also reported to have included non-Muslims among the beneficiaries of *Ṣadaqa* by virtue of their being destitutes, *'masākīn'*.[116] The other policy that he liked to press was about the per-head share of distribution. He believed in giving a quantity to each beneficiary which could make him well-off[117] and thus be able to dispense with *Zakāt* the next year. In the list of beneficiaries 'Umar II included the non-Muslims in order to induce them to Islam. He is reported to have given a *biṭrīq* (patriarch) 1,000 dīnārs to 'reconcile his heart'.[118] He wrote to his governors to relieve the resourceless debtors of their liabilities and pay for the dower of the needy persons.[119] He also pressed for an equal distribution of *Ṣadaqa* among the Arabs and non-Arabs.[120]

The policy of distribution of *Zakāt* collections pursued by the rulers can also be inferred from the way they practically utilized these funds. As stated above, *Zakāt* funds were distributed within the tribes of the paying locality for as long as there were deserving cases. In the case of dire necessity the centre could take some or the whole of it. After the minimum level of incomes of the beneficiaries was achieved – when they were no more entitled to receive *Zakāt* – the entire amount of *Zakāt* could be transferred to the centre. It is reported that Mu'ādh remitted a portion of *Zakāt* to Caliph 'Umar on the ground that it exceeded the requirement of his district. Within the next two years the whole of the *Zakāt* receipts are reported to have been declared by him as surplus to local requirements and remitted to Madina.[121] The report suggests that in the district, the general level of incomes was relatively higher than in other districts and as a result the number of deserving persons was also smaller. Moreover, through the process of redistribution of wealth a certain minimum level of incomes was achieved so as to remove them from the list of beneficiaries. The policy seems to have been pursued even in the far-flung newly-converted Muslim communities of Barqa and Zawīla[122] where *Zakāt* collections were distributed *in toto,* during Caliph 'Umar's time. The report that 'Umar II returned the *Zakāt* proceeds of 'Umān for local distribution[123] suggests that at least some of the rulers before him did not care much to satisfy the local requirements. But along with it, the report that the *Zakāt* of Banū Kalb was declared surplus to local requirement and was retained for expending the following year[124] suggests that by that time the distribution of *Zakāt* had already brought some degree of satiety at some places.

The centre spent the *Zakāt* funds generally on items as laid down in the Qur'ān. Some instances of such expenditures give an idea of the interpretation the early rulers gave to these items. According to Abū Dā'ūd, Abū Bakr gave 12,000 *sā'* of food-grains from *Ṣadaqa* of Yamāma in lieu of the hundred camels which were payable to Mujjā'a by way of blood-money.[125] When Salma b. Qays, the messenger of an army commander was returning to join his army unit, Caliph 'Umar gave him two camels from the *Bayt al-Māl* and advised him to give them to the poorer man he found than himself.[126] It was perhaps *Zakāt* funds which were utilized by Caliph 'Umar in setting up meal-houses for the destitute wayfarers and in storing along the route between Makka and Madina 'what would relieve those unable to continue their journey'.[127] Caliph 'Uthmān used to distribute meals in the mosques presumably among the devotees, the wayfarers and the destitute.[128] He also utilized *Zakāt* money to buy a prisoner (of war) for digging graves.[129] Many of the Umayyad rulers used *Zakāt* funds in perfuming and decorating the Prophet's Mosque on Fridays and during the month of Ramaḍān.[130] 'Umar II wrote to his governor that debtors may be helped to discharge their liability with the help of *Zakāt* funds collected from Banū Kalb but declared as surplus from local claims and carried forward for the next year.[131] He fixed a pension of three dirhams (per month?) for each destitute and fifty dirhams for each of the crippled in Baṣra, probably from *Zakāt* funds.[132] He also provided, with *Zakāt* money, bread and curry to the prisoners.[133] Walīd was among those Umayyad rulers who took great interest in public welfare activities. But his period was perhaps the most fertile period for the *Bayt al-Māl.* It cannot, therefore, be claimed that all these welfare services were rendered with *Zakāt* money, nor can they be categorically attributed to general incomes. That he spent the amount from the *Bayt al-Māl* is clear; but from which account, one cannot say. In any case, if he spent these funds from general sources, the *Zakāt* funds must have far exceeded the requirements of the genuine beneficiaries. It will, therefore, be interesting to mention some of the welfare services that he rendered. Ya'qūbī treats him as the first person who set up hospitals *(bīmāristān)* and guest houses, fixed subsistence for the blind, destitute and lepers and distributed meals during the month of Ramaḍān.[134] 'He used to arrange for circumcision of orphans and appoint teachers for them; assigned to those crippled by disease, persons to attend them and for the blind those to lead them; settled a daily allowance on the doctors of law; forbade the poor from begging and assigned to them what would suffice them for their maintenance. He used to give platters of silver which were divided among the readers of the Qur'ān at the Mosque of Jerusalem.'[135] While most of these expenditures could be made from *Zakāt* money, it is not known if Walīd did so.

Administration of *Zakāt* Funds

Zakāt was one of the sources of income to the *Bayt al-Māl* but its management could not possibly be like the management of other incomes due to the multiplicity of factors. Firstly, a portion of it was due to be distributed locally and thus it was bound to become partially a provincial subject and partially – sometimes even nominally – a central one. Secondly, the heads of *Zakāt* expenditure were strictly confined as compared with general incomes. Thirdly, it was receivable in a variety of kinds ranging from fish to camels and from honey to lentils. Although the *Zakāt* levy could be exchanged in terms of money or a suitable commodity the *Zakāt*-payer would generally find it convenient for him to hand over the commodity which had been assessed. As a result, the collection of *Zakāt* goods brought with it the problems of providing godowns for storing commodities and cattle farms for rearing animals. It is possible that perishable items like green vegetables and fruits were exempted from *Zakāt* because of storage problems. To overcome the problem of storage of non-perishable commodities and rearing the animals, godowns were built and cattle farms earmarked. Like the Prophet (peace be upon him), Caliph 'Umar could also be found personally taking care of the camels of *Zakāt* and preparing a list of the thousands of animals according to their colour and age.[136] The Prophet (peace be upon him) and the early caliphs continued to earmark public lands as *Ḥimā* according to requirements. In order that general incomes and *Zakāt* incomes were not mixed up, separate officers were generally appointed to look after these accounts. This is confirmed by the lists of officials under Umayyad caliphs. Whether there was any mismanagement of *Zakāt* funds can indirectly be inferred. The period of the Pious Caliphs cannot be presumed to have developed any such tendency and, for that matter, the reign of Mu'āwiya too. *Zakāt* was treated as a ritual *('ibāda)* and not a worldly affair *(mu'āmala)* and any deviation from the early conventions could offend the senior Companions of the Prophet (peace be upon him) and even Mu'āwiya would not take the risk of offending them. But the latter situation of anarchy with four different persons claiming caliphate and controlling their respective regions[137] did great harm to the proper functioning of different institutions, including that of *Zakāt.* The confusion, however, cleared in a few years during 'Abd al-Malik's reign. Abū 'Ubayd's report that during the last years of Sa'īd b. Jubayr there arose some grievances about corruption in the expenditure of *Zakāt*[138] is vague but not improbable in a general sense. Mas'ūdī's report that 'Abd al-Malik asked for money to be distributed as pensions and the fact that on one of the bags brought to him, was written 'The head of *Ṣadaqa*'[139] helps us in reaching an interesting conclusion, although the purpose of the story apparently seems to be to give the impression of 'Abd al-Malik's dislike of Banū Hāshim who were given this bag and were chided by 'Abd al-Malik when they refused to accept it.[140] The story suggests that receipts from different items were kept in bags. Secondly, bags containing the receipts of *Zakāt* at least were inscribed with their special head lest they should be mixed up with other incomes. As regards the other part of the story it can be safely suggested that 'Abd al-Malik would have passed on the bag quite inadvertently because he was an intelligent and well-behaved prince and knew how to observe the decorum of his throne. This cheap method of offence was not becoming of him.

During 'Umar II's reign the whole administration was streamlined. The *Bayt al-Māl* was divided into separate departments, each comprising the income of one head only. Thus *khums* incomes were kept separate from *Zakāt,* and *Zakāt* incomes separate from *Ghanīma,* and so on.[141]

The integrity and character of the *Zakāt* collectors and their officials would have been largely responsible for the nature of public response to this levy. A dishonest and unscrupulous official would harm the popularity of the institution. The general revolt in Ḥaḍramawt during Abū Bakr's reign was caused simply by the irresponsible behaviour of the collector.[142] Such incidents do not seem to have been repeated later on. What is interesting to observe is that 'Umar-like rigidity in character was not found in all the officials at any time. The Prophet (peace be upon him) censured his collector Ibn al-Lutbiyya for accepting gifts from the tribes in his jurisdiction. When Mu'ādh, during Caliph 'Umar's reign, returned to his house empty-handed, his wife criticized him and compared him with 'other officers who returned home with loads of gifts with them'.[143] This is a meaningful comment on the general behaviour of the officials and justifies Caliph 'Umar's punitive action against them by taking away half or in some cases the whole of their property.[144]

In spite of this tendency in the very early period it does not seem to have taken appalling proportions till late in the Umayyad period, although this period is assumed to be permeated with evils in the government, as also in the society. How, then, during this period was *Zakāt* managed? This can be inferred from the speech given by Yaẓīd III. This speech is, in fact, a statement of 'confessions' of the misdoings of the past governments and also reflects the main grievances of the people. If this statement does not contain any confessions about the mismanagement of *Zakāt* funds or misbehaviour of the officials, it may imply that there was no popular agitation against the institution or its management.

> I shall also not transfer money from one place to another unless the place has been well protected and its people are given sufficiently to strengthen themselves,[145]

is the only sentence which, in the immediate context of the preceding discussion about the local distribution of *Zakāt,* may divert the mind to the transfer of the whole *Zakāt* to the centre before Yaẓīd III's period. But in view of the fact that ever since 'Abd al-Malik's period the people had become over-sensitive to the centre's supremacy over the provincial *Bayt al-Māl,*[146] the proposition that the statement alludes to *Zakāt* receipts cannot readily be accepted. And this fact implies the absence of any public grievance about the management of *Zakāt* funds.

Notes and References

1. Chapter 1, note on *Zakāt.*
2. For relevant basic details see Chapter 1, note on *Zakāt.*
3. Rev. A.H. Sayce, *Babylonians and Assyrians – Life and Custom,* London, 1900, p. 253.
4. Sira, 2, 381.
5. Sad., III, 2, 139.
6. Tab., 1, 1601; Tir., 3, 117, 148, etc.
7. Pp. 90 and 89 respectively.

8. Tab., 1, 1750.

9. *Ibid.*, 1600–1.

10. 2, 384, 387.

11. 1, 1750; 1, 1600–1.

12. 973.

13. 1, 75.

14. II, 1, 115, 116; IV, 1, 17; 2, 64, 76.

15. Sira, 2, 381; also see Chapter 1, discussion on *Zakāt.*

16. Abu Daud, 2, 141; Mus., 7, 73.

17. See pp. 171–2.

18. Abu Daud, 3, 230.

19. Tir., 3, 106–7.

20. Of late there has been some discussion on the authenticity of these letters. The writer is inclined to accept the findings of the latest work on the subject written by 'Awn ash-Sharīf Qāsim, entitled *A Critical Re-examination of the Treaties and Letters of Muhammad.* A thesis for M.A. (typescript) 1961–62, London University.

21. Sira, 2, 380–1.

22. 'Awn ash-Sharīf Qāsim, *op. cit.,* note 20.

23. *Ibid.*

24. *Loc. cit* (italics are mine).

25. *Loc. cit* (italics are mine).

26. Sad., IV, 2, 77.

27. Abu Daud, 2, 141; also *cf.* Chapter 1.

28. Tir., 3, 148; Maq. ('Ilm.), I, 433.

29. A.U., 1911.

30. Abu Daud, 2, 155.

31. See also below.

32. 'Umar Abū 'n-Naṣr: *'Umar ibn al-Khaṭṭāb,* Beirut, 1935, p. 185.

33. Sad., I, 2, 119.

34. Bal., 92.

35. *Ibid.*

36. Sad., IV, 1, 17, 40.

37. Bal., 48.

38. Waq., 682.

39. Abu Daud, 3, 230.

40. See p. 171.

41. For a study of this tribal relationship see Watt (Medina), pp. 366–8. The list also includes the collectors of *Zakāt (muṣaddiqs).*

42. Abu Daud, 2, 154–5.

43. *Loc. cit.*

44. IV, 1, 40.

45. Sad., IV, 1, 52.

46. Nas., 5, 32–3; Abu Daud, 2, 137–40.

47. See pp. 171–2. See in particular the italicized portion.

48. Tir., 3, 140–3; Bal., 68.

49. Abu Daud, 2, 148; Tir., 3, 140–1.

50. Yah., 525–6; Qasṭalānī, *Irshād as-Sārī, Sharḥ al-Bukhārī,* n.p., n.d., Vol. 3, 40–1.

51. Nas., 5, 20.

52. Sad., IV, 1, 17.

53. See Chapter 1, notes on *Zakāt* and *Infāq*.

54. Sira, 2, 380, 381.

55. Mus., 12, 220–1; Abu Daud, 2, 154–5.

56. Nas., 5, 89.

57. Bukh., Zakāt, 102.

58. A summary reproduction of Ṭabarī's report, pp. 1, 1871 *et. seq.*

59. Ṭabarī reports that only some of the notables of the tribes became apostates while the common people remained faithful (1, 1871).

60. Tab., 1, 1873.

61. Tab., 1, 1894.

62. Tab., 1, 1991.

63. Tab., 1, 1920.

64. Tab., 1, 1908–9.

65. *Ibid.*

66. Tab., 1, 1880–1. The names of the leaders of these contingents and their destination have been given as follows:

1. Khālid to Ṭulayḥa (immediate north), then to Mālik b. Nawīra.
2. 'Ikrima to Musaylima.
3. Muhājir to contingents of Aswad etc.; also Ḥaḍramawt.
4. Sa'īd b. al-'Ās to borders of Syria.
5. 'Amr al-'Ās to Quḍā'a, Wadī'a and Ḥārith.
6. Ḥudhayfa to Dubba; then to Mahara.
7. 'Arfaja to Mahara.
8. Shurḥabīl to Yamama; then to Quḍā'a.
9. Ṭarīfa to Banū Sulaym.
10. Suwayyid to Tihāma.
11. 'Alā al-Ḥaḍramī to Baḥrayn.

67. Tab., 1, 1880.

68. Muhammad 'Īsa al-Tirmidhī: *Sunan,* Nawal Kishore, Lucknow, Vol. I, 1891, p. 195.

69. Tab., 1999 and below.

70. George Rawlinson, ed.: *History of Herodotus,* London, 1862, Vol. 2, p. 401.

71. ان العرب لا تطيب لكم نفسابالاتاوة فان انتم اعفيتموها من اخذ اموالها فستسمع لكم و تطيع و ان ابيتم فلا ارى ان تجتمع عليكم ،
(Tab., 1, 1880).

72. Tab., 1, 1895–6.

73. Tab., 1, 1884.

74. Tab., 1, 1880.

75. Bal., 92.

76. A.U., 1125.

77. A.U., 1127.

78. Yaq., p. 276. *Cf.* S.A.Q. Husaini: *Arab Administration,* Madras, 1949, p. 112. The story with the three names is reproduced by Saḥnūn more clearly: 'When Abū Bakr gave *'aṭāyā* to the people, he would enquire: Do you possess wealth on which *Zakāt* is payable? If (the receiver) answered in the affirmative, he would deduct *Zakāt* on his wealth; but if (the receiver) answered in the negative, he would hand over their *'aṭā'* without deduction.' Mālik has narrated the same story about 'Uthmān. His report suggests that Mu'āwiya was the first to deduct *Zakāt* from pensions. Saḥnūn b. Sa'īd al-Tanūkhī: *Al-Mudawwanat al-Kubrā,* Vol. II, Matba' Sa'āda, Misr, n.d., pp. 31–2.

79. Al-Kāsānī. 'Alā'uddīn Abū Bakr b. Mas'ūd: *Badā'i' al-Sinā'i'*. Vol. 2, Cairo, 1328 A.H., p. 7 (photo-copy), pub. by Said & Co., Karachi, 1400 A.H.

80. A grassy herb used for making face-powder and perfume. Bal., 85.

81. Bal., 68.

82. A.U., 1490.

83. Ag., 258.

84. Kh., 40, Abū 'Ubayd (894) also adds 'Umar's decision to levy 1/10 *Zakāt* on ornaments and ambergris taken from the sea. But he has expressed doubts about the authenticity of the report. His doubts are justifiable on the basis of analogy because the yields that involve risk and much human labour are generally subjected to the rate of 1/20 and not 1/10.

85. Bal., 85.

86. Mus., 7, 62.

87. A.U., 888.

88. Bal., 83.

89. Yah., 5013.

90. A.U., 1496.

91. A.U., 889.

92. A.U., 1391–2.

93. Ag., 241.

94. Yah., 207.

95. Yah., 200–10; Bal., 185–6; Kh., 68; for exemption limits see Chapter 1, note on *Zakāt*.

96. Bal., 142.

97. Ag., 368.

98. Yah., 548; Bal., 69.

99. Sad., III, 1, 223.

100. Al-Kharbūtlī, 360. The source referred to by the author is Vol. I of Ibn Ādam's *Kitāb al-Kharāj,* p. 7. The original source referred to by him seems to be an unpublished work, and could not be confirmed. This story is, however, not to be found in any of the sources referred to in this study.

101. See p. 184.

102. 296.

103. Bal., 361.

104. *Ibid.*

105. See Chapter 3, also Chapter 10, discussion on Agriculture.

106. Sad., III, 1, 216.

107. A.U., 1912.

108. A.U., 1914.

109. Bal., 226.

110. A.U., 1803–5.

111. See pp. 183–4.

112. A.U., 1786, 88, 89; Sad., III, 1, 105; Kath., 9, 5.

113. A.U., 1901.

114. A.U., 567–8.

115. A.U., 572.

116. Bal., 135; Kh., 72.

117. A.U., 1774.

118. Sad., 5, 258.

119. Sad., 5, 276. While it cannot definitely be claimed that these payments were made only from *Zakāt* money, there is valid reason to believe that because these heads are covered by the Qur'ānic heads of *Zakāt* expenditure 'Umar II would have utilized these funds for them. This is confirmed by other reports too (see pp. 188–9).

120. A.U., 574.

121. A.U., 1911.

122. Bal., 226.
123. Bal., 88.
124. Sad., 5, 257.
125. Abu Daud, 3, 208.
126. Tab., 1, 2719.
127. Sad., III, 1, 203.
128. M.B.Y., 31.
129. Bal., 249.
130. Sad., 5, 245.
131. Sad., 5, 257.
132. Tab., 2, 1367.
133. Kh., 88.
134. 3, 36; also Tab., 2, 1271.
135. Tab., 2, 1271; Sti., 228.
136. Athir, 3, 43.
137. Yaq., 3, 10.
138. A.U., 1811.
139. Mas., 3, 324–5.
140. *Ibid.*
141. Sad., V, 295.
142. See p. 180.
143. A.U., 1912.
144. Chapter 2, p. 107.
145. See Chapter 4, p. 140 for full speech.
146. *Ibid.*

CHAPTER 7

Jizya and *Kharāj*
(Poll-Tax and Land-Tax)

The Qur'ān does not prescribe any rate of poll-tax *(Jizya)* nor does it suggest if it is to be levied per head or in aggregates. It was levied on non-Muslim communities of Arabia during the Prophet's time.

Definition of the Term

The words *kharāj* and *kharj* are used in the Qur'ān three times but not in the sense of land-tax: *'am tas'aluhum kharjan? fa kharaju rabbika khayr'* (or dost thou ask of them any tribute? But the bounty of thy Lord is better . . .). In the *Ḥadīth* the word has been repeated many times and used to signify a variety of meanings in addition to the Qur'ānic sense of return, reward or bounty. Many a time the words *Jizya* and *Kharāj* have been interchanged in the works on *Ḥadīth* and history. For example, the Prophet's advice narrated by Abū Dā'ūd recommends a reduction in the amount of *Kharāj* on one Abū Ṭība who cupped him.[1] Here the word *Kharāj* is used in the sense of a master's levy on his slave.[2] Balādhurī reports that the Prophet (peace be upon him) asked two Najrānite priests to take a serious oath with him *(mubāhala)* but they agreed to pay *Kharāj*.[3] Here the word *Kharāj* is used in the sense of poll-tax. When the same Balādhurī reports about later representations made by the Najrānites he uses the word *Jizya*: 'Najrānites requested 'Umar II to reduce their *Jizya*.'[4] But the more interesting thing is that the reported copy of the letter of treaty with them also uses the word *Kharāj* for *Jizya* levied on them: *'fa mā zādat ḥulal al-kharāj aw naqaṣat 'an al-awāqī',* ('thus whatever exceeds the suits of (stipulated) *Kharāj* or falls short of the *ūqiyya* of silver, will be adjusted . . . ').[5] When Caliph 'Umar ordered his officer in Sawād to allot somebody a stretch of land for horse-rearing he is reported to have written: 'If it is not a "*Jizya*-land" and no "*jizya*-water" flows through it, then give it to him.'[6] Here by the word *Jizya*-land is meant *Kharāj*-land. 'Umar II is reported to have ordered the abolition of the prevalent un-Islamic taxes in the name of *Kharāj*.[7] He is reported to have used the word *ṣadaqa* too to signify general taxes, *Jizya* and *Kharāj*.[8] These are only a few of the many instances of interchange of the two terms. In the following discussion, however, the two words will be used in the meaning fixed by the later jurists and generally understood.

The Origin of *Kharāj* (Land-Tax)

Albeit the words convey the sense of levy, the question is if the Prophet (peace be upon him) or the early caliphs levied any tax on non-Muslims over and above the per-head levy termed as *Jizya*? Of late there has been some controversy on the issue. Some scholars suggest that the concept of *Kharāj* as distinct from *Jizya* originated with 'Umar II, while others attribute it to even a later period.[9] But Dennet's masterly work on the subject[10] repudiates many of the arguments of these scholars and with great skill, candour and sympathy, attributes both the taxes to 'Umar I's reign. His approach leads one to assume – although he did not directly deal with the point – that a double tax on non-Muslims did not enjoy explicit or tacit approval of the Prophet (peace be upon him) – it was 'Umar's innovation. There is some evidence to justify setting aside any such assumption. But it seems more appropriate to first evaluate the issue on the basis of common sense.

It cannot be denied that *Zakāt* is prescribed for Muslims and *Jizya* for non-Muslims. It also cannot be denied that *Zakāt* is incumbent on all the Muslims if they possess gold, silver, articles of trade, camels, livestock, and land produce, irrespective of age, sex or profession. On the other hand, poll-tax *(Jizya)* is not to be levied on women, children, the old and infirm, and monks. It also cannot be denied that the rate of *Zakāt* ranges between two and a half and ten per cent of the holdings while the rate of poll-tax that was levied by the Prophet (peace be upon him) was one dīnār per head. Now if it is believed that the Prophet (peace be upon him) prescribed only these two levies, one for Muslims and the other for non-Muslims, it will imply that he treated non-Muslims as a more privileged and superior class of citizens. That is why children, very old men, infirm persons, women and priests making up about two-thirds[11] of the population were exempted from the levy of poll-tax while almost none of the Muslims possessing wealth beyond the exemption limit were exempted. Similarly the non-Muslim population got off after paying one dīnār per assessed head while the Muslims had to surrender two and a half and ten per cent of their wealth. In an agricultural or nomadic society – and, for that matter, in any modern society – where Muslims and non-Muslims have a similar level of affluence, the Muslims will have to pay many times more than the non-Muslims. Moreover, the *Zakāt*-paying class is deprived of enjoying even the indirect benefit of *Zakāt*[12] while the *Jizya*-paying class can also enjoy the benefits of the payments if the amount is spent on public welfare projects. Even the non-Muslim destitute have been included among the beneficiaries of *Zakāt* funds without contributing anything to it.[13] Furthermore, the amount of poll-tax can be reduced but the rates of *Zakāt* cannot be revised from what have been prescribed by the Prophet (peace be upon him). These points place the Muslims at a great disadvantage as compared with the non-Muslims. This assumption goes against the Qur'ānic spirit of poll-tax, and there is reason to believe that the Prophet (peace be upon him) should not have neglected this point while taxing the two communities otherwise, as discussed above, the non-Muslims will always have an edge over the Muslims. This is an interpretation with which it is difficult to concur. Perhaps the conflict could be resolved by casting doubt on the reports regarding the rates and subjects of *Zakāt* or the meagre measure of the poll-tax. But this presumption cannot be supported by any convincing argument. Another way of solving the problem could be the examination and analysis of statistical evidence but unfortunately the relevant statistical data are missing. The only course that remains is to refer to history. Let us proceed with the premise that Caliph 'Umar levied a land-tax over and above the poll-tax; this he should also have done in Arabia. And had it been so there should naturally have been a reaction to this new pinching measure. Historians have been very careful in recording any tendency of reaction or protest which was caused as a result of any policy measure or as a result of alleged injustice by any ruler. They have been so meticulous in this respect as not to spare even the Prophet's actions and their reaction.[14] But books of history do not record any such reaction in Arabia or even report of Caliph 'Umar's changing the policy of taxing the Arabs. It also cannot be claimed that most of the Arabs had embraced Islam before Caliph 'Umar could think of any such measure because, accepting the initial assumption, Islam was an economically expensive affair and the obligation of *Zakāt,* as compared with one dīnār of poll-tax, was a disincentive to embracing Islam. Caliph 'Umar exiled some of the Jewish and Christian tribes. But this was confined to Khaybar, Fadak and Najrān. The people of Khaybar were working as labourers and were not required to pay any tax. The people of Fadak were required to pay half of their produce but no poll-tax. Other Jews, Christians and Magians generally remained where they had been. This means that Caliph 'Umar did not introduce any change in taxation in Arabia; the non-Muslims paid only what they had been paying during the Prophet's time. Now if it is accepted that the Prophet's period was a '*Kharāj*-free' period it will lead us back to the starting point of controversy that non-Muslims were given a more favoured treatment as compared to Muslims and this assumption makes it irreconcilable with the Qur'ānic objective of levying *Jizya* (poll-tax). Fortunately we have some pieces of evidence in history that give a clue to get us out of this tangle and save us from groping in the dark.

'Yaḥyā reports, on the authority of Ḥasan ibn Ṣāliḥ, that . . . any land that belonged to the Arabs – from whom no *Jizya* is accepted but only conversion or war – is *'Ushr* land. Thus acted the Prophet (peace be upon him) with regard to any Arab land captured by him. He did not impose *Kharāj* on it, but it became *'Ushr* land.'[15] According to Abū Yūsuf: 'The lands of Arab idolaters and the lands of all those from whom *Jizya* is unacceptable and who have to choose between conversion to Islam or death, are *'Ushr* lands, even if the ruler has conquered the land by force. The reason is that the Prophet (peace be upon him) conquered many Arab regions and left them (undistributed) so they were to be treated as *'Ushr* lands to the Last Day.'[16] Balādhurī reports the following situation about Baḥrayn: 'Early in the year A.H. 8 the Prophet (peace be upon him) deputed al-'Alā', to Baḥrayn . . . The two princes (of Baḥrayn) embraced Islam and with them all the Arabs and some of the non-Arabs, Magians, Jews, and Christians made a treaty with al-'Alā', which reads as follows: "In the name of God . . . etc., this is a covenant which is agreed between al-'Alā' and the people of Baḥrayn. It has been agreed in the document that they will share with us their dates keeping the Muslims away from labour. Cursed be the one who does not fulfil it! And per-head *Jizya* will be one dīnār from each man of age." '[17] According to another report by Balādhurī, al-'Alā' reported that he used to collect *'Ushr* from Muslims (of Baḥrayn or Ḥajar) and *Kharāj* from non-Muslims *(mushrik)*.[18] According to a third report by the same historian: 'The Prophet (peace be upon him) did not (need to) have a war against Baḥrayn. Some of the people willingly accepted Islam while some others agreed to pay half of (the produce) of grain and dates.'[19] This evidence is suggestive of the situation that the payment of land-tax by the pagan Arabs, by way of *Zakāt ('Ushr)* was taken for granted. *Jizya* was imposed only on those who had a 'foreign' religion: Jews, Christians, Magians. The reason is also to be found in the same evidence. Arabia had become the nucleus of Islam. It was perhaps taken for granted that because Islam originated in Arabia, the Arabs were to follow no religion other than Islam. If they followed a religion which originated outside the peninsula, they were to be treated as non-Arab. That is why the organized communities of Jews and Christians were gradually ousted from Ḥijaz although they were still within the Muslim lands while individual Jews and Christians were not disturbed. The report that there was a tax-paying Christian in Makka during the Prophet's time is surprising but not unbelievable.[20]

The above leads us to the following points: In the case of land produce Muslims and the pagans of Arabia had to pay similar rates of taxes, and this levy was treated as *'Ushr.* Thus in a sense land-tax was not levied on them because they were prospective Muslims. In another sense land-tax was levied on them with the same rates and conditions as those of *Zakāt* and this tax was termed as *'Ushr, Ṣadaqa* or *Zakāt.* This was over and above the poll-tax which was levied on Jews, Christians, and Magians whose position was somewhat different from pagan Arabs. The non-Muslims of Baḥrayn were required to share their produce over and above the payment of a per-head tax.[21] The Christians and Jews of Najrān were required to pay 2,000 dresses *(ḥulla),* each being worth forty dirhams.[22] This may be a lump sum of tax payable in two equal instalments. It is possible that the aggregate amount was fixed keeping in view the number of heads. For example, there might be 8,000 Jews and Christians who were required to pay the tax at a rate of one dīnār per head. But as a community they were allowed to pay the amount in the shape of dresses of the required amounts. Other charges on them were the loan of war material and provisioning of Muslim messengers for a month. In view of such a large number of dresses, it seems, they were generally craftsmen and not land owners or farmers. The Jews of Maqnā' were to pay a quarter of their woven and spun material, horses, coats of mail and produce of fruits.[23] The Scriptuaries of Tabāla and Jurash were levied a per-head tax amounting to one dīnār each and provisioning of Muslims for three days.[24] Similar conditions were made for the small communities of Ayla, Adhruḥ and Jarbā'.[25] But these seem to have been very small communities probably dwelling in a village or two with small holdings and as a result having too meagre resources to pay anything more than one dīnār per head. This becomes clear from their total payable amount, viz., 300, 100 and 100 dīnārs respectively.[26]

The Prophet (peace be upon him) levied a per-head charge in some cases and a tax on produce or stock-in-trade in others. But both of them could not be termed as *Jizya* which, according to the Qur'ān, was leviable only on non-Muslims. The Prophet (peace be upon him) is also reported to have said that there is no *Jizya* on Muslims and that if anybody accepted Islam he would be exempted from *Jizya.*[27] And yet we find that the caliphs and the later rulers levied land-tax on the Muslims without offending them and with the concurrence of the jurists. This simply means that land-tax was different from *Jizya.* The Qur'ān has expressly prescribed *Jizya* for the Scriptuaries and the Prophet (peace be upon him) extended it only to the other non-Muslim communities. Thus while it is certain that he levied a tax on some groups of non-Muslims over and above *Jizya* (poll-tax) it is not certain as to how he named it. This levy in some cases was a share in total land produce, while in other cases it was the provisioning of Muslims for a few days, or the supply of some arms etc., by way of a loan.[28]

The Spirit of the Poll-Tax

According to the Qur'ān, the spirit of the poll-tax seems to be an expression of non-Muslim subservience (to Islam or to Muslims).[29] But since the very beginning poll-tax and protection *(dhimma)* became interdependent and the concept of guaranteeing protection to the lives and properties, etc. of non-Muslims overshadowed the Qur'ānic concept of subservience and humility *(wa hum ṣāghirūn)*. The Prophet (peace be upon him) is reported to have said: 'Beware! whosoever perpetrated any injustice to a protected person *(dhimmi),* or broke a promise given to him or burdened him beyond his capacity or took away from him anything without his free will, I shall plead for him on doomsday.'[30] The treaties of the Prophet (peace be upon him) reveal emphasis on the responsibility of the state to guarantee protection. Professor Watt attributes this emphasis to the early nomadic custom.[31] Whatever the exact cause, the concept seems to have overshadowed the Qur'ānic spirit. The treaties in Iraq and Syria can be adduced in support of this theory.[32]

The Ethics of Land-Tax

The policy of land-tax was similarly based on the moral principles of justice and equity. And this concept underlay, at least in principle, throughout this period. When Sawād (Iraq) was conquered and assessed for the levy of land-tax, Caliph 'Umar called for two local persons competent to report about the pre-Islamic levy.[33] He then fixed the rate of tax in the light of their evidence. He always insisted that his collectors be kind and just in assessing and levying land-tax. He is reported to have reminded his successors not to tax the protected communities beyond their capacity.[34] When Egypt was conquered Caliph 'Umar advised his governor to find out from the local officials the fiscal secrets of its prosperity, and then devised his policy of taxation in Egypt. In this case also he liked to have direct personal evidence of a local Copt and ensure that justice was observed.[35] When a community was taxed on this principle, no more was to be exacted even if they could bear it. But if they were unable to pay it, the levy was to be made easier for them so that they were not burdened beyond their ability. And this policy was adopted everywhere.[36] In spite of this basic principle of policy, the Caliph repeatedly enquired of his collectors if they had done full justice to tax-payers, whenever they sent to him their tax collections. He continued to warn his officers who were compelled to assure him that the amount of taxes was easily payable by the assessees.[37] During Caliph 'Uthmān's reign one of the conditions that was laid down in the treaty with the prince of Herat was that he would equally distribute the burden of tax among his subjects, which he had agreed to pay to the Muslims.[38] Caliph 'Alī advised his officers not to sell the horses of the tax-payers nor their oxen or cows, nor their summer or winter clothing and insisted on their being kind and lenient and on giving them convenience.[39] According to Yaḥyā, a man from Thaqīf reported: "Alī b. Abī Ṭālib appointed me to supervise Buzurja Sābūr and advised me not to flog anyone or sell his provisions, his winter or summer garments, nor the beasts he works with, and never to let a man stand (in the sun) in order to collect dirhams. So I said: "O Commander of the Faithful! Then I shall return to you as I left you!" And he replied: "Even if you return as you left! Beware! We are ordered to collect from them with 'leniency', *('afw)* which means 'favour'."[40] During Mu'āwiya's reign, when the governor of Iraq was informed of some injustices done by the Muslim collectors, he replaced them with the natives.[41] His standing orders for the collectors were to behave leniently with the tax-payers and not to compel them to sell food-grain and livestock in order to pay their taxes.[42] Ḥajjāj, unnerved by the decline in taxes in Iraq, requested 'Abd al-Malik to allow him to enhance the rates. 'Abd al-Malik declined his request and advised him to be content with whatever he got and to refrain from greed. He also advised him to 'leave something for the farmers so that they may live a comfortable life.'[43] 'Umar II was meticulous in collecting only as much as was just and clean *(ṭayyib)*.[44] He wrote to his governor: 'The religious spirit of the economic laws is justice *('adl)* and generosity *(iḥsān)*. Survey the lands. Appraise the crops. Do not put the burden of barren lands on the fertile nor do it otherwise. Tax an infertile land only as much as it can bear.'[45] He had decreed that the tools and implements of the protected people could not be sold (for taxes).[46] He is also reported to have followed the practice of administering an oath to a delegation of the local population attesting that the collections were made fairly. Once, two such witnesses refused to take an oath before him which led 'Umar II to suspect it to be an unfair collection and so he dismissed the officer concerned.[47] It would not be without interest here to make a mention of the behaviour of some 'notorious' officers in Egypt. While the Muslim historians have treated Qurra b. Sharīk as a tyrant officer, the editor of the *Aphrodito Papyri* is inclined to acquit him of the charges of injustice, oppression and high-handedness.[48] Reference may also be made of the policy speech of Yazīd III which sheds ample light on the policy of taxation which he promised to follow perhaps by reforming the malpractices of his predecessors.[49]

Administration of Land-Tax

The above discussion is sufficient to give an idea of the ethics of taxation of the non-Muslims which most of the rulers generally made a point of following. Justice and generosity are urged. How far these principles were practically adopted remains to be seen.

Before giving a historical account of taxation some basic facts may be laid down. In the Prophet's time, as already discussed above, land-tax was paid by the Muslims as well as by the non-Muslims on their produce. Poll-tax was an additional levy on non-Muslims only. The later conquests of territories outside Arabia raised for the first time the problem of taxing the lands occupied exclusively by the non-Muslim subjects, who were not necessarily prospective Muslims. The taxation background of these lands was entirely different from those in Arabia. They were more fertile, their yield was high, their taxes were many and varied and the rates of taxes were also higher than the five per cent or the ten per cent rates of *Zakāt.* Moreover, the proceeds raised by way of *Zakāt* were to be spent on some specific purposes. Running a big, expanding administration, and waging an unceasing war required general sources of revenue to finance the various requirements. These facts led Caliph 'Umar and his successors to organize the administration of taxes. Thus land-tax as different from *Zakāt,* was extensively levied. Officials of the old pre-Islamic machinery were retained and entrusted with the task of collecting taxes from their respective communities so that the Muslims were not involved in an unpopular and corruptible task and were spared for warfare. Another important limitation of the Muslims was their lack of experience in maintaining account books. In any case, the policy-making authority and the overall supervision of the administration rested with the Muslim officers. Day-to-day routine work was generally looked after by the local staff who used Persian, Greek and Coptic languages. But when they posed a challenge to the Arab capability to run this office, it took the latter no time to switch over to Arabic and hand over tax administration to the Arabs or Arabicized non-Arabs. If the non-Muslim officers in the lower ranks of local assessment and collection were still retained, it was perhaps a matter of convenience without any bias to the concept of doing justice to the protected people. With these introductory observations the history of taxation in different regions can be studied.

ARABIA

About 9 A.H., the Prophet (peace be upon him) wielded his authority over almost the whole of Arabia. There were a large number of people who had not embraced Islam during the Prophet's lifetime. They included Jews, Christians, Magians and pagans *(mushrik)*. Details about the levy of poll-tax on the pagans are not recorded and, as discussed above, they were supposed to be prospective Muslims or were otherwise to be purged out. The following table (Table 4) will help in the study of the position of the *Jizya*-paying communities during the Prophet's time.

Administration and Levy

In Arabia at least the government appointed its own assessors and collectors who were also responsible for collecting *Zakāt* from the Muslims. They often belonged to the tribe to which they were deputed. These arrangements continued during Caliph Abū Bakr's reign, the only exception being a brief period of jeopardy due to apostasy.[50] Caliph 'Umar shifted the Jews and Christians of Khaybar, Fadak, and Najrān to the newly-conquered territories in Syria and Iraq. The Magians were not disturbed and took their time in merging themselves into the Muslim *umma*. Thus the income from poll-tax should have gradually declined to nothing. Caliph 'Umar was too sensitive to allow any non-Muslims into Madina.[51] Yet outside the city there were a substantial number of Jews and Christians. Many of the Jews has settled in Ṭā'if and paid poll-tax.[52]

Table 4
Assessment of *Jizya*-Paying Communities During the Prophet's Time

Community of non-Muslims at	Rate or quantity	Total in dirhams
1. Najrān[53]	2,000 dresses, valued 1 *ūqiyya* (40 dirhams) each, payable in two equal instalments + loans of coats of mail, horses, camels, and arms, 30 each + 30 days provisioning of Muslims	80,000
2. Baḥrayn[54]	Not given, but the total annual receipt including *Zakāt*	80,000
3. Ayla[55]	1 dīnār per head	3,000
4. Adhruḥ[56]	1 dīnār per head	1,000

(Continued on page 206)

(Continued from page 205)

5.	Yemen[57]	1 dīnār per head or mantles or dresses	–
6.	Ḥimyar[58]	1 dīnār per head	–
7.	Jarbā'[59]	1 dīnār per head	1,000
8.	Makka[60]	1 dīnār on the only Christian	10
9.	Maqnā'[61]	Commodities, horses and coats of mail	–
10.	Magians of Hajar and 'Umān[62]	Rate not given	–
11.	Dūmat al-Jandal[63]	Rate not given	–
12.	Taymā'[64]	Rate not given	–
13.	Tabāla and Jurash[65]	1 dīnār per head and provisioning of Muslims	–
	Total of recorded figures only		165,010

In the later period Muḥammad b. Yūsuf, the governor of Yemen, levied a fresh land-tax over and above *'Ushr* which was later withdrawn by 'Umar II but re-imposed by his successor.[66]

The Estimate of Collections

While incomplete figures of the collections in the Prophet's time are available, figures for the following period are more scarce. It would be reasonable to assume that income by way of taxes like those of *Zakāt* must have gradually increased. Baḥrayn paid 80,000 dirhams in the Prophet's time while the amount rose to 500,000 dirhams in Caliph 'Umar's time.[67] Ya'qūbī reports that *Kharāj* from Baḥrayn and Yamāma during Mu'āwiya's reign rose to 10 million dirhams.[68] The figures are too exaggerated to be accepted. Had the rate of increase in revenues been so high, the government at Madina would not have been waiting for funds from outside Arabia in order to meet its normal requirements. 'Send to the people of Madina their pensions because they too are sharers in your collections', thus wrote Caliph 'Umar to his collector in Sawād, and every year received some twenty to thirty million dirhams[69] which were distributed as pensions. Likewise 'Amr, the Governor of Egypt, was required to send half of the collections of Egypt to Madina.[70] These incomes were over and above the incomes received by way of the fifth of booty. When the famine of A.H. 21 threatened the lives of a large segment of the population of central Arabia, Iraq, Syria and Egypt rushed to the rescue and an impending catastrophe was averted.[71] But for these resources, the people of Madina and its surroundings might have starved to death.

Map 3. *Jizya*-Paying Communities Under the Prophet

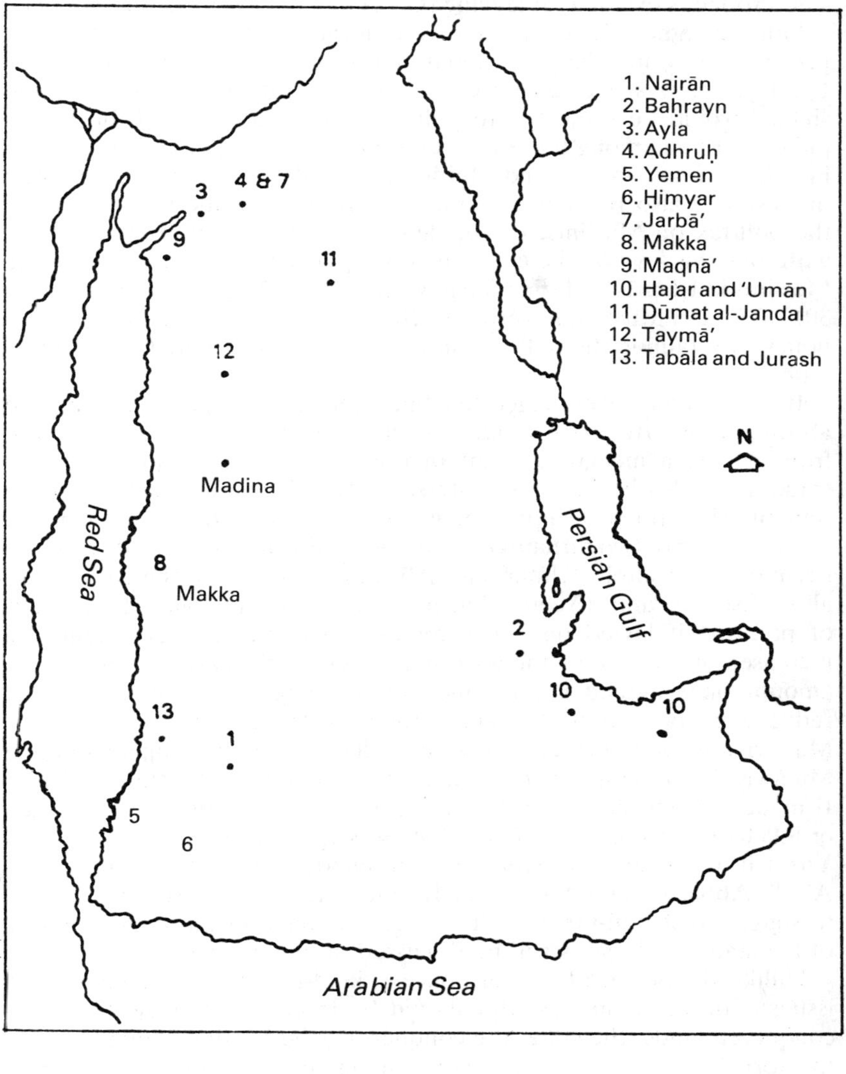

THE CONQUERED LANDS

New Issues and Decisions: Poll-Tax

The Muslim conquests outside Arabia brought many new problems. The Prophet's example of levying poll-tax on the Magians was extended to other communities of the non-Scriptuaries. Caliph 'Umar levied the tax in Persia while Caliph 'Uthmān did so in the case of the Berbers in Ifrīqiyya. It was decided by Caliph 'Umar that only those men who shaved would be subjected to poll-tax; viz., who attained the age of puberty. Even among these the very old and the crippled were exempt in addition to women and children.[72] Similarly the monks in their monasteries also remained exempt. There was no question of levying the poll-tax on Muslims, old or newly converted. Yet, Ḥajjāj did not withdraw this levy on the converts in Iraq. The number of *Jizya*-paying Muslims in Khurāsān during the governorship of Naṣr b. Sayyār reached 30,000.[73] Abū Muslim, governor of Ifrīqiyya also tried to follow Ḥajjāj's policy of retaining the poll-tax on converts, but was killed by an angry mob.[74]

It has already been suggested that land-tax was payable over and above poll-tax. But in case a man did not possess land, he was not spared from paying a meagre amount of poll-tax. He was required to pay trade-tax on his business or profession. The slave craftsmen who were sent by Mughīra to Caliph 'Umar paid a tax with the same name of *Jizya* at a rate of two dirhams daily or, according to Ibn Sa'd 100 dirhams per month.[75] Caliphs 'Umar and 'Alī levied this tax on the earnings of all craftsmen[76] and it seems that it was never withdrawn. The amount of poll-tax, if levied on any community without a treaty, could be increased or reduced by the government, but in the case of a treaty, the amount once agreed upon could not be increased. Caliph 'Uthmān reduced the poll-tax on Najrānites (now settled in Iraq) by 200 suits.[77] Mu'āwiya made a further reduction by 200 suits.[78] But Ḥajjāj withdrew Mu'āwiya's concession and reimposed the levy of 1,800 suits.[79] 'Umar II made a drastic cut of 1,600 to 200 suits, valued at forty dirhams each or 8,000 dirhams *in toto*.[80] This rebate was again withdrawn by governor Yūsuf b.'Umar and this situation continued until the 'Abbāsid Caliph Abu'l 'Abbās refixed it at 'Umar II's amount.[81] There are certain cases to suggest that poll-tax was altogether condoned in the larger interest of the state. Such cases will be discussed in due course.

Unlike the per-head levy of poll-tax, land-tax involved a number of issues. The question was who should be treated as the owner of the conquered lands: the state, the conquerors, the Muslim community, or the former owners who were now subjugated? In case the state was declared as its owner, who would possess, occupy or use it? What should be the nature of the right of the state or the conquering soldiers if it was to be retained and used by the former owners? What should be the considerations of the transfer of ownership? How should the government organize the machinery to guarantee the different rights over these lands? All these questions were decided by the caliphs in consultation, or sometimes without consultation, with the senior Companions of the Prophet (peace be upon him). The first Muslim conquest outside Arabia was Iraq and it was in this context that the Companions were divided on determining the policy about land – whether it should be treated as booty and distributed among the conquerors or as *Fay'* to be retained as a common property of the Muslims. Caliph 'Umar voted for the second alternative and got it approved. As regards the lands which were surrendered under an agreement, the terms of the agreement were followed. Thus most of the conquered provinces had two broad categories of land: the one conquered by force *('anwatan)* and the other governed by the terms of an agreement *(ṣulḥī)*. The ultimate ownership in both cases was vested in the state. The lands were left with whomsoever they were before the conquest. They were required to pay not only a tax on their heads *(Jizya)* but also a tax on their land. If any of them embraced Islam, the poll-tax was withdrawn but not the land-tax.[82] Where unoccupied land was reclaimed by a Muslim, it was treated as *'Ushr* land but not *Kharāj* land. The lands which were treated as *Fay'* were the common property of the Muslim community and inalienable.[83] A *Kharāj* land which was bought by a Muslim was subjected to land-tax but not *'Ushr*. As regards the other questions about land they were differently decided at different places, depending on the circumstances of the conquest and the preceding system. In the following sections an account will be given of those regions which the Muslims had conquered and where revenue administration had already taken definite shape during the first century. Spain (Andalus), which was overrun by the Muslims at the end of the century, and where administration took a definite shape by the end of the period, has not, therefore, been included.

IRAQ (as-Sawād)

The Treaties and the Amount of Tax

The conquest of Iraq was inaugurated by Khālid's treaties with the representatives of Ullays, Bāniqiyyā', Bārūsmā, and Ḥīra. Ṭabarī has given two different amounts of money agreed upon with the people of

Bāniqiyyā', and Bārūsmā (in the second treaty the name of the place is given as Basmā, not Bārūsmā): 1,000 dirhams and 10,000 dīnārs.[84] About the treaty of Ḥīra, the following amounts are given in different sources.[85]

Yaḥyā b. Ādam	1,000 dirhams
Abū Yūsuf	60,000 dirhams
Balādhurī	80,000; 84,000; 100,000 dirhams
Khalīfa b. Khayyāṭ	90,000 dirhams
Ṭabarī	90,000; 190,000; 400,000 dirhams

Yaḥyā's report seems to be very confusing and may be set aside. The question now arises as to which of these many amounts should be treated as the figure agreed on with the people of Ḥīra? Ṭabarī while giving the many amounts agreed on in the various treaties also mentions that the people of Ḥīra revolted two or three times, and, after each revolt was suppressed the amount of treaty was enhanced. Balādhurī's report on the authority of Yaḥyā, and Abū Yūsuf's report are comparable in respect of the heads on which poll-tax was computed, and as a result also in respect of the total amount which was probably initially levied. Abū 'Ubayd reports that the people of Ḥīra came of the tribes of Tamīm, Ṭayyi', Ghassān and Tanūkh[86] – branches of four tribes. Thus Abū Yūsuf's report that Ḥīra had 7,000 men of whom 1,000 were very old and invalid and were exempted, the remaining being taxed for a total of 60,000 dirhams,[87] seems to be more plausible. Balādhurī reports the same thing with a relative difference in the value of dirhams: 84,000 dirhams weighing five carats[88] which is equivalent to Abū Yūsuf's 60,000 dirhams weighing seven carats each. In this way Balādhurī's and Abū Yūsuf's statements if interpreted with Ṭabarī's report about three revolts, will give the following figures:

	dirhams
Amount originally agreed	60,000
Amount revised after suppression of the first revolt	90,000
Amount revised after suppression of the second revolt	190,000
Amount revised after suppression of the last revolt	400,000

But this gives rise to one difficulty. According to Ṭabarī, the amount of 190,000 dirhams was fixed by Khālid which means that it happened after the suppression of the second revolt. The amount of 400,000 dirhams was fixed by Sa'd when he suppressed the last revolt. But Ṭabarī himself mentions one more revolt which was suppressed by Muthannā and after which the amount of tax was again enhanced.[89] Muthannā commanded these areas after Khālid and before Sa'd. It means that Ṭabarī has missed quoting the amount fixed by Muthannā and also forgotten to include it in his account. Thus a more probable position seems to be that the amount of treaty initially agreed upon was 60,000 dirhams which gradually rose to 400,000 after the fourth and last revolt was suppressed.

As regards the treaties with the people of Bāniqiyyā' and Bārūsmā there seems to be confusion of a different nature. Khālid's debut in Iraq begins with this treaty involving 1,000 dirhams. But after suppression of the second revolt, he is stated to have entered into, with the people of Bāniqiyyā' and Basmā, not Bārūsmā, and the surrounding areas along the river Euphrates, a treaty involving 10,000 dīnārs, at a rate of four dirhams each.[90] These reports involve three confusions. Firstly, if it is supposed that Bāniqiyyā' and Bārūsmā were the first to come to terms, the agreed amount of 1,000 dirhams is suggestive of an insignificant area and population. But the geographers mention that Bārūsmā was a suburb *(ṭassūj)* in central Bihqubādh[91] and this, along with Nahr al-Malik, jointly fetched 122,000 dirhams of tax in addition to quantities of wheat and barley in A.H. 204.[92] The name of Basmā is nowhere to be found, at least in the books of Muslim geographers. Secondly, Bārūsmā, which at the time of the first treaty was a partner of Bāniqiyyā', has been replaced by Basmā without reappearing at any further stage of the treaties. It is probable that the name of the village was actually Bārūsmā which was later exposed to fabrication in reading or writing. Thirdly, this assumption is also supported by the fact that Khālid is reported to have expressly exempted Bāniqiyyā' and Basmā because a separate treaty had already been made with them. It meant that this Basmā also was situated within Bihqubādh and had already settled terms with Khālid. If Bārūsmā was a different place from Basmā it should also have been excluded because a treaty with its people and of Bāniqiyyā' had been signed which is not reported to have been violated.

It transpires from the above discussion that Basmā was not a different village from Bārūsmā, a suburb of Bihqubādh whose people, like the people of Bāniqiyyā', wished to get the treaty renewed and extended to a wider area, now covering the belts along the Euphrates. And in this agreement too the well-known Ṣalūbā family has been an active intermediary as in the earliest treaty with Bāniqiyyā' and Bārūsmā.[93] The amount was now enhanced to 10,000 dīnārs, reportedly at a rate of four dirhams per head.[94] If this rate is treated as correct the number of tax-paying members of the community will be 25,000 or a total population of 75,000, quite a big town for that time. Moreover, this seems to be a fairly unusual rate in the whole chain of treaties. The usual rate so far had been one dīnār per head or even more. Another doubtful thing is the unit of currency reported by historians. Iraq was a dirham area and most transactions involving money are reported in terms of dirhams and not dīnārs. Examples in the immediate context of the discussion are the four other treaties in Iraq. Thus both figures, the total amount of levy and the per-head rate, seem to be doubtful. It is difficult to suggest a solution because many assumptions are admissible. If both the figures are revised according to the above criticism, the amounts will have to be read as 10,000 dirhams, at a rate of one dīnār per head. But while there is the possibility of a misunderstanding between dirham and dīnār – inadvertently reporting dīnār for dirham – there can hardly be a possibility of misreporting four dirhams for one dīnār. Another assumption may be that while the total amount of 10,000 might be correct the per-head rate is wrongly reported as four dirhams rather than four dīnārs – a punitive increase in the usual rate of one dīnār per head. A third assumption may be that the rate of four dirhams per head is correctly reported and indicates the per-head average levy on the total population and not on the taxable population only. This would seem to be a more appealing interpretation and the rate per head of taxable population would in this way be around one dīnār. However, none of the interpretations are supported by any evidence and they stand as nothing but assumptions.[95]

The last of the treaties in Iraq was made with the people of Bihqubādh (Central and Lower). Here again Ṭabarī has given two different figures: the one involving 2 million dirhams on the authority of Mughīra, and the other involving one million dirhams on the authority of 'Ubayd Allāh. The following points lead us to choose the lower figure:

1. The treaty made with the people of Bihqubādh was the first treaty with them and the amounts generally fixed under the treaties were easy to pay.

2. During Ḥajjāj's governorship over Iraq, and even after him, agriculture in Iraq had some set-backs. Many lands were deserted; production and taxing capacity were reduced. There was a gradual decline in land revenue during the later Umayyad period, and the decline continued until the 'Abbāsid period. The total revenues raised by the 'Abbāsids in A.H. 204 from Bihqubādh (Upper, Central and Lower) amounted to 2,064,800 dirhams in addition to a quantity of grain.[96] But this amount also included the collections from Upper Bihqubādh while Khālid's agreement covered only the Central and Lower which, during the 'Abbāsid caliphate paid about 1.25 million dirhams.[97] If this was a full-capacity levy during the 'Abbāsid period, it should have been a mild levy during Khālid's period. This is also guess-work, but keeping in view the above-mentioned premises, we are inclined to choose 'Ubayd Allāh's report which is on the lower side and also demonstrates the early norm.

Other Conditions of the Treaties

In addition to the amounts involved in the treaties, there were certain other conditions that were made binding on the subject communities; namely:

1. The representatives of these communities were made responsible for collecting the amount of levy and paying it to the Muslim officials.[98] The government offered any necessary assistance through the services of the Muslim staff on condition that the charges incurred on this staff would be borne by the *Bayt al-Māl.*[99] This implied that charges incurred by the subject collectors or agents were not treated to be the liability of the *Bayt al-Māl.*
2. Lands were left in the possession of the former owners, except the lands and valuables owned by the emperor of Persia[100] and his family.
3. It was agreed that the amount of poll-tax would be receivable only when the Muslims protected these people.[101]
4. In some cases, the subject collectors were explicitly required to distribute the burden of this tax equitably among all the male population according to their respective incomes.[102] This meant that even assessment was sometimes left to the non-Muslim representatives.
5. Tax in the case of treaty lands is not poll-tax *(Jizya),* because it seems to have been levied in a lump sum without any consideration as to future fluctuations in population due to births, deaths or conversions. While the number of heads might have been taken into account at the time of fixing the original amount, this consideration was set aside in the case of revised treaties after the suppression of a revolt. Thus, though the amount of 60,000 dirhams might represent a calculated levy on the taxable people of Ḥīra, the latter amounts of 190,000 dirhams or 400,000 dirhams did not represent any such consideration. It was a punitive tax on the whole community.

These treaties were made perhaps within two months of Khālid's entry into Iraq and fetched a total of 1.41 million dirhams over and above some valuables. The people of Bihqubādh are stated to have paid their 1 million within fifty days.[103] The remaining part of Iraq was occupied by force of arms although these treaties took their final shape after the Muslims had fought it out in six pitched battles within an area of about forty square miles.[104] The remaining part of Iraq was conquered within the next four years after the most decisive battles of Madā'in, Qādisiyya and Jalūla'.

The Issue of the Distribution of Land

The first question to be decided by Caliph 'Umar was the government's policy towards the ownership of land. While a number of Companions of the Prophet (peace be upon him) were pressing for the distribution of conquered land among the fighters, Caliph 'Umar, supported by an almost equal number of Companions, voted against it and decided to treat it as *Fay'*.[105] Thus the following rules are known to have been observed by 'Umar and followed by his successors.

1. The part of Iraq, which was conquered by force, belonged to the Muslims and was declared inalienable,[106] while the part which fell under peace treaties, belonged to the former owners and its ownership could be transferred.[107]
2. *Kharāj* was to be levied on all those lands which were conquered by force even if the owner later on embraced Islam.[108] Such a converted owner was exempt from *Jizya*.[109]
3. The former owners of the lands conquered by force were allowed to occupy their land provided they were agreeable to pay poll-tax and land-tax.[110] Later on, the jurists sanctified it as a self-imposed commitment or a contract.[111]
4. The unoccupied lands, which were reclaimed and cultivated by Muslims, were treated as *'Ushr* lands. Thus the lands of Baṣra, for example, were to pay *'Ushr* but not land-tax.[112]
5. Collection of taxes in the case of non-treaty lands also was made the responsibility of the landlord.[113]
6. Land-tax was levied per *jarīb* of cultivable land whether or not it was cultivated, but not on the individuals.[114] In the case of cultivated land, rates were fixed according to the nature of the produce.[115]

The Assessment of Taxes and Collections

In order to manage the affairs of the land, Caliph 'Umar, first had experienced persons survey it[116] and then conduct a census of the population[117] which was also to be subjected to poll-tax. It is not known how large a team of assistants they took with them because a survey of the whole province could not be undertaken by only one or two men in a reasonable time. There are reports of attempts by local persons to mislead one of the surveyors, Ḥudhayfa[118] but the nature of these is not recorded. Residential areas and houses were excluded from survey.[119] Similarly the undergrowth, area covered under water, or the area inaccessible to water, and mounds *(talā)* were also excluded.[120] Thus the total area of surveyed land was reportedly 36 million *jarīb*[121] or 125 *farsakh* in length and 80 *farsakh* in breadth or 10,000 square *farsakh*.[122]

In order that people should not evade poll-tax by pretending to have been counted, a seal was fixed on their necks after they had been counted. A man without a seal was declared to be unprotected.[123] Thus about 550,000 persons were dealt with in this way.[124]

When these basic data were available, Caliph 'Umar had to decide about the question of fixing land-tax. Before Noshirwān, the government took from the landlords between one sixth and one third of the yield;[125] Noshirwān levied a payment in money and in kind, each measure of ground being taxed at a dirham and one fixed measure of the produce. These payments, which applied only to sown land, were never increased, and in consequence the cultivator was free to work for his own benefit, sure of reaping what he sowed. It is stated that an annual survey was made of all lands under cultivation. This is difficult to believe on account of the enormous staff the work would have required; but it is certain that there was a remarkable improvement in efficiency.[126] In addition to land-tax there was an assessment of fruit trees, a tax on property and poll-tax. Payment of the taxes was made in three instalments, at intervals of four months, and to prevent oppression, the Magians were allowed to act as inspectors.[127] According to Balādhurī, the amount of poll-tax which Noshirwān levied was twelve dirhams for the well-to-do, eight for the average, and four for the poor.[128] That Caliph 'Umar knew all these details, cannot be doubted, particularly when his favourite poet Zuhayr had made a mention of the general practice of the levy of *qafīz* and dirhams (per *jarīb*) in Iraq.[129] Abū Yūsuf in one of his reports[130] suggests that Caliph 'Umar levied the same rates whether or not land was cultivated. According to another report from the same source, 'Umar first sent for a delegation of the Iraqi landlords to have direct information about the pre-Islamic taxes. The landlords informed him that they had to pay to the Persians twenty-seven dirhams but 'Umar did not like this rate and fixed for each *jarīb* of land where water was available a *qafīz* of wheat or barley and a dirham.[131] According to Ṭabarī, Caliph 'Umar levied the same rates in Sawād as were levied by Kisrā (Persian Emperor).[132]

It will be seen that all the reports are almost identical except for the addition of Abū Yūsuf's story about the pre-Islamic levy of twenty-seven dirhams. The story does not explain the nature of the monetary payment exclusive of any commodity payment. Whether it was the monetary value of the total taxes in money and kind, on the lands of these landlords, or an average per person or average per unit of land, is not clear. It is, however, clear that Caliph 'Umar did not like the idea and fixed it at per unit of land in terms of money as well as produce. This was over and above the poll-tax which he levied on them. But it seems that after the situation normalized he changed the general rule of levying

Table 5
Caliph 'Umar's Monetary Levies on Different Crops in Iraq

Crop	Source	Kh., 20–2							Bal., 270			Yaq., 2,142	Yaqūt, *cf.* Yaq.	I.K., 12
	S. No.	1	2	3	4	5	6	7	8	9	10	11	12	13
Grain		1+1*				1+1	1+1	1+1						
Grapes		10	10	8	10			10	10	8	4	5	5	6
Dates		5	8	10	5						10			8
Wheat			4		1+1									4
Barley			2		1+1						2			2
Oilseed								5		8				
Vegetables								3						
Cotton								5	5					
Gourds												10	10	6
Inferior dates							Nil	Nil	1					
Lentils					1+1					8				
Bamboo†			6											

*1+1 signifies one dirham plus one measure *(qafīz)*. All other figures indicate levies in terms of dirhams.

†In many countries bamboo is a forest produce. But its inclusion in the list as farm or garden produce suggests that, if the report is correct, bamboo was also cultivated on farms. It is also likely that garden bamboo might be of a different variety from what is generally understood.

a fixed amount on all lands and changed it to varying amounts depending on the quality and value of the yield. The early sources have reported different amounts for the different crops which may be arranged in tabular form. (See Table 5.)

It will be seen in the above table that while the inferior quality dates were exempt, the rates on superior quality fresh dates were the highest. Barley was treated as the cheapest crop with two dirhams per *jarīb* of levy. The list seems to have covered almost all the crops that might have been grown in Iraq. The rate of poll-tax was fixed at forty-eight dirhams for the well-to-do, twenty-four dirhams for the middle, and twelve dirhams for the poor class, per annum.[133] It has already been mentioned that this per-head poll-tax was over and above the land-tax which was levied on per *jarīb* of land and the amount of taxes collected from Sawād either included both or was only land-tax exclusive of poll-tax. The point is easily understandable due to the fact that the number of heads on which poll-tax was imposed and the total collections are recorded by most of the historians without any formidable difference.

The total taxable population in Sawād has been recorded as some five to six hundred thousand.[134] In order to conjecture the probable total amount of poll-tax we shall have to assume different ratios of class strata. Suppose that the number of the well-to-do persons was 5,000, the middle class 50,000 and the poor 550,000. The total amount of poll-tax with this hypothesis will come to 8,040,000 dirhams per annum. This, it will be observed, seems to be quite a modest estimate of class-division. In order to remove the possibilities of any objection to this estimate, let us also calculate the amount of annual collections on the basis of a maximum allowance to the assumed number of the higher strata of population. Thus, suppose the class ratio would be 1:2:3 – although improbable. In this way the number of the well-to-do who would be taxed at forty-eight dirhams would be 100,000; of the middle class 200,000; and of the poor 300,000 or say, fifty per cent of the total. The total collections by way of poll-tax would amount to not more than 13,200,000 dirhams. Thus while the amount of 800,000 dirhams could be a modest estimate, the amount of 13.2 million would be the maximum in a medieval agricultural society of Persian territory. A reasonable figure must be much less than that.

The question whether the amount of poll-tax is included in the total figures of revenue collections as quoted by the historians is not certain except on the evidence of Yaḥyā's statement that when two men from Ullays embraced Islam ʻUmar reduced the amount of poll-tax from the total land-tax[135] which indicates that the collections were inclusive of both taxes. The following table presents the amount of collections from Iraq throughout the period under study:

Table 6
Amount of Collections from Iraq

Period	Dirhams (in Million)
Caliph ‘Umar’s	100[136]
Caliph ‘Uthmān’s	100[137]
Caliph ‘Alī’s (Governorship of Ziyād)	100[138]
Mu‘āwiya’s (Governorship of ‘Ubayd Allāh)	120[139]
‘Abd al-Malik’s (Governorship of Ḥajjāj)	40[140]
‘Umar II’s	80[141]
Hishām’s (Governorship of Yūsuf b. ‘Umar)	100[142]
(Governorship of Khālid al-Qisrī)	100[143]
(For comparison): Harūn al-Rashīd’s	100[144]

The above table gives an almost uniform figure for about 150 years, but for a short period intervening Ḥajjāj’s governorship till a period of recovery during ‘Umar II’s caliphate, which could be a period of about twenty-five years. The increase during the governorship of ‘Ubayd Allāh was, presumably, the result of his withdrawing Arab officials and replacing them by natives[145] although these natives had already been working at lower levels since the very beginning.[146] On the contrary, ‘Abd al-Malik’s period witnessed a sharp decline in the revenues from the record 120 million dirhams to 40 million dirhams. The cause of this decline is not difficult to see. This should not actually be treated as the figure for the whole of Iraq, nor for the entire period of the twenty years of ‘Abd al-Malik’s reign. It was a period when a number of claimants of caliphate were actively operating in the Ḥijāz and Iraq and they practically controlled these regions. Over and above these claimants (Ibn Zubayr and Mukhtār) who were taking away a chunk of the taxes of Iraq, the Khārijites (Shabīb and his followers) also exacted taxes wherever they operated.[147] The situation could be restored to normalcy only after suppressing all these elements, but in A.H. 82–83 the mutineers, who also robbed the farmers of taxes,[148] set on fire all the revenue records and this encouraged evasion of taxes, and other malpractices, and it would have taken a long time to improve the situation. By the time of ‘Umar II the situation had improved only partly and the total revenue of 40 million dirhams increased to 80 million. After ‘Umar II, however, the figure again reached the pre-Mu‘āwiya figure of 100 million dirhams and remained so throughout the period.

Ḥajjāj's Levy of Poll-Tax on Muslims

An important development that took place during this period was Ḥajjāj's policy of the non-withdrawal of poll-tax on fresh converts to Islam. The reports of Ḥajjāj's rudeness and cold-bloodedness might have some truth but his policy of levying poll-tax on the converts, if examined in proper perspective, does not strengthen the allegations against him. The question that requires examination in this respect is whether the amount of poll-tax could really be so large as to affect the total government revenues of the province. It cannot be believed that if poll-tax was withdrawn – as it should have been – the entire population of non-Muslims was prepared to embrace Islam forthwith. Supposing that a maximum of 50,000 taxable persons were willing to accept Islam during the period when the question of withdrawal of poll-tax arose, the total amount involved would not be more than 1 million dirhams out of a total collection of 40 million dirhams. Was this small amount such a potential threat to cause sensible Ḥajjāj to misbehave in such an arrogant way? Conversion was no threat to the amount of land-tax because it was to be paid even after embracing Islam. In fact, monetary benefit in the case of their conversion could have accrued in the form of their contribution by way of *'Ushr* and this could have added more to the public treasury than the per-head levy of poll-tax and thus more than offset the loss. It can be mentioned here that a similar situation took place in Khurāsān thirty years later and a close examination of the two events suggests one common factor that was responsible for an unjustifiable reaction of the governors. This common factor was the emotional and religious attachments of the tax officers whose sympathies lay with the non-Muslims. They did not like these conversions but could not fight this 'menace' on a religious plane without offending the Muslims – the ruling community. The best and most intelligent way to discourage this tendency was to get the converts punished by the government and they partly succeeded in their manoeuvring. It is unfortunate that early historians have disposed of this particular aspect of the story in a summary way, yet these brief reports give a clue to the tax officials' over-emphasizing the real situation and thus misguiding the governors. In the case of Khurāsān the officer concerned reported that the man whom the governor sent for preaching (and whose preaching proved effective) 'had created dissatisfaction and unrest among the people; and peace and order was threatened'.[149] This is the literal sense that the historians found fit to record. It can roughly be conceived in what way the officers would have made out their case. A simple metaphorical or emotional sentence could hardly prompt an intelligent and sensible governor to take drastic action, thus prejudicing his own religious bias.

These officers would probably have made out a theoretically strong case to attain their objective – with written reports, personal representations, fake stories of insolvency of the local treasury and imaginary over-ambitiousness of the converts or their hypocrisy, as clearly happened in Khurāsān under Ashras.[150] As for Ḥajjāj he was already in the doldrums. Suppression of unceasing revolts and mutinies required increased funds but the revenues of the province were, at the time, declining. When the revenue officers painted an extremely dismal picture of the future finances due to conversions and migrations from village to city, and by implication about the future of Ḥajjāj's governorship, he probably became unnerved and in a fit of neurosis acted upon the suggestions of tax-officers by re-imposing poll-tax on the converts and pushing them back to the villages. It was Ḥajjāj who at the time of levying taxes convened a large meeting at Wāsiṭ, perhaps to distribute the burden of taxes equitably[151] as used to happen in Egypt.

By the time of 'Umar II the trend had already changed. Stability had set in long ago, yet the caliph was unable to get the pre-Ḥajjāj amount of revenue. This may be attributed to his leniency and his efforts to compensate for past injustices. A tax-payer has always the wherewithal to pay his taxes and any leniency on the part of the tax-collector encourages him to evade his liabilities.

Incomes from land-tax do not include other incomes from land. Caliph 'Umar's rigid policy was to disallow the possession of *Fay'*-land by Muslims in Iraq.[152] He applied this rule even in the case of those lands which were formerly owned by the Persian royal family. As a result vast tracts of land were lying idle. Caliph 'Uthmān changed this policy and took the initiative to put these lands into use by allotting them to Muslims. While income from such state lands in Caliph 'Umar's time was 9 million dirhams, it shot up to a figure of 50 million under Caliph 'Uthmān.[153] Many such lands were later on picked up by Umayyad rulers as their 'chosen' property *(ṣafī)*.[154] The so-called anti-Umayyad historian Ya'qūbī reports that Mu'āwiya received 50 million dirhams and perhaps later on, 100 million dirhams[155] from his chosen properties. Whether or not the report is a hundred per cent correct, it is certain that the lands of Sawād which were directly under state ownership were widespread[156] and brought sufficient revenues to the state. The chaotic condition that prevailed during Ḥajjāj's governorship ended about A.H. 82–83, but the lack of land records, after they were set ablaze during the mutiny, was still a formidable obstacle in restoring state revenues to normalcy. Yazīd II, the successor of 'Umar II, advised his governor to again survey the lands and prepare fresh records.[157] This then formed the basis of future taxation and the situation improved.

SYRIA (ash-Shām)

The Administrative Set-up

The circumstances of the conquest of ash-Shām (Syria) were entirely different from those of Iraq. In the latter case the entire region had a centralized administration under Persian rule and over-running of a certain part or region did not finalize its conquest unless the Persian armies were driven out of the last boundaries of the region and any future threat of an offensive was crushed. In the initial stages the regions contiguous to Arab borders (Ḥīra and surrounding villages) saved themselves from the Arab onslaught by a fake commitment but, as soon as they knew of a counter-offensive by the Persians, they turned back again and again and tried to rid themselves of the Arab yoke. After the defeat of Persian contingents in six pitched battles within an area of about forty square miles near Ḥīra, the subjugated people lost all hope of restoration of the former position and reconciled themselves to the new rulers. Contrary to it, Syria was, administratively, not one unit when the Muslim armies invaded it. It was administered by separate local bodies, independent of each other. These units were based on fiscal considerations and the main features of these fiscal institutions dated from the reforms of Constantine and Diocletian. The latter emperor had a census made of lands and people, resulting in the rough division of the country into units, equal not in acreage, but in the value of the crop produced. The unit was called *iugum;* and each *iugum* paid the same fixed tax. The census took note of the numbers of *iugera* of each municipality with its dependent lands, villages, and estates; and once a year when the basic tax per *iugum* was announced, the municipal *curiales* were compelled to collect a sum equal to the basic rate multiplied by the number of *iugera* ascribed to the municipality. The keynote in the fiscal structure, then, was the municipality, and this explains why the Arabs, in taking Syria, made not one but many treaties.[158]

The Terms of Treaties

Thus when the Arabs began their operations in Syria, they found it easy to deal with these municipal bodies one by one. Each of them, finding it difficult to defend itself, entered into a treaty with them. Thus while most of Iraq was conquered by force, Syria, including Jordan and Palestine, was subjugated by treaties made with the municipal bodies of the respective cities. Cyprus also agreed to enter into a treaty with the Muslims who, administratively, merged it with Syria. Thus these treaties encompass more than thirty cities and their suburbs.

As regards the terms of the treaties with these cities, they varied from one another only slightly. Balādhurī reports that the people of Buṣrā agreed to pay a dīnār per head and a measure *(jarīb)* of wheat on each *jarīb* of land.[159] According to another report, the supply of oil and vinegar was also included in the treaty.[160] Later on (during Caliph 'Umar's time) they were subjected to a poll-tax per head and a separate tax on their lands.[161] The terms of the treaty with the people of Emessa, Damascus, and Jordan, according to Ṭabarī, were similar.[162] Some agreed to pay a fixed sum without any consideration of future economic conditions, while others agreed to pay according to their capacity.[163] The treaty of Damascus contained the payment of cash, sharing the land with the Muslims, a per-head levy of one dīnār and a levy of one *jarīb* of produce per *jarīb* of land. The properties of the royal family and its entourage were treated as booty *(Ghanīma).*[164] The same terms were settled with the people of Ṭabariyya and Bisān.[165] According to Khalīfa b. Khayyāṭ, the city of Damascus was subjugated under a treaty while the entire land was conquered by force.[166] Ibn al-Faqīh, the geographer, has mentioned that four-fifths of the governorate of Damascus was covered by treaty.[167] Ṭabarī has repeated almost the same terms of taxes for Emessa while giving details, as in the case of Damascus.[168] Balādhurī has reported that the people of Emessa[169] like the people of Bā'labak and some other towns paid poll-tax and land-tax,[170] but he fails to report about the proportionate amount of levy. He records the same terms for the payment of poll-tax and land-tax for Faḥl and many other cities of Jordan.[171] The terms of treaty with the cities in Palestine were also basically similar.[172]

The contents of the treaties recorded by Ṭabarī and Balādhurī suggest that in many cases the nature and the amount of levy were not defined immediately after the conquest. The confusion in the use of the terms *Jizya* and *Kharāj* is more pronounced in the case of many reports about cities in Syria than anywhere else. It seems, as already discussed earlier in this chapter, that the two have sometimes been taken to mean tax or tribute without any regard to its nature. For example, Khālid is reported to have written to the people of Damascus that 'They will be well treated if they pay *Jizya.*'[173] This simply means that the taxes and the liabilities were yet to be levied on them. Moreover, 'the officer of Adhru'āt requested the Muslim commander to offer him the same terms as were offered to the people of Buṣrā and to declare the lands of al-Bith'thīna as *Kharāj* lands. The commander agreed to it.'[174] 'Abū 'Ubayda . . . appointed Yazīd b. Abī Sufyān in his place and started for Emessa and settled an agreement with the people of Emessa that . . . whoever among them will stay will have to pay *Kharāj*';[175] 'So the lands in Emessa were given to them on condition that they pay *Kharāj* without any regard to boom or scarcity.'[176] In all these quotations the word *Kharāj* has been used to convey the sense of both taxes and tribute. Similarly Balādhurī reports that the people of Jerusalem 'agreed to pay something in lieu of the properties that were left within the fort'[177] and suggests that they were to pay something like *Kharāj* but not *Jizya,* but Ṭabarī reports that they agreed to pay *Jizya* and opened the gates for him (for Caliph 'Umar).[178] The fact is that, as other reports suggest, they were made to pay both the taxes. All such instances simply reflect confusion in reporting. But all the reports taken together and reconciled to each other suggest two to three stages of taxation during Caliph Umar's time. In the first stage the absolute term of *Jizya* or *Kharāj* was settled without any mention of rates. In some cases a dīnār and a measure of produce of land was levied while in some other cases this was the second stage of taxes – the implementation of the levy. This was in comparison with the terms that were decided after the conquest of Sawād (Iraq) – a dirham and a measure of the produce of the land. Supply of provisions for the army was over and above this condition and it stands to reason that this should have been levied in the very first stage. The next stage began with Caliph 'Umar's visit to Jerusalem while he defined the taxes as per-head levy *(Jizya)* of money and per-*jarīb* levy of land produce. Then came the last stage of Caliph 'Umar's reorganization of the tax system when he revised the rates. According to Balādhurī: 'In the beginning the poll-tax in Syria was in terms of *jarīb* and a dīnār per head. Then Caliph 'Umar levied on "the people of gold" four dīnārs and on "the people of silver" forty dirhams and divided these people according to the wealth of the wealthy, the poverty of the poor and the average resources of the middle class.'[179] According to another report by Balādhurī, Caliph 'Umar wrote to the army commanders to levy poll-tax on all those who shave, at a rate of forty dirhams for 'the people of silver' and four dīnārs for 'the people of gold' and he also advised the commanders to make themselves responsible for supplying provisions at a rate of two *modī* of wheat and three *qisṭ* of oil, and fats and honey for every Muslim person in Syria and Mesopotamia.[180] Thus the government, as Dennett has observed in the case of Mesopotamia, 'placed on the countryside the exclusive burden of providing food for the *jund* (army) . . . therefore, if the country people had to bear the exclusive burden of providing the tax in kind it would seem proper to assume that the city people had the exclusive burden of paying the money tax.'[181] The new system perhaps followed a general census in respect of population in 639–40 (A.H. 18–19) and of all lands, men, animals and palms.[182]

Cyprus was conquered during Caliph 'Umar's reign. But it chose to impose upon itself the suzerainty of both the warring powers, Byzantine and Muslim. It agreed to pay 7,000 dīnārs to each.[183]

Tribute Paid to the Byzantine Ruler

Successful military operations continued up to Caliph ʻUthmān's time. During ʻAlī's caliphate, Muʻāwiya seceded from the centre and the Muslim-Byzantine war took the form of a 'see-saw'. While at loggerheads, Muʻāwiya, the ruler of Syria and Egypt, was compelled to pay 'some wealth' to the Byzantine ruler[184] to save the cities under his control. How much Muʻāwiya had to pay and for how long, has not been reported by any of the Muslim historians. But because this has also escaped the notice of the early Christian historians it seems that it was a purely temporary arrangement in respect of some particular Byzantine expedition. ʻAbd al-Malik also faced the same situation in A.H. 70 and agreed to pay the Byzantine ruler 1,000 dīnārs per week.[185] The Muslim historians are again very brief on the point while some details are available in the Christian sources. Agapius (Mahboub) de Manbidg records: 'The treaty between ʻAbd al-Malik and the Byzantine Emperor provided for a ten-year period of peace and that the Emperor Justinianus should return from the Lebanon hills. In return ʻAbd al-Malik was to pay 1,000 dīnārs daily *(sic)* and horses and slaves. Moreover Cyprus was to be common between them.'[186] But it seems this agreement was also not respected for long because shortly afterwards we find ʻAbd al-Malik despatching his expeditions along the Byzantine borders.[187]

Table 7
Amount of Collections from Syria and Palestine

	Amount in dīnārs		
	Muʻāwiya's reign[188]	ʻAbd al-Malik's reign[189]	A.H. 158 (for comparison)[190]
Damascus	450,000	400,000	420,000
Emessa, Qinessrīn, ʻAwāṣim	170,000[191]	800,000[192]	990,000
Jordan	180,000	180,000	97,000
Palestine	450,000	350,000	310,000
Cyprus	7,000	8,000	7,000
Total	1,257,000	1,738,000[193]	1,824,000

The total income from these levies is not given for the early period. For Emessa, the amounts levied on different cities are also not recorded. However, incomplete figures given by Ya'qūbī and Balādhurī can be helpful in giving some idea about the amount of collections, and are reproduced in Table 7.

Changes in the Rates of Levy

Table 7 suggests an increase of about forty per cent during 'Abd al-Malik's reign over Mu'āwiya's which is perhaps the figure for his pre-reform period. Before Mu'āwiya's reform the taxes on an estate were payable by the possessor of the estate, who collected the amount from the peasants by way of rent. But Mu'āwiya, after his general reorganization of the empire, introduced the practice of collecting all taxes directly from each peasant without intermediation of the landlord.[194] Michael the Syrian reports that in the year 980 of the Greeks, 9 of Mu'āwiya and 54 of the Arabs, Abu'l A'war made a census of the Christian peasants for the tribute in all Syria.[195] It would possibly be after this census that Mu'āwiya introduced his reforms. Another reason for the increase in the amount in the later period could be Yazīd's raising of the rates of poll-tax in Jordan and Palestine[196] and the levy of an additional tax on land over and above the levy by way of provisions for the army.[197] Yazīd is stated to have enhanced the amount of poll-tax to five dīnārs per head[198] in the case of Sāmira in Palestine. The tax in Cyprus, which was then 7,000 dīnārs, was raised by 'Abd al-Malik to 8,000 but reduced by 'Umar II to the original 7,000. This was again raised to 8,000 by Hishām and remained so until the 'Abbāsid caliph Manṣūr reduced it again to the original amount.[199] Like the Banū Taghlib of al-Jazīra, the people of al-Jarjūma, the Nabaetians of the suburbs of Antioch, who had helped the Muslims during war and who were a threat to peace and defence, were, in A.H. 89, exempted from the payment of poll-tax. Not only were they taxed like the Muslims – a higher privilege than that enjoyed by Banū Taghlib, but they were also made entitled to *salab,* pensions *('atā'),* and provisions like Muslim soldiers.[200] So far the practice had been to link poll-tax with the granting of protection. Now it was also treated as a charge for exemption from military service. That is why when al-Jarājima fought with the Muslims, poll-tax was withdrawn. Though such instances applied to individual cases only, the wider and more general application of this rule carried significance for the later jurists.

To Sum Up

The terms of the treaties and the nature of the later developments arrive at the following main points of the taxation policy in Syria (including Palestine and Jordan):

1. Unlike Iraq almost the whole of Syria was conquered through treaties. These treaties were made with the separate municipal units that were functioning under Byzantine rule.

2. Caliph 'Umar employed two methods of levy in Syria: a fixed tax of one dīnār on each man plus a quantity of grain on each *jarīb,* and a proportional tax on the harvest.

3. The old administrative structure was retained for some time but because the government then wished to exercise more and direct control over taxation with a view to eliminating unnecessary intermediation, it took upon itself the responsibility of assessment. Collection was, however, left in the hands of the local people. They were also required to hand over monthly supplies at the headquarters.

4. While the cities and the occupied lands enjoyed the privilege of treaty relationship, the royal estates and unoccupied and deserted lands were taken under state ownership and control.

5. Although the task of assessment of taxes was taken over by the Muslims, collection was still the responsibility of the local people. This should have involved some expenditure, but to whose account this expenditure was debited is not given by historians. In the case of Iraq the government had promised to bear the expenses of Muslim officials if the local people required their services. But it seems that the expenses incurred by the locals were the responsibility of the local people themselves. It appears, therefore, that these local collectors in Syria, as also perhaps in Sawād, transferred this burden to the assessees, and thus levied tax over and above that which was to be transferred to the government. Although there is no concrete proof in support of this assumption in the case of Syria, the levy of such a tax in Egypt, as will be discussed in the relevant pages, provides ground for it.

MESOPOTAMIA (al-Jazīra)

The Conquest and the Levy of Taxes

The region lying to the north of Iraq (Sawād) and stretching between the Euphrates and the Tigris was conquered by the Muslims after the conquest of Iraq and Syria. Agapius de Menbidg has given the following account of the conquest:

'Abū 'Ubayda sent 'Ibād b. 'Āthim[201] *(sic)* with a large army . . . Then he ('Ibād) turned to al-Jazīra and conquered all her cities and granted them security under the agreement that they will send to him 100,000 dīnārs every year provided that none of the Arabs crossed the Euphrates (to enter al-Jazīra) . . . The people sent to 'Ibād b. 'Āṣim Kharāj of one year and this was done by the patrician Būlīs (Polis?) whom Heraclius had appointed governor of al-Jazīra. Heraclius dismissed him and exiled him to Ifrīqiyya and appointed patrician Baṭlīmūs as governor.'

The statement is not confirmed by Muslim historians on a number of points. Firstly, a lump-sum agreement for the whole of al-Jazīra was not made. Like Syria, al-Jazīra also fell not at once but city after city under separate treaties – all of them following the terms settled with ar-Ruḥā (Edessa), the capital. The condition that Muslims would not cross into al-Jazīra is also contrary to the Muslim historians' records which give the following details:

"Iyāḍ b. Ghanam, according to historians, began his operations in the border town of ar-Raqqa *en route* to Edessa, the capital of the Byzantium part of the region. According to Balādhurī, 'Iyāḍ spread his soldiers around ar-Raqqa where they arrested the countrymen and took food and provisions. It was harvesting time there and when some five or six months elapsed in this way, the city officer conveyed to 'Iyāḍ a request for the grant of protection to which 'Iyāḍ acceded and granted protection to the lives, properties, children and the city of these people and made a treaty with him and said, "But the land is ours because we have trodden over it and secured it *(qad waṭ'anāhā wa aḥraznāhā)*." Then he left all their land with them on the condition of paying land-tax, and gave to the Muslims those lands on the condition of paying *'Ushr* about which they did not agree. He also levied on all of them, except women and children, a poll-tax of one dīnār per head and fixed some *qafīz's* of wheat and quantities of oil, vinegar, and honey. When Mu'āwiya became ruler, he levied these things on them as poll-tax . . . It is said that 'Iyāḍ fixed a tax of four dīnārs per head but it is not correct; actually when 'Umar appointed 'Umayr b. Sa'd after 'Iyāḍ, he ordered him to fix four dīnārs per head as had become the case with every "person of gold". Then 'Iyāḍ reached Ḥarrān where the people offered to accept the conditions which would be settled with the people of the capital Edessa. 'Iyāḍ then reached Edessa . . . After a few days the people of Edessa requested for protection and treaty. 'Iyāḍ agreed to their request and gave them the following document. "In the name of God . . . this writing is from 'Iyāḍ b. Ghanam for the bishop *(usquf)* of Edessa. If he will open for me the gate of the city on the condition that he shall pay on behalf of every man a dīnār and two *modii* of wheat, he shall have security for himself and his property and for his fellows and followers. It is incumbent on him to guide the lost travellers, to repair bridges and roads, and to evince goodwill to the Muslims . . .'[202]

Abū Yūsuf has given a more comprehensive account of the conquest and the levy of taxes in al-Jazīra. A summary of the relevant portions is as follows:

'Al-Jazīra was partly under the Byzantine and partly under the Persian Empire. Abū 'Ubayda sent 'Iyāḍ for al-Jazīra. 'Iyāḍ started for the capital city of the Byzantine part and laid siege on the city. The governor, along with most of his army got off and the people of the city, the Nabaetians, sent their emissary to make a treaty with 'Iyāḍ who conveyed their desire to Abū 'Ubayda. Abū 'Ubayda asked Mu'ādh for his advice whereupon Mu'ādh said: "If you make a treaty with them on a fixed thing which, later on, they fail to pay you shall have no right to kill them, but the only alternative will be to cancel the agreed amount. On the other hand, if they become more well-to-do, they will be able to pay the amount without feeling the burden which God has desired them to feel. It is, therefore, suitable to accept their request for treaty but on condition that they shall pay land-tax according to their capacity." '

Abū Yūsuf continues: 'Abū 'Ubayda wrote this advice to 'Iyāḍ who informed the people of the city about the condition. The reports about the later events differ. Some say they accepted the condition of paying according to their capacity while some others say that they agreed to pay only a fixed amount. In any case 'Iyāḍ agreed to what these people wished. He then went to Ḥarrān, the people of which also agreed to these terms. Similar was the situation in respect of other towns and villages. After full control over the area, the caliphs gave the people of the villages the same treatment as to the townsmen. But the provisioning of the army was made the responsibility of the countrymen and not of the townsmen. Some knowledgeable scholars say the caliph did so because the countrymen had fields and farms but the condition of the townsmen was different.

'As regards the Persian part of al-Jazīra, the population had already vacated it after the fall of Qādisiyya. But those who failed to migrate embraced Islam.

"Iyāḍ fixed on their chiefs a rate of two dīnārs per head plus two *modii* of wheat and two *qisṭs* each of olive oil and vinegar. He computed a class of people (under each chief). When 'Abd al-Malik became ruler, he deputed Ḍaḥḥāk b. 'Abd ar-Raḥmān who found their levy very light. He, therefore, took a fresh census of the chiefs and treated all the people as labourers under them. He calculated the gross annual earnings of every person, deducted from it the cost of food and other requirements and of the festivals and found that this still left them with a surplus of four dīnārs which he fixed for every man alike. While levying the tax he also took into consideration the factor of nearness to the city, and levied a dīnār each for every 100 *jarībs* of land near the city, and for every two hundred *jarībs* remote from the town. Similarly a dīnār each on every 100 gourds of vine and every 100 trees of olive near the city and every 200 gourds and 200 olive trees far from the city. The same technique was followed in Syria and Mosul.'[203]

The above narrations depict almost all the important points about taxation in al-Jazīra. Yet Balādhurī has recorded a few more details which fit the chain of events and make them more intelligible. These details are summarized as follows:

1. The towns and villages of al-Jazīra were conquered under treaties *(ṣulḥan)* but their lands were conquered by force[204] *('anwatan)*.
2. The terms of treaties with most towns were identical.[205]
3. The commissioner of Bidlīs (*ṣāḥib* Bidlīs) was made responsible for collecting the *Kharāj* of Khilāṭ and (the tax on) its heads and also the amount due to the patrician of Khilāṭ.[206]
4. Ra's al-'Ayn was captured by 'Umayr b. Sa'd who levied four dīnārs per head as poll-tax while the land was treated as being under the ownership of the Muslims.[207]
5. Al-Jazīra continued to supply oil, vinegar and food for the Muslims for a time. Caliph 'Umar then reduced the poll-tax to forty-eight, twenty-four and twelve dirhams. Before this concession every man was to pay two *modii* of wheat, and two *qisṭs* each of vinegar and oil in addition to his poll-tax.[208] This point is also perhaps confirmed by Theophanes and Michael the Syrian who observe that Caliph 'Umar wrote to his governors to straighten *(taqsīṭ)* the *Kharāj* system in all the places under their respective jurisdictions. So the registers *(Dawāwīn)* were maintained and *Kharāj* was levied town to town, village to village, city to city and suburb to suburb, and the taxes and *Ṣadaqat* were collected.[209]
6. As was the case with al-Jarājima in Syria, Banū Taghlib, an Arab race, perhaps Christians (Naṣārā) in al-Jazīra, were exempted from poll-tax and land-tax but subjected to *Ṣadaqa (Zakāt)* at double the rate levied on Muslims.[210] Unlike al-Jarājima who rendered military service for Muslims, the consideration in this case was purely negative. The government did not want this tribe to join their enemies. But they were not agreeable to pay poll-tax because, as they argued, they were Arabs. The compromise was effected on their paying double *Ṣadaqa* on the '*Zakāt*-able' items.[211]

The above details emphasize the following points about the system of taxation in al-Jazīra:

1. Most of al-Jazīra was conquered under treaty which followed the pattern of treaty settled by the people of Edessa and which provided for a tax in money as well as in kind.

2. Land was treated as conquered by force and some unoccupied or deserted lands were also allotted to Muslims who paid *'Ushr* on their produce. Thus the land was treated as *Kharāj*-land unlike the lands in Sawād which were generally treated as *Fay'*.

3. In the beginning a per-head tax of one dīnār was levied over and above the supply of food-grains, vinegar, oil and honey. But later on Caliph 'Umar introduced reforms and taxed the townsmen only for money at forty-eight, twenty-four, and twelve dirhams per head[212] and the countrymen only for provisions. The per-head monetary collection in the case of the townsmen was enhanced in lieu of the provisions which they had previously paid. In the same way it also stands to reason that the commodity levy in lieu of money should also have been enhanced for the countrymen.

4. While assessment was done by the Muslims, the responsibility for the collection of taxes was laid on the local officials. Here again the *Bayt al-Māl* is not reported to have committed itself to bear the expenses of collection which, it can be presumed, was probably the responsibility of the local community.

5. For assessment purposes the population was, in the early stages, divided into towns or village communities. Mu'āwiya is stated to have introduced his reforms in al-Jazīra too but the details about them are not recorded. It is presumable that they might be in line with what he introduced in Syria.[213]

'Abd al-Malik again streamlined tax administration in al-Jazīra. He reconstituted the units of assessment by treating a number of workers working under a chief head as one unit and the chief head was made responsible for collecting and paying the taxes on their behalf. He also revised the taxes on land by taking into consideration the factor of nearness to the city. The way of taxing land before this period in al-Jazīra is not explicitly recorded but it is likely that this was not much different from what it was in Iraq.

As was the case with al-Jarājima in Syria, the Banū Taghlib in al-Jazīra were also exempted from poll-tax and land-tax but, unlike the former, were subjected to a double *Zakāt* on the negative consideration of stopping them from crossing into enemy country.

EGYPT AND THE WEST (Miṣr and al-Maghrib)

The Circumstances of the Conquest

Almost all historians have recorded the role of 'Amr b. al-'Āṣ in sending relief supplies to Madina during the famine *('ām ar-ramāda)* which occurred in Arabia in A.H. 21. This suggests the capitulation of Egypt before this year.[214] Immediately after the conquest of Egypt, al-Maghrib was seized and Caliph 'Umar stopped his advancing general from crossing the borders of Ifrīqiyya which was destined for 'Abd Allāh b. Sa'd b. Abī-Sarḥ on the orders of Caliph 'Uthmān.

The account of the conquest of Egypt and particularly al-Maghrib (west of Egypt) is discussed by historians briefly perhaps because the Muslims did not have to exert as much force here as in Iraq or in Syria, and also because the whole of this region was conquered by 'Amr in less than two years. The Byzantine armies were already engaged in Syria and after its fall, in saving the remaining borders of the mainland. This hampered them from sufficiently reinforcing the garrisons stationed in Egypt and thus they lost the richest province which fed a large number of Roman and Byzantine people free bread for centuries.

'Amr started his operations from Pelusium (al-Faramā'). The local Copts were probably reluctant to resist him. The Byzantine garrisons stationed at different places resisted in vain and were either routed or they capitulated on condition of a safe return to their mainland. An agreement was reached for the whole province. But the treaty did not last for long. Heraclius disapproved of it and dispatched fresh contingents to reinforce the defeated armies who again arrayed themselves against the Muslims. By A.H. 25 Alexandria had revolted twice and been reduced.[215] The original treaty was obviously abrogated. It is said that during this period also, the local population did not actively support the Heraclian troops and sought an under-cover agreement with the Muslim commander. When Alexandria was fully and finally conquered after suppressing the revolt, Zubayr pressed 'Amr to distribute the land as the Prophet (peace be upon him) had done in Khaybar. But Caliph 'Umar decreed what he had done in the case of Iraq.[216]

Leaving aside the chronology of events, the names of persons and the terms of the treaties involved, this general story is discernible from the different sources, mainly Balādhurī. Severus observes that when the Muslims crossed Jordan to enter Egypt Heraclius concentrated his forces at Aswān. 'Amr defeated the Romans and captured a number of cities, advanced to Babylon between Ṣa'īd and Rīf, pitched his tents and named it Babylon al-Fusṭāṭ. The Muslims vanquished the Romans after three battles.[217]

The above statements suggest that at the time of the first capitulation of Egypt an agreement was reached. But later on the treaty was violated and thus abrogated. What terms and conditions were originally settled and what changes were made after the abrogation of the treaty are not precisely explained by historians. Moreover, while in other regions different terms were settled with people of different cities, the terms of treaty in Egypt seem to be different for different communities; the followers of the ruling church and the local Copts with a different church. It was natural, therefore, that the policy of taxation should also have been different for different communities.

Conquest by Force or by Treaty?

But this situation seems to have confused the early historians in deciding if the whole of Egypt was taken by force or by treaty. They have recorded both views on different authorities with stronger evidence for the former view. Later developments also suggest continuing confusion throughout the period. What the caliphs generally did suggested that they treated it as a land occupied by force. The confusion arises due to a number of conflicting reports which have been mixed up by historians without suggesting the chronology and the exact place of events. It seems worthwhile, therefore, to record the different reports on the subject.

When the prince of al-Yūna (Babylon) sorted out his own affairs and the affairs of its citizens, he settled the same terms for all the people of Miṣr as he had done for al-Yūna. They were agreeable to it and said: 'When these well-guarded people *(mumtani'ūn)* have had an agreement, we are more in need of protection because we are exposed.' *Kharāj* was levied on the lands of Miṣr which amounted to a dīnār for every *jarīb* of land, three artabas of wheat and two dīnārs of poll-tax on each head.[218]

Al-Muqawqis agreed with 'Amr to let the willing Romans go and to allow those who wished to stay on agreed terms. They also agreed that the Copts should pay poll-tax at two dīnārs per head. When the Byzantine ruler learnt about it, he was annoyed and despatched reinforcements who shut the gates of Alexandria and gave an ultimatum to 'Amr. Al-Muqawqis then came to 'Amr and said: 'I beseech you for three things: firstly, do not show that leniency to Romans which you showed to me because they have treated me as a traitor; secondly, do not abrogate the treaty for the Copts because they have not violated it; and, lastly, bury me in such and such a church in Alexandria when I die.' To this 'Amr replied: 'This (last) condition is most acceptable to me.'[219]

According to Yazīd b. Ḥabīb, al-Muqawqis, the ruler of Miṣr agreed with ‘Amr to levy two dīnārs as poll-tax on Copts. When Heraclius knew of it, he was very annoyed and sent armies towards Alexandria and they shut its gates. Then ‘Amr conquered it by force.[220]

According to the same source, a second treaty was made with the tributaries of Miṣr which required them to pay two dīnārs for wheat, oil, honey, vinegar, in addition to two dīnārs per head.[221]

According to Abu'l ‘Āliya, ‘Amr said: ‘I am sitting here at my seat and I am not committed to any treaty with any of the Copts of Miṣr. I may kill them if I will, I may take the fifth *(Khums)* of their properties if I will, or I may sell them if I will. But the matter of Anṭābalus is different because they have a treaty which will be respected.’[222]

According to ‘Abd-Allāh b. Ja‘far, Mu‘āwiya wrote to Wardān asking for an increase in tax of a carat each on the Copts, to which Wardān replied how could he do so while there was a treaty committing for no increase on them.[223]

According to Sufyān b. Wahab, when Miṣr was conquered without a treaty Zubayr stood up and exclaimed: ‘O ‘Amr! Distribute it among us.’ ‘Amr said: ‘No! Unless I write to ‘Umar!’ So he wrote to Caliph ‘Umar who decreed to leave it as it was, so that posterity would also benefit from it.[224]

Ibn An‘ām's grandfather, who took part in the expedition against Miṣr, and ‘Abd-Allāh b. Hubayra, have reported that Egypt was conquered by force.[225]

Ziyād b. Jaz' who was also present on the expedition has reported that Miṣr was conquered by treaty and he criticized the policy of the Umayyad rulers of treating it as land conquered by force.[226]

Ḥusayn b. Shufayy said: ‘When Alexandria was conquered the number of surviving slaves was six hundred thousand excluding women and children. There was a disagreement between most of the Muslims and ‘Amr, on the question of their distribution. ‘Amr referred the matter to Caliph ‘Umar explaining to him about the conquest and the general opinion about distribution (of slaves). Caliph ‘Umar wrote to him to leave them undistributed so that their *Kharāj* becomes *Fay'* for the Muslims and a source of strength in waging war against the enemies. So ‘Amr spared them, counted them, and levied *Kharāj* on them. Thus the whole of Miṣr became a conquest through treaty *(ṣulḥī)*, paying two dīnārs for each person, not to be increased except that they are able to pay it corresponding to increase in the productivity of land outside Alexandria. Thus they (people out of Alexandria) paid both *Kharāj* and *Jizya* at a rate which was determined by their officers. Alexandria, on the other hand was conquered by force and without any treaty or condition, and the people there have no treaty or protection.’[227]

According to Layth, Yazīd b. Ḥabīb used to say that the whole of

Miṣr was conquered by treaty except Alexandria which was vanquished by force.[228]

According to Yazīd b. Ḥabīb, Mu'āwiya wrote to an officer to allot to 'Uqba a stretch of land measuring one thousand square ells. The officer declined on the ground that he had treaty land. At this 'Uqba observed that the treaty contained only six conditions: nothing will be snatched away from them or from their women or their children, nothing will be increased on them, and protection will be given to them and they will not be overburdened; and I am a witness to these conditions.[229]

It is said that Mu'āwiya wrote to Wardān to increase their tax by one carat. Wardān wrote back to him: 'How would you increase when the agreement provides for no increase on them.'[230]

According to Yazīd b. Ḥabīb, when 'Amr conquered Miṣr, he settled with them that all the Copts should pay two dīnārs each major person excepting the women and children. They counted these assessed persons who numbered 8 million.[231]

Many other reports, on the other hand, claim that Egypt was conquered by force and without any treaty or conditions.[232]

Miṣr, a City or a Province?

All the above reports have been made by Balādhurī, Ṭabarī and Ibn 'Abd al-Ḥakam, without generally suggesting the context of these reports and this has confounded the whole issue. The sources suggesting the capitulation of Egypt do not mention if the terms of capitulation pertain to the first round of conquests or the last. In order to reach a precise conclusion, the following points also need clarification:

1. Why the ruler (or more correctly the competent officer) of Bāb al-Yūna (Babylon) settled the terms for all the people of Miṣr? Was he the governor? Moreover, was Babylon the seat of the governor?
2. Why did the people of Miṣr fear their unprotected position as compared with Babylon? Was there only one fortress at Babylon in the whole of the province of Miṣr (Egypt) with the only protecting army at Babylon?

Along with these questions the frequently occurring mention in early records of Alexandria as exclusive of Miṣr is also meaningful. 'Zubayr earmarked two plots of land in Miṣr and Alexandria.'[233] "Amr stayed for some time after he conquered Miṣr and then wrote to 'Umar for permission to advance towards Alexandria.'[234] 'Miṣr and Alexandria were conquered in the year A.H. 20.'[235] These are only a few of the similar statements which are reproduced by historians. It is no less important to note that Muslims were not the first, nor for that matter the last, to distinguish Miṣr from Alexandria. Even centuries before the Muslims, Egypt was sometimes known as *Alexandria ad Aegyptum.*[236] In the later period the tenth-century Patriarch Severus mentions: 'When Khusroes conquered Miṣr and controlled it, he made preparations to conquer the great city of Alexandria.'[237] In view of the above statements the question arises was Alexandria at that time not a part of Egypt?

The early Muslim sources do not clarify these points and this is the main cause of confusion. The solution to this problem may solve other problems too. Let us, therefore, look at other sources. A clue is given by John of Nikiu who reports the capitulation of the city of Miṣr[238] and is supported by Abū Ṣāliḥ when he describes the church at the 'Island of Miṣr.'[239] Severus also mentions the 'district of Miṣr and other cities'.[240] Muslim historians suggest that Miṣr capitulated consecutive to Babylon, and after the capitulation of Babylon and Miṣr the Muslim armies set out for Alexandria. This leads us to infer that the confusion among the different historians was because they did not distinguish between the city of Miṣr[241] and the whole province which was also known by the same name. The questions listed above are answered if this is kept in mind. Thus the answer is that Miṣr, in the context of many (not all) reports of historians was a city near Babylon, poorly protected and thinly populated mainly by the Copts. According to Ibn Duqmāq, ancient Miṣr was located on the site of present-day Fusṭāṭ.[242] Evetts locates it on the 'north of Raudah or Roda, the large island near the Nile nearly opposite to the old city of Cairo.'[243] Moreover, the rationale behind 'Amr's seeking Caliph 'Umar's permission to advance towards Alexandria after the conquest of Miṣr is understandable in the context of Miṣr being situated east of the Nile. When 'Amr conquered the east bank of the Nile he did not like to cross it to advance towards Alexandria without prior approval of the caliph who did not encourage sailing across the waters.

The Person of Muqawqis

It transpires from the above discussion that the first stage of the conquests ended with the capitulation of the city of Miṣr – on the eastern bank of the Nile. The second stage started after Caliph 'Umar had given permission to cross the river *en route* to Alexandria. This fact can also be inferred from 'Amr's son, 'Abd-Allāh's statement[244] but in view of a general confusion it escaped a clear understanding. As regards al-Muqawqis, he is found communicating at Babylon and then encouraging 'Amr to crush the Romans, and then resisting the Muslim onslaught at Alexandria and then suggesting his people come to terms with the Muslim armies. Long before this a Muqawqis was also to be found sending some gifts to the Prophet (peace be upon him).[245] All these traditions taken together suggest that Muqawqis was not the name of a person but the name of an office – the chief officer of the principal city. Balādhurī reports that when Alexandria revolted, Muqawqis withdrew from the revolt. 'Amr reinstated him and his colleagues in their offices; but some say that he was dead even before this war.[246] In view of the suggestion about Muqawqis the reports can be reconciled without contradicting each other. A Muqawqis of Alexandria (Cyrus) was called back by Heraclius after the first treaty with the Arabs. Another Muqawqis (Manuel) was killed by the Muslims in the fighting for Alexandria; there should have been a third Muqawqis to replace Manuel, and come to terms with 'Amr.[247]

The above discussion leads to the following conclusion: 'Amr had settled the terms of treaty after the capitulation of the city of Miṣr. Then the same terms, or with some changes, were reconfirmed at Alexandria, now for the whole of Egypt – Miṣr or the eastern bank of the Nile, and Alexandria or the western bank. After the revolt of Alexandria, the treaty was abrogated. When 'Amr was reminded of the supporting role of the Copts, and the retention of the treaty for them, he did not clearly commit it. Yet he behaved generously, spared them and levied a tax on them, rather than killing or enslaving them according to the prevalent custom of war. When a similar behaviour was adopted with the people of Iraq it was later on taken to mean a self-imposed treaty. The confusion in the case of Egypt was further caused by ignoring the sequence of events and the chronology of the conquest. It also seems that in some cases full reports were not reproduced. For example, the statement attributed to 'Amr's son 'Abd Allāh suggesting the truth behind the misunderstandings, seems to have been only half-produced and thus it has distorted the real picture.

While the treatment of the issue given above is a short cut to explain the question, in essence, it is generally in line with the comprehensive work produced by Butler[248] who has skilfully combined the early Muslim and the Christian records of history and cleared up many confusions and ambiguities. But unfortunately the work is not so helpful for our purpose which is outside the scope of his work. Bell has tried to compensate for this lack but, as Dennett put it, he 'was not an Arabist and dependent, therefore, on the evidence of Becker for the information to be derived from Arabic sources.'[249] As a result his work is exposed to all those objections which apply to Becker's work.

The Terms of the Treaty

While the confusion in the chronology of events could be largely cleared up by combining and reconciling the Muslim and Christian records, the confusion in respect of the terms and conditions of the treaty still remains to be thrashed out. As regards the social and political concessions contained in the treaty, it can be believed, as is also evident from different sources, that they were not different from those given elsewhere. They include protection of life, properties and churches, freedom of religion and exemption of women, children, the elderly and monks from poll-tax. But, unfortunately, the differences among historians reach their climax on the point of the amount of tax. The following are some of the amounts which are reported to have been levied.

According to Ṭabarī, ʻAmr settled the following conditions:

ʻ . . . And the people of Miṣr if they are agreeable to this treaty shall pay the *Jizya* (poll-tax); when the inundation of their river has subsided, fifty million . . .[250] and as for those who will not enter into this treaty the sum of the poll-tax shall be reduced in proportion; but we are not responsible for their protection. If the rise of the Nile is less than the usual the tax shall be reduced in proportion to the decrease . . . The collection of taxes shall be in (instalments of) one-third at each time . . . ʼ[251]

According to ʻAbd Allāh b. ʻAmr, the treaty which originally covered the people up to the city of Miṣr (Babylon) called for a poll-tax of two dīnārs per head and a levy of two dīnārs on the owners of land; in addition to three artabas of wheat, two *qisṭs* each of oil, vinegar and honey. ʻAmr also required them to supply clothes for his soldiers each year. These terms, according to ʻAbd Allāh, were extended to the whole of Miṣr (Egypt). The lands of Egypt were subjected to land-tax at a rate of one dīnār per *jarīb* plus three artabas of wheat and two dīnārs on each adult.[252] According to Yaʻqūbī, when the whole of Egypt was conquered ʻAmr collected 14 million dīnārs at a rate of a dīnār per head and two artabas of wheat per hundred artabas.[253] As regards the total receipts under this treaty Yaʻqūbī has given figures of 14 million dīnārs,[254] Maqrīzī 12 million,[255] Balādhurī 2 million,[256] Ibn ʻAbd al-Ḥakam 12 million as compared with 20 million dīnārs which, according to him, al-Muqawqis used to collect before Islam.[257] The most paradoxical figure is given by Severus for a period when, according to Muslim historians, the amount had much decreased, viz., 200 million dīnārs excluding the charges for so many other expenses during the early ʻAbbāsid period,[258] although according to Abu Ṣāliḥ the total of receipts during Mahdī's period amounted to 1,828,000 dīnārs[259] while in Hārūn's period, according to other sources, it was 4 million dīnārs.[260] Saʻīd (Eutychius) is inclined to suggest an amount of 12 million while he confirms that the number of taxable Copts in Egypt was 6 million who were taxed at two dīnārs per head.[261]

Some sources also give the amount of collections exclusively for Alexandria. Balādhurī has given two different versions: (1) 13,000 dīnārs and two dīnārs per head on Copts and, (2) 18,000 dīnārs.[262] According to Mahboub al-Manbidg (Agapius) the treaty between ʻAmr and Qurra,[263] the patrician of Alexandria, provided for the payment of 200,000 dīnārs per annum, provided ʻAmr did not overrun Egypt. Qurra lived there for three years and no Arab entered there during his time. ʻThen some Egyptians reported to Heraclius Qurra's payment of wealth to Arabs . . . and of his payment of *Kharāj.* Heraclius was annoyed and sent patrician Manuel to dismiss Qurra . . . When the Arabs again came to collect their money, Manuel was displeased. ʻAmr invaded Alexandria and pushed them out and conquered Egypt.'[264] According to Maqrīzī, ʻAmr collected 600,000 dīnārs from the *ahl adh-dhimma*[265] in Alexandria. According to his other report the amount stood at 12,000 dīnārs in the beginning and rose to 36,000 dīnārs in Hishām's time.[266]

The Population of Alexandria and Egypt

The above figures give a very intriguing picture of the real situation. While the minimum amount of land-tax and poll-tax for Egypt is reported by Balādhurī at 2 million dīnārs the maximum amount as suggested by Severus stands at 200 million for the ʻAbbāsid period. If any credence is given to the latter report the amount during the early period will come to between 300 and 400 million dīnārs. The matter does not end here. Some historians have added to the confusion by suggesting very high figures for the population of Alexandria and Egypt.[267] ʻYaʻqūbī, while he gives the amount of 14 million at one dīnār per head, admits the population at 14 million persons; Eutychius at 6 million of taxable persons,[268] Ibn ʻAbd al-Ḥakam too at the latter figure at a rate of two dīnārs per head, and according to yet another version 8 million taxable persons at a similar rate.[269] For Alexandria alone Maqrīzī has reported the Jewish population at 600,000 during the Roman rule and an equal number of taxable persons after the Muslim conquest. His third version suggests a taxable population of 300,000.[270] Ibn ʻAbd al-Ḥakam has reported 100,000 only of Romans, and forty to seventy thousand Jews excluding the Copts.[271]

With the above figures one may hastily infer that some historians have based their estimates of population on the recorded total collection: so much money divided by two, the rate of per-head poll-tax, will give its quotient in terms of taxable population. This is no doubt an easy calculation but it can be convincing only when, contrary to all historical records it is believed that, firstly, there was no other levy except poll-tax and, secondly, there was no increase in the rate of levy. But all the historians agree that at the stage of conquest by force land-tax was also levied in addition to poll-tax. Moreover, Balādhurī has reported that Caliph 'Umar himself replaced the levy in commodity by two dīnārs making the total levy four dīnārs.[272] There seems to be no reason to suspect the authenticity of the report mainly in view of the fact that similar reforms were carried out in other provinces too.

As regards the figures of total population ranging between 14 million and 24[273] million there seems to be grounds to suspect the validity of such a fantastic estimate. It may be argued that counting the population entails counting the living human beings. If in the first century of Hijra (A.D. seventh) the population was 14 million persons, the population of the country should have reached about 150 to 250 million, even rejecting the Malthusian theory of growth at geometric ratio. If it is not so, there should be some reports of large-scale toll of human life through epidemic or wars. If there is no such report, there should be some proof of large-scale migration or exodus of the population to another place. In the latter case there should have been reports of an explosion in population in that part of the world where it migrated. But in the absence of supporting demographic evidence it appears safe to believe that the figures of the early population of Egypt that have come down to us are based on some sort of misunderstanding. And as this misunderstanding occurred in Egypt, in overestimating its population, the same situation seems to have occurred in underestimating the population of Alexandria. A poll-tax of 12,000 or 18,000 dīnārs will credit Alexandria with 6,000 or 9,000 taxable persons or an approximate total population of 20,000 or 30,000 persons. Alexandria, at the time of the conquest, was not that small a city of only 30,000 persons. Severus has reported the presence of 600 busy churches *(dayr 'āmir)* in Alexandria during the same period.[274] This figure can also be discredited as easily as the reports that it had 4,000 bath houses, 400 playhouses and 12,000 grocery shops and the like.[275] But that Alexandria was a big and densely-populated city cannot be doubted. The size of the population can be guessed at by the fact that at the beginning of the seventh century John the Almoner could find only 7,500 persons in Alexandria who needed charity[276] and this number was considered to be a very small segment of the total population.

A census of population was conducted by both the Roman and the Byzantine rulers. But unfortunately the records giving the number of heads have not yet come to hand. In the early Islamic period too a census was conducted; not once, but at least four times by the end of the Umayyad period. 'Amr might have relied on the figures furnished by the continuing officers in the initial stage of his governorship. Severus attributes to 'Abd-Allāh b. Sa'd the first maintenance of registers and organization of administration.[277] According to another report, 'Ubayd Allāh conducted a census of men and livestock and surveyed land and trees during Hishām's caliphate.[278] Before him Ibn Rafā'a had also conducted an intensive census and surveyed lands in the whole region accompanied by a large number of staff working for several months.[279] During this period there also appear reports of the recompilation of the registers and perhaps the administrative structure too. While Severus names 'Abd-Allāh b. Sa'd as the first to set up taxation registers (*dīwān* or offices), al-Kindī names 'Amr as the founder of the administrative machinery who also took a census and conducted a survey followed by 'Umar II's governor. Later on Qurra and Bishr b. Ṣafwān also did the same in their respective governorships.[280] Ibn 'Abd al-Ḥakam includes Ibn Rafā'a among those who conducted an intensive survey of land, livestock and men. His report is very emphatic in suggesting a very large population in the province. He reports that when Ibn Rafā'a became the governor of Egypt he undertook a census in order to reassess the taxes. He worked for six months and reached Aswān with a team of assistants and scribes. He spent three more months in the lower part of Egypt. There were more than 10,000 villages and even the smallest of them accommodated no less than 500 tax-paying persons.[281] This brings the minimum total to about 5 million persons.

With all these details about censuses and surveys it is difficult to believe that the early historians used only wild guesses when calculating the total population. They must have had a reason to believe in the reports quoting such high figures. But it is now very difficult to put a finger on the source of this misunderstanding. It would require a great deal of demographic research to prove that the race to which the Copts belonged was tending to decline in rate of growth. There remains, therefore, no other course than to put aside the factor of population in discussing the revenues of Egypt, at least at this stage.

Pre-Islamic Taxes

Before discussing the question of the total collections in Egypt, note must be taken of the volleys of criticism from modern historians who have reacted oversensitively to the figures reported by Muslim historians. Butler, and following him Johnson, criticize the figures of total collection by observing that 'If these figures were divided by ten they might be more credible.'[282] Gibbon is also startled by these figures, but did not insist upon the formula of dividing them by ten.[283] But unfortunately the basis of the information of the first two is the extremely insufficient fragmentary evidence about the pre-Islamic period from which one cannot make out a reliable statement of fact. As a result the economic history of pre-Islamic Egypt is replete with presumptions and wild guesses. The most important source of information about this period is now supposed to be the Greek Papyri which cover only a few isolated villages and give some incomplete figures for different periods, sometimes even undated. These Papyri are frequently exposed to various conclusions at one and the same time and can be used by scholars to fit in with the many *a priori* theory and *idee fixe*.

In spite of this weakness in the study of the economic statistics of pre-Islamic Egypt, it would not be advisable to altogether ignore the available information. It can, to some extent, provide the tools to break fresh ground.

While criticizing the early Muslim figures Johnson has tried to estimate the probable total collections of Egypt during Justinian's period (around A.D. 540) and has compared them with the Muslim period (A.D. 643, A.H. 41). According to his presumptions the wheat levied by Justinian, if converted into money, would be worth 800,000 solidi. The *largitionalia* would normally add 500,000 solidi. The gold annona at Aphrodito was normally about a sixth of the canonica, and probably all of these should be reckoned as part of the revenue sent to Constantinople. If we add the customs dues, taxes on vineyards, gardens, and trades, the revenues from imperial estates and government monopolies, it is possible to estimate the total income of the Byzantine rulers at 2 million solidi annually.[284]

Before commenting on this figure it is worthwhile to list the taxes that are supposed to have been levied in Byzantine Egypt, although there is much obscurity as to the total amount of tax that was raised by the Byzantine Empire. Fragmentary evidence suggests the existence of a multiplicity of taxes that were inherited from the Roman period and which still continued. The amount which was contributed by Egypt was a matter for special consideration by the Emperor year by year. He not only decided how much revenue was to be raised in the province, but issued special instructions as to the manner in which it was to be collected. The most important of all the taxes levied in Egypt was the corn tax, *embole,* which was collected in kind from the villages and used to furnish the tribute of corn sent to Rome.[285] One of the lists available for the period apparently refers to this tax, and the rates vary from two and a half to seven artabas per aroura, the commonest being four and twenty-seven fortieths artabas.[286] In the sixth century Justinian set the grain tribute at 8 million units, presumably artabas. This amount would be sufficient to supply approximately 600,000 people daily.[287] Another tax, payable like the *embole* in corn, was *annona.* Details of this tax are rare, but it appears probable that it was for supply of the allowance of corn made to Alexandria as the *embole* was for that to Rome and Constantinople.[288] A further charge upon the village granaries was met in the form of certain payments for charitable purposes, which was made in corn payable either through a special tax or chargeable upon the common property of the village.[289] The gardens were also liable to a tax payable in money. The rate of taxes on trees and plantations cannot be determined but in one case the tax was ten drachmae per *aroura,* in another it was from twenty to forty.[290] There were other taxes on lands payable in money, the nature and amount of which is obscure. A charge of *'naubian'* is mentioned several times; but there is nothing to show what its precise object was, beyond the fact that it appears among other imposts levied on real property; nor what its rate was except in one instance, where it seems to have been assessed at approximately 100 drachmae per *aroura.*[291] Entries for receipts for *'geometrica'* are also found on the same list as the one named *'arithmeticon',* apparently on house property, along with most of the taxes already mentioned; but the particulars relating to these charges cannot be determined.[292] House property was subject to tax presumably at 100 drachmae for each house.[293] Cattle-tax was levied on various kinds of flocks and herds separately.[294] All inhabitants of Egypt between the ages of fourteen and sixty, with the exception of certain privileged classes were liable to pay a poll-tax.[295] According to Hussey the system of taxation in the Byzantine Empire since the third century A.D. had been that of the *ingatio-capitatio* and with many alterations it remained in force during the whole Byzantine period. As the name indicates the system established on the one hand a taxation according to the yield of the soil, on the other a capitation fee per head of the labouring population.[296] But Johnson thinks that the urban population was exempt from this tax.[297] Romans and Alexandrians were also exempt from most capitation levies.[298] In addition to income from monopolies, customs dues became an important source of revenue. These included *octroi* as well as an import duty.[299] Other indirect taxes which were formed in the same way as the customs duties were the *enkyklion,* a fee of ten per cent on sales, a fine of five per cent on inheritance and one at a similar rate on manumission of slaves.[300] Greek Papyri suggest that Justinian also introduced 'air tax', which was levied as an addition to the ordinary tax but the nature of the tax is not explained.[301] A tax was also paid by traders of all descriptions, the sum payable being reckoned on the monthly receipts of the business. This was therefore a kind of income-tax.[302] Another burden which was laid upon the inhabitants of Egypt consisted of the posting rights claimed by officials although in principle it had been restricted by the decree of the prefect.[303] The work of repairing dykes and clearing canals was somewhat of the nature of liturgy inasmuch as it was compulsory though it was joint labour for a common purpose.[304] Temple property was not, as such, exempt from taxation. It paid the ordinary taxes; and there were in addition special taxes levied under the names of altar tax, tax on offerings and *'lesonia'*.[305] The priest also paid a special tax known as *epistatikon*.[306] Records also suggest the exaction of some levies called *diagraphae* and these have been explained as poll-tax.[307]

The above list cannot be claimed to be comprehensive or conclusive because of the nature of the evidence on which it is based. It is possible that records of many more taxes have not so far reached us; it is equally possible that a particular tax that has been inferred from some incomplete record did not exist at all, and the amount actually refers to some other transaction which is misunderstood. Similar is the case of the few rates of levy at isolated places, that have come down to us. In spite of these formidable obstructions in his study Johnson has tried to estimate the probable total collections on the basis of Justinian's assessment and has come to the conclusion that the Byzantine rulers would have received 2 million solidi annually;[308] an amount which Balādhurī seems to have suggested for Caliph 'Umar's period.[309] The question arises: Are Johnson and his predecessors justified in their criticism of the figures reported by early historians when comparing them to the figures of A.D. 530–50? A mention has already been made of the source of their information which can be of some use in formulating various theories but not necessarily in arriving at facts. Apart from this, these scholars have totally ignored the difference in the boundaries of the governments of Egypt between Justinian's and the Muslim period. In Justinian's period, as Johnson himself records, certain parts of Egypt were transferred to Libya, while under the early Muslim rule the whole of Egypt including Libya was under the governorate of Egypt. Even the conquered lands of the south were merged with it. And this remained so up to the period when most of Ifrīqiyya was conquered and a separate governor was appointed to control al-Maghrib and Ifrīqiyya, and Mu'āwiya again merged the entire western provinces with Egypt under Maslama who appointed a lieutenant governor, Abu'l Muhājir, to look after his western region.[310] Mūsā b. Nuṣayr the governor of al-Maghrib had his capital at Qayruwān when 'Abd al-Malik advised him to prepare for further conquest[311] (see also map on p. 247). Moreover the amount suggested by Johnson refers to what would have been actually received by the emperors at the centre but not what would have been actually collected, while the amount referred to by the Muslim historians is what was collected and not what was remitted to the centre. What portion of the collections was retained by the Roman collectors is not discussed by these sources.

In view of the above-mentioned differences between the areas of the governorate of Egypt before and during early Muslim rule (see also map on page 247) any comparison of revenues during the two periods having a gap of about a century is meaningless. Yet the figure which Johnson has suggested as an estimate of the total area under cultivation during Justinian's time may provide ground for working out new figures. He is of the view that Justinian's levy of 8,000,000 artabas of wheat would require 6,400,000 arouras of arable land[312] which means an area of about 1,760,000 hectares[313] or about 4,460,000 acres of land under cultivation. If it is taken for granted that the total area under cultivation did not change during the preceding 100 years the figure may provide a basis for estimating the total population engaged in agriculture and its complementary and allied industries and trades. Let us suppose that with primitive methods of cultivation the average crop area per inhabitant would be about 1 acre. It is not a rash assumption because up to the forties of this century the average crop area per inhabitant in Upper Egypt was 0.51 feddan.[314] With this estimate, which should be treated as modest, the total population of Egypt necessary to cultivate 6,400,000 arouras of land and engaged in all the allied and complementary trades would be about 4,500,000 persons or in other words about six to seven hundred thousand families (each family comprising of six to seven persons). This gives a taxable population of about 1.5 million (being one-third of the total) at a rate of two dīnārs. It is guesswork and not necessarily correct, but in the absence of any reliable evidence the figure may tentatively work as a datum.

Collection of Tax During the Islamic Period

Among the different figures quoted by the historians, Ṭabarī and Balādhurī are regarded as the most important and reliable sources of information, but both give two different figures for Egypt. According to Balādhurī, Wāqidī and Yazīd have reported that total receipts of land-tax and poll-tax amounted to 2 million dīnārs. The amount rose to 4 million during Caliph 'Uthmān's caliphate.[315] According to the same source, the original agreement required the payment of poll-tax at a rate of two dīnārs per head and a land-tax of one dīnār per *jarīb* of land.[316] According to Ṭabarī, the agreed maximum amount was 50 million in case the Nile inundated its banks extensively; otherwise less.[317] It should be noted that Ṭabarī has not mentioned the unit of currency, which, common sense would suggest as dirhams, equivalent to 5 million dīnārs. Secondly, it was not a fixed amount, but was commensurate with natural phenomenon. The only fixed condition seems to be that the levy would not exceed 5 million; it could be reduced. Apparently this report conflicts with Balādhurī's reports adduced on the authority of Wāqidī and Yazīd. But in fact the latter may accommodate a number of interpretations. Firstly, the amount refers to the eastern bank of the Nile, or in other words, Miṣr, exclusive of Alexandria. Secondly, this refers to the amount which was remitted to the centre after deducting expenses of administration, salaries, pension and stipends, repairs and constructions. Thirdly, this amount refers to the collections during the first three years of the conquest but not the period after the suppression of the revolt led by Manuel, after which, as was done in the case of Ḥīra in Iraq the amount was increased by way of punishment. Fourthly, the amount refers to one-third of the total annual taxes, because as Ṭabarī reports, the agreement contained the payment of tax in three instalments. Arguments can be adduced in support of each interpretation, but curiously none contradicts Ṭabarī's report; they are all reconcilable to his. As pointed out earlier, Ṭabarī does not give a fixed annual amount of land-tax, he gives a maximum which could be reviewed every year, in determining the extent of reductions. Now if it is supposed that the Nile had full-flooded inundation, and the land could produce enough to bring the maximum of tax the situation would be as follows:

Land-tax	5,000,000 dīnārs
Poll-tax @ 2 dīnārs per head, on 1.5 million taxable persons	3,000,000 dīnārs
Total	8,000,000 dīnārs

Keeping in mind the above figures it becomes easier to accept Ibn 'Abd al-Ḥakam's report about total collections amounting to 12 million dīnārs. It has been pointed out that al-Maghrib and the southern lands of Egypt up to the frontiers of Nūbiya had already fallen during the same period and been merged with the governorate of Egypt. Balādhurī has given the following report on the conquest of al-Maghrib in A.H. 22 in 'Amr's words which he addressed to Caliph 'Umar:

> I have entrusted 'Uqba ibn Nāfi' with al-Maghrib. He has reached up to Zawīla and the situation from Barqa to Zawīla is fully under control. Its people are fully subdued and whosoever among them has embraced Islam, paid *Ṣadaqa.* Those who came to terms have agreed to pay *Jizya.* I have levied on the people of Zawīla, and on those between Zawīla and my place, a tax which they can bear. I have advised all my officers to collect *Ṣadaqa* and distribute it among the needy, and to remit to me the amount of *Jizya.* I have also advised them to levy on the Muslims at a rate of one-tenth and half of one-tenth and on the tributaries according to the agreed terms.[318]

None of the historians has given any statistics about al-Maghrib except the fact that the city of Barqa agreed to pay 13,000 dīnārs.[319] It is, however, reported that al-Maghrib was also the land conquered by force.[320] Thus the difference between the amount of total tax as calculated above and that reported by Ibn 'Abd al-Ḥakam can be made up with the collections from the southern regions of Egypt (up to Nūbiya[321]), and from al-Maghrib. The total of 12 million dīnārs largely tallies with 100 million dirhams that was collected from Iraq during Caliph 'Umar's time, although its area and population were less than those of the governorate of Egypt. This however does not tally with the collections from the governorate of Dimashq (Syria and Palestine) amounting to 1.25 million dīnārs because all the cities there capitulated under treaty and because most of the lands bordering Byzantine lands or waters were allotted to Muslims and made tax-free.[322]

The situation in Egypt, however, did not remain the same. During 'Uthmān's caliphate a part of Ifrīqiyya was conquered and it also added to the revenues of Egypt. But later on the provinces of al-Maghrib and Ifrīqiyya became part of another province, and their revenues too. Another reason for the decline in revenue, as suggested by Ya'qūbī, was the gradual conversion of the people. The following figures for the total amounts of revenue have been reported by historians, for different periods:

Table 8
Amount of Collections from Egypt

Period	Amount
Caliph 'Umar's[323]	12 million dīnārs
Caliph 'Uthmān's[324]	14 million dīnārs
Mu'āwiya's[325]	5 million dīnārs
For comparison:	
Hārūn's[326]	4.2 million dīnārs
Ma'mūn's[327]	4 million dīnārs

As in other provinces, women and children, the very old, and monks were exempt.[328] John of Nikiu reports the exemption of churches too.[329] But this exemption would not, perhaps, cover the extensive landed properties owned by the church. That some of the Papyri also suggest the names of the priests as tax-payers can be interpreted in this context.

As mentioned elsewhere, the treaty with Egypt called for the payment of an amount which was not fixed; only a maximum limit was fixed.

Map 4. Tax-Paying Areas of Egypt and the West

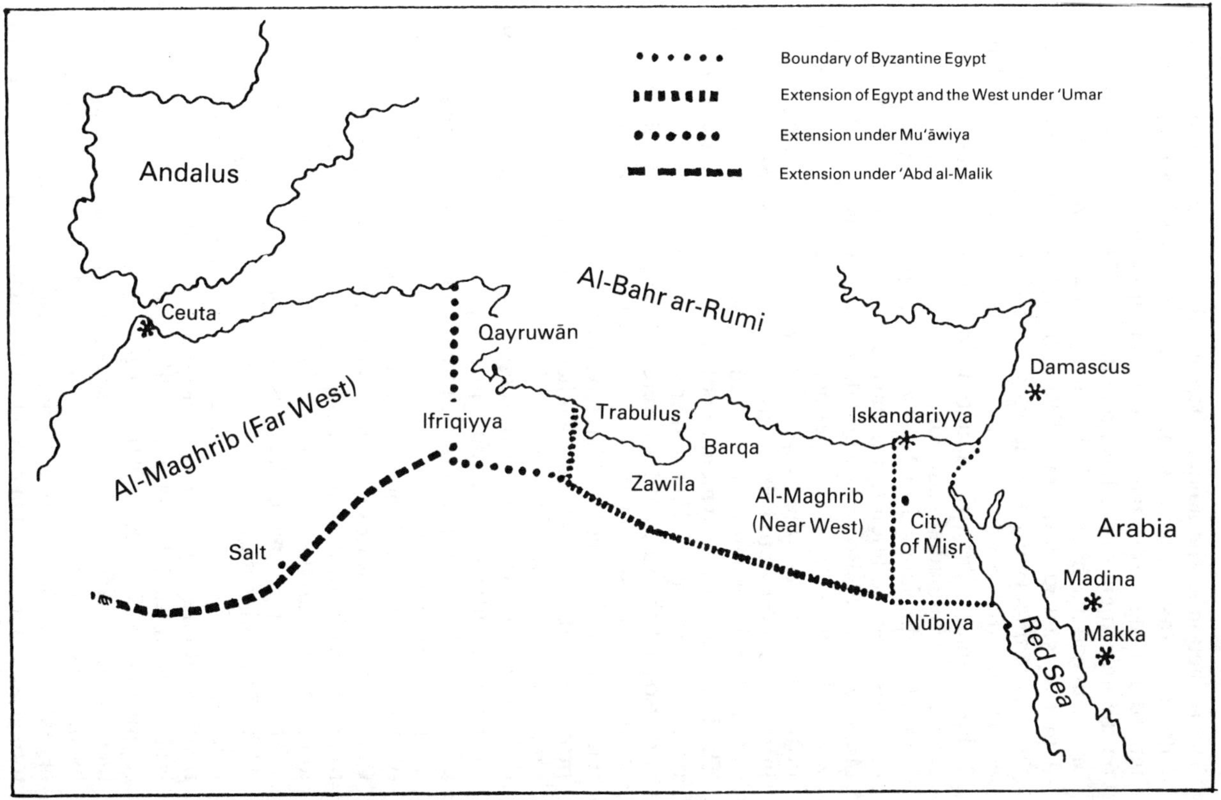

The reduction in the amount depended on the poor inundation of the Nile. This was a consideration which the preceding rulers also did not ignore. In order to estimate the extent of inundation 'Amr had to depend on the judgement of the local population. He had fortunately inherited an organized machinery of administration which he fully utilized. Caliph 'Umar as usual advised him to first find out from competent local persons the secret underlying the development of land and thus increase its economic efficiency. 'Amr asked Muqawqis about it and informed Caliph 'Umar. When the situation favourably normalized 'Amr reorganized revenue administration.[330]

Initially, the supply of wheat, oil, vinegar, and honey was also made compulsory in addition to the payment of two dīnārs. But as was done elsewhere, here also the commodity payment by the urban population was replaced by two dīnārs per head. Thus the burden of the supply of provisions became the responsibility of the landowners. Mu'āwiya introduced reforms to bring consistency to the system followed by 'Abd al-Malik; but the nature of the reforms in respect of Egypt is unknown. The Papyri showing payment of both money and commodity by the land owner suggest that Caliph 'Umar's policy had long since been changed and also that the rates of levy were increased. The details given by Ibn 'Abd al-Ḥakam suggest the levy of taxes for the benefit of clergy and public utilities like baths which have not been reported about any other province.[331] It was traditionally inherited from the Byzantine period and retained by the Muslims. There is reason to believe that the entire collection and disbursement of these funds would have been entrusted to the local officers and, thus, in perspective of the 'Green' (Coptic Church) – 'Blue' (Orthodox Church) antagonism, exposed to many malpractices. Severus, himself a Copt, has cited a number of instances of the 'rivals' injustice and tyrannies' but he does not tell us how the Copts behaved towards their adversaries. It is through him that we come to know about 'Amr inviting Benjamin the Coptic bishop to return and look after the affairs of the church and his community.[332]

The amount of total collections is reported to have increased during 'Uthmān's caliphate due to the conquest of some regions in Ifrīqiyya. According to Wāqidī and Ibn Ka'b, 'Abd Allāh b. Sa'd concluded a treaty with Gregory for payment of 2.5 million dīnārs.[333] The amount is also reported as 300 *qinṭārs* of gold.[334] According to Khalīfa, Subayṭala capitulated in A.H. 27 at 200,000 *riṭl* of gold.[335] Another reason for an increase in the amount of taxes was perhaps the strict vigilance exercised by the new governor. Severus is inclined to credit him as the first to organize tax administration,[336] but he probably means that 'Abd-Allāh took a personal interest in revenue affairs and did not leave them entirely in local hands as 'Amr had done. During Mu'āwiya's reign more conquests were made in the western parts of Ifrīqiyya but the impact of these is not known. During his early period 'Amr again took over as governor, now enjoying full powers. But Mu'āwiya's period is known only for a decline in revenues. There was no question of a substantial number of prompt conversions after 'Uthmān. The reason for this decline may be attributed firstly to the weakening authority of the centre during 'Amr's governorship and after him the separation of the account of Egypt and al-Maghrib from the centre. The rise in the number of the privileged class, exempt from poll-tax, may also have been a cause of decline but its impact should have been negligible. In the case of land-tax, the exemption of any number of people would not affect the total collections because it was deemed to be a collective liability of each village. But poll-tax depended on the number of heads which were taxed and exemption from this tax would mean loss to the government. That is why we find 'Umar II advising his governor to withdraw the exemptions and levy poll-tax on all the *dhimmīs*.[337] The report that Mu'āwiya advised one of his officers to increase the poll-tax by one carat[338] per head suggests that the earlier policy of non-increase in taxes was now abandoned. Although the officer is reported to have refused to obey the caliph's order, he could not stop the proposed increase because another newly-appointed officer would be obliged to take his place and change the policy. The proposed increase by a meagre amount such as one carat, however, could not compensate for a substantial decline. There might have been some attempts to increase the taxes after Mu'āwiya's reform throughout his empire, as mentioned elsewhere, but the main taxes remained the same; *viz.*, land-tax and poll-tax. It is not surprising to find that the Aphrodito Papyri do not mention a third tax up to the end of 'Abd al-Malik's period[339] (A.H. 86; A.D. 705). When further taxes were officially levied cannot be dated precisely, but the evidence that people began to desert their lands in A.H. 90 (A.D. 709) is suggestive of the impact of burdensome taxation during Walīd's caliphate. Severus reports about the fugitives during Qurra's governorship[340] who, according to al-Kindī, took over in that very year (A.H. 90; A.D. 709). This means that Qurra was the first governor either to himself inaugurate a policy of an increase in taxes or to allow the local officers to give extraordinary exemptions to some favourites and overburden some others. Which of the different factors was responsible for burdensome taxes cannot be explained in the absence of complete and conclusive evidence.[341] Even the Aphrodito Papyri do not help in giving any hint at the probable situation. These fragmentary documents which cover a period of twenty-two years ending A.H. 103 (A.D. 722) only suggest that taxes which were levied during this period were of two kinds: public and extraordinary. Public taxes comprised land-tax, poll-tax, and other expenses *(dapāne)*. The first two were by far the most important while the third was a charge for salaries and maintenance of the collectors and other local officials. While poll-tax was paid by adult males, land-tax was payable by the owners of land in addition to their share of poll-tax. Those who did not possess land but pursued any other trade were not exempt from this levy. They paid a sort of trade-tax on their earnings which corresponded to land-tax.[342]

The evidence cited above simply confirms the fact that, by the end of A.H. 103 (A.D. 722), the government had the benefit of only two traditional taxes. Other taxes were levied and utilized only locally. As regards the rate of increases made during the period of the last eighty years, the information found in the Papyri is incomplete and inconclusive. The following tables compiled from different lists in the Papyri sufficiently prove the point:

It will be evident from the tables that the figures of taxes given in the Papyri are hopelessly bewildering. Fractions and odd amounts of land-tax can be interpreted to have occurred due to differences in the area of land but no such explanation is possible in the case of poll-tax which is supposed to have been levied at a uniform rate for each person. Anyhow it will be noticed that in a large number of the records of the Papyri the rate of two dīnārs is the most usual rate of poll-tax while the rate of one dīnār for every four aroura of land is the most common rate of land-tax.[343]

Table 9
Rates of Taxes in Egypt (Number of Holdings)

Number of holdings	Amount in dīnārs			
	Land-tax	Poll-tax	Levy in kind (artabas)	Other expenses
One holding	2 1/3	2/3	2 1/3	
" "	2	3	3	
" "	1 1/2	1	1 1/2	
Two holdings	2 1/2	0	3	
One holding	3	0	3	
Two holdings	2	1	3	2
One holding	3	1	8	5
" "	1	0	2	1/6

Cf. Pap. IV. Gen. Intr., pp. XXXVIII and XXXIX.

Table 10
Rates of Taxes in Egypt (Area of Holdings)

Area of holdings (aroura)	Amount in dīnārs Land-tax	Poll-tax	Levy in kind (artaba)	Other expenses
16	4	0	4	0
4	1	0	2	0
4	1	0	2	0
8	2	3	0	0

Cf. Pap. IV. Gen. Intr., p. XXXIX.

Table 11
Rates of Poll-Tax in Egypt

Number of persons	Amount in dīnārs
95	230
5	7 1/6
7	17
15	38 1/2
7	20 1/2
5	13
12	25 1/6
14	108 2/3

Cf. Pap. IV. 1420–3, 146f. *Cf.* AST., p. 198.

Another money tax which is mentioned in a number of Papyri seems to be a charge for local officers, not intended for the provincial government.[344] Over and above these taxes the local population was also supposed to contribute physical service in repairs and construction of public utilities.[345] Whether or not they were also paid for this service is a question which can be argued both ways. But it can be supposed that in this respect also they would have continued the preceding Byzantine practice of imposing five days' labour or its equivalent in terms of money. Similar is the case with taxes in kind *(embole)* which, sometimes, seem to have been paid for, but not in all cases.[346] The accounts mention the contributions of articles like oil, salt, mats, palm, ropes, poultry, butter, iron, milk, naval supplies, sewn leather, and ready-made clothes.[347]

The Issue of the Non-Muslim Officials

Egypt was a country where the Muslim influx was not as rapid and large as in Iraq and Syria. As a result the entire revenue administration was at the mercy of local officials. It was they who determined the extent of inundation of the Nile, the leviable total of land-tax, its distribution among districts and villages and the per-person share in that tax depending on the area and produce of land, the levy of extraordinary taxes for officials and religious and public utility services and the method of collection. As the Muslims for a long time did not penetrate deep inside smaller towns and villages, they were unaware of the functioning of these officials and thus they could easily be misguided and duped. For centuries the sectarian jealousies of the 'Blues' and the 'Greens' had continued. After the Muslim conquest the 'Greens' (Copts) won the confidence of the Muslim governor and used him to take revenge upon the Greek 'Blues' (Orthodox Church). As a result the 'enemy' also did not miss any opportunity to retaliate. While the Copts were in power Theodosius went to Yazīd I at Damascus and got a patent as governor of Alexandria independent of the governor of Egypt. And as Severus put it, 'he was an enemy of the Coptic Patriarch, and used his position to vex him. He exhorted from him thirty-six dīnārs yearly as a tax for disciples, the governor's share of the requisitions of the fleet, besides other money'.[348] But during 'Abd al-Malik's time, we find Athnasius as the tax commissioner and the supervisor of churches. He belonged to the Coptic Church, and led a delegation to the governor to request that the Church of Alexandria be taken over by some body because it had possessions that were liable to heavy tax. He also suggested a person who could manage the affairs of that church. The governor agreed to Athnasius' suggestion and acted accordingly.[349] How they took their revenge is not reported by Severus. Such sectarian intrigues continued along with normal routine and the governors were made to be convinced of the rationale behind such acts. To what extent this behaviour affected the tax-payer cannot be determined.

The priests and monks were exempt from poll-tax but not land-tax. When burdensome taxation made the rural population flee from their land, the governor ordered that they be brought back to their villages.[350] The reason behind the governor's policy seems to have been concern for the maintenance of the agricultural economy, and not the amount of land-tax because this was the communal responsibility of the village, and primarily of the district without any consideration of individuals. The Aphrodito Papyri too confirm this fact.[351] Many fugitives took refuge in the churches and monasteries. As a result the monks were required to wear a ring on their hand to distinguish themselves from the fugitives.[352] Governor Aṣbagh and his successor Usāma issued passports to the rural population[353] and forbade the monks to accept any newcomers, and at the same time removed the profit motive by making the monks themselves pay poll-tax.[354] Severus describes the tax imposed on the monks for the first time as by 'Aṣbagh the pagan'.[355] The rate of this poll-tax on monks is given by him as one dīnār in general and two dīnārs annually for the monks in districts.[356] 'Umar II abolished the tax on clergy, which is observed by Severus in the following words:

> He was good to the people and bad to God. He ordered for abolition of tax on clergy and priests and withdrew (additional)[357] taxes, inhabited the cities which had been deserted, and the Christians and the churches became in peace and relief. After all this he began to act maliciously and wrote that those who wished to retain government posts should embrace Islam . . . He also ordered that all the non-Muslims should pay poll-tax although they were not traditionally used to it. So God did not give him much opportunity to rule the country because he was like a 'Dajjāl', anti-Christ.[358]

These observations speak for themselves. Up to this time the local officers were in control of the financial affairs of the province and they practised a selective policy of levying poll-tax. 'Umar II decreed to levy poll-tax on all. This strict policy would have induced many to embrace Islam. That is why we find the governor of Egypt complaining of the financial implications of conversions, which offended 'Umar II.[359]

Yazīd did not toe 'Umar II's line and reimposed the taxes which had been abolished by his predecessor. During Hishām's caliphate a fresh census was made of men, livestock, lands, and trees; followed by a further increase of tax by one carat.[360] According to Severus, people over twenty years of age were subjected to poll-tax[361] but this seems to be his misunderstanding because there was apparently no reason to increase the age limit which had been fixed at puberty.

Details about the provinces west of Egypt are not recorded fully in the early history books but it can be assumed that the regions formerly under Byzantine control would have had a similar administration and the Muslims retained them to the extent they did in Egypt. In the beginning local non-Muslim officers looked after the affairs of these regions. Mu'āwiya, however, began to replace them by Muslims who surveyed the land and re-organized administration.[362] An interesting development that took place in Ifrīqiyya in A.H. 102 was the governor's policy of collecting poll-tax even from the converts and returning them from the city to their former villages. However a mob of converts killed the governor and elected another one which the caliph confirmed.[363]

Administrative Set-Up

The machinery of administration that functioned in Egypt is explained by Ibn 'Abd al-Ḥakam and confirmed by Aphrodito Papyri.[364] The report gives a general idea about administration. It runs as follows:

> When 'Amr b. al-'Ās had gained complete control over Egypt, he established for the Copts the taxation that had prevailed under the Greeks, which was equitable *(bi't-ta'dīl)*. If a village were prosperous and its population numerous, the taxation was increased. If its population were few in number, and it had decayed, the taxation was decreased. The knowledgeable persons and the chiefs of every village used to assemble and discuss the prosperity or decline [of the village] until, when they had determined on the quotas to be increased they returned to their districts with their quotas. There they came together with the chiefs of the villages and divided that quota according to the cultivated area of the villages. Then every village would take back its quota, and they would add to these quotas the *Kharāj* of every village and its cultivated land. Thereupon they would subtract two *feddans* from the land for their churches, baths and ferries out of the total acreage of the land and subtract from it also the amount for the entertainment of Muslims and for the visit of the authorities. When they had finished this work, they inspected the artisans and the labourers in every village and allotted them their portion according to their capacity but usually only to domiciled or married men. Thereupon they calculated the *Kharāj* that remained and divided it among them [the villages] according to the amount of land and then divided that [land] among those who were willing to cultivate it, according to their capability. If anyone were weak and complained that he was unable to cultivate his land, they divided what he was unable to cultivate according to capacity. And if anyone desired more land, he was given what the weak were unable to cultivate. If there were disputes, they divided land according to number. Their quota was made according to the carats of the dīnār, 24 carats to the dīnār on which basis they divided the land . . . They were taxed artaba of wheat on each *feddan* and 2 waiba of barley, but there was no impost on clover. The waiba was then equal to six mudds.[365]

At places the Papyri make reference to the treasury of Aphrodito, and also mention the main treasury at Babylon and sometimes at Alexandria. Fusṭāṭ is also mentioned as the place of the main treasury. It is believable, therefore, that while the provincial *Bayt al-Māl* should have been located at the provincial capital, the main treasuries looked after the revenue of districts like Aphrodito where local treasuries were set up.[366]

PERSIA AND THE EAST

Iraq and Eastern Mesopotamia (al-Jazīra) were part of the Persian Empire when they were invaded by the Muslims. But the subjugation of these provinces did not decide the fate of the whole empire. The battle of Nihāwand crippled the effective defence potential of the Persians; yet the complete conquest of the empire took many more years. In the meantime, frequent raids were made into Armenia, Sijistān, and Western India which was not taken until the end of the century. And because the Muslim armies were engaged on several fronts in the east, north and west at one and the same time, and their internal differences provoked internecine struggle, the conquered regions continued to revolt frequently against their conquerors in the hope of regaining their lost position. Thus there is reason to believe that the treaties made with a number of cities in the Persian provinces would have undergone considerable changes. But historians have devoted themselves to describing the circumstances of conquests and reconquests, neglecting to enumerate the revised treaties. The case of Ḥīra in Iraq has been reported earlier to explain how, after suppressing frequent revolts, the originally agreed amount of 60,000 dirhams was increased to 400,000 dirhams.[367] But operations during the years A.H. 20 to 35 were so swift and so multi-lateral that many of their details escaped the notice of historians. As a result, a reader is confused about the precise chronology of different conquests and reconquests. The series of conquests started after the fall of Nihāwand which ensured a tribute of 800,000 dirhams annually.[368] Ṭabarī begins this series with the conquest of al-Jibāl.

Al-Jibāl

The treaty of Iṣfahān, according to Ṭabarī, provided for the payment of *Jizya* which was to be assessed according to the capacity of the subject people.[369] Balādhurī gives some details about the different stages of the

Map 5. Classification of Taxes in the Eastern Regions of the Muslim Empire

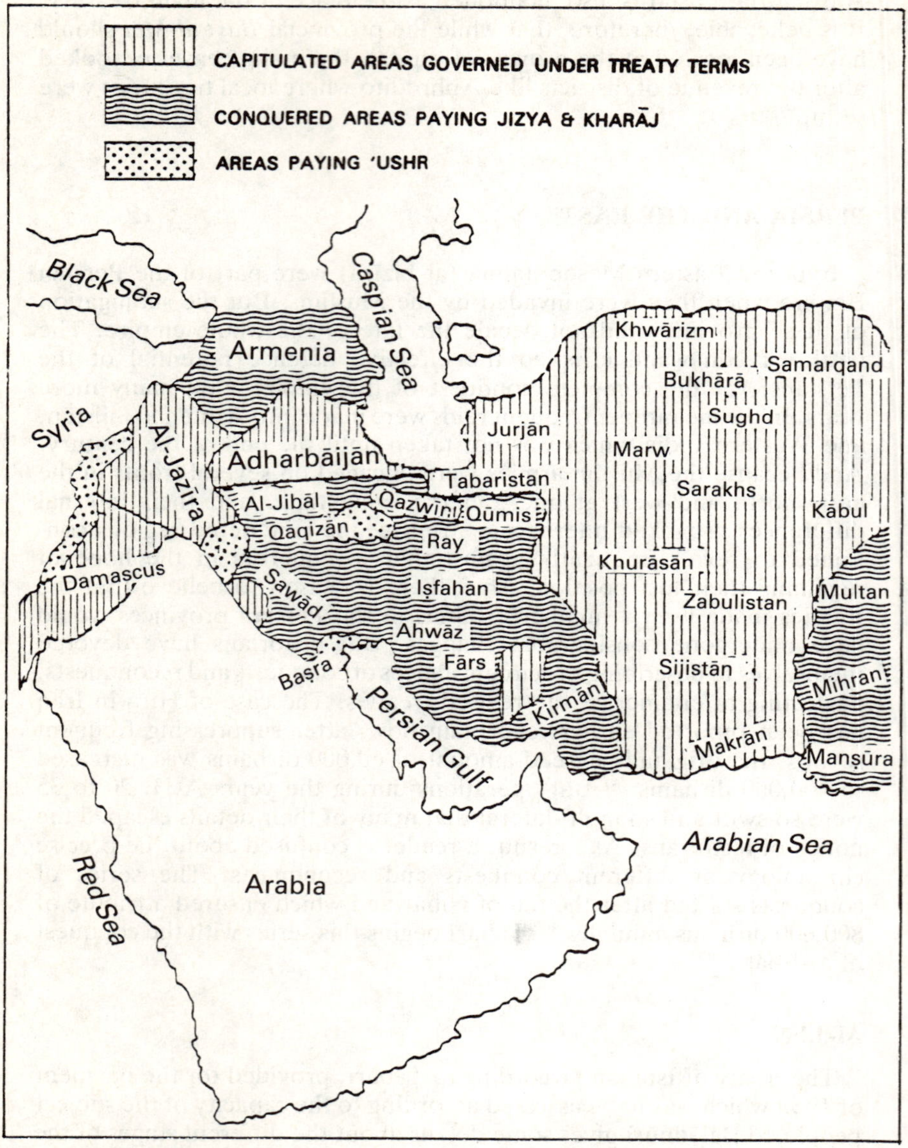

conquest of the region. While he does not give details of the financial arrangements with the people of Ḥulwān and Qirmāsīn,[370] Dīnawar and Iṣfahān are reported to have capitulated on condition of the payment of poll-tax.[371] Ray and Qūmis capitulated on payment of a lump sum of 500,000 dirhams and the condition of the payment of poll-tax and land-tax.[372] The people of Barā'a, Qazwīn and Qāqizān opted for Islam rather than for paying poll-tax, and their lands were treated as *'Ushr* lands.[373]

The total collections from Iraq and al-Jibāl jointly amounted to 21 million dīnārs or 210 million dirhams during 'Umar's caliphate.[374] Thus, if the collections from Iraq for that period are deducted from the total the revenue of al-Jibāl comes to 90 million dirhams. During Mu'āwiya's caliphate the collections from the district of Ray alone amounted to 20 million dirhams which had declined to 12 million by Māmūn's time.[375] Whether the comparison of the figures about Ray or any other district will be valid in the absence of the precise delimitation of boundaries in different periods is doubtful. And this confusion remains for the entire period.

Khūzistān

Khūzistān, with its headquarters at Ahwāz, was conquered by force. The details of the arrangements the Muslims made with the people or their Marzubān are lost in the accounts of Hurmuzān's defeat, his march to Madina and conversion to Islam. According to Khalīfa b. Khayyāṭ, it agreed to pay 2,890,000 dirhams in A.H. 16 when Mughīra conquered it,[376] but the amount was increased to 14 million when Abū Mūsā suppressed a revolt a year later.[377] During Mu'āwiya's time the total collection from Khūzistān (Ahwāz and suburbs) amounted to 40 million dirhams.[378] It is possible that the amount included the tribute of Rāmhurmuz amounting to 800,000 dirhams, as reported by Balādhurī and Khalīfa.[379]

Ādharbāijān

In the case of Ādharbāijān, Ṭabarī reports the text of a treaty calling for the payment of a poll-tax on the adult males according to their capacity to pay. Women, children, monks and priests were, as usual, exempt.[380] But, according to Balādhurī, Ādharbāijān capitulated on 800,000 dirhams weighing eight ūqiyyas each.[381] According to Ibn Isḥāq, the agreed amount was 100,000.[382] The three different stories can be reconciled keeping in view Balādhurī's report that Ādharbāijān revolted many times and after each suppression, additional taxes were levied on its people.[383] This means that initially there was a general agreement to pay the poll-tax. In the next stage an amount was fixed. At another stage, maybe the last, 800,000 dirhams per annum were imposed.

Jurjān-Ṭabaristān

Jurjān and Ṭabaristān also revolted many times. The amount of treaty with Jurjān was 200,000 dirhams[384] and with Ṭabaristān, 500,000 dirhams.[385] When Ṭabaristān was reconquered in A.H. 98, it was made to pay 700,000 dirhams in addition to quantities of saffron, 400 slaves, dresses, and silver.[386] Mosul, Ṣāmighān and Shahrabādh agreed to pay poll-tax and land-tax.[387]

Fārs-Kirmān

The cities in Fārs and Kirmān were also mostly conquered by force. Some of the cities, however, agreed to pay the two taxes or a lump sum.[388] According to Khalīfa, the cities of Imrān and Dar'abjard agreed to pay 220,000 dirhams each, or according to another report, the latter agreed to pay 520,000 dirhams.[389] Balādhurī reports that it agreed to pay some cash.[390] Sābūr capitulated on payment of 3,300,000 dirhams.[391] In the cities that were conquered by force, the farmers during the early period are reported to have been regularly paying a share of their produce which varied from one-tenth to a third.[392] Arrajān and Shīrāz agreed to pay poll-tax and land-tax.[393]

Armenia

The Armenian expedition, according to Balādhurī,[394] started with the conquest of Qālīqalā. The inhabitants either left the city or agreed to pay poll-tax. After Qālīqalā, Daybul capitulated on the condition of paying the two taxes.[395] The same terms were settled for Nushwā, Bifirjān, Sīsjān, Tiflis, Kafarbīs, Kasāl, Khānān, Samsakhī, Jurdamān, Khazar, etc.[396] Some of the cities capitulated on the condition of paying slaves and/or quantities of corn. Sarīr agreed to pay every year five hundred male slaves and an equal number of female slaves in addition to 200,000 mudd of corn. Wazīkarān payed 50 slaves and 10,000 mudd. Hamzīr payed 500 slaves once and 30,000 mudd every year. Sadd payed 100 slaves once and 5,000 mudd every year, and Ṭabarsarānshāh 10,000 mudd. Similar arrangements with varying quantities were made with Lakz, Sharwān, etc.

Operations in Armenia started during 'Umar's caliphate immediately before his death and continued till the end of the Umayyad period. The native officers and princes continued to govern the regions under the agreement and were made responsible for levying and collecting the tribute. The lack of direct Muslim control can be ascertained from the fact that they did not survey the land throughout the Umayyad period.[397] Some of the cities capitulated without war and agreed to pay an annual tribute *(itāwa)*.[398] The semi-autonomous position of the province induced the princes to revolt frequently. The last such revolt during the Umayyad period was perhaps suppressed by Marwān in A.H. 100, who levied a tribute of 1,000 slaves and 100,000 mudd of wheat every year.[399]

The ruler of Bāb, who promised to assist the Muslims during war, was exempted from tax.

How much Armenia brought in every year is not recorded. Ibn Khurdādhabih and Qudāma give 4 million dirhams as the amount of annual collections made sometime during the third century.[400]

Khurāsān

Khurāsān was the only province of the Persian empire which did not risk the hazards of a war and capitulated on the condition of paying a fixed annual amount of money. When the Muslim armies reached any city the ruling chief hastened to reach an agreement. Thus the different cities agreed to pay different amounts of tribute. In the cases of Hirāt, Būshanj and Bādaghīs, the amount of tribute was fixed and the ruling chief was warned to divide the amount equitably among the people.[401] But later developments suggest that these chiefs did not take this warning seriously. In any case, they themselves became the assessors and collectors and the Muslim officers' only concern was to collect the stipulated amount from these chiefs. The following table gives the amount of the annual tribute that was originally settled.[402]

Table 12
Amount of Annual Tribute of Khurāsān

	Dirhams
Ṭabasayn	60,000[403]
Qūhistān	600,000
Nīsābūr	700,000[404]
Nasā	300,000
Abīward	400,000
Ṭaus	600,000
Hirāt etc.	1,000,000

(Continued on page 260)

(Continued from page 259)

Marw Shāhjahān	2,500,000
Ṭakhāristān	300,000
Marw Rawz	60,000
Bukhārā	1,000,000
Samarqand	700,000
Khwārizm	400,000
Total	8,500,000

Khalīfa also describes the agreement with Sarakhs at 150,000, with Bayhaq at 1 million, in addition to a quantity of food-grain, and with Balkh at 400,000 dirhams.[405] Thus the total amount agreed in the case of Khurāsān did not exceed 10 million dirhams, a very much lighter burden compared with other regions that were conquered by force. Syria also enjoyed the same privilege by virtue of its capitulation without risking a war. But the difference was that in Khurāsān the ruling chiefs enjoyed a semi-autonomous position in determining, assessing and collecting the taxes. Yet these chiefs did not reconcile themselves to the new arrangement. Ṭabarī reports three revolts in Khurāsān during 'Uthmān's caliphate.[406] They also revolted during Caliph 'Alī's time. Balādhurī reports that the Marzubān of Marw called on Caliph 'Alī who appointed him the chief commissioner of taxes and wrote to all the landlords to pay him their future dues. At this the people of Khurāsān violated the treaty. Caliph 'Alī sent Ja'da to suppress the revolt but he was not able to do so. Unrest continued even during Mu'āwiya's reign[407] and the amount of tribute also remained the same.

Sijistān

The expeditions against Sijistān (Sīstān) continued till the conquest of Zarang. The Marzuban agreed to pay 1,000 slaves, each with a gold cup in his hand.[408] But it revolted after three years and was penalized to pay 2 million dirhams and 2,000 slaves.[409] The conquest of Sijistān opened the way to Kābul and to confrontation with Ratbīl the most obstinate prince. In the first few encounters Ratbīl gave in and agreed to pay 1 million dirhams.[410] But not long afterwards he hit back at the Muslims who were then forced to pay him 500,000 dirhams by way of ransom.[411] The die-hard Ratbīl and, after him, his son, proved uncontrollable and their land a problem-province; they frequently claimed a heavy toll of Muslim lives and money. In A.H. 80 again the Muslim army was entrapped by him and got off only on paying a ransom of 700,000 dirhams.[412] When Ibn Ash'ath took refuge with him, Ḥajjāj offered him a peace-treaty for 7–9 years without having to pay anything. After the lapse of this period, however, he was required to pay farm-produce valued at about 900,000 dirhams annually.[413] Both parties honoured the treaty. But Ratbīl's son again backed out of the treaty during Sulaymān's reign and later on refused to pay anything. Thus the Umayyad rulers were deprived of this tribute[414] after Ḥajjāj although even he could not regularly collect it.[415]

Apart from Khurāsān, which had a treaty relationship, most of the other regions then under the Persian empire and in the east were conquered by force and the terms and conditions governing these provinces were based on the circumstances of the conquest. In some cases a tribute was levied. In others poll-tax and land-tax were imposed. The amount of taxes was not always pre-determined. In most cases if the subject people violated the treaty the terms were revised but not always. While Iraq had been made a separate province, the remaining parts of the Persian empire were divided into three administrative units: Ādharbāijān, Khurāsān and Sijistān, not much different from the pre-Islamic division.[416] After the conquest of Sind a new administrative unit was created. Land surveys preceded the levy of land-tax in the regions which were conquered by force and where land-tax was to be levied. It is, therefore, natural to believe that the conquered lands in the Persian empire were surveyed like the lands in Iraq and Egypt. It is reported that in Qum alone the lands were surveyed as many as four times.[417] Fārs was surveyed twice during Caliph 'Alī's rule.[418]

Reconquests and Reassessments

Historians have mentioned several conquests of the same city or region in different periods which suggests their reconquests after revolts. In A.H. 87–88 Samarqand was reconquered and made to pay 2.2 million dirhams as against the original 700,000 dirhams annually.[419] This was perhaps over and above a fine of procuring 30,000 slaves.[420] Revolt in Jurjān was suppressed in A.H. 93 and cost 500,000 dirhams in addition to clothes and slaves.[421] Khwārizm and Ṭabaristān were also penalized in A.H. 93 and A.H. 98 respectively.[422] According to Balādhurī, Ṭabaristān had to hand over 4 million dirhams as a lump sum, 700,000 dirhams per annum, slaves and a variety of goods.[423] The suppression of the fourth revolt in Bukhārā bound it to a payment of 200,000 dirhams to the caliph and 10,000 dirhams to the Amīr of Khurāsān every year, perhaps in addition to the originally agreed amount.[424] Half of the dwellings were to be vacated for the Muslims. The inhabitants were also required to supply forage and fuel.[425] The revolt in Sughd was also suppressed in the nineties and it was now made to pay 2,200,000 dirhams annually in addition to a number of slaves.[426]

The Issue of the Non-Muslim Officials

Sporadic attempts to overthrow the Muslim rule in Armenia and Khurāsān continued until the end of the Umayyad period, and every time the revolts were suppressed and the tribute refixed. This was perhaps the factor, or at least one of the factors, that led the Umayyad rulers to seriously reconsider the problem. In Khurāsān, then, the chief Rabbi collected the taxes from the Jews, the Bishop from the Christians and the Marzubān from the Magians or Zoroastrians.[427] Quite naturally they had their religious loyalties and prejudices. The conversion of their co-religionists should have been pricking their conscience. All the religious communities were reconciled to each other under the Sassanid rule and co-existed without conflict. The situation completely changed under Islam which emerged as a fast-spreading religion and began to enlarge its circle at the expense of the numerical strength of other communities. In all the provinces the old administrative staff were retained as workers and helpers, while the Muslims busied themselves with policy-making and overall supervision and control. In the Persian provinces of Khurāsān and Armenia the native officers were working more autonomously than elsewhere. This fact, while it partly explains the cause of unceasing and increasing turmoil in these lands, also provides material to understand how before it, Ḥajjāj was wrongly convinced of retaining the poll-tax on converts in Iraq,[428] thus adding fuel to the fire. It is possible that this policy in Iraq was adopted by him after Khurāsān and Sijistān were also consolidated under his governorship.

The Politics Behind Poll-Tax on Muslims

As already explained, the cities of Khurāsān had to pay a fixed amount of tribute; not land-tax and poll-tax. But this tribute was collected from the local population. What the considerations were for distributing the burden of the tribute can be understood from the report brought to the notice of 'Umar II: that the burden of taxes on non-Muslims and the converts was uniform. It meant that the subjects were to share this burden through multiple levies, perhaps with different names. The levies were assessed for each person.[429] Another probable way of assessing these persons might be their distribution according to the preceding Persian pattern in which poll-tax was also collected from persons of twenty to fifty years of age.[430] In any case, 'Umar II freed the converts from poll-tax.[431] But later developments suggest that the converts continued to be discriminated against, not only in relief from tax but also in other respects. Ṭabarī states that a delegation brought to the notice of 'Umar II that 20,000 *mawālī* (confederates) were taking part in *Jihād* without receiving any pensions and rations as were admissible to them under the rules. They also reported that an equal number of converts were being made to pay their taxes as before.[432] The story may raise many questions but the answers will be found in the explanation that the officers in charge of assessing taxes did not like the fact that conversion was encouraged by withdrawing poll-tax levied on the converts, nor did they like to have their names entered in the pension/rations registers to feed them free and make them contented soldiers. ‘Umar II wanted to improve this situation but he did not live long enough to check the results of his instructions to abolish poll-tax on converts or to enter their names in pension/rations registers. But because he had abolished a number of levies over and above poll-tax, the impact of these liberal withdrawals should have been felt by his successors.[433] Ibn Sa‘d has clearly mentioned that the main reason for the decline in revenues was ‘Umar II's withdrawal of one dīnār tax on the Persians, one dīnār on servants (or slaves?) and five dirhams tax on farms.[434] He also abolished a number of other taxes and exactions that were a source of substantial income.[435] This brought a sharp decline in revenues. Had all the other taxes and levies been re-introduced – barring the poll-tax – the deficiency in income would have mostly been made up. But it seems that of all these levies, most emphasis was placed on the re-introduction of poll-tax on converts. The story about conversion and the levy of poll-tax in and after A.H. 110, with all its ambiguities, is meaningful and supports the above view. Ṭabarī reports that Ashras, the governor of Khurāsān, said to his officials: ‘Find me a man who is pious and virtuous and I shall send him to Transoxania to summon people to embrace Islam.’ They recommended to him Abu'ṣ-Ṣaydā' Ṣāliḥ b. Ṭarīf, a *mawlā* of Banū Ḍabba. Abu'ṣ-Ṣaydā' said: ‘I shall go on condition that *Jizya* shall not be taken from him who embraces Islam, for the *Kharāj* of Khurāsān is only on the head of men.'' Ashras agreed. . . . Then Abu'ṣ-Ṣaydā' went to Samarqand, where the governor and the collector of *Kharāj* was al-Ḥasan b. Abu'l Amarraṭa al-Kindī. Abu'ṣ-Ṣaydā' invited the people of Samarqand and its environs to become Muslims on condition that *Jizya* would be removed from them, and the people hastened to respond to his call. Whereupon Ghūrak (the native prince) wrote to Ashras that the *Kharāj* was ‘going broke’, *inkasara*. Ashras wrote to his lieutenant: ‘Verily in the *Kharāj* is the strength of the Muslims. I have learnt that the people of Sughd and the like have not become Muslims sincerely. They have accepted Islam only to escape *Jizya*. Investigate this matter and discover who is circumcized, performs the required acts of devotion, is sincere in his conversion to Islam, and can read a *Sūra* of the Qur'ān. Relieve that man of his *Kharāj*.’ Later Ashras relieved his lieutenant Ibn Abu'l Amarraṭa of his duty as collector of *Kharāj* and appointed Hānī b. Hānī as collector. Meanwhile the *mawla* Abu'ṣ-Ṣaydā' succeeded in preventing the collection of *Jizya* from the converts, with the result that the Dahāqīn of Bukhārā came to Ashras and said: 'From whom you are going to get the *Kharāj* when everyone has become an Arab?' Thereupon Ashras wrote to Hānī b. Hānī and his officials: 'Collect the *Kharāj* from those whom you used to collect it and restore the *Jizya* on those who have become Muslims.' As a result 7,000 people of Sughd seceded. Abu'ṣ-Ṣaydā' protested against this treatment and was imprisoned. His friends revolted under Abū Fāṭima but were soon disposed of. Then the Arab supervisors of *Kharāj* insisted on collecting it in full, and they maltreated the Persians. The clothing was torn from the Dahāqīn, their girdles were hung around their necks in derision, and they took the *Jizya* from the converts who were weak.[436]

The story is suggestive of some points worthy of consideration: Ashras, the governor willingly agreed to waive the poll-tax on the converts. According to the original arrangement, Khurāsān was to pay a fixed amount of tribute but not poll-tax and land-tax. In the absence of any report about alterations in the arrangement the governor's agreement to withdraw poll-tax implies two conclusions: firstly the assessors and collectors were distributing the burden of the tribute over each head through a per-head levy and a tax on earnings. This was the system that the officers practised in pre-Islamic Persia and the native officers would have retained it,[437] and the government recognized it *de facto;* secondly, the governor, while giving his consent to Abu'ṣ-Ṣaydā', would not have been unmindful of the fact that if the amount of per-head levy, the so-called poll-tax, was withdrawn the revenues would not substantially suffer. Even the collector of Samarqand did not fear it; that is why he allowed Abu'ṣ-Ṣaydā' to work freely. It was Ghūrak, the native prince, who hastened to dissuade Ashras from his offer. Ṭabarī gives the sense of Ghūrak's message in only four words, *innal kharāj qad inkasara.*[438] How and in what detail Ghūrak argued in his letter is not mentioned, but Ashras' reaction by advising the scrutiny of 'sincere Muslims' suggests at least one point: 'you should have no soft corner for these converts simply because they have joined your religion; they are hypocrites and have embraced Islam simply to evade their tax.' Yet Ashras did not withdraw his offer; he suggested the application of a criterion to test the *bona fides* of Ghūrak's letter and retained his offer if the conversion was sincere. Now it was the Dahāqīn's turn to dissuade Ashras. They were practically the real collectors and they stopped work and called on Ashras to paint a very gloomy picture of the state of collections: 'From whom are you going to get the *Kharāj* when everyone has become an Arab?' Whether the Dahāqīn themselves took the initiative to call on the governor or they were prompted by Ghūrak, is not clear. But Ghūrak's part in the events is most mysterious. In the beginning he apparently demonstrated his loyalty to the Muslims and his grave concern for the finances of the government. But when the government, acting upon his advice, turned against the converts, he betrayed it and joined Khāqān with whom his son was already fighting against the Muslims.[439] He continued to fight against the Muslims as 'one of the slaves of Khāqān'.[440]

Why the native princes, like Ghūrak and Dahāqīn, were against the abolition of *Jizya,* does not remain a secret or a point of presumption. This is further strengthened by the later events which suggest that the matter of the abolition of *Jizya* did not have as significant financial implications as religious and political ones. In order to appreciate these events the following facts should also be noted:

At the time when Abu'ṣ-Ṣaydā' started for Samarqand, Ḥasan al-Amarraṭa was entrusted with army-command and revenue. Ashras after receiving Ghūrak's letter dismissed him from revenue. But when *Jizya* was reimposed on the converts he was relieved of army-command too and was replaced by al-Mujashshir. A few months later al-Mujashshir was also replaced by Naṣr b. Sayyār who, about ten years after these events, was promoted to the governorship of Khurāsān. He can rightly be believed to be a most reliable witness to these ugly happenings and to the real causes underlying them. His analysis of the revenue situation during this period is worth studying for the observations he made in his speech as governor. Naṣr said:

'Did not Bahrāmsīs favour the Magians, helping them and protecting them, and putting their burdens on the Muslims? Did not Ishbadād b. Jarījūr in like manner favour the Christians, and did not 'Aqība favour the Jews? Shall I not favour the Muslims, helping them and protecting them and relieving them of their burden which I shall impose on the unbelievers? Shall I accept anything but the full payment of the *Kharāj* according to what has been written and made known? Therefore I have appointed as special officer Manṣūr b. 'Umar b. Abū Kharqa and I have ordered him to act with justice to you. If there is a single Muslim from whom the *Jizya* on his head has been taken, or on whom the *Kharāj* is a heavy burden while it is correspondingly lightened for the unbelievers, let him report the matter to Manṣūr who will transfer the burden from the Muslims to the unbelievers.'[441]

'And the second week had not passed before 30,000 Muslims came to him who were paying *Jizya* on their heads while 80,000 unbelievers had been relieved of their *Jizya* by the officials. Thereupon he put the *Jizya* on the unbelievers and removed it from the Muslims. Then he reclassified the *Kharāj* and put it in order *(ṣannafa'l Kharāj ḥattā waḍa'ahū mawāḍi'ahū)*. Then he assessed the stipulated tribute *(waẓīfa)* according to the treaty of capitulation. And 100,000 used to be taken from Marw in Umayyad days in addition to *Kharāj*.'[442]

The speech and the later developments, if read in the context of the above arguments do not need further explanation; they are self-evident and reveal the truth underlying the whole story. The figures of 80,000 and 30,000 are suspicious to Wellhausen[443] but there seems to be no obvious reason to suspect these figures because of either of the two probable situations: firstly it suggests the composition of the entire population of the whole district which wrongly suffered and which was wrongly benefited; or, secondly, the governor announced this policy not for the city of Marw but for the whole of the province and the figure reflects the fortnight's progress. These figures, however, add another point to our hypothesis that aspersions on the financial impact of *Jizya* were mischievous because even ten years after Ashras the number of converts had not assumed those serious proportions, although Islam had completed a century in Khurāsān. It is worthwhile to reproduce a similar story about Bukhārā during Asad's governorship:

'It is reported on the authority of Muḥammad b. Ja'far through Muḥammad b. Ṣāliḥ al-Laythī that a man arrived and began to preach Islam among the *dhimmīs*. Some people became converts. But the native prince Tughshādā resented it because he had not sincerely embraced Islam. He, therefore, wrote to the governor of Khurāsān, Asad[444] b. 'Abd Allāh that a man was "creating unrest among the people and advising them to announce Islam superficially in order to evade *Jizya*, and inciting them to oppose the government." Asad got them (the converts) arrested through his collector of revenue and handed them over to Tughshādā for punishment. Some were punished, some others were expelled or sent to Khurāsān. But they did not desert Islam.'[445]

The facts stated above easily lead to the causes underlying the offensive decision of retaining poll-tax on converts and do not require any further discussion. It can, however, be observed that the Muslims had not yet achieved that degree of expertise in politics, diplomacy and administration which was to be found in their rivals. And yet they had a complete hold over their lands and they held their own.[446]

Total Collections

The total amount of taxes etc., collected in different districts is not available except in the case of Khurāsān. But the arrangement made with individual cities has been dealt with in the above pages. Details of the frequent changes that were made are also not available. In most cases, it seems the original arrangement was retained and a penalty for revolt was imposed as a lump sum. Like the ruler of the Persian city, Bāb Fīlānshāh and Ṭabarsarānshāh were also exempted from tax because they had promised to assist the Muslims in war,[447] while the prince of Sharwān who also promised to side with them payed ten thousand modi of wheat every year.[448]

Ya'qūbī has given the following figures for Mu'āwiya's period,[449] for some of the regions.

Table 13. Amount of Annual Collections During Mu'āwiya's Reign

	Dirhams
Fars	70,000,000
Ahwāz and suburbs	40,000,000
Kūr Dajla	10,000,000
Nihāwand	
al-Jibāl (Dinawar and Hamadhān)	40,000,000
Ray etc.	30,000,000
Ḥulwān	20,000,000
Moṣul	45,000,000
Ạdharbāijān	30,000,000
Total	285,000,000

The total collection from the provinces of the Persian empire are calculated at 650 million dirhams as compared with the pre-Islamic collection of 600 million as reported by Qudāma who has also produced the average of total revenues for the first half of the third century.[450] As regards the individual units, the figures can only be of value if their precise boundaries are known, otherwise it would be rash to insist on any conclusion. Qudāma, for example, has divided the Persian provinces into about twenty units in the later period while Ya'qūbī has divided them into eight for Mu'āwiya's period. As a result, Mu'āwiya's Ādharbāijān earns 30 million dirhams while Qudāma's, with its districts, only 4.5 million;[451] Ahwāz brings in 40 million but Qudāma's with its seven districts, only 18 million;[452] and so on. Similar differences are to be found if the two lists are compared with Ya'qūbī's figures for the 'Abbāsid period. Ya'qūbī, however, reports that the entire amount of the revenue of Sijistān was spent on maintaining the army, police, and borders within that country.[453] This means it did not carry forward any balance for the province or for the centre.

The Conquest of Sind

Sind, the western region of Hind (India) was first conquered when Spain was reduced. The only financial detail that Balādhurī has reported for the period is the balance sheet of the conquest: the expedition cost 60 million dirhams and brought 120 million by way of booty.[454] But the general turmoil and the political unrest followed by the return of the conqueror, Muḥammad b. Qāsim blurred the situation. The Umayyad dynasty survived for forty years after the conquest of Sind but the effects of the functioning of economic machinery could not be judged from across the turmoil-stricken lands of Sijistān and Khurāsān. It is, however, certain that Sind was conquered by force and agreement was reached on the payment of *Kharāj* (land-tax).[455] What amount was involved is not known, but the fact that the Muslims settled there for a time without debiting the accounts of the central or the provincial treasury suggests that they raised sufficient funds there. Balādhurī reports that the governor of Sind sent 40 million dirhams to the centre and retained an equal amount after distributing some funds. This suggests that the total collection must have been substantial.[456] When a new governor took charge of the treasury, he found a balance of 18 million dirhams.[457] But a report about the later period mentions that the governor sent 7 million dirhams to Ma'mūn after deducting the local expenditure.[458] This means that in the beginning the government did not have the expense of running the administration of this region.

Notes and References

1. Abu Daud, 3, 363.
2. al-Qasṭālānī, *Irshād as-Sārī* (commentary on al-Bukhārī), Vol. 4, p. 40.
3. Bal., 75, 76.
4. Bal., 78.
5. Bal., 76.
6. Yah., 43.
7. A.U., 120.
8. Sad., 5, 227.
9. For example, Wellhausen, J.: *The Arab Kingdom and its Fall,* tr. Margaret Graham Weir, Khayat, Beirut, 1963. pp. 282, 284, etc.; Bell, H.I.: 'The Administration of Egypt under the Umayyad Khalifas', *Byzentinische Zeitschrift* 28 (1928), pp. 280–2; Al-Rāwī, Thābit Ismā'īl: *al-'Irāq fī 'aṣr al-Umawī,* Baghdad, 1965, p.56. Also Becker, C.H.: *Bietrage,* Vol. II, p. 82; Caetani: *Annali dell Islam,* Vol. V, pp. 282–3; Lammens, 'Le Califal de Yazid I er', *Melanges de la Faculte Orientale,* Universite Saint Joseph, Beyrouth, V (1911), pp. 712–24; Grohmann: *Zum Steuerwesen,* pp. 124–5; *cf.* Dennett, Daniel C. Jr.: *Conversion and the Poll-Tax in Early Islam,* Harvard University Press, 1950, pp. 4–6.

10. See note 9.

11. For computing these figures here and hereinafter see the formula in Chapter 13 under the note on 'Population'.

12. See Chapter 6.

13. *Ibid.*

14. History is replete with such instances; for example the reaction of the Companions against the Prophet's consent to strike off from his name the words 'The Apostle of God' (rasūl-Allāh) in the document of treaty with the Quraysh at Ḥudaybiyya in A.H. 7. Then the general reaction of the Muslims on the Prophet's advice to slaughter their animals and return from Ḥudaybiyya without pilgrimage. Or, the *Anṣārs* (Helpers) protest over the Prophet's policy of distribution of the spoils of war at Ḥunayn *(Passim).* Apart from such group protests, accounts of individual protests abound.

15. Yah., 45.

16. Kh., 39.

17. Bal., 89.

18. Bal., 90.

19. Bal., 90–1.

20. Yah., 230.

21. Bal., 89.

22. A.U., 502.

23. Bal., 71.

24. Bal., 70.

25. Bal., 71.

26. *Ibid.*

27. Abu Daud, 3, 231–2.

28. See pp. 205–6.

29. See Chapter 1.

30. Abu Daud, 3, 231.

31. Watt (Prophet), 219–20.

32. See below.

33. Kh., 21.

34. Kh., 21; A.U., 334; Yah., 232.

35. I.A.H. (M), 161.

36. Yah., 29; Kh., 23; A.U., 106, 114.

37. A.U., 106; Bal., 226.

38. Bal., 396.

39. A.U., 116.

40. Yah., 234.

41. Tab., 2, 458.

42. Agh., 21, 27.

43. Maw., 338.

44. Sad., 5, 260.

45. A.U., 120.

46. A.U., 258.

47. *Akhbār Majmū'a fī Fatḥ Andalus,* pp. 22–3, ash-Shāṭibī, 277–8.

48. Pap. IV, General Introduction, XXXV.

49. For full reproduction of the speech see p. 140.

50. See Chapter 6, pp. 177–82.

51. Sad., III, 1, 250 reports Caliph 'Umar's refusal to permit even non-Muslim slaves.

52. Bal., 67–8.

53. Abu Daud, 3, 227; Bal., 75, 79; A.U., 67.

54. Bal., 89, 91, 92.

55. Tab., 1, 1702; Bal., 71.

56. Sira, 2, 338; Bal., 71.

57. Abu Daud, 3, 227; Nas., 5, 26; Bal., 82–3; Yah., 228–9; A.U., 64.

58. Tab., 1, 1718–20; Sira, 380–1.

59. Waq., 1032 (Sira, 2, 338, amount not given). Waq. has mentioned the Prophet's writing of treaty to both the people of Jarbā' but in the text of the letter Adhruḥ alone is mentioned. Ṭabarī (1, 1701) says that the Prophet (peace be upon him) wrote a letter to all of them, the people of Adhruḥ and Jarbā' *(wa kataba Rasūl-Allāh ṣallalāh 'alaihi wa-sallam li kullin kitāban).*

60. Yah., 230.

61. Bal., 71.

62. Abu Daud, 3, 229; Tir., 7, 84–6; Tab., 1, 1600–1.

63. Waq., 1027; Sira, 2, 339; Sad., II, 65; Abu Daud, 3, 226.

64. Waq., 711; Bal., 47.

65. Bal., 70.

66. Bal., 84.

67. Sad., III, 1, 216.

68. Yaq., 2, 221.

69. Yaq., 2, 142.

70. I.A.H. (M), 158–9.

71. Sad., III, 1, 224; I.A.H. (M), 162–3.

72. Yah., 231; I.A.H. (M), 70, 152.

73. Jurjī Zaydān, *History of Islamic Civilization,* Part IV, tr. D.S. Margoliouth, London, 1907, p. 98. (For full details see discussion on Khurāsān); also Tab., 2, 1689.

74. Tab., 2, 1635; Jahs., 57.

75. Sad., III, 1, 250; Mas., 3, 64.

76. Yaq., 2, 142.

77. A.U., 504.

78. Bal., 78.

79. *Ibid.*

80. *Ibid.*

81. *Ibid.*

82. Bal., 268; Yah., 24; A.U., 231.

83. A.U., 256.

84. Tab., 1, 2017, 2049.

85. Yah., 143; Kh., 85; Bal., 244–5; Khal., 101; Tab., 1, 2016, 2017, 2029, 2042, 2045.

86. A.U., 68.

87. Kh., 84–5.

88. Bal., 245.

89. Tab., 1, 2045.

90. Tab., 1, 2049–50.

91. I.K., 8; Qud., 236.

92. Qud., 237.

93. Tab., 1, 2050.

94. See above.

95. There still remains one minor point of dating. Ṭabarī mentions that this treaty was signed by Khālid after he suppressed the second revolt of Ḥīra. The treaty of Ḥīra involving 190,000 dirhams gives the month of Rabī‘ I of A.H. 12. But the treaty with Bāniqiyyā, and Bārūamā ends with Ṣafar, A.H. 12 (Tab., 1, 2050). It means that this treaty was signed before Khālid set about suppressing the second revolt of Ḥīra (1, 2045).

96. Qud., 237–8.

97. *Ibid.* (calculated amount).

98. Kh., 85; Tab., 1, 2050–1.

99. Kh., 85.

100. Tab., 1, 2028, 2031, 2050–1.

101. *Ibid.*

102. *Ibid.*

103. Tab., 1, 2054.

104. Tab., 1, 2042 *et sqq.*

105. Kh., 13–15, full story.

106. Yah., 148–63.

107. Yah., 144.

108. Bal., 268.

109. A.U., 231 *et sqq*.

110. Tab., 1, 2028, 2031, 2370.

111. Kh., 16; Yah., 126–8; Bal., 266.

112. Ist., 82.

113. A.U., 134.

114. See p. 215.

115. See p. 217.

116. Kh., 20.

117. Kh., 21. The names of the two officers are given as ‘Uthmān b. Ḥunayf and Ḥudhayfa b. al-Yamān.

118. Kh., 22.

119. A.U., 182.

120. Yaq., 2, 142.

121. Kh., 20.

122. I.K., 14. *Farsakh* = 3,600 sq. yds.

123. A.U., 134.

124. Kh., 73; I.K., 14.

125. Jahs., 4.

126. Sykes, 1, 462.

127. *Ibid.*

128. Bal., 93. (Almost the same points with varying details are to be found in Tab., 1, 961–2; Christensen (Arthur): *L'Iran sous les Sassanides,* Paris, 1936, pp. 54–6, 98–105, 118, 361–2; Noeldeke (T): *Geshcheste der Perser und Araber zer zeir der Sasaniden,* Leiden, 1879, pp. 243–5, 246. *Cf.* Denn., 14–16.)

129. فتغلل. لكم ما لا تغل لاهلها   قرى بالعراق من قفيزو درهم

Cheikho, 519: also *Sab'a Mu'allaqa*, Zuhayr, line 33.

130. Kh., 48.

131. Kh., 21.

132. Tab., 1, 2371.

133. Kh., 20–1.

134. For detailed discussion see chapter on Economic Indicators, s.v. Population.

135. Yah., 21.

136. Bal., 270. According to Kath., 9, 137, 'Umar II is reported to have said that the collections from Iraq during Caliph 'Umar's time were 11 million. This is irreconcilable with any of the above figures unless it is treated to be in terms of dīnārs (Iraq was a dirham area).

137. al-Ṣūlī, p. 219; *cf.* S.A.E., 135.

138. *Ibid.* The figure compares with the total during 'Umar's period although Balādhurī (pp. 270–1) has given a somewhat different table of the rates of levy during 'Alī's period.

139. Yaq., 2, 221. Balādhurī, *Ansāb al-Ashrāf* (Mss); *cf.* S.A.E., 135. Mu'āwiya is also reported to have added *ṣawāfī* lands which, according to Yaq., 2, 207, fetched 50 million dirhams over and above land-tax and which later rose to 100 million dirhams, pp. 2, 221–2.

140. Bal., 270.

141. Kah., 9, 136–7.

142. Hamadānī, K. al-Buldān. f.86 A (Mss.), *cf.* S.A.E., 135.

143. Jahs., 63.

144. *Ibid.*

145. Tab., 2, 457–58.

146. See above. Also Tab., 2, 941.

147. Tab., 2, 907–8.

148. Agh., 6, 46.

149. For a thorough discussion on the subject see note on Khurāsān, pp. 323–31.

150. For full story see note on Khurāsān in the same chapter.

151. Mok., 129.

152. For this and the following discussion on land policies also refer to Chapter 3.

153. See p. 130, note 34.

154. See Chapter 3.

155. Yaq., 2, 207; see above.

156. See above. See also Chapter 10, note on Agriculture.

157. Yaq., 3, 57.

158. J.B. Bury: *History of the Later Roman Empire,* London, 1923, Vol. I, pp. 40–8. *Cf.* Denn., 51.

159. Bal., 120.

160. Bal., 157.

161. *Ibid.*

162. Tab., 1, 2392.

163. *Ibid.*

164. Tab., 1, 2154.

165. Tab., 1, 2159.

166. Khalifa, 1, 112.

167. I.F., 105.

168. Tab., 1, 2392.

169. On another authority Bal., 136 has given a fixed amount of 17,000 dīnārs as levy on Emessa. This was perhaps the first stage of an agreement which was later made uniform with other cities.

170. Bal., 136–7.

171. Bal., 120–2.

172. Bal., 144; Tab., 2405–7.

173. Bal., 128.

174. Bal., 132.

175. Bal., 137.

176. Tab., 1, 2392.

177. Bal., 144.

178. Tab., 1, 2403.

179. Bal., 131.

180. *Ibid.*

181. Denn., 45–6.

182. Michael the Syrian II, Fasc. III, p. 426, and Theophanes 55. *Cf.* Denn., 60–1. This evidence also indirectly confirms the different stages of taxation. A survey of the entire land and adoption of a uniform policy was impossible unless the whole of Syria etc. was captured which took some six to seven years. The cities already conquered in the early stages could not be left tax-free pending the entire conquest. So some sort of provisional taxation policy was adopted in the beginning.

183. Bal., 158; Tab., 1, 2826.

184. A.U., 445; Bal., 163.

185. Yaq., 3, 16; Tab., 2, 796.

186. Patr. Or., 8, 497. But, according to Ya'qūbī, 1000.

187. Tab., 2, 853.

188. Yaq., 221–2.

189. Bal., 197.

190. Ibn Khal. *Cf.* Lestr. p. 45. The figures have been included only with a view to judging the authenticity of the other figures, by comparison.

191. The amount pertains to Emessa only in the first stage of the treaty.

192. Or according to another tradition 700,000 dīnārs.

193. Or with the amount given in f.n. 5, 1,638,000 dīnārs.

194. Denn., 62 *(sic.)*.

195. Michael the Syrian, II, Fasc. III, p. 450. *Cf.* Denn., 62. Dennett has criticized the corresponding dates.

196. Bal., 162.

197. *Ibid.*

198. *Ibid.*

199. Bal., 159.

200. Bal., 164, *et seq.*

201. Patr. Or., 8, 476. 'Ibād b. 'Āthim seems to be a mistake in deciphering. The original name is 'Iyād ibn Ghanam.

202. Bal., 178.

203. Kh., 23–4.

204. Bal., 179.

205. Bal., 180.

206. *Ibid.*

207. Bal., 181.

208. Bal., 187.

209. Theophanes, 341; Cedr. I, 752; Mich. the Syrian II, 424. *Cf.* Patr. Or., 8, 478.

210. Bal., 186–7; Kh., 69.

211. *Ibid.*

212. As discussed in the case of Iraq and Syria, the amount differed according to the resources of the tax-payer.

213. See above.

214. For a useful and brief discussion on the chronology of the first conquest of Alexandria, see S.L.P., 13 fn. For a detailed discussion see Butler, *The Arab Conquest of Egypt,* Oxford, 1902.

215. Bal., 224; Severus, 107–8.

216. Bal., 220.

217. Severus, 107–8.

218. Bal., 216–17.

219. Bal., 217.

220 *Ibid.,* 220.

221. *Ibid.,* 218.

222. Bal., 219.

223. *Ibid.*

224. Bal., 220.

225. *Ibid.,* 221.

226. Tab., 1, 2581–4.

227. I.A.H. (M), 84.

228. *Ibid.*, p. 84.

229. *Ibid.*, pp. 85–6.

230. *Ibid.*, p. 86.

231. I.A.H. (M), 87.

232. *Ibid.*, pp. 88–9.

233. Bal., 216.

234. *Ibid.*, 221.

235. Tab., 1, 2580.

236. A.C.J., 139.

237. Severus, 103.

238. S.L.P., 3 fn.

239. A.S., 112 fn.

240. Severus, 108.

241. Also called Masra, *cf.* Gibbon 5, 447.

242. Bal., 231.

243. A.S., 112 fn.

244. Supra, p. 237.

245. Watt (Medina), 345.

246. Bal., 223.

247. For another possible interpretation see But., 508–26.

248. Butler, Alfred J.: *The Arab Conquest of Egypt* and *The Last Thirty Years of the Roman Dominion,* Oxford, 1902.

249. Denn., 7.

250. Lane-Poole (S.L.P. 6n.) suggests that this is probably a slip for 'pay the poll-tax [of two dīnārs a head] and fifty million dirhams in land-tax' *(Kharāj)* for it would be the land-tax not poll-tax that would be modified in proportion to the fertility dependent upon the extent of inundation. He may be correct but another interpretation would be that the historians have, as usual, misused the word *Jizya* for *Kharāj.* Examples of such misuses have been cited above *cf.* (pp. 197–8).

251. Tab., 1, 2588–9.

252. Bal., 217.

253. Yaq., 144.

254. Yaq., 2, 144; Yaq. (B), 339.

255. Maq., (Kh.), 1, 98.

256. Bal., 217, 220.

257. I.A.H. (M), 161.

258. Severus, 204–5.

259. A.S., 83.

260. Yaq. (B), 339; Maq. (Kh.), 1, 81.

261. Scr. Ar., VII, 24.

262. Bal., 224.

263. Perhaps 'Cyrus'.

264. Patr. Or., 8, 471.

265. Maq. (Kh.), 1, 79.

266. *Ibid.*

267. Yaq., 2, 144.

268. Scr. Ar. VII, 24.

269. I.A.H. (M), 70.

270. Maq. (Kh.), 1, 62, 66, 79.

271. I.A.H. (M), 82.

272. Bal., 218.

273. Computed with 8 million taxable persons.

274. Severus, 103.

275. I.A.H. (M), 82; Scr. Ar., VII, 26.

276. J. and W., 237.

277. Severus, 111.

278. *Ibid.,* 154; Kindi, 73.

279. I.A.H. (M), 156.

280. Kindi, 71.

281. I.A.H. (M), 156.

282. A.C.J., 126; J. and W., 264.

283. 5, 458.

284. A.C.J., 126.

285. J.G.M., 118.

286. Pap., 267; *cf.* J.G.M., 119.

287. J. and W., 236.

288. J.G.M., 120.

289. *Ibid.*

290. *Ibid.,* 120; A.C.J., 128.

291. J.G.M., 120–1.

292. *Ibid.*

293. *Ibid.*

294. *Ibid.;* A.C.J., 128.

295. *Ibid.;* J.M.H., 2, 73.

296. J.M.H., 2, 73.

297. A.C.J., 109, 112, 122.

298. *Ibid.*, 109.

299. *Ibid;* J.G.M., 123.

300. J.G.M., 124.

301. Pap. IV., Intr. 1357.

302. A.C.J., 109; J.G.M., 122.

303. J.G.M., 126.

304. *Ibid.*

305. *Ibid.*

306. *Ibid.*

307. A.C.J., 122.

308. *Ibid.*

309. Bal., 217, 220.

310. Tab., 2, 93.

311. I.F., 88–9; Khalifa, 1, 417.

312. A.C.J., 124.

313. J. and W., 237 n.

314. Issawi, Charles: *Egypt: An Economic and Social Analysis,* London, 1947, p. 47.

315. See above.

316. See above.

317. See above.

318. Bal., 236.

319. *Ibid.*, 225; I.A.H., 34; Yaq., 2, 146.

320. Bal., 219.

321. Nūbiya is excluded. Historians (Bal., 238) report that the Muslims made an agreement with the people of Nūbiya to have a number of slaves in exchange for a quantity of food-grain. Ṭabarī (1, 2593) has termed it as a gift. Ibn Khaldūn reports that the agreement with the Nūbiyans also provided for permission for free trade and peace. (Khal., 2, 115. Supplement). The agreement was made during ʻAbd-Allāh b. Saʻd's governorship.

322. See note on Syria p. 221 *sq*. and note on Agriculture, p. 310 *sq*.

323. I.A.H. (M), 161.

324. *Ibid.*

325. Yaq. (B), 339.

326. *Ibid.*

327. Maq. (Kh.), 1, 81.

328. I.A.H. (M), 70; Bal., 215, 216, 220.

329. *Cf.* S.L.P., 12.

330. I.A.H. (M), 161.

331. I.A.H. (M), 153.

332. Severus, 109.

333. Tab., 1, 2818; Bal., 228.

334. *Ibid.,* Khalifa, 1, 165.

335. Khalifa, 1, 165.

336. Severus, 111.

337. Severus, 153.

338. Bal., 219.

339. Pap. IV, Intr. p. 82.

340. Severus, 149.

341. Aphrodito Papyri, IV, 1345, 1354, 1356, 1365, however, seem to absolve Qurra of the allegations of high-handedness levelled by some Muslim historians. The Papyri confirm Qurra's care for the interests of the people and also describe the restrictions which he imposed on four persons who levied fines on the defaulters.

342. Pap. IV, Gen. Intr. XXXV.

343. Pap. IV, Intr., p. 172.

344. *Ibid.,* pp. 173, 264.

345. Pap. IV, Gen. Intr. XXVI.

346. *Ibid.,* Intr., pp. 158, 261.

347. Pap. IV, Intr. pp. 126, 129, 159, etc.

348. Severus, 122.

349. Severus, p. 142.

350. Pap. IV, Intr., 1343.

351. *Ibid.*

352. Severus, 151.

353. Denn., 81; Maq. (Kh.), 2, 493.

354. Denn., 79.

355. Severus, 143.

356. *Ibid.*

357. Parenthesis mine.

358. Severus, 152–3.

359. Sad., 5, 283.

360. Severus, 154; Kindi, 73.

361. Severus, 154.

362. Bal., 229.

363. Jahs., 57; Tab., 2, 1435.

364. Pap. IV, Intr., p. 174.

365. I.A.H. (M), 152–3.

366. Pap. IV, 1405, 1412.

367. See p. 209 *et seq.*

368. Khalifa, 1, 148.

369. Tab., 1, 2641.

370. Bal., 299.

371. 304 *et sqq.*

372. Bal., 306.

373. Bal., 318–19.

374. Sad., III, 1, 202.

375. I.F., 270. How large the district was during Mu'āwiya's reign and into how many districts the region was divided is not discussed by geographers. Even the boundaries of al-Jibāl are not precisely defined. Ibn al-Faqīh, for example, observes that it included Hamadhān, Māsabazān, Saymara, Qum, Nihāwand and Qirmāsīn, the Pehlavī cities, but not Ray, Isfahān, Qūmis, Ṭabaristān, Jurjān, Sijistān, Qazwīn, etc. (p. 209). Muqaddasī although he excludes them (p. 386) as Pehlavi cities, includes them within al-Jibāl.

376. Khalifa, 1, 124.

377. *Ibid.,* 126.

378. Yaq., 2, 221.

379. Bal., 372; Khalifa, 1, 132.

380. 1, 2662.

381. Bal., 321.

382. *Ibid.*

383. 322.

384. Bal., 330. According to another report *(Ibid.)* it involved 300,000 dirhams.

385. Tab., 1, 2659. Khalifa, (1, 266), also mentions clothes and 300 slaves.

386. Khalifa, 1, 424.

387. Bal., 327, 329.

388. Bal., 378, 380, 383; Tab., 1, 2695–6, 2704 *et sqq.*

389. Khalifa, 1, 164.

390. Bal., 380.

391. Khalifa, 1, 163.

392. Ist., 158.

393. Bal., 380.

394. Bal., 200 *et seq.*

395. *Ibid.* The rate of land-tax on vineyards in Caliph 'Uthmān's period is reported as 100 dirhams. The same amount was payable by those who owned mills.

396. *Ibid.*

397. Bal., 212.

398. *Ibid.,* 205.

399. Khalifa, 2, 367.

400. Qud., 246; I.K., 124.

401. Bal., 396.

402. For all the figures see Bal., 394 *et sqq.*

403. Or 75,000 (Bal., 394).

404. Or 1,000,000 (Bal., 395).

405. Khalifa, 1, 173–4.

406. Tab., 1, 2689.

407. Bal., 399.

408. Bal., 386.

409. *Ibid.*

410. Bal., 389.

411. *Ibid.*

412. Tab., 2, 1037.

413. Bal., 391; Tab., 2, 1134 mentions a seven-year truce.

414. Bal., 392.

415. Tab., 2, 1036.

416. Yaq. (1, 154) reports about (1) Khurāsān, (2) Ādharbāijān and (3) Fars, in the pre-Islamic period.

417. S.A.E., 10 n.

418. *Ibid.*

419. Bal., 410.

420. Bal., 416.

421. Khalifa, 1, 422.

422. Khalifa, 405, 424.

423. Bal., 333.

424. Narshakhi, 53.

425. *Ibid.*

426. Tab., 2, 1245.

427. Well. 478.

428. See pp. 219–20.

429. Tab., 2, 1507.

430. Denn., 116.

431. Bal., 415.

432. Tab., 2, 1354.

433. His own governor of Khurāsān sought his permission to be stricter in collecting revenues but he declined. Tab., 2, 1355.

434. Sad., 5, 277.

435. See page 287.

436. Tab., 2, 1507–10.

437. Christensen, L'Iran, 118–24, 362. *Cf.* Dennett, 116. Dennett (121) has assumed that by A.H. 110 there seems to have been some change in the taxation system of Khurāsān. But the difficulty is that there is not a single report to support this assumption. Moreover the terms of the revised treaties in different parts of Khurāsān essentially retain the same system of a fixed tribute. A third point to note is Ṭabarī's report (2, 1689) that Manṣūr reimposed the amount of the agreed tribute which also suggests that a formal revision was never made by the government. The report *(Ibid.)* that 'after the reorganization Marw paid one hundred thousand dirhams more than the amount of treaty' is suggestive of the possibility that this amount would be a penal impost over and above the agreed amount of treaty. The treaty was intact even during the 'Abbāsid period when 'Abd-Allāh b. Ṭāhir intended to revise the policy in Nīsāpur (an-Nīsābūrī, Muḥammad b. 'Abd-Allāh: *Ta'rīkh Nīsābūr,* abridged by al-Khalīfa an-Nīsābūrī, Tehran, n.d., p. 130).

438. 2, 1508. (The *Kharāj* has surely gone broke.)

439. Tab., 2, 1516.

440. Tab., 2, 1542.

441. Tab., 2, 1688.

442. Tab., 2, 1688–9.

443. Well., 479.

444. Asad preceded Naṣr.

445. *Narsakhi: The History of Bukhara,* tr. Richard N. Frye, Cambridge (U.S.A.), 1954, pp. 59–60.

446. For detailed study on the subject see Chapter 2 on Moral Foundations.

447. Bal., 211; Khal., 2, 120 Supp.

448. Bal., 211.

449. Yaq., 2, 221.

450. Qud., 249–52.

451. Qud., pp. 242–6 for all cities.

452. *Ibid.*

453. Yaq., (B), 286.

454. Bal., 427.

455. Bal., 425.

456. Bal., 429–30.

457. *Ibid.*

458. Ibn Ṭayfūr, 39.

CHAPTER 8

Miscellaneous Incomes

Commodity Levies

It has been pointed out above that a number of levies comprised payment of commodities and slaves.[1] In the discussion on the amounts of taxes the commodities or their values have not been accounted for. These commodities, apart from slaves, included food-grain and provisions like wheat, barley, honey, oil, vinegar, clothing and utensils.[2] In most cases provisioning of the Muslims was also made a condition of an agreement. The Egyptians were required to supply the army in Egypt with gowns, mantles, caps, trousers, and socks.[3] In most agreements entertaining the Muslims for three days or so was made a condition of the treaty. But such arrangements have an invisible economic effect and their value cannot be ascertained. The commodities and clothing were collected by the government, stored in godowns, and distributed among deserving persons.

The *'Ushūr*

Apart from the tributes and taxes the *Bayt al-Māl* also received some other incomes, most important of which were customs duty *('ushūr)* and later on purchase/sales tax. Before Islam, each tribe or a group of tribes inhabiting a town collected these taxes on the trade goods imported by a 'foreign' tribesman for sale in their market.[4] These levies were deducted at ten per cent of the value of the goods and perhaps a dirham per transaction and the collector was called *ṣāḥib maks* or *'āshir*. But it seems that after the establishment of an Islamic state in Arabia many tribes were still asserting their pre-Islamic authority and collecting these taxes even from the Muslims who, in principle, had transcended these tribal imposts. That is why the tone of the *Ḥadīth* on this subject is very severe.[5] The aim seems to be the elimination of extra-state authority, and the subjugation of the pre-Islamic tribal authorities to the Islamic state. It is, therefore, not surprising that the very sources that narrate the Prophet's serious views against *'ushūr,* also narrate that Caliph 'Umar was the first to introduce *'ushūr* in Islam. As a result, they have tried to reconcile the Prophet's sayings with Caliph 'Umar's practice. Abū 'Ubayd has suggested that it was the pre-Islamic practice which the Prophet (peace be upon him) intended to abolish. He banned it and substituted *Zakāt* which amounted to two and a half per cent of the value of goods as against the pre-Islamic ten per cent *('ushr,* pl. *'ushūr).* Thus the receiver of the two and a half per cent will not be called *'āshir* (the collector of a tenth) because he is actually collecting two and a half per cent.[6] As regards the tenth collected from *ḥarbīs* or the twentieth collected from *dhimmīs,* it was based on treaty.[7]

The rationale behind this tax as given by Abū Yūsuf is more convincing. He has adduced two stories to suggest the origin of the tax:

1. Abū Mūsā al-Ash'arī wrote to Caliph 'Umar that the Muslim traders were being taxed at a rate of one-tenth in *ḥarbī* lands. 'Umar advised him to reciprocate and further suggested that he charge five per cent from *dhimmīs* and two and a half per cent from the Muslims, provided the value of the goods exceeded two hundred dirhams.[8]

2. The traders of Manbij, an enemy *(ḥarbī)* nation across the waters, wrote to Caliph 'Umar to allow them to enter his country for trade on payment of one-tenth of the value of goods. 'Umar consulted the Companions who voted for it. Thus it was the first nation to pay *'ushūr.*[9]

Whatever the rationale, Caliph 'Umar levied customs duty on imports. In the beginning some Companions were reluctant to accept the job of collecting *'ushūr* because of the Prophet's condemnation of the *'āshir* (the collector of the tenth)[10] but they were soon convinced. 'Umar appointed tax collectors at different centres.[11] They checked the incoming traders at a central point. The rate of tax was ten, five and two and a half per cent for the 'Romans', *dhimmīs,* and the Muslims respectively.[12] Nabaeteans, who frequented the markets in Madina, were also taxed at a rate of ten per cent but, in order to encourage imports of oil and wheat, these two commodities were taxed at a rate of only five per cent.[13] These taxes were collected on an article once a year subject to a minimum value of 200 dirhams.[14] Manumitted slaves were exempt from paying this duty on their own articles for trade.[15] At first the place of levy was the border post through which goods passed. But, because there were no fixed routes of entry, a trader could cross the border at any point and travel through the country unnoticed by the customs collector. As a result markets were also made centres of levy.

The proceeds of customs duty are not recorded for the period. But there is no doubt that the levy continued throughout the period. 'Umar II, in order to streamline the administration of this tax, advised his officers to issue an official receipt so that a double charge was not made on the same goods during the same year.[16] He abolished the system of checking at border posts or canals and bridges, etc., and appointed city-collectors.[17]

Other Levies

When *maks* or the transaction-tax was introduced, is not known. But 'Umar II's condemnation of the tax and its abolition suggests that it was prevalent before his caliphate. Reports also suggest the existence of unofficial collectors which particularly led 'Umar II to abolish it along with some other taxes known as *mā'ida* (table) and *fidya* (ransom), the exact nature of which is not known.[18] Some trade-tax was also reported to have been collected from the traders and craftsmen in lieu of land-tax. 'Umar II abolished all such excesses.[19] He also prohibited his governors from collecting excise duty on wine.[20] Ṭabarī mentions his decree aimed at abolishing the charges of minters *(ujūr-aḍ-ḍarrābīn),* the presents made on the eve of the Persian festivals of Nawroz and Mehrjān, the 'price of the book' *(thaman ṣuḥuf),* charges in the income of carriers *(ujūr-al-fuyūj* or *al-futūḥ),* house charges, and wedding charges *(dirāhim al-nikāḥ).* Almost the same words are reported by Abū 'Ubayd.[21] The nature, the impact and the incidence of these taxes can only be guessed at. It is, however, clear that they were in force before 'Umar II, and can be presumed to have been levied some time during and after Mu'āwiya's reign. Whether or not these taxes were reintroduced after 'Umar II cannot be definitely stated. But because most of the decisions taken by him were reverted by his successors, so might be the case with these levies.

Other Sources of Income

Over and above these levies, there were also some minor and negligible sources of income to the *Bayt al-Māl.* Since 'Umar's time the *bequest* of the heirless deceased was transferred to the *Bayt al-Māl.*[22] Later on half of the *blood-money* of a tributary was taken over by the state, the other half being passed on to the claimant.[23] Another source of income was the *seized properties* of the officers. This practice started in Caliph 'Umar's time[24] and seems to have continued throughout the period. During Umayyad rule, however, there were clear cases of corruption and many of the corrupt officers were caught.[25] The amount received by way of *ransom* of enemy captives had also been a source of income since the Prophet's time.[26] Caliph Abū Bakr received the ransom of the apostates at 400 dirhams each.[27] 'Umar II is reported to have charged, in some cases, 100,000 dirhams for a captive and 100 *mithqāl* of gold for another.[28] *Seigniorage,* after the government took over the minting of coins, also became a source of income, the normal rate being one per cent of the value of the coin.[29]

Debts and Donations

Apart from these sources of income, the government always had a last resort in cases of emergency: *loans* from individuals. How the Prophet (peace be upon him) utilized this source, has been discussed earlier.[30] During ʻAbd al-Malik's reign, his governor of Khurāsān borrowed from the traders sufficient funds to prepare for war.[31] The governor of Egypt under ʻUmar II borrowed 20,000 dīnārs to distribute as pensions.[32] An interesting case of attracting income is Walīd's requisition of money, material and technicians from the Byzantine ruler, for the reconstruction of the Prophet's mosque[33] in A.H. 98. According to Ibn Kathīr, Walīd demanded of the ruler the necessary material.[34] According to Ṭabarī, the ruler sent 100,000 *mithqāl* of gold, 100 masons, and forty camel-loads of marble.[35]

Muʻāwiya and the later rulers and their governors received the *presents* given on the occasion of non-Muslim festivals.[36] While it is not certain if these gifts and presents formed a portion of the income to the *Bayt al-Māl,* it is certain from ʻUmar II's decree of abolition of the tax that the governor received it.[37]

Notes and References

1. The slaves were, apparently indispensable to the socio-economic institution of the age. But the Qur'ān and the *Sunna* of the Prophet (peace be upon him) coming down to us enjoin a behaviour that first of all tends to replace the institution of slavery with that of a respectable household servant or personal attendant, and then gradually abolish it. One of the positive measures that the Qur'ān takes in this regard is earmarking a portion of the *Zakāt* fund for the freeing of slaves *(wa fi'r-iqāb).* It seems that Abū Bakr and ʻUmar were conscious of this spirit and took measures to discourage it. But later on the Muslims realized that it was too early to completely abolish the institution without first replacing it with an alternative that could fit the Islamic set-up. There was the need for somebody to look after their household affairs, to help them in farming and gardening and to take care of their riding animals. The ruler himself needed to have an entourage of faithful and submissive persons. The tribal Arabs were not 'tamed' to act as submissive servants. These factors probably induced them to acquire foreign slaves and elevate their status to that of a household servant. ʻUthmān's governor ʻAbd-Allāh b. Saʻd, for the first time settled an agreement to receive a number of slaves from Nubia and after him it became a regular practice to haul up the largest possible 'herd of slaves'. But the generous treatment that was extended to them created political problems followed by their control of absolute political power in almost the whole of the Muslim world. Beginning gradually from the status of the teachers of religious disciplines and soldiers, they rose to the position of rulers in a political but not at all a religious upheaval.

2. Chapter 7.

3. *Ibid.*

4. For example a pre-Islamic poet, Jābir b. Hānī, says (Cheikho, 189):

وفى كل اسواق العراق اتاوة　　وفى كل ما باع امرؤ مكس درهم

And there is a payment in each of the markets of Iraq and in the case of each article that a man has sold the deducting of a dirham. The literal meaning of *Mikas* or *Mumakisa* is: he diminished or deducted from the price of selling or buying (Lane, *Arabic-English Dictionary*).

5. See p. 175.

6. A.U., 1638.

7. A.U., 1668, *ḥarbī,* one who belongs to a nation locked in war against an Islamic state.

8. Kh., 78; Yah., 638–9.

9. *Ibid.*

10. Sarakshī, *Sharḥ Siyar,* 4, 282; Tab., 1, 2642.

11. I.A.H. (M), 109. Abū Yūsuf has given the names of Anas b. Mālik and Ziyād b. Ḥudayr, pp. 78–9.

12. A.U., 1655 *et sqq.* Kh., 78.

13. A.U., 1659–60.

14. According to Yaḥyā, *ḥarbīs* were charged at 10% if they stayed for less than six months. But if they stayed for a year they were required to pay 5% (Yah., 635).

15. Kh., 79.

16. Sad., 5, 288–9.

17. *Ibid.,* 279.

18. Sad., 5, 254, 290; A.U., 1628.

19. A.U., 120, 1653.

20. Sad., 5, 280.

21. Tab., 2, 1366–7; A.U., 120.

22. Sad., III, 1, 61.

23. Umm, 6, 97; Agh., 13, 15. *cf.* A.S.T., 180.

24. Chapter 2, p. 107.

25. Chapters 2 and 10 D.

26. Chapter 4, p. 143.

27. Bal., 112.

28. Sad., 5, 258, 260–1.

29. Bal., 454.

30. See p. 143.

31. Tab., 2, 1022.
32. Maq. (Kh.), 1, 78.
33. Tab., 2, 1194.
34. Kath., 9, 146–7.
35. Tab., 2, 1194; Yaq., 3, 30.
36. Tab., 2, 1366, 1635; A.U., 120; Jahs., 24.
37. See p. 287.

CHAPTER 9

Centre-Province Relationship

'O Amīr al-Muminīn! Retain something in the *Bayt al-Māl* for the future too.'

'This has been put into your mouth by Satan. God save me from his evil. It will become an ordeal for those who will come after me.'[1] Thus responded Caliph 'Umar to the advice of one of his Companions in the early days of his rule. But after a few years, he wrote to one of his governors: 'By my life a regular income *(Jizya qā'ima)* which continues for us and our posterity is more desirable to me than the *Fay'* which is distributed and exhausted as nought.'[2]

Establishment of the Provincial *Bayt al-Māls*

Caliph 'Umar had now changed into an administrator with vision and realism. The Muslim armies were treading the remote north, east and west. More than 100,000 soldiers needed regular provisions, arms and riding animals for themselves and in many cases for their families, too. Thousands of Arabs were to be settled in the conquered lands. A fully-fledged administrative machinery was to be organized. Construction for the economic infrastructure and for defence was an urgent requirement for retaining the conquests. Caliph 'Umar now realized that what he had refused to do earlier should now be done by his governors in the provinces. As controller of the central *Bayt al-Māl* he needed large amounts to finance the ever-increasing requirements of an expanding state. These amounts could not be donated by the Arab provinces. The newly-conquered lands were expected to help finance the government requirements at the centre too. As a result, provincial *Bayt al-Māls* were set up and placed under an officer separate from the provincial governor. The functions of these provincial organizations were to cover all their expenditure within their jurisdiction and send the remaining portion to the centre. Thus the provincial *Bayt al-Māl* was supposed to support the central *Bayt al-Māl* but not to call upon it for support unless an unusual situation arose.

The central *Bayt al-Māl* was located in Madina. Caliph 'Alī transferred it to Kūfa while Mu'āwiya took it to Damascus.[3]

The provincial *Bayt al-Māl* was located in the governor's city, with branches at all the centres of collection. The function of the latter was to collect levies and remit them to the provincial headquarters which utilized them according to requirements. In the early period, the centre was responsible for allocating pensions and, therefore, a regular and quick remittance of funds was very necessary. But later on many of the centre's functions were transferred to the provinces. Yet the centre was not self-sufficient even in respect of its local needs. 'Send me for the Madinans their pensions as they are also the sharers of your *Fay*" wrote Caliph 'Umar frequently to his governors.[4] When Mu'āwiya had full control over the government, he asked his officers in Iraq to expedite sending him funds to relieve him of his liabilities.[5] The same advice he sent to his officers at Baṣra[6] and Khurāsān, but in the latter case only for gold and silver procured in booty.[7] It is doubtful if he received anything from Egypt during 'Amr's governorship because some historians have reported that he had bestowed upon him the income of Egypt and al-Maghrib.[8] In any case the centre was so needful of provincial funds that the pensions of the Syrians were delayed unless funds from Egypt were received.[9]

The Condition of the Central *Bayt al-Māl*

In spite of its claim on the provincial resources, the centre in the early days was not well off. Caliph 'Umar did not have resources enough to pay his soldiers generously.[10] Caliph 'Uthmān had sufficient funds in his treasury, but Caliph 'Alī had to face a financial crisis followed by Mu'āwiya's secession. Even the provinces of Fars and Kirmān which were under him refused to pay their share.[11] In the later period, the centre generally kept its head above water. Walīd I and Hishām were in this respect the most fortunate rulers in that they had a treasury bulging with surplus funds. While the income of the provinces was certain, the resources of the centre were at the mercy of the provinces. The favouritism and nepotism of the rulers paid politically but hit them financially. Mu'āwiya seems to have been deprived of the resources of Egypt and the West for as long as 'Amr was the governor.[12] Under Marwān I his son 'Abd al-'Azīz was posted as governor of Egypt and he remained there until his death in the middle of 'Abd al-Malik's reign. Both the caliphs thus deprived themselves of the privilege of claiming the funds of Egypt and the western provinces. When 'Abd al-Malik was angry with his brother, he wrote to him to remit the centre's share. 'Abd al-'Azīz replied: 'Do not disturb me. We both are the oldest men in our family and God knows who will die first.'[13] Early in Marwān's period he sent only 7,000 dīnārs to the centre;[14] 'Abd al-Malik tried to persuade the governor of Khurāsān to desert his rival Ibn Zubayr and take the province as his personal property for seven years.[15] This, however, did not materialize. The native prince of Kabul was granted a *Kharāj*-free period for seven to nine years.[16] A similar case was that of Iraq and Khurāsān during Yazīd II's reign when his brother Maslama was in charge of the taxes of both provinces.[17] Though Walīd experienced some hard times during his early period,[18] he managed to increase the rates of taxes, reorganized the finances and thus, within a short time, had sufficient funds to undertake mammoth construction and public welfare projects.[19] 'Umar II had difficulties in the first year of his reign because he withdrew from a number of 'unjust' incomes. Iraq, which had been the most faithful supporter of the central *Bayt al-Māl,* felt in need of support.[20] The general state of the treasury was also unsatisfactory. While granting a pension to Ibn Sīrīn, the caliph regretted that he could not restore the pensions of the deprived Basrites simply for want of funds.[21] But not long after this several reports suggest a miraculous recovery in the financial position of his government. It is reported that the governor of Iraq found it difficult to dispose of the funds of the *Bayt al-Māl* even after generous distribution among new heads.[22] Governor Abū Bakr b. Ḥazm also admitted the same situation for his province. Another probable reason for this situation was his decision to distribute *Zakāt* funds within the provinces, which had perhaps been sent to the centre before him.[23] Moreover, there were regions where incomes fell short of their requirements, and they became a liability for the centre. An example is the border regions of Syria where *Kharāj*-free lands were in abundance. Muslims had occupied them and paid *'Ushr* on their produce. *'Ushr* alone could not, perhaps, cater for the military requirements of the border belt.[24] Armenia had no surplus to be remitted and in the event of a military operation it became a liability of the centre.[25] The general increase in the pensions of the soldiers and expenditure on heavy administration during Walīd II's reign created a strain on the resources of the central *Bayt al-Māl.* The ruler not only pressed his governors to remit him more funds,[26] but also began to bargain with the governorships.[27] However he managed to improve matters, so much so that he bequeathed a *Bayt al-Māl* of 47 million dīnārs.[28]

The Condition of the Provincial *Bayt al-Māls*

While the central *Bayt al-Māl* was experiencing both good and bad days, most of the provincial *Bayt al-Māls* were in a relatively better position. When Zibriqān offered to grant Caliph Abū Bakr the *Kharāj* of Baḥrayn for ensuring the loyalty of the people there[29] he was obviously convinced that the province would give abundant surplus. The officers in Syria were the first to assure Caliph 'Umar of the free supply of fine quality rations to the Muslims stationed there, because as they admitted: 'God has abundantly supplied wealth, resources and taxes.'[30]

Egypt contributed large funds to the centre. Mu'āwiya is stated to have been left with 600,000 dīnārs every year, after providing for the provincial requirements.[31] Ibn 'Abd al-Ḥakam reported it to be the richest province during Walīd's period.[32] The governor is reported to have complained to the caliph about the lack of accommodation for storing wealth.[33] The Greek Papyri reveal the existence of several district treasuries throughout Egypt.[34]

Iraq had been a source of regular income to the centre. In Caliph 'Umar's time it was divided into two financial zones: Kūfa and Baṣra. Kūfa alone donated 20 to 30 million dirhams every year.[35] But because most of the army that was deployed on the northern and in particular on the eastern front was financed by these two zones, resources fell short of their requirements. As a result, these zones were extended by adding the paying districts of Dīnawar and Nihāwand.[36] The practice was that the branches collected the funds and sent them to the provinces. The provinces, after deducting the estimated local expenditure, passed on the remainder to the centre. For example, the collectors of different districts of Baṣra sent their collections to Caliph 'Alī's governor Ibn 'Abbās who passed them on to Caliph 'Alī.[37] Kūfa had branches at Anbār, Madā'in, 'Ayn Tamr and Wāsīṭ.[38] Irmiyya, Ḥawr, Khawmī and Salmās sent their collections to Mosul.

During Mu'āwiya's reign, Ziyād became the sole collector in charge of the whole of Iraq and Khurāsān. The jurisdiction of Ḥajjāj was extended to its farthest eastern frontiers. During a time of crisis, he wanted to raise the taxes but the caliph disapproved of it.[39] By Walīd's time, Iraq remitted 25 million dirhams every year.[40]

Sind is reported to have paid to the centre 40 million dirhams,[41] but it is not certain if the same amount was regularly remitted.

Malpractices in the Provinces

In view of their relatively better position, the provincial *Bayt al-Māls* could have performed a more important role, had there been regular audits and strict vigilance over the accounts. How Caliph 'Umar exercised control over these treasuries has already been discussed elsewhere. In the later period also, reports suggest the auditing of the provincial treasuries, but the incidents of corruption suggest that, firstly, it was not a regular practice and secondly, the offices of administration and revenue did not remain strictly separate. When 'Abd-Allāh b. 'Āmr, the governor of Baṣra, called on Mu'āwiya, he requested him not to check his accounts. Mu'āwiya agreed to this and spared him.[42] Yazīd I asked his governor of Khurāsān, 'Abd ar-Raḥmān about the amount he had brought with him. '20 million dirhams', answered the governor. Yazīd then said: 'If you wish to continue your job, submit the accounts; but if you do not want to surrender the amount, resign.' The governor chose the second option.[43] The period from Yazīd to the middle of 'Abd al-Malik's reign was not in this respect a happy one. The eastern provinces were under Ibn Zubayr's control. In 66 A.H. Mukhtār took nine million dirhams from the treasury in Kūfa.[44] 'Abd al-'Azīz was not remitting the revenues of Egypt. Even Ibn Zubayr's governors were not behaving fairly towards him. Ḥamza, the governor of Baṣra, deserted with the entire funds of the *Bayt al-Māl*.[45] The Kharijites were exacting taxes from the people of the lands under their influence. Defaulting tax-payers had banded together and killed many tax-collectors.[46] Sulaymān's deputy governor, Yazīd, misappropriated about six million dirhams but was caught by 'Umar II.[47] Hishām's governor, Khālid, amassed a large fortune and misappropriated government properties.[48] How much the office of revenue collection had become a source of corruption can be ascertained by the report that when a person in 105 A.H. went to take over from a revenue officer, the latter offered him 300,000 dirhams to withdraw from the job.[49]

The Provincial Bias

In the face of the above instances of corruption and frequent loss to the government, two points emerge clearly. Firstly, the government never showed any signs of financial insolvency, although it experienced many a hard time. Secondly, the Muslim society looked down upon the corrupt officials whenever they were exposed. It was conscious of the concept of *māl-al-Muslimīn* (Muslim common weal); and if it found anything suspicious, it rushed to protect its *māl*. But unfortunately the concept, in the absence of proper discipline during Umayyad's reign, was distorted and narrowed down to provincialism. When Ibn 'Abbās intended to transfer the funds to Baṣra, the people there objected because they wanted to have their pensions before sending any money to the centre.[50] When Ziyād advised his officer to send to the caliph the entire quantity of the precious metals of the booty, he assembled the soldiers and put the proposition to a vote.[51] 'Ubayd Allāh b. Ziyād, perhaps sensing this tendency, and to win the support of the people, announced in his inaugural address that the caliph had advised him to distribute 'their' *Fay'* only among them and not to transfer it.[52] When

Ziyād, the governor of Baṣra, intended to transfer the surplus funds to the centre he was mobbed by the people who said that the funds belonged to them and should be distributed only among them.[53] A similar situation arose when Ḥamza b. Zubayr was trying to take away the provincial funds.[54] Governor Ibn Ziyād had enormous funds with him when Salma revolted against him. He, perhaps with a view to winning the people's support, distributed these funds among them by calling them 'their own wealth' *(Fay')*.[55]

While the above instances suggest a consciousness of the concept of *Bayt al-Māl* as the common property of the Muslims, the narrower outlook of the region, or the tribal affiliations of that society are all the more pronounced. This narrow-mindedness fed by the pre-Islamic tribal prejudices seems to have continued and by the end of the period, grown to the extent that when the people of Iraq were given their usual pensions, the Syrians objected in these words: 'Why are you giving the wealth gained by us, to our enemies.'[56] This objection was later withdrawn by the Syrians, but during the same period Yazīd III officially reconfirmed this provincialism in his first announcement to reform the financial policies.[57]

Notes and References

1. Tab., 1, 2414–15.
2. Tab., 1, 2582.
3. Well., 131.
4. Yaq., 2, 142; Maq. (Kh.), I, 78.
5. Yaq., 2, 207.
6. *Ibid.*
7. Chapter 2, p. 114.
8. Yaq., 2, 210–11; Kindi, 31.
9. Yaq., 2, 222.
10. Bal., 438.
11. Dh. (Ibar), 31.
12. Yaq., 2, 210; Kindi, 31.
13. Tab., 2, 1167; Athir, 4, 410.
14. Kindi, 55.
15. Tab., 2, 832.
16. Chapter 7, pp. 260–1.
17. Tab., 2, 1432.

18. Yaq., 3, 36.

19. See chapter on Expenditure.

20. Sad., 5, 252.

21. Sad., 5, 256.

22. A.U., 621.

23. Chapter 6, p. 187.

24. Qud., 255.

25. Bal., 176.

26. Tab., 2, 1778–9.

27. Athir, 5, 125.

28. Yaq., 3, 77.

29. Tab., 1, 1920–1.

30. A.U., 607.

31. I.A.H. (M), 102.

32. I.A.H. (M), 132.

33. *Ibid.*

34. Pap. IV. General Introduction, p. XIX.

35. Yaq., 142–3.

36. Bal., 303.

37. Tab., 1, 3440.

38. Rawi, 68.

39. Chapter 7, p. 203.

40. Yaq., 3, 36.

41. Bal., 429–30.

42. Tab., 2, 69; Kath, 8, 28.

43. Tab., 2, 189; Yaq., 2, 225.

44. Tab., 2, 634.

45. Kath., 8, 293.

46. Tab., 2, 941.

47. Bal., 333; Tab., 2, 1213.

48. Tab., 2, 1655.

49. Tab., 2, 1470.

50. Balādhurī, *Ansāb al-Ashrāf* (Ms. Paris) f. 450A.; *cf.* S.A.E., 122.

51. Chapter 2, p.114.

52. Ad-Dīnawrī, *al-Akhbār aṭ-Ṭiwāl,* 247; *cf.* Kharbutlī, 386.

53. Agh., 20, 17; *cf.* Kharbutlī, 386.

54. Tab., 2, 752.

55. Tab., 2, 439.

56. Tab., 2, 1854.

57. See p. 140 for full speech.

CHAPTER 10

Expenditure

A. PENSIONS AND RATIONS

While the expenditure of the proceeds of *Zakāt* was confined to particular heads,[1] the most important items of expenditure from the general funds of the *Bayt al-Māl* were pensions, followed by defence and development.

Pension, in its present-day limited sense, is a misnomer to the sense of *'aṭā'*[2] and *arzāq* (sing. *rizq*), as used in the early works of Muslim history; but the same has been adopted to signify this sense throughout this study for want of a really appropriate word and because of its currency in contemporary literature. The aim of granting annual pensions was to distribute wealth throughout the society and particularly to the Muslims who were supposed to volunteer themselves for the defence of the faith and the state. It also included salaries (*waẓā'if,* sing. *waẓīfa*) that were paid to the civil employees who were exempted from military service.

Principles of Distribution and Entitlement

In the early days the policy was to distribute all incomes whenever they were received. The need to hoard money was not realized mainly because distribution of wealth was much emphasized in the Qur'ān and by the Prophet (peace be upon him).[3] The Prophet himself (peace be upon him) distributed among the Muslims whatever and whenever he got anything. So did Abū Bakr. But during this period the resources for distribution were scanty and the per-head share was negligible. The situation changed after the conquest of Iraq and Syria which brought in substantial wealth to Madina. Then a permanent settlement with the people of these lands and the conquest of some more regions ensured a regular flow of income to the *Bayt al-Māl.* These regular resources were further supplemented by the frequent loads of the fifth of booty that were received after each successful expedition.

What was distributed among the people is divisible into two heads:

annual pensions *('aṭāyā),* and monthly rations *(arzāq)*. According to Ṭabarī, "'Umar fixed the pensions for those on whom God bestowed *Fay'*. They were the dwellers of the cities and had moved to Kūfa, Baṣra, Dimashq, Ḥimṣ, Urdunn, and Filasṭīn. 'Umar said: "The booty is for these urban people and for those who are with them; assist them and stay with them." He did not fix anything for others. These very people were staying in the cities. They were a party to the treaties. Poll-tax was paid to them. They were also responsible for guarding the frontiers and facing the enemy.'[4] But as regards rations, Balādhurī observes that wheat, oil, and vinegar were meant for all the Muslims including the slaves.[5] This is confirmed by Ibn Sa'd, who reports that Caliph 'Umar gave rations to the people of the suburbs of Madina *('Awālī)* while 'Uthmān added clothes too.[6] Thus, while pensions were, in the early stage of distribution, fixed for those who could join and did join the army, rations were perhaps given to most of the population. The same policy, in respect of pensions was adopted by Abū 'Ubayda, the military governor in Syria, who turned down the request of the countrymen to grant them pensions. He gave two reasons for his refusal: firstly, the funds could not suffice even the urban population and, secondly, the countrymen did not join the congregation in the city.[7]

In view of the above-mentioned policy it was probable that the rural population was not supposed to be eligible for any share in the *Fay'*. Abū 'Ubayd has adduced much evidence to prove that the right of countrymen to *Fay'* was accepted and respected but Caliph 'Umar did not grant them regular pensions as he did in the case of town-dwellers. Instead, he, like the Prophet (peace be upon him) supported them whenever they fell in need.[8] Reports also suggest that during the last year of his life, he had made up his mind to include among the beneficiaries even the countrymen and to increase the minimum limit to equalize the benefits to the Muslims. He is reported to have said: 'By God! If I am spared for the widows in Iraq, I shall care for them so that they will not need support of any ruler after me.'[9] On another occasion he said: 'If I survive the shepherd in far away hills of Ṣan'ā will surely get his share from this wealth although he will be at his place.'[10] And: 'If I survive, I shall bring the senior and the junior to the same level.'[11] He also wished to increase all pensions to 4,000 dirhams per annum: 1,000 for travel, 1,000 for arms, 1,000 for household, and 1,000 for riding animals.[12]

Extension of the List of Beneficiaries

The above evidence suggests that it was the ultimate policy of the caliph to extend the list of distribution to the countrymen and to increase the amount of pensions to equalize the benefits to the Muslims. But he died before he could implement his scheme. Even if he had lived, it is doubtful if the resources of the *Bayt al-Māl* would have allowed him to do so, in fact the resources never seem to have been sufficient for this.[13] The list in the later days was extended to cover a larger number of persons but never the whole population. It was always recognized that regular pensions pre-supposed military service in the past, present or future, if the recipient was not engaged in any other service of the state, for example, the civil service. Even those who received the pension pre-supposed it as a moral obligation to discharge military service whenever they were called upon to do so. When 'Abd al-Malik ordered the despatch of an army to Khurāsān, the pensioners transferred their pensions to those who could represent them on the battlefield.[14] Hishām had made it compulsory for the Marwānids to participate in war. Many of them, however, sent their substitutes.[15] 'Umar II wrote to his governor: 'Order fixed pensions for the army. Take care of the townsmen and neglect the countrymen because they neither join the congregation nor do they take part in wars.'[16] Thus pensions continued to be granted as a return for expected war service. This also included prospective or potential soldiers. The newly-born children of the pensioners were also included in the list.[17] Fresh converts and even non-Muslims who could be expected to assist the Muslims were also given pensions. Examples are the *dahāqīn* and the *asāwira* of Persia and the non-Muslim residents of Jarjūma in Syria.[18] In this way all the Muslims, and a sizeable number of non-Muslims, who were available for war service were eligible for fixed pensions.[19] Caliph 'Umar had exempted Makkans from this service; as a result, he did not fix their pensions.[20] Traders were also excluded from the list because they could not devote themselves to war.[21] By the end of 'Abd al-Malik's time, a large number of persons receiving very high payments had died, and thus the inequality in the scales of pensions had largely narrowed down. A sizeable number of villagers had joined the townsmen and volunteered for military service. Thus the list of beneficiaries had expanded. Yet complete equality in distribution and a universal distribution of wealth could never be achieved. The Prophet (peace be upon him) and Caliph Abū Bakr distributed incomes equally.[22] Caliph 'Umar simply wished to do so. After Caliph 'Umar the higher scale of pensions could not be curtailed perhaps for fear of the seniors' resentment. But it could also not be enhanced in order to introduce equality due to scarce resources. In spite of this constraint, when Caliph 'Alī is reported to have distributed any other incomes he maintained equality. It is reported that he once entered the treasury of Baṣra and ordered an equal distribution of the entire funds among his followers including himself and his sons.[23] Similarly, he is also reported to have expedited the distribution of funds whenever he received them. Abū 'Ubayd reports that he received some funds thrice a year and soon distributed them. When, in the meantime, he received funds from Iṣfahān too, he instructed his followers to distribute them among themselves the next day.[24] It seems that any such bonus was also distributed by the following rulers if they had spare funds. Mu'āwiya is reported to have distributed such an amount by announcing: 'Some funds remain in your *Bayt al-Māl* after the distribution of pensions. They are now being given to you. If a surplus remains the next year too, it will be distributed in the same way, but if otherwise, do not be annoyed. It is not my property. It is God's *Fay'* which He sends for you.'[25]

Other Considerations for Pensions

As the Prophet (peace be upon him) used to give a larger share to a married man than to a single man,[26] women were also made eligible for a share in pension in Caliph 'Umar's time, although at a lower rate than men. The Umayyad rulers had privileged the members of the ruling family to receive special pensions.[27] If the funds exceeded the pension requirements, Caliph 'Umar extended the list of soldiers, including persons of sound character, *murū'a* and good company, *ṣuḥba*.[28] He also fixed pensions for those who were memorizing the Qur'ān but later withdrew it.[29] Mu'āwiya appointed officers for different tribes to find out if any of the Muslims had entertained any guest, in which case the host was entitled to an allowance.[30] Walīd added to the list all the destitute and invalid persons,[31] 'Umar II granted an allowance for pilgrimage to Makka,[32] and continued the policy of fixing pensions of the decrepit and the weak.[33] In the case of higher pensions, he advised his officers to disburse the amount after ensuring that the recipient had in his possession an Arab horse and all the conventional weapons of war.[34]

The Origin and Development of the Institution

The report that Caliph 'Umar introduced the scheme of distribution after Abū Hurayra brought the revenue collections of Baḥrayn amounting to 500,000 or 1,000,000 dirhams[35] seems to be incomplete because this amount alone would not have been sufficient to cover even a part of his ambitious scheme.[36] With the rates given in the early records, the total collection should have been many times more than Abū Hurayra's. It is possible that many more funds and the receipts of *Khums* might already have been lying with the caliph. Balādhurī's view that Caliph 'Umar introduced the scheme when he received the taxes of Iraq and Syria in A.H. 20[37] may be more convincing but with some reservations about the year.[38]

The Rates of Pensions

Historians have given different rates which Caliph 'Umar fixed for different categories of persons. But these differences occur mainly in the case of the first two categories. The rates for the following eight categories are almost the same everywhere. The following annual amounts are the most commonly reported:[39]

Table 14. Rates of Pensions Fixed by Caliph 'Umar

Category of persons	Dirhams each
The Prophet's wives	12,000
The Prophet's uncle and grandsons	5,000
The Badrites	5,000
The Uḥudites	4,000
Migrants to Abyssinia	4,000
Migrants of the pre-Makkan conquest	3,000
The sons of the Badrites	2,000
Converts at the conquest of Makka	2,000
The children of all Emigrants and Helpers	2,000
Muslims in Syria and Iraq	200 to 2,000
Those who fought at Qādisiyya	2,000[40]
Those who conquered Ubulla	2,000[41]
Those who took the oath at Ḥudaybiyya	2,000[42]
Makkans (not *Muhājirs*)	600 to 700[43]
Yemenites	700[44]
Muḍar and Rabī'a	200 to 300[45]
Women	200 to 500[46]
All others[47]	250
Newly-born children	100
Converted Persian landlords	2,000
Unclaimed children	100[48]

Apart from these fixed scales of pension, other scales were given in special cases. The main considerations were high office, courage and bravery, generosity, conquests or loyalty to the Prophet (peace be upon him).[49]

Over and above these pensions each Muslim including slaves was allowed a *mudī* of wheat, two *qisṭs* of vinegar and two of oil.[50] In Syria the per-head quantity was perhaps larger.[51]

When 'Uthmān became caliph he increased the pensions by 100 dirhams each.[52] Whether the increase was general or in the case of low pensions only is not known. He also supplemented rations with dresses.[53] Caliph 'Alī increased the pensions of his followers in Iraq.[54] Mu'āwiya ordered an equal increase in the pensions of Kūfans,[55] but reduced the scale of the pensions of honour *(sharaf)* from 2,500 dirhams to 2,000 dirhams.[56] Mālik has treated this cut as the deduction of *Zakāt*[57] but the prescribed rates of *Zakāt* on this amount would allow an annual deduction of sixty-two and a half dirhams only. If it is treated as a deduction of *Zakāt* on other wealth of the recipient, the amount would not be identical in all cases. The only plausible interpretation can be that this reduction was discretionary. During his time Egypt alone had 40,000 Muslims, of which 4,000 were on the 200-dirham list.[58] His governor Ziyād added many new names to the list and assigned to 500 persons 300 to 500 dirhams each.[59] It is stated that he distributed 60 million dirhams to 60,000 persons in Baṣra.[60] Mu'āwiya granted to confederates *(Mawālī)* a pension of fifteen dirhams, perhaps every month. 'Abd al-Malik increased it to twenty; Sulaymān to twenty-five; and Hishām to thirty.[61] Ḥajjāj discontinued the pensions of the confederates but 'Umar II restored them.[62] In Egypt governor 'Ābis also increased the scale of pensions.[63] 'Umar II ordered a further increase in Egypt[64] as he had done in Syria;[65] but the increase in Egypt was later withdrawn by Yazīd II.[66] 'Umar II also made many additions to the list of recipients and placed new names on the 40-dirham list.[67] A higher scale of 100 dirhams was given to some whose names were drawn by ballot.[68] The poor and the invalid were also given pensions although at a meagre rate. He abolished the practice of giving pensions to the new-born and fixed it instead from the age of weaning.[69] He also discontinued special pensions to the privileged.[70] He wrote to one of his governors instructing him to fix pensions for all except traders.[71] The minimum age fixed by him for full pension was fifteen years before which a boy was treated as a dependant.[72] During Hishām's time 15,000 more persons from Khurāsān were included on the roll.[73] Pensions distributed in Egypt during Hishām's time and throughout the Umayyad period totalled about 1,700,000 dīnārs.[74] By the end of this period more additions were made in Iraq and Egypt.[75] Walīd II recommended an overall increase in the scales but these were reduced by Yazīd III.[76]

The Personal Element

Along with the general policy outlined above, the personal inclination of the ruler or high officials also affected the policy of granting or withdrawing pensions. An army officer promised to award a pension to a non-Muslim and his family for locating a way into an enemy city.[77] Twenty-five soldiers who had displayed exemplary courage and bravery at Qādisiyya were granted 500 dirhams each.[78] Yazīd I restored the pensions of Madinans as a gesture of goodwill to the visiting Madinan delegation.[79] 'Abd al-'Azīz (Egypt) increased the pension of one who criticized him for not saying 'if God wills' *(inshā' Allāh)*.[80] The killer of a Kharijite was rewarded by 'Abd al-Malik with a pension of 2,000 dirhams.[81] Ḥajjāj celebrated the end of Ibn al-Ash'ath by allowing a general increase in pensions in his province.[82]

There are also instances of pensions being withdrawn by way of punishment or displeasure. Caliph 'Umar cut the pension of one poet by 500 dirhams and raised another's by the same amount.[83] Caliph 'Uthmān was displeased with Abū Dharr, Ashtar and Ibn Mas'ūd, but the magnanimity with which he treated them was not displayed by the later rulers. In the case of Abū Dharr, he not only did not discontinue his pension amounting to 4,000 dirhams but gave him a flock of sheep, a herd of camels, and two slaves before he was allowed to leave Madina.[84] Ashtar was exiled from Iraq, but his pension continued to be paid to him in Syria.[85] Ibn Mas'ūd's pension was discontinued, but 'Uthmān himself apologized to him and paid the arrears.[86] Mu'āwiya punished a man by holding back his pension because he complained to him of the debasement of a coin which was minted under his instructions.[87] Ibn Ziyād punished a man by reducing his pension by 400 dirhams because he intended to marry his own deceased wife's mother. 'With this knowledge of law 300 dirhams will suffice you', observed Ibn Ziyād.[88] Zuhrī's pension was withdrawn because his father was anti-government.[89] Some followers of Ibn Ash'ath were deprived of their pensions but had them restored after three years after they appeased Ḥajjāj.[90] However, another person whose brother had joined Ibn Ash'ath was unable to win his pleasure.[91] All the Asāwira and Zaṭṭ were similarly deprived because they supported Ibn Ash'ath.[92] 'Abd al-Malik discontinued the pension of a political opponent who eulogized his rival Muṣ'ab.[93] 'Abd al-'Azīz deducted 100 dīnārs from a pension because the pensioner spoke incorrect Arabic.[94] Walīd took a census of the pensioners and dropped as many as 20,000 names from the list.[95] 'Abd-Allāh b. 'Ulā, Ḥasan and Ibn Sīrīn were out of favour before 'Umar II took over and restored their pensions.[96] Even prince Walīd, son of Hishām, did not escape his father's wrath and lost his *sharaf 'atā,*[97] honorarium.

Administration of Pensions

The administration of pensions and rations was organized by maintaining two registers *(dīwans)*. One of them contained the census records and the amount that was payable to each pensioner; the other contained the statement of revenues.[98] In Arabia both registers were maintained by the Arabs[99] but in the provinces the first kind was maintained in Arabic and the second in the provincial language, *viz.* Coptic, Greek, or Persian, and was looked after mostly by native officers.[100] ‘Abd al-Malik and Ḥajjāj switched over to Arabic in Syria and Iraq, Walīd in Egypt, and Hishām in Khurāsān.[101] Each province depended on its own revenues. But in case the population of a province exceeded the resources of the province, revenues of some other areas yielding surplus were allocated to the deficit province. For example, the governor of Baṣra requested Caliph ‘Umar to merge some surplus districts in the province because the *Kharāj* of the province had fallen short of its requirements.[102] Thus pensions were also a factor in delimiting the area of a province.

The register contained the names of the beneficiaries with all relevant details. Mobility of the Muslim population was not infrequent and this, in addition to births, deaths, and conversions, called for frequent revisions of the list.[103] The beneficiaries were issued with pension cards and ration cards which contained the name of the beneficiary, his tribe, and the amount of entitlement.[104]

Pensions were paid twice a year while rations were issued every month. But if the soldiers were mobilized they were paid in advance.[105] Many a time payment of pensions was delayed because of shortage of funds or as a punishment of the pensioners.[106] Payment of cash in lieu of rations was also practised.[107] Pensions were generally distributed from the *Kharāj* fund.[108] Payment from the *Zakāt* fund was treated as an indignity, and resented.[109]

While money taxes were collected locally but remitted to the provincial headquarters, commodities were transported to the nearest distribution point. For example, the distribution of rations in Baṣra was effected from the commodities that were received from Kaskar.[110]

Mu‘āwiya introduced a system of deducting penalties from the pension payments. He wrote to the *Qāḍī* (Judge) of Egypt telling him to compute the nature of the wound of the wounded person and to send a note to the master of registers *(ṣāḥib ad-dīwān)*. Qāḍī Sulaym, for the first time, sent such a note to the register master ordering him to deduct the amount of compensation from the pension of the offender, in three equal instalments. However he continued to be issued with rations as usual.[111]

The pensions reached the recipients in a well-organized manner. In the beginning, the administration followed the pattern set by the Prophet (peace be upon him) for organizing the army. The commander-in-chief had under him group commanders each of whom controlled a number of contingents; each contingent was represented by a flag-bearer *(ṣāḥib ar-ra’ya),* who controlled the tribal units. Each tribal unit was led by a tribal chief who approached the individual soldiers through a commandant (*'arīf)* who was in charge of ten persons.[112] Thus the order from the bottom to the apex was *'arīf* – who was also made responsible for distributing salaries to individuals at their houses – tribal chief, flag-bearer, group commander, commander-in-chief. The system was called *a'shār,* the system of tens, and continued till the founding of Kūfa and Baṣra after which it was changed. The group was then composed of seven persons. One hundred *'arīfs* were appointed in an army, each *'arīf* having at his disposal 100,000 dirhams. Among the Qādisiyyites, a group consisted of 43 men, 43 women, and 50 dependants, and was paid 100,000 dirhams. The pre-Qādisiyyite *(aḥl al-ayyām)*[113] group consisted of 20 men each in the 3,000-dirham list, 20 women and 100 children, assigned a total of 100,000 dirhams. The post-Qādisiyyite group had 60 men, 60 women, and 40 children. These men were entered in the 1,500-dirham list and all of these 160 persons got 100,000 dirhams. Distribution was effected thus: *amīr,* the commander received money and distributed it among the *asḥāb ar-ra'yāt,* flag-bearers, who were Arabs. The flag-bearers redistributed it among the different *'arīfs* under them. Each *'arīf* paid it to the different *amīns* (trustees) under him and the *naqībs,* who handed it over to the beneficiaries at their houses.[114] Some changes were, however, effected from time to time. For example, Ziyād reconstituted the groups into fours, but the basic organization remained undisturbed.[115]

B. DEFENCE

The note on pensions and rations reveals that the distribution of wealth in this account can also be characterized as expenditure on defence. Although the Muslims since the very beginning, were supposed to offer themselves for military service without any expectation of return or reward, yet, once involved in their various economic pursuits, it would have been difficult to dislodge them from their business and employ them as trained professional fighters. Since the very beginning they were, no doubt, entitled to booty but this arrangement prerequisited victory in war which was not generally predictable. Thus the institution of pensions kept them ever available for war. During the first twenty years they hardly got a 'fair' material return for their services and sacrifices. Fixation of pensions, however, added a factor to bind them to volunteer themselves for military service without any excuse. In this way defence became a big claimant of the resources of the *Bayt al-Māl.* The expenditure in this account called for a contented army ready to advance and strike: large teams of riding animals or a fleet of ships, traditional weapons, cantonments where the army was permanently stationed and kept in a state of readiness near the borders, forts, castles, and also ready money to mobilize the army, to give an incentive to the soldiers by way of prizes and awards, and to ransom captured Muslim soldiers.

Since pre-Islamic days almost all Arabs were supposed to be well-versed in the art of warfare. It was a matter of personal honour to be well-trained and to own at least some effective arms to defend themselves and to organize raids on their enemies. Riding animals facilitated quick movements but they were too expensive to be maintained by everyone; let alone a horse which was very expensive to keep.

Arms and Horses

The early Islamic state encountered two major problems: arms and horses. How these problems were tackled in the Prophet's time has been discussed earlier. By Caliph 'Umar's time the resources of the state had expanded and it was possible to provide a large number of camels and horses. Provision of arms – simple and few as they were – was no problem for the Muslims during the period of affluence. However a horse was still an expensive animal to maintain. Caliph Abū Bakr used to spend money from the *Bayt al-Māl* to buy horses, camels and arms, and distribute them among the soldiers.[116] Caliph 'Umar had a number of public grazing farms from where horses and camels were supplied to the fighters every year. According to Abū Yūsuf these horses numbered 4,000[117] in addition to a very large number of camels, which, according to Ibn Sa'd, numbered 30,000 and were given along with their equipment.[118] That is why all the soldiers at Madā'in were mounted on horseback.[119] It can be supposed that later on the practice of supplying riding animals must have continued because of the vast increase in the area of operation. Ibn Sa'd reports that horses were taken to Sulaymān for distribution. But he expired before he could distribute them; so 'Umar II did so.[120] He also provided 500 horses and provisions for the safe and quick return of Maslama's contingents from the Syrian border.[121] Ṭabarī reports an interesting instance of Caliph 'Umar exchanging a weak camel for a strong one, for a fighter.[122]

Naval Fleet

Maintaining a naval fleet was a much more expensive affair than supplying traditional arms and riding animals. It required large workshops with a very large number of workers. War on water was started by Mu'āwiya, the governor of Syria, under Caliph 'Uthmān. In the beginning he used the newly assembled Phoenician and Egyptian fleet and took Cyprus, then Rhodes and Cos and finally defeated Emperor Constans II in a sea-battle off the coast of Lycia.[123] In Egypt also when the Byzantine fleet had crossed to Egypt, the Muslims, under the command of 'Amr, had two hundred ships,[124] although this was still well below the number of enemy vessels. But against Constans II, Mu'āwiya commanded a fleet of 1,700 ships.[125] When he became ruler he set up a workshop *(ṣanā'a)* to assemble warships in Jordan.[126] 'Abd al-Malik set up another workshop in Tunis,[127] also for manufacturing instruments. The Greek Papyri allude to a workshop in Alexandria during Walīd's time.[128] Hishām is reported to have moved the workshop in 'Akkā (Jordan) to Ṣūr.[129] Hussey's report that the Muslim Navy used 2,500 ships in its expedition against Constantinople in 717 A.D. (A.H. 99)[130] supports the assumption that the workshops would have been in a position to assemble this number of ships by the end of the century. Balādhurī reports that the Umayyad rulers always kept their ships on the alert for any possible confrontation with Byzantium.[131]

Cantonments

After the conquest of a number of foreign lands, Arabia had become secure from the enemy. But the lands they had conquered were exposed to the enemy's retaliation. Caliph 'Umar set up a number of cantonments *(jund)* in Palestine, Al-Jazīra, Moṣul and Qinnesrīn, etc., over and above the centres that existed in provincial capitals and principal cities. He was also the first to recruit for a regular army.[132] Governor Mu'āwiya also recruited an army to be posted on the borders of Al-Jazīra.[133] He was also advised by the caliph to repair the castles and forts, arrange for a guard, and illuminate the posts.[134] Abū 'Ubayda did the same during his command in Syria.[135] Caliph 'Uthmān arranged for the permanent rehabilitation of the Muslims in the border areas.[136] 'Abd al-Malik fortified the exposed cities and undertook the repair of weak defence constructions.[137] 'Umar II and Hishām also paid full attention to construction, renovation and repairs.[138] In addition to these regular jobs, rehabilitation of new cities also served the purpose of an army centre.

The Cost of Army Operations

There are not many reports to give an exact idea about the expenditure on an army operation in the different stages of its accomplishment. But it can be assumed that this involved heavy expenditure. The conquest of Sind involved 60 million dirhams.[139] The expedition against Sijistān in A.H. 80 cost 2 million dirhams excluding the regular salaries paid to the army.[140] 'Abd al-Malik granted the entire funds of some regions to finance a local military operation, in addition to the incomes of two districts.[141] Crossing an inundated valley cost Ibn 'Āmir, the governor of Makrān, 4 million dirhams by way of awards to boost their morale.[142] There are several instances of prizes being awarded for gallantry, courage and leadership, some of which have already been mentioned in other chapters.

Corresponding to the awarding of prizes there are also instances of fines that the government had to pay for its weaknesses. It has been mentioned earlier that Mu'āwiya and 'Abd al-Malik had to pay tribute to Byzantine rulers during some hard times. 'Umar II had to pay ransom for a large number of Muslim soldiers who had been captured at Lāziqiyya.[143] He had also to pay ransom to get back a number of Muslim men, women and children from the Aden coast.[144] When the army was hard pressed in Cyprus, Yazīd I sent 'large amounts of bribe' to ensure that it returned safely.[145]

The above list, although not claimed to be complete, gives at least a sketchy idea about the nature and extent of the financial implications of defence: active and unceasing wars throughout the whole period, fortification of the borders from Sind to the remote west, and mobilization of armed contingents in an area extending over about 4,000 miles from Multan to Gibraltar.

C. AGRICULTURE

The encouragement given to agriculture and horticulture on the religious plane has been discussed on Chapter 1. The policy of recognizing the user's right over unowned barren land had been in practice since the early days of Islam. Caliphs 'Umar, 'Alī and 'Umar II are reported to have followed the same policy.[146]

BASIS OF CLASSIFICATION OF LANDS

Ownership

The classification of land in the early Islamic period can be made in a variety of ways. From the point of view of ownership, there were three kinds of land:

1. State ownership
2. Collective ownership
3. Private ownership

The lands not in possession of anybody were state-owned. In the case of conquered lands this rule was applied even to those lands whose owners were killed during war, or who had fled away. The ownership of Imperial lands in Egypt, Syria, and Iraq, was also transferred to the Islamic state.

The concept of collective or communal ownership is not unknown in Arabia. It has been a cornerstone of the nomadic economy. But in the Islamic period, collective or communal ownership was recognized and practised, even in the agricultural society where private ownership was the prevalent rule. The lands of Khaybar were collectively owned by those Muslims who took part in the war on Khaybar.[147] The lands which were conquered without a treaty were taken into the collective ownership of the Muslim community.[148] In Khaybar the rights of ownership were alienable but it was not so in the case of the lands in Iraq and Egypt for quite some time. Later on, however, the principle was not rigidly adhered to. In the case of treaty lands, the right of the owner was respected.

Levy of Taxes

From the point of view of taxes, lands were divided into two categories: *'Ushr* land and *Kharāj* land. The lands in Arabia were, from the beginning, treated as *'Ushr* lands. The barren lands anywhere else which were reclaimed by the Muslims were also subjected to *'Ushr.*[149] Similarly the lands taken over by the government and then transferred to the Muslims also paid *'Ushr,* as was also the case with lands which were abandoned by the original owners and passed on to the Muslims. In Syria, *'Ushr* land was that unclaimed land from where the inhabitants had been expelled and which was then allotted to the Muslims. This land was thus reclaimed with the permission of the government,[150] and lay mostly in those areas which were contiguous to Byzantine borders. The lands outside Arabia which were occupied by the subjugated people were treated as *Kharāj* lands. The rate of the tax was fixed by the government[151] and collected in cash, kind, or both; the last being the most prevalent way during this period. The policy of assessing in this way continued in Iraq apart from when the 'Abbāsid ruler Mahdī changed it to share-cropping.[152] The treaty lands continued to pay according to the terms agreed upon.

Tenancy

Another basis of classification may be from the point of view of tenancy. In Arabia lands were generally owner-cultivated. The conquest of Khaybar and the capitulation of Faḍak transferred the ownership of these lands to those who did not cultivate them. Land-lordism was already prevalent in parts of Iraq[153] and other Persian provinces and continued along with owner-cultivated lands. In Egypt there were a large number of domain lands which were cultivated by the local people. The terms of tenancy varied at different places. Letting out land in exchange for a share in the crop was a controversial issue among the Prophet's Companions although it was practised by many. Cultivators in Khaybar were given land on the condition of sharing half the produce.[154] In the case of Najrān lands were given on the condition of two-thirds share for the state and one-third for the cultivator if it was irrigated by natural means, and vice versa if otherwise.[155] Investment of capital and labour was made by the tenants – the Jews in Khaybar and the Muslims in Najrān.

Protection for Farmers

The conquest of lands outside Arabia brought vast territories under Muslim control. While large portions of land were cultivated, vast tracts of land were lying idle. They comprised dry lands, thickets, swamps, forests and water-logged areas. As the mainstay of these provinces was agriculture, efforts to maintain and develop this industry could hardly be over-emphasized. The caliphs, from the very beginning, addressed themselves to the challenge and adjusted their policy to meet it. They did not disturb the existing set-up, put new lands into use and made Herculean efforts to reclaim land that was lying uncultivated.

While Caliph 'Umar believed in the user's right to unclaimed barren land,[156] he ensured that the interdictor utilized the land properly. 'It is not given to you to interdict it from others. Take only as much as you can reclaim; return the rest',[157] thus Caliph 'Umar advised one of the allottees. When the Muslim armies conquered Iraq, they did not disturb the farmers.[158] Caliph 'Umar knew that it was not possible for the Muslims to utilize these lands and advised the Muslim commanders to spare the cultivators if they were detained and return the lands in their possession.[159] Under the prevalent laws of war, the subjugated people, if spared, were treated as slaves and had no guarantee of protection of life and property. Caliph 'Umar wrote to his governors: 'Fear God in treating subjugated peasants. Do not kill them unless they wage war against you.'[160] 'Umar II also urged his governors to ensure their protection.[161] These cultivators even where land was conquered by force were treated as *dhimmīs* (the protected) whose life and property could not be harmed. A problem arose when they began to embrace Islam and desert their lands to join the ruling Muslim community in the cities and thus probably claim their right to pensions as were fixed for the town-dwelling Muslims. It was not only the shortage of funds but also the fear of disruption in agriculture that forced Ḥajjāj to drive them back to their villages.[162] The same situation arose in Egypt when governor Qurra increased taxes.[163] As a result he also had to drive the farmers back to their lands. This compulsory return must have been effected by force but there are no records to suggest any ruthless persecution of the farmers. In any case when once the farmers were disinterested in their lands the agricultural economy was bound to suffer. But the adverse effects of this tendency were offset by the increased interest of the Muslims in farming.

Reclamation and Development of Land

Lands were granted to Muslims even by the Prophet (peace be upon him) and the succeeding caliphs. But Caliph 'Uthmān was, in a sense, the first to grant fiefs to a large number of Muslims in Syria and Iraq. Thus the masters changed but the land tenancy system perhaps remained the same. He also allowed alienation of lands and a number of Muslims bought them. A large number of Muslims were granted fiefs in the border areas of Syria and Al-Jazīra where they settled as farmers.[164] In the later period they acquired lands in Egypt as well.[165] While the Muslims had an incentive to cultivate their lands by paying only tithes on their produce, the newcoming non-Muslims were also sometimes encouraged to cultivate lands. The expelled Najrānites were not only given lands in Iraq but were also exempted from land-tax for two years.[166]

Over and above the growing rush for cultivation the rulers themselves became interested in adding to their landed properties. They occupied vast tracts of barren lands and developed them. Such occupation is reported to have begun with Mu'āwiya and continued throughout the Umayyad period.[167] The development of the lands required a net-work of canals and bridges, clearing forests, drying and filling up ponds and repair of the existing irrigation system – work which could be discharged only by a government.

In the early period, state lands were developed at government expense. Caliph 'Uthmān left them to persons who possessed the ability to improve them.[168] It was, perhaps, because of this element of personal ownership of the rulers and cultivators that the factors causing adverse effects on agriculture, due to burdensome taxes and desertions of land in the later period were greatly offset. There are many instances which suggest an increasing government interest in development of land. Ḥajjāj used to go to the farmers to personally inquire about the techniques of farming and the effects of taxation.[169] 'Abd al-Malik used to receive periodical newsletters about the quantity of rainfall in Iraq.[170] When agricultural activities increased, draught animals fell short of requirements. Ḥajjāj restricted the slaughter of cows with a view to protecting and multiplying them.[171] 'Umar II wrote to one of his governors: 'Look into the lands in your province and distribute them on the condition of share-cropping at 50% of the yield; and a poorer quality at one-third for the state; or even less, reducing the state share to a tenth. However, if the land is so unfertile that nobody likes to cultivate it even at a tenth, give it for nothing. If even then there is nobody to accept it, spend on it from the treasury of the Muslims so that no land under your control is neglected.'[172]

The Provision of Canals and Dams

While the owner or the cultivator of the land was supposed to look after the development of his field, the task of providing rich arable land was taken up by the government. Most of the arable lands were already under cultivation. What was left were the cultivable wastes or barren lands. The government cleared the forests and brushwood, filled and dried water cisterns and dug canals for irrigation and reclamation of water-logged areas. The canals, as usual, were also used for drinking water and for many other purposes.[173] Caliph 'Umar wrote to his governor, Abū Mūsā, telling him to get a canal dug for the people of Baṣra[174] with the primary object of supplying drinking water.[175] He also advised his governor in Egypt to re-open the choked-up canal linking the Nile to the Red Sea with a view to facilitating the transport of corn to Madina.[176] Apart from transport facilities the irrigation system of Egypt was also improved. 'Amr developed the productiveness of land by irrigation[177] and it is reported by historians that the system kept 120,000 labourers at work during winter and summer maintaining and improving the dams and canals.[178] Governor Sa'd, during the same period, started the construction of a canal at Anbār (Iraq) but the work was discontinued because of the hilly terrain. This was, however, later completed by Ḥajjāj.[179] A canal was also dug in Madina and extended and improved by Caliph 'Uthmān and Walīd.[180] Later on a canal was dug between Tā'if and Uḥud.[181] The canals dug during 'Uthmān's caliphate are rarely mentioned in history, but this can be safely assumed in view of his greater interest in reclamation of land than that of his predecessors. Caliph 'Alī is reported to have once written to his governor: 'The protected people have reported a canal which is choked-up in your jurisdiction, and the Muslims are bound to repair it. You should inspect the site along with them and get the work done. To me, improving and developing the lands is preferable to having the inhabitants desert them.'[182]

These are a few instances of the early stage of development activities of the government. To what extent this government interest developed in the Umayyad period may not be usefully detailed here. Balādhurī has given the names of more than a hundred well-known canals in Iraq alone which were constructed by these rulers.[183] A study of early geographical works gives a many times larger number of such canals. In a nutshell, Iṣṭakhrī reports the existence of 120,000 canals linked to each other around Baṣra many of which were used even for transport.[184] The figure becomes more easily believable if it is assumed that it also included the small channels in the fields, linking the canals. Along with these canals, bridges, culverts, and dams would naturally have been built. Balādhurī speaks of the construction of a dam as far away as the River Indus in the present-day province of Sind. The dam, Sakr-al-Mīd, was built to canalize the water of the river.[185] The repair and maintenance of the network of canals and bridges, etc., would naturally have required a large force of technical staff and labourers and involved huge funds. The details of this administration are not known. The details as to how management of land was made can be inferred from the following story:

Yazīd b. 'Abd al-Malik wrote to 'Umar b. Hubayra: 'Amīr al-Mu'minīn does not possess, along with his possessions, any piece of land in Arabia. Go to the lands and check up. If there is any piece of land that is yet to be allotted reserve it for him.' 'Umar toured the places. He went from one land to another, investigated them, and surveyed the lands [to compare them with the documents] and at last came across a piece of land [which had no document]. He asked the occupant of the land as to who it belonged to. 'How did you acquire it?' asked 'Umar. The occupant retorted a couplet saying that he had inherited it from his forefathers and would, in the same way, bequeath it to his posterity.[186]

Land Records

The records of these lands were also centrally maintained in each province. The followers of Ibn Ash'ath burnt them in A.H. 83,[187] and this paved the way for disorder and corruption. The records of Egypt were burnt by Marwān during the last years of Umayyad rule.

D. PUBLIC WELFARE

While the development of agriculture and subsidiary projects was in full swing only after the conquest of Iraq and Syria, other public welfare projects had been in force since the very first day of the inception of the Islamic State. The reason is that public welfare is a vital duty of an

Islamic state. The very success of the moral and legal system of Islam depends upon the satisfactory performance of this duty. That is why public welfare has always formed the datum of the fully-fledged implementation of Islam. But the Islamic concept of public welfare does not coincide with the modern concept under which the theory of welfare either leads to self-centred, materialistic capitalism or results in regimentation and turns human beings into paupers who must look to the government as the only sustainer and provider.

An Islamic state introduces prosperity with austerity and affluence with abstinence. Islam treats economic pursuit as a virtuous act but inculcates in its followers a spirit of self-control and contentment *(qanā'a)*. It allows attainment of the highest economic position but does not leave any person or group of persons to monopolize those heights. If some person or persons reach this height, it compels him or these persons to share their fortune with many more persons. It may be an unearned income for the new sharers but Islam introduces this element of distribution by force of law. These distributive instruments are the law of inheritance, the law of subsistence and *Zakāt*. *Ṣadaqa* and gift are voluntary acts but they are recognized by Islamic law as valid forms of the transfer of wealth.

The Islamic concept of public welfare calls for the satisfaction of the basic requirements of life. It does not reconcile itself to the situation in which a person is unable to demonstrate his worth for want of the basic requirements of life. These basic requirements are food, clothing, shelter, education, medical care and insurance against unforeseen events. A man is inclined to set aside ethical and religious doctrines if compelled by hunger and want, and this poses a challenge to the society. The society for its part is handicapped in the optimum utilization of its potential human resources. It is for these reasons that Islam, from the very beginning paid full attention to public welfare. In the early days of his rule the Prophet (peace be upon him) compensated for the shortage of resources with over-emphasis on *qanā'a* but it was perhaps not an everlasting and dependable alternative to the material necessities of life. As a result state responsibilities increased with the increase in its resources. The Prophet himself (peace be upon him), during the last days of his life when the resources of the state had increased, announced: 'If somebody dies leaving behind undischarged debts on him I shall pay them off; but if somebody leaves wealth, it is for his heirs.'[188]

It was this concept of public welfare that compelled the caliphs to personally visit the trade centres and listen to public grievances. They also insisted that their governors take care of public welfare. It was this concept that led to the introduction of *ḥisba,* inspection of public places. It was with a view to ensuring this welfare that they generally tried to spend *Zakāt* within the community from where it was collected. The concept converted the state treasury into God's wealth and the common prosperity of the Muslims. The concept inspired the rulers to undertake welfare projects on a large scale throughout the empire. Some such activities have been enumerated in the earlier chapters. Some other activities are listed in the following lines. The list includes every welfare activity except education which had a different institutional form than the one we now conceive of.

Setting up Townships

The problem of providing houses, markets and cultivable lands arose when the Prophet (peace be upon him), along with his Companions migrated to Madina. Migration (*Hijra*) in the Prophet's early Madinan period was a matter of merit and thus the influx of population continued throughout his life. The disposal of the Jewish population in Madina provided some support in accommodating a number of refugees. New markets were also built, plots of land were allotted for housing and new lands were brought under cultivation. Fresh conquests made it necessary to rehabilitate the armies in the newly-conquered provinces and to found new cities with all the amenities that were required during those days. Ibn Sa'd names Caliph 'Umar as the first to 'urbanize' *(tamaṣṣara)* or found the cities of Kūfa, Baṣra and Mosul and others in Syria and Egypt. He rehabilitated the Arabs in these cities and earmarked different areas for the tribes.[189] He also 'urbanized' Baḥrayn.[190]

The building-up of a city followed the selection of a site which suited the physical requirements of the Arabs. Madā'in was the first choice to build up a city, but Caliph 'Umar, knowing that camels could not stay there because of the mosquitoes refused to allow the Arabs to settle there. Kūfa was the next choice,[191] located near the village of 'Āqūl.[192]

Construction was inaugurated with the building of a mosque and the governor's house[193] within the market area. Land was divided into units, each for a tribe.[194] This plan was followed at the time of the building-up of Baṣra and Moṣul;[195] the latter was a small town before the arrival of the Muslims.[196] Al-Jīza,[197] Tawāj,[198] and Sanjar[199] were also colonized during 'Umar's caliphate in Egypt, Persia, and Al-Jazīra respectively. Qayruwān in al-Maghrib, Nushwā in Armenia, and Mar'ash in al-Jazīra were founded during Mu'āwiya's period.[200] The city of Bazra'a was rebuilt.[201] Ḥajjāj founded the city of Wāsiṭ in A.H. 83 at a cost of 43 million dirhams.[202] 'Abd al-'Azīz founded Ḥulwān in Egypt.[203] Muhammad b. Qāsim founded a city near Dībal in Sind and settled 4,000 Muslims there.[204] After him, his son founded al-Manṣūra[205] and Ḥakam b. 'Iwāna founded al-Maḥfūẓa.[206] Mūsā established a town in Ṭanja in

A.H. 89[207] and Sulaymān the city of Ramala.[208] Caliph Hishām built ar-Ruṣāfa[209] while his governor, Asad established a city near Balkh.[210]

Town Planning

The founding of a city called for the establishment of the basic amenities of life, like offices, mosques, houses, roads, supply, and grazing fields for cattle. Some of these facilities were supplied by the inhabitants themselves and some provided by the government. Reports suggest that the government constructed godowns for storing food-grains. In A.H. 20 two godowns were built at the port of Jār, near Madina.[211] There is also evidence of godowns at Anbār, Armenia, and Malṭiyya,[212] and it can be assumed that there was universal construction of such godowns because the government needed them to store commodity taxes and *Zakāt*.

In the new cities the governor's house was the first building to be constructed after erecting a mosque. In old cities, sometimes, a house was requisitioned for offices. Mu'āwiya bought 'Ikrima's 'Dār-an-Nadwa' (club house) at Makka and converted it into a 'Dār-al-Imāra' (government house).[213]

Setting up Markets

Apart from the founding of new cities other public welfare activities were not ignored. The Prophet (peace be upon him) founded a market in Madina.[214] Shopping centres were established in the heart of the newly-founded cities near the mosque. The market in newly-founded Kūfa was so noisy as to compel the governor, Sa'd to fix a big gate on his house which invited Caliph 'Umar's wrath.[215] Caliph 'Uthmān's governor, Ibn 'Āmir founded a market in Baṣra.[216] Hishām's governor, Khālid had a number of shops constructed and arranged for the accommodation of the shop-keepers near to their shops. His brother, Asad also founded a new shopping centre in a village.[217] The income from the Kūfan market was utilized for the requirements of the army.[218] Baṣra had three shopping centres including one for camels. Wāsiṭ had a big market, Moṣul had three and Ḥīra one.[219]

Construction of Mosques

The mosque, since the early days, has been a focal point of Muslim architecture. Caliphs 'Umar and 'Uthmān expanded the Prophet's mosque.[220] Caliph 'Uthmān's governor, Ibn 'Āmir had pools constructed at 'Arafāt and linked them with a canal.[221] Mu'āwiya decorated the

Kā'ba.[222] His governor, Ziyād had the mosques of Kūfa and Baṣra renovated at great expense and set up seven new mosques.[223] Wālid founded the mosque of Damascus, spending fabulous amounts on its construction and decoration.[224] His governor at Madina further expanded the Prophet's mosque.[225] The Ka'ba was also renovated at a cost of 30,000 dīnārs. Ibn 'Abd al-Ḥakam reports that Walīd founded several mosques in Egypt.[226] He also advised his governor to level up the hilly tracks leading to Madina and sink wells in the city.[227]

Amenities for Wayfarers

The importance of hotels, inns and rest-houses cannot be over-emphasized, particularly along caravan routes. Caliph 'Umar ensured that wayfarers had water and shelter along the route between Makka and Madina.[228] His governor, Abū 'Ubayda had rest-houses built at Qinnesrin.[229] 'Umar II did the same in Khurāsān.[230] According to Ibn Sa'd, 'Umar II exempted the local population from the obligation of entertaining Muslims and provided government guest-houses for them.[231] It is possible that these guest-houses were constructed by Walīd. Hishām provided a rest-house at Ṣūr[232] while his governor, Asad provided such facilities even in lonely deserted places.[233]

Communications

Mu'āwiya and his governor, Ziyād spent 4 million dirhams setting-up a mail-service.[234] The service had become so effective by Ḥajjāj's time that a message from Kūfa could reach Sind within three days.[235] Greek Papyri mention the existence of post-offices even in the small towns of Egypt.[236]

Free Ration Depots

People were permitted free rations in all the cities. This required the setting-up of provisions stores and ration depots *(dār ad-daqīq)* where rations were stored for monthly distribution. Caliph 'Umar was the first to fix rations and set up ration depots. They stored plain flour, baked flour *(suwīq)*, dates, raisins and other provisions for free distribution.[237] These commodities could also be used by wayfarers and guests. A similar ration-depot is mentioned in Egypt.[238] There is also mention of one in Kūfa during 'Alī's caliphate.[239] Ziyād is reported to have set up such a depot in Baṣra.[240]

Hospitals

To Walīd can be attributed the setting-up of hospitals *(bīmāristān)* and leprosy centres.[241] Agapius mentions one such hospital at Naṣībīn even before Islam, which a Patriarch visited to read some books.[242] This suggests that these centres were also used as teaching hospitals. Iṣṭakhrī (d. A.H. 318) found one of Walīd's hospitals still functioning in his time.[243] Walīd was also the first to provide free food to the deaf, the destitute and the decrepit.[244]

Grant of Loans and Subsidies

Besides these routine programmes of construction and development of public welfare centres and amenities, the *Bayt al-Māl* took upon itself a number of other functions to give direct support to the different classes of society. It granted loans for consumption, trade and agriculture.[245] Reports suggest the advance of consumption loans even to Abū Bakr, 'Umar and Sa'd.[246] Hind, 'Utba's daughter (Abū Sufyān's wife) borrowed 4,000 dirhams from the *Bayt al-Māl* for trade.[247] One of the functions of the *Bayt al-Māl* since the Prophet's time had been the relieving of undischarged debtors. 'The debt outstanding against a deceased person is our liability but the wealth bequeathed by him is for his heirs', is narrated to have been declared by the Prophet (peace be upon him) in his last days.[248] When 'Umar II had improved the financial position of his treasury he wrote to his governors to relieve the debtors with government funds.[249] The *Bayt al-Māl* also functioned as a trustee.[250] Caliph 'Umar compulsorily advanced as business loans an orphan's fund which was under the trust of the *Bayt al-Māl.*[251] Ḥajjāj and 'Umar II are reported to have advanced agricultural loans to farmers.[252] 'Umar II spent public funds in bearing the marriage expenses of the poor.[253] Unclaimed children were treated as the liability of the *Bayt al-Māl.*[254] When Caliph 'Umar withdrew vast tracts of land from the tribe of Bajīla, he paid to their chief, Jarīr eighty dīnārs from the *Bayt al-Māl,* perhaps in appreciation of his sacrifice, but not at all as compensation.[255]

Other Welfare Activities

Instances of the advance of loans are not many in the later period because the line of distinction between the personal resources of the rulers and public wealth had been blurred. They frequently used – or misused – the funds carelessly. While they did not stop the necessary and permissible expenditure, they spent or even overspent, unnecessarily. And because the beneficiaries were only too glad to draw this benefit, the practice was not generally criticized. Rather, this generous behaviour was appreciated perhaps because it was in keeping with the old traditional virtue; the more liberally a ruler distributed his wealth the more popular he became. As against it, the early standard was modest. An observer summed up the behaviour of Caliph ‘Umar’s governor, Sa‘d in the following words: ‘Collects for the people grain like an ant, behaves affectionately like a mother; is a Bedouin in his care for date-trees and Nabaetean in supervising taxes; distributes equally and arbitrates justly.’[256] Another observer summed up the conduct of the governor of Egypt thus: ‘He gives a camel if somebody loses his own, gives a slave if somebody misses one, gives money if somebody is needful of it.’[257] Ziyād, the governor of Iraq declared in his first speech: ‘I shall not hide myself if any needy person comes to me even at the dead of night.’[258]

This was not mere talk. The very concept of the *Bayt al-Māl* or *‘māl al-muslimīn’* called for this approach and attitude. It was considered the responsibility of the state to ensure a subsistence level to all its citizens, and to relieve them of the pressure of exigencies.

Among the functions of the *Bayt al-Māl* were also the freeing of slaves and the payment of ransom of Muslim prisoners in enemy camps.[259] It also shouldered the responsibility of paying blood-money or compensation to claimants in cases where the culprit could not be charged or punished.[260]

Notes and References

1. See chapter on *Zakāt.*
2. Sometimes also called *waẓīfa,* salary.
3. Refer to Chapter 1.
4. Tab., 1, 2414.
5. Bal., 446–7.
6. Sad., III, 1, 214.
7. A.U., 558.
8. A.U., 558–68. One example of distribution in need is the generous grant of subsidies and rations to all during the famine of 21 A.H. *(‘ām-ar-ramāda).* It is narrated (A.U., 644) that a Bedouin’s daughter came to Caliph ‘Umar and said that her father had fought with the Prophet (peace be upon him). Caliph ‘Umar fixed for her a subsistence allowance. Ibn Sa‘d (III, 1, 224) narrates that during the year of famine the entire caravan of relief provisions was diverted towards the countrymen who had swarmed around Madina. When the relief operations were ended after the rains Caliph ‘Umar distributed provisions and camels among them and allowed them to go (*ibid.,* 229).
9. Yah., 240; Bukh. (Faḍā’il ‘Uthmān), 5.
10. Sad., III, I, 216.

11. *Ibid.*, 217; A.U., 649.

12. *Ibid.*, 214 (or 3,000 dirhams, *Ibid.*, 219); also Tab., 1, 2414.

13. This is also partly proved by the fact that Ḥajjāj was keen to push back the converts to their villages in Iraq, (see above).

14. Tab., 2, 1028.

15. Tab., 2, 1731.

16. A.U., 559.

17. A.U., 581–6; Kath., 7, 214; Sad., III, 1, 214.

18. Bal., 165, 166, 366, 374, 444; A.U., 304.

19. Kindi, 76; Bal., 153, 209, 279, 350–1, 359, 401, 412, etc.

20. A.U., 562.

21. Sad., 5, 254–5.

22. See p. 144. (also A.U., 67–73 for 'Alī).

23. Mas., 3, 116–17.

24. A.U., 671–3.

25. A.U., 620.

26. Abu Daud, 3, 188.

27. Sad., 5, 275.

28. A.U., 641.

29. *Ibid.*, 641–2.

30. Maq., (Kh.), I, 94.

31. See above.

32. A.U., 120.

33. A.U., 119.

34. Sad., 5, 255.

35. Kh., 26.

36. 500,000 dirhams at a rate of 5,000 dirhams to each of the Badrites could suffice only 100 persons. The number of persons will double if the total amount is doubled yet it will not solve the problem.

37. Bal., 435–6.

38. The same year has been reported by Ibn Sa'd, III, 1, 213. But in principle the period after the fall of Iraq and Syria following the battles of Qādisiyya and Jarmuk appear to be a convincing date because a permanent settlement with the farmers after they had returned to their lands and reconciled themselves to paying their taxes to the Muslim government could be a possible natural condition of receiving a substantial amount of taxes. But the insistence on the year A.H. 20 would also require scrutiny of the report that Caliph 'Umar's general, Abū 'Ubayda b. al-Jarrāḥ also fixed pensions for the Muslims. The historians agree that Abū 'Ubayda died of plague in A.H. 18. Ṭabarī (1, 2411) has

suggested the year A.H. 15 for pensions. Ya'qūbi has suggested that rations were fixed for the Muslims in A.H. 18 and pensions in A.H. 20 (Yaq., 2, 139, 143). Patriarch Agapius (Maḥbūb al-Manbij) has reported (Patr. Or., 8, 581) that it took the Muslims five years to restore normalcy and levy taxes. The period, if calculated from the beginning of the expedition to Iraq suggests the year A.H. 17, but if calculated after the fall of Qādisiyya, makes the year A.H. 20.

39. Sad., III, 1, 213 *et sqq*; (also Kh., 25–6 with some minor changes. Similarly Bal., 435 *et sqq;* Tab., 1, 2412 *et sqq*).

40. Or 1,500 dirhams. Sad., III, 1, 215. But the one above is most frequently reported. See for example Tab., *op. cit.,* also 1, 2307.

41. Tab., 1, 2385.

42. I.A.H. (M), 145.

43. Yaq., 2, 139.

44. *Ibid.*

45. *Ibid.*

46. Tab., 1, 2413.

47. Who these 'all others' were is vague. It is possible that they included those who had not taken part in any war till that time but could be mobilized. Thus they may have been those countrymen or nomads who lived near the cities and frequented the social and religious gatherings.

48. Sad., 5, 65; Yah., 185–6.

49. A.U., 549 *et sqq;* Kh., 27; Tab., 1, 2412; Bal., 442 *et seq.*

50. A.U., 609–10.

51. A.U., 607 *et sqq.*

52. Tab., 1, 2800.

53. See p. 300.

54. Isfahani, *Maqātil aṭ-Ṭālibīn* 55; *cf.* Kharbutli 424.

55. Agh., 14, 175.

56. Kalbī, Ansāb, 836; *cf.* S.A.E., 111.

57. *Cf.* S.A.E., 111.

58. Maq. (Kh.), I, 94; I.A.H. (M), 102. Probably a new scale introduced for the fresh recruits.

59. Tab., 2, 77 and 78.

60. Mas., 3, 282–3.

61. 'Iqd., 4, 400; *cf.* Kharbutli, 417.

62. Tab., 2, 1354.

63. Kindi, 313.

64. Kindi, 68.

65. Yaq., 3, 50.

66. Kindi, 70.

67. Tab., 2, 1367; Bal., 415 reports that he fixed pensions for the converts.

68. *Ibid.*

69. A.U., 586.

70. Sad., 5, 278.

71. Sad., 5, 254–5.

72. Sad., IV, 1, 105.

73. Bal., 418.

74. Maq. (Kh.), I, 99.

75. Tab., 2, 1855; Kindi, 90.

76. Yaq., 3, 76.

77. Bal., 373.

78. Tab., 1, 2343.

79. Kath., 8, 215.

80. Kindi, 50.

81. Tab., 2, 1020.

82. Kath., 9, 126.

83. Aghānī. ed. II, 18, 165; *cf.* A.S. Tritton, 'Notes on the Muslim System of Pensions', *Bulletin of the School of Oriental and African Studies,* 16 (1954) 170, hereinafter referred to as AST (Notes).

84. M.B.Y., 74–5.

85. Athir, 3, 109.

86. Yaq., 2, 160; Sad., III, 1, 113–14.

87. Naqsh, 6. Also Tab., 2, 194; Kath., 8, 96, for other examples.

88. Kath., 8, 284; Tab. (2, 816) has reported these figures in connection with 'Abd al-Malik's act of punishment. It may be a matter of coincidence in figures or a confusion in reporting.

89. Kath., 9, 346–7, was later restored. *Ibid.*, 341.

90. Mas., 3, 358.

91. Kath., 9, 124.

92. Bal., 367.

93. Agh., 5, 79.

94. Kath., 9, 57.

95. Yaq., 3, 36.

96. Sad., 5, 256.

97. Tab., 2, 3744. For some other names, see AST (Notes), *op. cit.*, 170.

98. Jahs., 38.

99. Athir, 3, 43; Sad., III, 1, 214.

100. Jahs., 38, 40, 67; Maq. (Kh.), 1, 98; Kindi, 58–9; Bal., 298, Patr. Or., 8, 498; Khalifa, 1, 395.

101. *Ibid.* (all sources).

102. Tab., 1, 2672.

103. Maq. (Kh.), 1, 94; Kindi, 71; Yaq., 3, 36.

104. Kath., 9, 57 inference.

105. Bal., 318.

106. Kath., 8, 50; 9, 41; AST (Notes), *op. cit.,* 171.

107. Kindi, 354.

108. A.U., 234.

109. Chapter 6, p. 190.

110. Yāqūt, *Buldān,* 4, 275; *cf.* S.A.E., 120.

111. Kindi, 309.

112. Tab., 1, 2224–5.

113. Those who fought during the Prophet's lifetime.

114. Tab., 1, 2496; Maq. (Kh.), 1, 93.

115. Tab., 1, 2495, 2486.

116. Sad., III, 1, 151.

117. Kh., 27.

118. Sad., III, 1, 220; Abu 'Ubayd, 742 reports 40,000.

119. Tab., 1, 2451.

120. Sad., 5, 293.

121. Tab., 2, 1346.

122. Tab., 1, 2703.

123. J.M.H., IV, 2, 41.

124. Kindi, 13.

125. Patr. Or., 8, 480.

126. Bal., 124, 125.

127. Maq. (Kh.), 1, 200.

128. Pap, IV. Gen. Int. XXXII, also Introduction to 1369.

129. Bal., 125.

130. J.M.H., IV, 1, 63.

131. Bal., 167.

132. Bal., 436.

133. Bal., 183.

134. Bal., 134.

135. Bal., 155.

136. Bal., 134.

137. Bal., 124, 148.

138. Bal., 139, 169, 179.

139. Bal., 427.

140. Tab., 2, 1046.

141. Tab., 2, 1004.

142. Athir, 3, 147.

143. Bal., 139.

144. Sad., 5, 260.

145. Bal., 158.

146. Bukh. (Muzāra'a), 15; A.U., 716.

147. Chapter 3, n. 28.

148. Chapter 3, p. 123.

149. Bal., 84 *et sqq*.

150. Bal., 157.

151. Kh., 16.

152. Bal., 271.

153. Abū Yūsuf reports that Caliph 'Umar, after the conquest of Iraq handed over 500,000 cultivators to their landlords. Balādhurī reports that when the Arab newcomers bought lands from the Persians ('Ajam) in Ādharbāijān, the villagers became their peasants (Kh., 73; Bal., 324).

154. Bukh. (Ijārāt) 25; Muq., 10, 208–10; Kh., 29.

155. Kh., 49.

156. A.U., 700–1.

157. A.U., 712.

158. Tab., 1, 2026.

159. Bal., 370–1; Yah., 28.

160. Yah., 132.

161. Yah., 134.

162. Chapter 7, pp. 219–20.

163. *Ibid.*

164. Chapter 3, pp. 121–3, also Bal., 157, 184.

165. See above; also Kindi, 74, 76–7.

166. Kh., 41.

167. Bal., 288, 291, 325, 356; Qud., 241 etc.

168. Ag., 509.

169. Jāḥiẓ, *al-Bayān wa't-Tab'īn,* 273. *Cf.* Kharbutlī, 341.

170. *Ibid.,* 3, 235; *cf.* 341.

171. Rustam, Abd as-Salām: *Al-Manṣūr,* Cairo, 1965, p. 105.

172. Yah., 195.

173. Bal., 352–3.

174. Jahs., 19.

175. Bal., 352.

176. I.A.H. (M), 163. The canal connected Babylon to the Red Sea (S.L.P. 20). 'Amr sought Caliph 'Umar's permission to dig out a long canal linking the Mediterranean Sea with the Red Sea across Pelusium (al-Faramā), but 'Umar declined on the ground that the 'Roman' pirates would cause problems for the travellers to Makka. (Abu'l Fidā', Geography, Mss Fol. 102, Paris. *Cf.* Syed Sulayman Nadvi: *'Arbon Kī-Jahāz Rānī,* Azamgarh, 1935, p. 55.)

177. Lane-Poole (S.L.P. 20) calls it a corvee system perhaps because it was so in the Byzantine period. But Bell observes that this personal service 'was not exactly forced labour in the ordinary sense since the persons requisitioned whether as sailors or workmen received wages. It was, in fact, conscription'. Pap IV, General Introduction XXXI.

178. S.L.P., 20.

179. Bal., 273–4.

180. Muq., 80.

181. Bal., 26.

182. Yaq., 2, 192.

183. Bal., 149, 155–6, 172, 184, 284, 288–9, 292–3, 327–8, 356–64, etc.

184. 1st., 80.

185. Bal., 432.

186. Bal., 359–60.

187. See p. 218.

188. Al-Bukhārī, Muḥammad Ibn Ismā'īl: *Ṣaḥīh,* text with Urdu trans., Muhammad Said & Sons, Quran Mahal, Karachi, III, 173.

189. Sad., III, 1, 202.

190. *Ibid.,* 204.

191. Khalifa, 1, 129; Tab., 1, 2482 *et sqq;* Bal., 274–5.

192. Patr. Or., 13, 625.

193. Bal., 275–6.

194. *Ibid.*

195. Bal., 256, 327, 341; Tab., 1, 2378.

196. Aḥmad Ṣūfī: *al-Athar wa'l Mabānī al-'Arabiyya fi'l Mawṣil,* Moṣul, 1940, 5.

197. I.A.H. (M), 128 *et sqq.*

198. Dh. (Tar.), 2, 39.

199. Bal., 181.

200. Bal., 192, 207, 230.

201. *Ibid.*

202. Bal., 288; Tab., 2, 1126.

203. Severus, 139.

204. Bal., 425.

205. *Ibid.,* 431.

206. *Ibid.,* 430.

207. *Ibid.,* 232.

208. *Ibid.,* 149.

209. *Ibid.,* 185.

210. Tab., 2, 1490. Nājī (*'Urūba al-mudun al-Islāmiyya,* Baghdad, 1964, 47–55) has picked out the names of as many as twenty-eight cities that were built during the whole period.

211. Yaq., 2, 145.

212. Bal., 191, 209, 247.

213. Sad., I, 1, 45.

214. See Bal., 28.

215. Kath., 7, 75.

216. Sad., 5, 33.

217. Yaq. (B), 310–11; Bal., 284.

218. *Ibid.*

219. I.F., 181, also Kharbutlī, 373, with many other names.

220. See p. 124.

221. Sad., 5, 34.

222. I.F., 20.

223. Bal., 275, 342; Kath., 9, 148.

224. Ist., 60; I.F., 107; Khalifa, 397.

225. *Ibid.*

226. I.A.H. (M), 132.

227. Tab., 2, 1195.

228. Bal., 64–5.

229. Bal., 150.

230. Bal., 415; Sad., 5, 254.

231. Sad., 5, 258.

232. Bal., 124.

233. Tab., 2, 1637.

234. Kharbutli, 419.

235. Bal., 424.

236. Pap. IV, 1347 (intr.)

237. Sad., III, 1, 203.

238. Bal., 216.

239. Tab., 1, 3135.

240. Tah., 2, 77.

241. Yaq., 3, 36; Tab., 2, 1199.

242. Patr. Or., 8, 530.

243. Ist., 241.

244. Yaq., 3, 36.

245. There are no instances to prove that the Qur'ānic provision of the prohibition of interest was violated by the government or by other Muslims even long after the period under study. There is valid reason to believe that these loans were granted without interest.

246. A.U., 659; Sad., III, 1, 198; Athir., 3, 45, 63.

247. Athir., 3, 48.

248. See p. 316.

249. A.U., 621; Kindi, 68–9; I.A.H. (Umar), 68.

250. Sad., 5, 61–2.

251. A.U., 1303.

252. A.U., 621; I.K., 15.

253. A.U., 621.

254. Sad., 5, 45; Bal., 446.

255. Yah., 109–10; also Chapter 3, n. 88.

256. Bal., 278.

257. Mus., 12, 212.

258. Tab., 2, 75.

259. Sad., IV, 1, 56–7; Yah., 55.

260. Sad., III, 1, 259; Yaq., 2, 212; Tab., 2, 172; Mas., 3, 341.

CHAPTER 11

The Economic Policy of the Islamic State

Chapter 1 gives the basic principles which underlie the economic system of Islam. These were the principles which guided the early caliphs to consciously lay down an economic policy and which they pursued during their caliphate. A change in strategy was often necessitated due to changed socio-economic institutions in the newly-conquered lands but this did not bring about a change in the policy. The levy and collection of poll-tax, the administration of land-tax and the introduction of *Zakāt* as discussed in the foregoing chapters are suggestive of the government's policy of removing injustice, relieving the burden of the oppressed classes and bringing about a forced distribution of wealth among the poor of the society. The expenditure of government revenues over different sectors of the economy as discussed in Chapter 10 gives an idea of the government's desire for economic growth and public welfare in addition to an increase in its defence potential. It would not be out of place to list the objectives which the economic policy of the caliphs was intended to achieve.

The Qur'ān enjoins the cardinal values of equity, justice, mutual co-operation and self-sacrifice for reorganizing the socio-economic milieu of the society.[1] The Prophet (peace be upon him) said: 'If God makes anyone in charge of some job of the Muslims and he neglects their requirement, He will also neglect him in time of his need.'[2] He further said: 'An office is a trust: it is a humiliation except for those who rise equal to the task and pay everyone his due.'[3] Again, 'If somebody in a community sleeps hungry until the next morning, Allah will withdraw from His security for that community.'[4] It was on this basis that Caliph 'Umar declared: '('Umar) the son of Khaṭṭāb would be answerable (to God) if a camel starves to death along the Euphrates.'[5]

A study of the teachings of the Qur'ān and the Prophet's sayings suggests the objective of setting-up an economic order which enforces justice, stops exploitation and establishes a contented, satisfied society.

It is a real welfare state. What in precise terms the early Islamic governments did to achieve this objective has been discussed in relevant chapters and can be recapitulated as follows:

(1) Improvement in the Pattern of Consumption

Islam discards the contemporary outlook of an ever-increasing higher standard of living[6] as the object of economic pursuits. While officially it seeks to increase production and distribute income and wealth on a broader level, it does not allow its followers to make it an ultimate object of their life. Firstly, the Qur'ān and the *Ḥadīth* prohibit the use of many luxurious items of wealth like precious metals, and silken clothes for men and strong drinks for everybody. Secondly, simplicity is made a norm[7] and austerity treated as commendable. The Pious Caliphs set their own examples before other government officials to emphasize simplicity and austerity.[8] Apart from the stories about the Pious Caliphs quoted in the foregoing pages,[9] there are innumerable instances to suggest that in spite of an increase in opulence after the conquests of Persia, Iraq, Syria and Egypt the level of consumption of the common man did not substantially change from a simple mode of living. The frequent reports about distinguished persons' large bequests[10] suggest that large incomes were not lavishly spent and consumed. This simple living was inspired by Islamic teachings and by the examples of the rulers in contrast with the life-styles of the well-to-do Persians who were accustomed to big, beautiful houses, costly robes, sumptuous dishes and expensive jewellery.

(2) Improvement in the Distribution of Income and Wealth

The Qur'ānic policy of distribution helps a lot in introducing a broader basis of the distribution of income and wealth and discouraging accumulations and concentrations. It assures that in the process of distribution none of the factors of production is deprived of its share nor does it exploit the other. Land, labour and capital jointly create value. As a result the land owner, the labourer and the owner of capital should jointly share in their production. In addition to this policy it compulsorily retains a portion of this produced wealth for those who are prevented from contributing their share in production due to some social, physical or economic handicap.

The former aim was achieved by the Prophet (peace be upon him) and the caliphs through prohibiting a large number of exploitative and unjust techniques in trade.[11] A study of *Ḥadīth* literature is suggestive of those measures which include disciplinary restrictions on landlords and the farmer, the employer and the employee, and the producer and the trader. The latter aim was achieved by the rulers through the levy of taxes[12] including the impost of *Zakāt* and enactment of the laws of sustenance *(nafaqāt),* in addition to the emphasis on philanthropy and generosity.

Distribution of income and wealth acquired by man is perhaps the most distinguishing feature of the Islamic economic system. The frequent emphasis on spending for a noble cause, occurring in the Qur'ān,[13] is not only voluntary but also to an extent compulsory. Moreover, Islam encourages such institutions as lead to a wider distribution of wealth. The concept of the *Bayt al-Māl* as a trust in the hands of the ruler, retained for expending for the betterment of the public, demonstrates the distributive bias of the financial policy of the State.[14] The levy of *Zakāt* is a unique impost in the sense that its direct *quid pro quo* is prohibited for the tax-payer. The Islamic law of sustenance binds all Muslims to share their wealth with their kinsmen. The State may, if the need arises, extend this law to cover even neighbours and remote relations.[15] The prohibition of interest makes possible investment alternatives which distribute the return on capital on a broader basis.[16] Even if these distributive measures leave some accumulations of wealth and large holdings, the law of inheritance compulsorily sub-divides them into relatively smaller fragments.[17] While the former measures are a regular though mild technique of distribution, the last is a long-term process and takes a generation to substantially disintegrate accumulations. It is a process of this redistribution through which the sharers of inherited wealth have to restart their economic struggle and prove their entrepreneurial capabilities. A really capable entrepreneur may exceed his legator but an incapable person may lose his existing resources. Thus the privilege of being wealthy is not monopolized by a few fortunate families forever.

(3) Stability of Prices of Essential Goods

Another objective of the economic policy of the state was price stability. A free-market economy prevailed in the early medieval societies. Prices generally reflected the point of equilibrium between aggregate supply and effective demand. It was, therefore, natural that the increase in opulence should increase the demand for goods and hence prices. In the early Islamic period the increase in demand was generally met from the import of goods from newly-conquered provinces. But due to slow means of transport supply often lagged behind demand. Moreover increased incomes and urbanization also influenced the standard of living of the people. As a result prices began to rise sharply.

A rise in prices, without a rise in income is more detrimental to the poor than to the rich. But the government's policy did not allow these factors to affect the people adversely due to a number of reasons: Firstly, the state provided free rations.[18] Secondly, a large number of able-bodied persons were granted annual pensions.[19] Thirdly, the very poor were supported from a general budget as well as from the *Zakāt* fund.[20] Fourthly, the rulers ensured that prices of essential goods did not rise beyond the reach of the common man.[21] In some cases they controlled prices and sometimes restricted the rate of profit. Control of prices and security of the supply of essential goods ensured stability of prices over a long period although prices of other non-essential items rose very sharply during the same period.

(4) Security of Supply

Security of supply was ensured by improved means of communication and transport. As already mentioned, it was Governor 'Amr b. Al-'Ās who first proposed the construction of a canal linking the Mediterranean and the Red Sea. Caliph 'Umar though disagreed with him and advised him to re-open the choked-up canal linking the Nile to the Red Sea,[22] to facilitate the transport of food-grains. In Iraq many canals were broad enough to be used for transport.[23]

Founding of new cities implied the construction of godowns[24] for storage of food-grains and roads for quick transport of goods from one city to another.[25] This was extensively done by the rulers and the supply of goods was ensured. The supply was further facilitated by ensuring the safety of the caravan routes which were, before the conquest, exposed to a number of hazards. An efficient means of communication throughout the Muslim empire was also established. Mu'āwiya and his governor Ziyād spent huge funds organizing a mail service.[26] This service had become so effective by Ḥajjāj's time that a message from Kūfa could reach Sind within three days.[27]

(5) Expansion in Production

Egypt and Iraq were already surplus areas; the former fed the Byzantines and the latter the Persians, before Islam. Their conquest added to the food resources of the Islamic state. But the early rulers continued to add to their resources. New lands were reclaimed and brought under cultivation by the Pious Caliphs and later rulers.[28] This not only added to the coffers of the state through land-tax but also provided large quantities of food-grains for the population and for export. Reports suggest the existence of 120,000 canals around Baṣra (presumably including field channels). In Egypt more than 100,000 persons were employed to maintain the dams and canals in working order.[29]

A very large number of canals, dams and water courses were built by the rulers. A historian mentions the construction of a dam in the first century of Islam, along the river Indus in the present-day province of Sind in Pakistan. The dam, Sakr al-Mīd, was built to canalize the water of the river.[30]

Apart from efforts to increase agricultural production, mining was also encouraged by exempting minerals from tax. Oil and mica are reported by a historian as an example in Iraq.[31] Handicrafts were not subject to tax and they flourished because, contrary to food items, they were not subject to the policy of price controls.

(6) Satisfaction of Collective Needs and other Welfare Activities

After food and clothing another basic necessity for man is housing. Early instances of founding new cities abound.[32] The basic policy was to avoid density of population as far as possible. This urbanization started in Caliph ‘Umar's time and continued for centuries. The founding of a city called for the establishment of amenities like offices, mosques, houses, godowns, roads, markets, bath-houses, communications, water supply and pastures for the cattle.[33] Some of these facilities were supplied by the inhabitants while others were provided by the government. Amenities were also provided for the wayfarer by constructing rest-houses and inns and by providing meal houses and supplying fresh water.[34] A free medical service was institutionalized by Walīd (A.H. 85) when he inaugurated a *bīmāristān* and also set up a number of leprosy clinics. Many such hospitals were also used as teaching hospitals.[35]

In addition to providing the above facilities the rulers ensured that nobody was handicapped in his economic pursuits or social accomplishments simply for want of essential necessities. The government gave direct and indirect support to the needy by advancing loans, relieving the undischarged debtor, and offering financial assistance.[36] The details of the welfare-orientated behaviour of the government are summed up by the historians in interesting words which shed sufficient light on the policy and approach.[37]

(7) Population Planning

It may be a point of argument that the Islamic approach to population is inspired by religious motives or economic requirements or both. The

Prophet's sayings allude to the desirability of an increase in population.[38] The religious justification for this policy is, beyond doubt, because the strength of a religion lies in the number of its followers which could increase either by force, or by preaching or by multiplying. Islam did not advocate direct pressure or force; it made use of the last two devices. Preaching was made a religious duty.[39] Polygamy favoured an increase in birth rate. Permission to marry non-Muslim female Scriptuaries[40] further increased the overall reproduction rate of the Muslims with a negative effect on non-Muslims.

Besides this religious factor the Qur'ānic condemnation of 'killing' the offspring for fear of poverty[41] alludes to the disapproval of freely practising birth control measures on economic grounds. The population planning that was practised in the early Islamic period not only aimed at an increase in the size of the population but also at changes in the structure of the population. Large-scale migrations and emigrations were organized and encouraged by the early Islamic governments, sometimes also for strategic and social reasons. The economic effects of these religious, social and strategic reasons were an increase in human capital and employment of extensive production techniques. The trend of increase and the changes that took place in the structure of population during this period are discussed in detail in Part III of this book.[42]

(8) Protection and Safeguards for the Consumer

It was not only the setting-up of markets which the government took upon itself in the early period; it also ensured, as already mentioned, that the trader did not exploit the buyer. Government interest in market conditions developed into the institution of *ḥisba,* the department of inspection which was responsible for stopping adulteration, under-weighing, etc., over-work by the employees, employment in risky jobs, encroachment on thoroughfares, unhealthy trades, unlawful professions and cruelty to animals.[43] This department, headed by a *muḥtasib,* performed more functions than present-day local government. There are numerous instances where the government intervened if the rules of justice and fair play were violated. The Prophet's treaties with the Thaqīf, Hawāzin and the people of Najrān required a ban on transactions involving interest.[44] Transactions involving uncertainty and any possibility of dispute as were banned in the *Ḥadīth*[45] were also banned. The Prophet (peace be upon him) appointed an inspector to ensure that unlawful transactions were avoided and also himself visited the market and advised the traders to observe moral principles in trade.[46] His successors were also active in controlling trade and commerce. Serious action was taken against adulteration.[47] Minting of coins was so regulated as to prevent debasement and dishonesty and save the general public from being defrauded.[48] The rulers were generally vigilant about the prices of different commodities in different markets.[49]

(9) Defence

The Qur'ānic emphasis on defence by laying down: 'And make ready for them all thou canst of (armed) forces and horses tethered, that thereby ye may dismay the enemy of Allah and your enemy, and others beside them whom ye know not',[50] inspired the Muslims to be always ready with their fighting power. Actually it was considered the duty of every adult Muslim to take part in warfare. But manpower was not the only requirement for war. It needed a large number of riding animals, workshops for manufacturing weapons, an efficient communication system, cantonments and forts, and if necessary, the manufacture of warships. A full account of the activities of the government in this regard has been given in the foregoing pages.[51]

Above are discussed the objectives of the economic policy that was pursued by the early rulers. These objectives included:

(1) Improvement in the pattern of consumption.
(2) Improvement in the distribution of income and wealth.
(3) Stability of prices of essential goods.
(4) Security of supply.
(5) Expansion in production.
(6) Satisfaction of collective needs and other welfare activities.
(7) Population planning.
(8) Protection and safeguards for the consumer.
(9) Defence.

Notes and References

1. See p. 34 *et seq.*

2. Abū Dā'ūd Sulaymān Ibn Ash'ath: *Sunan,* Qur'ān Maḥal, Karachi, n.d., Vol. II, p. 465. Hereinafter this edition to be referred to as Abu Daud (Quran Mahal).

3. Mus., 12, 209.

4. Abū 'Abd Allāh Aḥmad b. Muḥammad b. Ḥanbal ash-Shaybānī: *Musnad,* Vol. II, Maṭba' Maymana, Miṣr, 1333 A.H., p. 466.

5. Aṭ-Ṭabarī, Abū Ja'far Muḥammad b. Jarīr: *Ta'rīkh al-Umam wa'l-Mulūk,* Vol. III, Cairo, 1939 (1357 A.H.), p. 272.

6. See p. 53 *et seq.*

7. Ibn Māja, Muḥammad b. Yazīd: *Sunan,* Vol. II, Qur'ān Maḥal, n.d., 543.

8. See for examples p. 106 *et seq*.

9. *Ibid*.

10. See p. 358 *et seq*.

11. See p. 50 *et seq*.

12. For a thorough discussion on the levy of *Zakāt* and other taxes see relevant chapters.

13. For example 2: 272–3 and 280; 17: 26; 92: 6, etc.

14. See p. 137 *et seq*.

15. Details of the law of sustenance can be found in the books of *fiqh*. The law provides not only for the subsistence share of wife, children and other near relations but also pet animals, in the wealth of the guardian if he can afford it.

16. According to Islamic law the owner may offer his land or capital to a worker on the basis of share-cropping (*muzāra'a* and *musāqāt*) or of partnership on condition that he shares profit as well as loss.

17. The following verses of the Qur'ān give a comprehensive list of the sharers of wealth left behind by a deceased:

> Allah chargeth you concerning (the provision for) your children: to the male the equivalent of the portion of two females, and if there be women more than two, then theirs is two-thirds of the inheritance, and if there be one (only) then the half. And to his parents a sixth of the inheritance, if he have a son; and if he have no son and his parents are his heirs, then to his mother appertaineth the third: and if he have brethren, then to his mother appertaineth the sixth, after any legacy he may have bequeathed, or debt (hath been paid). Your parents or your children: Ye know not which of them is nearer unto you in usefulness. It is an injunction from Allah. Lo! Allah is Knower, Wise. (4: 11)

> And unto you belongeth a half of that which your wives leave, if they have no child; but if they have a child then unto you the fourth of that which they leave, after any legacy they may have bequeathed, or debt (they may have contracted, hath been paid). And unto them belongeth the fourth of that which ye leave if ye have no child, but if ye have a child then the eighth of that which ye leave, after any legacy ye may have bequeathed, or debt (ye may have contracted, hath been paid). And if a man or a woman have a distant heir (having left neither parent nor child), and (he or she) have brother or sister (only on the mother's side) then to each of them twain (the brother and the sister) the sixth, and if they be more than two, then they shall be sharers in the third, after any legacy that may have been bequeathed or debt (contracted) not injuring (the heirs by willing away more than a third of the heritage) hath been paid. A commandment from Allah, Allah is Knower, Indulgent. (4: 12)

18. See p. 300.

19. *Ibid*.

20. See pp. 177, 186–9, 319, 320–1.

21. See p. 128.

22. See p. 314.

23. See p. 315.

24. See p. 318.

25. *Ibid.*

26. See p. 319.

27. *Ibid.*

28. See p. 313 *et seq.*

29. See p. 314 *et seq.*

30. *Ibid.*

31. See p. 185.

32. See pp. 316–21.

33. See p. 318.

34. See p. 319.

35. See p. 320.

36. *Ibid.*

37. *Ibid.*, pp. 320–1.

38. Abu Daud (Quran Mahal), 2, 123. The Prophet (peace be upon him) is reported to have said: 'Marry a loving and very fertile (woman) because through you shall I multiply (my *Umma*).'

39. For example, Qur'ān 3: 104; 3: 110; 16: 112, etc.

40. Qur'ān 5: 5.

41. Qur'ān 6: 151; 17: 31.

42. For details see pp. 362–8.

43. Early scholars have discussed the functions of the institution in detail. For the most comprehensive work published exclusively on the subject *cf.* Ibn al-Ukhuwwa, Diyā' ad-Dīn Muḥammad b. Muḥammad al-Qurashi: *Kitāb Ma'ālim al-Qurbā fī Aḥkām al-Ḥisba*, ed. Reuben Levy, Cambridge University Press, 1938.

44. See p. 126.

45. See p. 50 *et seq.*

46. See p. 127.

47. *Ibid.*

48. *Ibid.*

49. See p. 128.

50. 8: 60.

51. See pp. 308–10.

CHAPTER 12

A Note on Coinage

Who can be credited with introducing coinage in Islam? Many modern scholars have tried to summarily dispose of the question by choosing any of the classical views; still, most of them are conditionally right. It is not worthwhile to deal with the question at any great length but the observation made by Lane-Poole seems to accommodate most of the different theories in this regard:

> The Khalif 'Alī or one of his lieutenants seems to have attempted to inaugurate a purely Muslim coinage, exactly resembling that which was afterwards adopted; but only one example of this issue is known to exist, in the Paris collection, together with three other silver coins struck at Damascus and Merv between A.H. 60 and 70 of a precisely familiar type. These four coins are clearly early and ephemeral attempts at the introduction of a distinctively Mohammadan coinage, and their recent discovery in no way upsets the received Muslim tradition that it was the Khalif 'Abd al-Malik, who in the year of flight 76 or . . . 77 . . . inaugurated the regular Muslim coinage, which was thenceforward issued from all the mints of the empire so long as the dynasty endured, and which give its general character to the whole currency of the kingdom of Islam.[1]

A study of important early material on the subject leads to the following further conclusions which also do not contradict Lane-Poole's opinion.

1. Arabia used to have Iraqi dirhams and Syrian dīnārs before Islam. Himyarite coins from Yemen, though in use, were not popular. They were accepted on their weight and not on their face value.[2] This situation continued even under Islam.[3]

2. Private money-changers were available to exchange gold or silver for the coins in use at moderate charges. They might use their own dies to mint the coins. They could also perhaps improve the dies.

3. In the beginning Caliph ‘Umar due to the scarcity of gold thought of issuing a new currency to be made of leather. He refrained from doing so when other Companions opposed the idea.[4] This was intended to perhaps serve as token money.

4. Caliphs ‘Umar and ‘Uthmān had the Persian dirhams minted. This was done on Persian lines. Caliph ‘Umar is reported to have suggested some additions to the inscription.[5] This was not unusual because the money-changer could make alterations to the die. The weight of Caliph ‘Umar's dirham was fourteen carats.[6]

5. Caliph ‘Umar's deputies in Syria also followed the same practice of making some minor additions along with the original Christian inscription.[7]

6. To Caliph ‘Alī can be attributed the introduction of a distinctively Muhammadan coinage.[8]

7. Mu‘āwiya also continued to issue his coins with a figure and a sword struck in it.[9] His deputy in Iraq, Ziyād, also issued dirhams.[10] These coins were also of the Persian style except for the addition of the caliph's name in Arabic.

8. To Ibn Zubayr can be attributed the minting of round coins in Ḥijāz, while Muṣ‘ab, his governor in Kūfa, minted the coins on Persian and Syrian patterns.[11]

9. Some recent finds include coins issued in A.H. 74 by Bishr b. Marwān and some even in A.H. 72 by the Kharijites. The latter were called *‘atawiyya*.[12]

10. ‘Abd al-Malik for some time followed the practice of his predecessors when issuing coins.[13]

11. So far coinage had been unorganized, irregular and a personal affair. New coins were only additions to the already prevalent Byzantine and Persian coins. All were acceptable currencies. ‘Abd al-Malik changed this state of affairs. Coinage was almost nationalized. Old Byzantine and Persian patterns were altogether discarded. New dies were made. Government mints were set up.[14] A uniform standard for each currency was prescribed and the minting of coins was subject to government authorization.[15]

The Role of the Government

‘Abd al-Malik's activities bring us to discuss briefly the government's role as a formal and permanent authority to control coinage.

In the early Islamic period the value of a coin depended on its weight.[16] A *mithqāl* of gold containing a grain less than 22 carats represented a full standard Arab dīnār but the dīnār in general use usually contained 20 carats,[17] and was sub-divided into 1/2 and 1/3 dīnār.[18] A dīnār could be cut into smaller pieces and used as gold – a medium of exchange *par excellence.* Caliph 'Alī, for example, cut off two carats of gold from a dīnār in order to buy meat.[19] Silver was weighed in terms of *ūqiyya* which was known to be equal to 40 dirhams in weight, and was sub-divided into *nash, ritl, nawāt* and *sha'īra,* representing 20, 12, 5 and 1/60 dirhams respectively.[20] But a standard and uniform weight of dirham was not adhered to mainly because coinage was a private business. The silver content of a dirham generally varied between 10 and 20 carats.[21] When Caliph 'Umar wished to mint dirhams he recommended an average weight of 14 carats for a dirham.[22] This was 7/10 of the weight of a dīnār which was 20 carats.[23] While Mu'āwiya is stated to have increased the weight by one carat, his governor, Ziyād still adhered to the earlier average weight of 14.[24]

The Weight and Value of Coins in Egypt

Although Egypt was governed by a strong central government from Rome and after that from Constantinople for the last few centuries before Islam, the situation in respect of coinage was not much different. Dīnār *(solidi)* was the coin in general use as was the case in Syria and it continued to be so even after Islam. The early Muslim sources do not give sufficient details about coinage in Egypt but the finds of the Aphrodito Papyri have to some extent compensated for the lack of earlier records. These finds belong to the early seventh century, mostly covering the reign of Walīd b. 'Abd al-Malik. The editor of the Papyri is inclined to suggest the prevalence of dīnārs of varying weights,[25] the biggest containing 24 carats with different smaller fractions, the smallest being 1/6 of a dīnār.[26] He also finds the existence of folles, which Jahshiyārī refers to as the coins of copper.[27] It was because of the varying weights of these coins that their value was determined by the weight of their gold content. Officers were appointed to appraise the real value of the coin, at least when receiving the government revenues.[28] Although 'Abd al-Malik fixed the weight of a dīnār at 22 carats less a grain[29] and 15 carats weight for a dirham,[30] yet Egypt seems to have been independent of this standard.

Setting-up Mint Houses

As already mentioned the government did not exercise any control over coinage before the reign of 'Abd al-Malik. At the most, they replaced counterfeit coins with genuine ones.[31] But Marwān treated the cutting of a coin as fraud and made it a punishable offence.[32] Before minting was formally started, Ḥajjāj, the governor of Iraq collected full information about its technique and the procedure that was being followed in Persia. He then set up mints and employed technicians.[33] Ḥajjāj also ordered the setting-up of mint-houses in all large towns[34] and advised traders to get new coins minted at moderate charges[35] of one dirham for every 100 dirhams.[36] Unauthorized minters were punished.[37] In order to further discourage the use of old coins, the government compelled the farmers to pay their taxes in old currency. It also prohibited even the private melting of coins and permitted hoarders and the rich to remit their old coins to the state mint.[38] While the minting of dirhams was organized in the 'silver areas', minting of the dīnār was started in Damascus and Egypt.[39] The seigniorage was equally moderate. Care was taken to ensure correctness in weight.[40] During Yazīd II's period, 'Umar b. Hubayrā took special care to use pure silver[41] and made the rules of money-changing more rigid.[42] Hishām's time was ideal for the issue of standard currencies. His governor, Khālid was known to be a very strict officer in enforcing government standards.[43] His successor, Yūsuf b. 'Umar was even more rigid, so much so, that when he found a dirham less in weight by one grain *(ḥabba)* he ordered one hundred lashes for each of the responsible persons.[44] He is also reported to have mutilated their hands and branded their skin with burning dies.[45]

By the time of Hishām new coins had already been widely circulated. It was, therefore, not feasible to run mints at different places so making it an expensive and cumbersome job with a large staff employed in every town. Hishām centralized the work and closed all the mint-houses except the one in Wāsiṭ.[46] The standard of the dirham was so well maintained by 'Umar b. Hubayrā, Khālid and Yūsuf that dirhams issued under their authority were the only valued coins even after the end of the dynasty.[47]

Dīnār-Dirham Ratio

The dīnār-dirham ratio throughout the period under study seems to have remained almost stable. For all practical purposes a 20-carat dīnār was treated as equal to ten 14-carat dirhams, giving a gold-silver ratio of 1:7.[48] It cannot be claimed that this ratio was fixed as a result of the interplay of the factors of demand for and supply of gold and silver. Augustus fixed a gold-silver ratio of 1:12 throughout his empire[49] and this was also the case in Egypt. Since the fourth century onwards there is some evidence to suggest that 10 grams of silver were collected for every one of gold.[50] In Syria, Iraq and Arabia under Islam the prevalent ratio of gold to silver was 1:7 and thus the dīnār-dirham ratio 1:10. The conquest of eastern lands gradually brought many silver mines into Muslim hands[51] but the gold-silver ratio remained unchanged for quite a long time. In the second century and early third century Muslim jurists generally treated the 1:10 dīnār-dirham ratio as real and practical.[52] But later on the ratio fluctuated in favour of the dīnār. Qudāma (d. A.H. 337) puts it at 1:15 in his period[53] although during the time of Ibn al-Faqīh (d. A.H. 289) it was 1:17.[54]

Other Monetary Instruments

The above discussion should not be taken to mean a universal prevalence of coins in the Islamic empire. Barter was more popular in villages and small agricultural towns than it is in the twentieth century in agricultural countries in the Orient. The *Ḥadīths* banning transactions involving interest in barter allude to its wide prevalence in the Prophet's time.[55] But this does not contradict the statements[56] about the developed trade and financial institutions of Makka even before Islam. It was the development of this institution later on that made popular cheques and bills-of-exchange even among the villagers, which is evident from a poetic message quoted by Ibn Qutayba (d. A.H. 276):

> Pay my compliments to the *amīr* when you see him and tell him that I am indebted to one of the villagers *(a'rāb)* which is the worst indebtedness. I owe him 1500 (in cash) and 250 in terms of an old bill of exchange . . .[57]

Notes and References

1. S.L.P. (Coins), 165.
2. Naqsh., 10.
3. Bal., 453.
4. Bal., 456.
5. Maq. (N), 8.
6. *Ibid.;* for weights and measures see Appendix.
7. Cheikho (Adab II), 385–7; also *cf.* Shalabī, 285.
8. See above.
9. Maq. (N), 8.
10. *Ibid.*
11. Kath., 9, 15; Maq. (N), 9; Bal., 454.
12. J. Walker: 'Notes on Arab Sassanian Coins', *Numismatic Chronicle,* 14 (1934), pp. 293, 297.
13. Sad., 5, 170. While different dates are suggested by authorities, the earliest available dīnār minted under 'Abd al-Malik's reform is dated the year 77. G.C. Miles: 'Some Early Arab Dinars', *American Numismatic Society Museum Notes,* 1948, pp. 94–6.

14. With the help of recent finds some definite information is now available about some of the places where mints were set up. They include Dara'bjarb, Sūq Ahwāz, Sūs, Jay, Manādar, Maysān, Ray, Abarqubādh. J. Allan: 'Unpublished Coins of the Caliphate', *Numismatic Chronicle,* 19 (1919), p. 195. J. Walker: 'Notes on Arab Sassanian Coins', *op. cit. Ibid.* G.C. Miles: 'Abarqubādh, a new Umayyad Mint', *American Numismatic Society Museum Notes,* 4 (1950), pp. 115–20.

15. Bal., 454; Maq. (N), 15; Naqsh., 11; Tab., 2, 939; ad-Damīrī: *Ḥayāt al-Ḥayawān,* 1, 76. *Cf.* Kharbutli, 424–5.

16. Bal., 452–3.

17. Bal., 451–2.

18. Naqsh., 11.

19. Abu Daud, 2, 186.

20. Bal., 452–3.

21. Bal., 451.

22. Ag., 264.

23. Naqsh., 12.

24. Maq. (N), 8, 9.

25. Pap. IV, 84, 85 Introduction.

26. *Ibid.*, p. 86.

27. P. 464, Introduction to Pap. IV, 1544; Jahs., 34.

28. Pap. IV, Introduction, 84–5.

29. Sad., 5, 70.

30. Maq. (N), 10; Naqsh., 11; But Balādhurī (Bal., 451) makes a general statement about the weights of the coins in the Islamic period, at 14 carats each for dirham and dīnār. The same value is derivable from Ṭabarī (2, 939) who observed that 'Abd al-Malik's 10 *mithqals* weighed 7 pre-Islamic *mithqāls* although his statement that a dirham weighed 1 grain less than 12 carats does not fit his earlier statement *(ibid.).* On the contrary there is evidence to suggest that 'Abd al-Malik reduced the weight of the dīnār. In modern weight the 4.55 gram weight per dīnār was reduced to 4.25 grams. (*E.I.*, II, art. Dīnār).

31. Bal., 455.

32. Bal., 456.

33. Bal., 454.

34. Bal., 453; also fn. 14.

35. Bal., 454.

36. *Ibid.*

37. Bal., 455.

38. Bal., 454.

39. Naqsh., 17.

40. Naqsh., 15.

41. Bal., 454.

42. *Ibid.*

43. *Ibid.*

44. Al-Bayhaqī, Ibrāhīm b. Muḥammad: *al-Maḥāsin wa'l Masāwī,* Leipzig, 1902, p. 199.

45. Bal., 454–5.

46. Maq. (N), 16.

47. Bal., 454–5.

48. Grierson calculates the mint ratio at 1:14 by treating the dīnār-dirham ratio at 1:20. But the works of history and literature suggest it as a very late development, perhaps long after the fall of the Umayyad dynasty. He has, however, admitted that before 'Abd al-Malik's reform the dīnār-dirham ratio was 1:10.5, *viz.* the mint ratio at about 1:7. It has already been reported that 'Abd al-Malik increased the weight of dirhams by one carat to fifteen carats while he decreased the weight of gold from 4.55 to 4.25 grams. Thus the change of the dīnār-dirham ratio after the reform in favour of the dīnār at 1:15 as suggested by him is not apprehensible. For Grierson refer to 'The Monetary reforms of 'Abd al-Malik', *Journal of the Economic and Social History of the Orient,* 3 (1960), pp. 259, 263. For other details see note 30 and *E.I.* II, art. Dīnār.

49. A.C.J., 4.

50. *Ibid.*, 65.

51. S.A.E., 158.

52. *Passim.*

53. Qud., 239.

54. I.F., 264.

55. See Chapter 1.

56. W.M. Watt, *Muhammad at Mecca,* Oxford, 1972, p. 3; De Lacy O'Leary: *Arabia Before Muhammad,* London, 1927, p. 182.

57.

ان اخيت الامير فقل ميلاء   عليك ورحمة الله الرحيم

واما بعد ذاک فلی غريم   من الاعراب قبح من غريم

له الف علی و نصف الف   ونصف النصف، فی صک قديم

دراهم ما انتفعت بها ولكن   وصلت بها شيوخ بنی تميم

Qut., 302–3.

PART III

ECONOMIC INDICATORS

- Prices and the Cost of Living
- Salaries and Wages
- Affluence and the Standard of Living
- Population

CHAPTER 13

Economic Indicators

A. PRICES AND THE COST OF LIVING

The efficacy of an economic system can be judged by a study of the key economic indicators of the society in which the system is made to work. It is with the help of these data that we come to know if wealth is justly distributed, if taxes are equitably and justly levied, if the level of prices is kept within the reach of the common man, and if an average standard of living can be enjoyed by a man of moderate means. This requires a study of the average level of prices, level of incomes and the standard of living of the town-dwellers.

In spite of the extreme significance of these indicators it is not surprising that the complete data which are necessary to reach a satisfactory conclusion are not available for the period under study. The only alternative that remains is to study the incomplete data and try to draw conclusions.

It seems that the most practical method of gaining an idea about the cost of living in the very early period is by a study of the exemption limits *(nisāb)* of *Zakāt* on different items.[1] Exemption was allowed perhaps with a view to providing a minimum level of subsistence to *Zakāt*-payers. Thus savings amounting to less than 200 dirhams or the produce of five *wasqs*[2] of grain were exempted from *Zakāt*. And this suggests that 200 dirhams was the level of the average annual requirement of the payer. While the amount of money was fixed in the case of cash savings, gold, silver, and articles of trade, the quantity of consumption but not its value was considered in the case of land produce. That is why the exemption limit of dates and grain is fixed at the same level of five *wasqs* without discrimination. In respect of animals and livestock the number and not the value of different breeds has been made the standard; the aim in view seems to be the price of an average animal. What can be inferred from these standards is the theory that the annual requirement of an average family could be met by 200 dirhams or five *wasqs* of dates or grain. The same amount is computable in the case of an average animal. For example, forty sheep or goats are exempt from

Zakāt, their average value amounts to 200 dirhams. Less than five camels are exempt and the minimum value of five camels comes to about 200 dirhams. This evidence suggests that in almost all cases the exemption limit has been made commensurate with the average annual requirements of a man. Incidentally, this was the minimum amount which Caliph 'Umar granted by way of pensions.[3]

The question remains whether this minimum standard was set for a comfortable living or just to enable one to keep his head above water. The following evidence suggests that the aim of fixing this minimum was the distribution of the burden of *Zakāt* as widely as possible, even where a man with a large dependent family could not comfortably afford it. While Caliph 'Alī observed about Baṣra that a man possessing 4,000 dirhams (per annum) was a rich man,[4] 'Umar II found that 20,000 dirhams were sufficient for 4,000 homes[5] (five dīnārs per month per home). These two figures suggest the maxima and the minima of living with two different standards, although 'Umar II's standard belongs to a very late period in Damascus. What 'Umar II might have considered sufficient to provide a comfortable living in a more urbanized society of Syria as late as A.H. 100. His own household expenses are stated to be two dirhams daily and this does not seem to be an exaggeration in view of another statement that one could pass his month with an expenditure of only two dirhams in Baṣra under Ziyād.[6] Thus the exemption limit of 200 dirhams for every owner of '*Zakat*-able' goods may ensure a comfortable living for an average family. And it is also not surprising because the exemption limit is granted on personal holdings but not on family holdings. Thus if there are four persons in a family who are liable to *Zakāt,* each of them will enjoy this exemption limit.

After this basic evidence, study may be made of the available prices in different regions. In some cases the prices of different articles have been inferred on the basis of arithmetic calculation. For example, in the case of blood-wit in Islamic law, 100 camels were considered to be equivalent to 1,000 dīnārs or 10,000 dirhams or 2,000 goats or 200 suits or 200 cows,[7] which meant that 1,000 dīnārs could command each of these lots or in other words a goat could be had for five dirhams, a suit for fifty dirhams and so on. Similarly when it is reported that a certain person retained with him two dirhams for expenditure on food during his expedition to Khaybar and left two dirhams for his household expenditure during his absence, it meant that two dirhams were sufficient for a family for its meal expenses for about fifteen days.[8]

The most important items of human necessity are food, clothing and shelter. Food prices for the early period are not given anywhere in clear figures. The principal diet of the Arabs was dates or barley. A quantity of dates valued at two dirhams or less was sufficient to feed a man for about fifteen days.[9] As regards the price of grain, it is only known that the price had fallen to a reasonable extent after imports of wheat from Egypt had started during Caliph 'Umar's time,[10] but they soared again during anti-'Uthmān agitation. Later on the prices in Madina are reported to have gone up during Ibn Zubayr's 'revolt' and rose to two dirhams for a modi of wheat;[11] while the average monthly consumption of wheat which was fixed by Caliph 'Umar for free supply was two modi per man.[12] A rough idea about low prices of wheat can be obtained keeping in view the reportedly 'high' price. This provides for justification to believe that the range of low prices should have been between one and one and a half dirhams for a modi. That is why the person going on expedition to Khaybar left a total of two dirhams for household meal expenses for about fifteen days.[13] It should not be ignored that barley, the common man's diet, was cheaper than wheat.[14] The rate of tax on land growing barley was fixed at half of that under wheat crop.[15] Mu'āwiya reduced by half the quantity of *ṣadaqat al-fiṭr* in terms of wheat than that fixed in terms of barley.[16] The price of an average goat was five dirhams[17] and of below average, three dirhams.[18]

As regards clothing, the cheapest quality of shirt could be bought for three dirhams,[19] and a mantle for four dirhams.[20] A pair of rough shoes was bought by Caliph 'Umar for one dirham.[21] The price of a trouser was four dirhams.[22] The following table gives the different prices of various items, as quoted by historians.

Table 15. Prices of Selected Commodities in Arabia and Iraq
(Prices in dirhams per unit unless stated otherwise)

Wheat[23]	1 to 2 per modi
Shirt[24]	2, 3, 4, 6 1/2, 8, 14, 400
Mantle[25]	4, 5, 8, 100, 200, 500, 1,000
Trouser[26]	4
Two-piece dress[27]	50, 500
Rough shoes[28]	1
Goat[29]	3, 5
Camel[30]	40, 70, 120, 300, 400
Coat-of-mail[31]	sold for a garden
Shield[32]	3
Arm (*silāḥ*)[33]	280
Saddle (camel's)[34]	13
Agricultural land[35]	100, 100,000, 170,000, 1,600,000
Garden[36]	Sold for a coat-of-mail
Date tree[37]	1,000
Slave[38]	8, 360, 400, 600, 800, 10,000, 40,000
Maid-Slave[39]	150, 200, 6,000, 10,000

The above prices were current mostly in Ḥijaz and Iraq. Greek Papyri give some prices that were current in Egypt during the middle of the period under study. They are reproduced below.[40] The figures can be accepted with the observation that they represent the most expensive period as observed by al-Kindī.[41]

Table 16. Prices of Selected Commodities in Egypt

Commodity	Period	Rate
Wheat	699 A.D. (A.H. 80)	20 artabas per solidi or dīnār
,,	706–07 (87–88)	12 ,, ,, ,,
,,	709 (90)	13 ,, ,, ,,
,,	715–16 (96–97)	10 ,, ,, ,,
Oil	711 (92)	20 xestes *(qisṭ)* ,, ,,
Dates	,,	12 artaba ,, ,,
Onions	,,	10 ,, ,, ,,
Raisins	,,	2 ,, ,, ,,
Boiled wines	,,	40 xestes *(qisṭ)* ,, ,,
Vin Ordinaire	,,	72 ,, ,, ,,
Poultry	,,	20 birds ,, ,,
Sheep	,,	2 heads ,, ,,
Vegetable	,,	60 bundles ,, ,,
Firewood	,,	16 centenaria ,, ,,

According to the same evidence, per-capita monthly consumption was calculated at 7 artabas of loaves, 1 1/6 artabas of pulses and 7 xestes of oil. The cost of provision (probably only oil and salt) of a man for 6 months was estimated to be 11 1/4 carats or about 1/2 solidus (dīnār).

The above generally includes the prices of those items which do not register any abnormal rise or fall in demand in ordinary circumstances. But in case a wide range of variation in prices of the same item is evidenced, it surely reflects the great difference in the quality of goods. A coarse plain shirt may cost three dirhams but it cannot be comparable with a superior silken shirt inlaid with golden embroidery. This is always the case with the prices of slaves and animals. The price of each and every slave must depend on his appearance, talents and accomplishments. The price of an animal is governed by its age, health, size and breed. The prices of land are sometimes governed even by those factors which are not to be found within the land itself. Development of the adjacent area, progress in the means of communication and transport or attachment of any historical, social or religious significance may cause a sudden increase in the demand for land and hence an increase in its price. These phenomena were actively at work in fast-developing Arabia and other Muslim lands and as a result the prices of such items witnessed an unprecedented increase. The land which Zubayr bought for 170,000 dirhams was sold for about 1,600,000 dirhams after his death.[42] A big house three miles away from Madina was sold for 300,000.[43] In Baṣra a house which cost 5,000 dirhams fetched 10,000 simply because of its neighbourhood.[44] Ibn 'Umar was offered 10,000 dirhams for his slave Nāfi'. He himself bought another one for 40,000.[45] There are many more instances of abnormal increases in the prices of these items with the passage of time and there seems to be no point in emphasizing the fact that the latter instances of possessing big buildings, land, good slaves or expensive horses are suggestive of the level of affluence of the owners.

B. SALARIES AND WAGES

After gaining a sketchy idea of the level of prices it is worthwhile now to examine if the salaries and wages were commensurate with them.

While prices were governed by the laws of supply and demand allowing for all its limitations, salaries were yet to be fixed by the newly growing Muslim state which had no previous experience or tradition of such administration. The Prophet (peace be upon him) is stated to have observed: 'Whosoever gets an office in our administration he may marry if he is unmarried; he may get a house if he does not possess it; he may have a riding animal if he does not own it; he may keep a servant if he does not have one. But if anybody hoards wealth or rears a flock of camels (with government funds) God shall make him rise up as the one who misappropriates or who cheats us.'[46] The Prophet (peace be upon him) did not fix any regular salaries. When he appointed 'Uttāb b. Usayd as his *'āmil* (officer) at Makka, he fixed for him one dirham per day.[47] When Abū Bakr became caliph he was not sure if he was entitled to a salary as a matter of right. While he was selling mantles as usual, 'Umar said: 'Come, Abū 'Ubayda shall provide for you.' Abū 'Ubayda said: 'I shall provide for you the allowance for one man of the Muhājirs and a garment for winter and one for summer.' Then he assigned unto him every day half a sheep, and shelter for him and his family.[48] According to another report, Abū 'Ubayda assigned him 2,000 dirhams. Abū Bakr thereupon said: 'Increase the sum for me for I have a family', so they gave him an increment of 500 dirhams.[49] When Caliph 'Umar set for himself a standard of his salary he would say: 'Two suits for the year are permissible for me: one in winter, another in summer; and a riding animal for pilgrimage and meal for myself and for my family of the standard of an average Qurayshite. After all this I am only one of the Muslims. I shall get what the other Muslims get.'[50] Caliph 'Uthmān was himself a rich man and did not like to take any salary.[51] Caliph 'Alī is also reported not to have taken the caliph's salary perhaps along with his pension. He did take a cotton stuffed shirt and dress.[52] 'Umar II, too, lived on his pension only.[53]

These concepts, though modest and impressive in themselves, could not be made applicable to everyone. And when salaries were to be fixed there was bound to be some realistic basis for it. Arabs within Arabia could continue to live in their traditional way but when they moved out of Arabia they had to observe the decorum of a ruling nation in a way that impressed the subjects. In the beginning, fixation of salary for any official in any part of the kingdom was generally the function of the caliph but later on the power passed to the provincial governors, so much so that they sometimes fixed their own salary.[54]

Caliph 'Umar is regarded as the first to fix regular salaries for officials. He fixed for the surveyor of Iraq five dirhams and a bagful of flour every day.[55] His governor in Iraq was also given an economical salary but he convinced Caliph 'Umar of the political need to have a reasonable amount.[56] Mu'āwiya, unlike all other governors under Caliph 'Umar, received 1,000 dīnārs annually.[57] The commander of the Muslim army in Iraq appointed Ziyād in charge of the spoils and paid him two dirhams daily.[58] But when later on Ziyād himself became governor of Iraq he fixed 1,000 dirhams each for his soldiers and 25,000 dirhams for himself.[59] *Qādī* Shurayḥ (judge) got 100 dirhams or, according to another report, 500 dirhams per month.[60] The judge at Fusṭāṭ got 300 dīnārs annually, during Mu'āwiya's reign,[61] while another judge of Egypt, Ḥudhayma, got 120 dīnārs.[62] During Marwān's reign the salary of the judge was 240 dīnārs per annum which equalled 200 dirhams per month. The person in charge of an office got 300 dirhams per month[63] and an ordinary clerk 30 dirhams. Governor Iyās b. Mu'āwiya was paid 2,000 dirhams.[64] Ibn Ḥujayra al-Akbar, the governor of Egypt in the early seventies, received 200 dīnārs each for his additional jobs of judge, preaching *(qaṣaṣ)* and the *Bayt al-Māl.*[65] This was over and above his pension amounting to 200 dīnārs and perhaps the same amount as the salary for his governorship.[66] It is stated that during 'Abd al-Malik's time the chief of the police was paid 100,000 dirhams[67] while Ḥajjāj received 500,000 dirhams[68] (per annum?). A shipbuilder in Egypt got 9 to 24 dīnārs, caulker 18 dīnārs, sawyer 22 dīnārs, labourer 8 dīnārs and a carpenter 15 dīnārs per annum.[69] 'Umar II fixed a salary of 300 dīnārs for his officers so that they would not commit any malpractices because of financial stringencies.[70] The early caliphs believed in austerity on the part of the officials but the later rulers had a different view and tried to keep the officers contented and carefree. To facilitate a glance at the overall picture of the salaries and wages the figures may be arranged as far as possible chronologically. They are given in terms of dirhams per annum at the dīnār-dirham ratio of 1:10.

365
2,500
1,800
4,400
4,000
3,300
5,500
1,000
3,600
2,400
10,000
1,200
2,000
2,000
2,000
2,000
2,000
25,000
100,000
500,000
3,000
1,200

The above discussion suggests that there was no uniform standard of fixing the pay for different jobs. While one governor got 2,000 dirhams another got 25,000 dirhams. Apart from some exceptional cases of high salaries, which cannot be unconditionally accepted, most of the incomes lie within the range of 2,000 to 5,000 dirhams per annum. These salaries belong to a class of people employed by the government. Over and above these salaries regard should also be given to the pensions and rations that Caliph ‘Umar extensively granted to early Muslims and soldiers and the list of which continued to expand throughout the period under study.[71]

Conclusion

Above a sketchy study of prices, wages and salaries has been made. It will be seen that the prices of food-grain and cloth were within the reach of even the poorest class of people. Wheat at twelve artaba per dīnār or one modi per dirham meant that a man with an average family, earning twenty dirhams per month, could spend six to eight dirhams on his monthly grain requirement and he could spend 80 to 100 dirhams on ordinary clothes every year. Land and houses in fast-growing regions had become expensive but even there a poor man's house normally cost him his own labour and a nominal investment in ordinary building materials. It was the rich man's mansion which had become expensive in densely-populated towns.

The question now arises, was the distribution of economic resources widespread or was it limited to a certain class of population or to certain areas? The question can be studied with the help of a similar set of incomplete data.

C. AFFLUENCE AND THE STANDARD OF LIVING

Books of history and biography are replete with descriptions of very important persons or of the Companions of the Prophet (peace be upon him) about whom special care was taken to record as much detail as possible. Thus a description of such names does not in any way give the maxima of the wealthy persons. There must have been numerous persons who were richer than them but they escaped the notice of the historians because of their insignificant religious or political position. Picturesque details about a number of such persons are to be found in literary works like al-Aghānī but they cannot be made a point of sober analysis in respect of this study mainly because their degree of reliability cannot be ascertained. Some of the sources which have been made a basis of the above and the following inferences are not without defect yet they are much more reliable than the works on literature and poetry.

How economic change of the whole society and of the individual was ushered in within a short period of the first forty years of Islam can be discerned from the following few instances. When on the occasion of the battle of Ḥunayn the *Anṣār* (Helpers) had some grievances about the distribution of booty, the Prophet (peace be upon him), addressing them, reportedly said: 'Were you not destitutes *('Āla)* when I came among you and after that God made you well-off?' The *Anṣār* are reported to have admitted it[72] which meant that they realized the overall economic change in Madina. How the condition of the Muslims in general underwent a change in this period can also be examined by the quality and quantity of the equipment which they possessed during their expeditions. While the 300 Muslims had seventy camels and two horses[73] in A.H. 2, they took with them 30,000 riders including 10,000 on horseback at Tabūk in A.H. 9.[74] Although the overall situation was not very impressive, the relative change over the former situation was but a promising development – a net increase in resources. The change that was gradually taking place can be judged in the context of the following stories:

Bukhārī reports that Ibn ‘Umar demonstrated the way of offering prayers in a single garment and then said: ‘We did not have even two-piece suits during the Prophet’s time.’ Bukhārī states that by this Ibn ‘Umar wanted to show how it was practically possible to offer prayers with a single piece of clothing.[75] The *Ḥadīth* not only reflects the state of poverty in the Prophet’s time but contrary to it, also the level of affluence of the people in the later period, who could not conceive of managing with a single dress. This story reflects the nature of change in the standard of living of the people. Another interesting report about the same Ibn ‘Umar appears in Ibn Sa‘d’s statement that he himself was very much affected by the opulence and sometimes covered himself with a mantle worth 500 dirhams.[76] This report becomes less interesting in the face of another report that Ibn ‘Abbās covered himself with a gown *(ḥulla)* worth 1,000 dirhams.[77] Another *Ḥadīth* transmitted by Bukhārī gives the two statements in simple words: Ibn Mas‘ūd said ‘Whenever the Prophet (peace be upon him) advised us to give *ṣadaqa,* some of us would earn one *mudd* of commodity after a full day’s labour; and now many of them own 100,000 dirhams.’[78] Ibn Mas‘ūd has, in his comment, given a very modest estimate of the riches of some of his contemporaries. The extent of their holdings can be gauged by some instances which have been given by historians about some of the well-known persons. That Caliph ‘Umar agreed to pay 10,000 dīnārs by way of dower to Kulthūm[79] could be suggestive of his regard for the Prophet’s grand-daughter but the point to note is that a rigid man in austerity, like ‘Umar, could arrange to have the amount paid from his own resources without compelling his sons to borrow from anybody.[80] Ibn Mas‘ūd and many other well-to-do Companions in Kūfa refused to accept their pensions and invested money in landed property. Ibn Mas‘ūd bequeathed 90,000 *mithqāl* in addition to slaves, goods, and livestock.[81] ‘Uthmān is known to have extensively allotted land to Muslims in the newly conquered territories. Its object was to utilize uncultivated land in order to add to the funds of the public exchequer and general welfare, and secondly, to rehabilitate Muslims in those areas which were absolutely under the practical control of the *dhimmīs*. This policy gave a fillip to agriculture and building activities. A group of Companions in ‘Uthmān’s time took to housing and estates, among them Zubayr b. al-‘Awwām who built his house in Baṣra which stood there till A.H. 333, and where the businessmen, the wealthy, and the people from the ships (sailors and travellers) stayed. He also built houses in Kūfa, Miṣr and Alexandria.

He bequeathed properties valued 50,000 dīnārs in addition to 1,000 horses, slaves, and other properties.[82] According to Ibn Sa'd, Zubayr bequeathed lands, eleven houses in Madina, two in Baṣra, one in Kūfa and yet he was indebted because he accepted others' deposits by way of loans and invested them in properties. Thus he became indebted for 2,200,000 dirhams. He bought the property of al-Ghāba for 170,000. His four wives received a share of 4,400,000 by way of inheritance which totalled 40 million dirhams.[83] During the same period Ṭalḥa b. 'Ubayd-Allāh also built a house in Kūfa. His daily income from Iraq alone was 1,000 dīnārs or even more. Ibn Sa'd puts his income at 1,000 dirhams, not dīnārs, and adds that he sold one of his lands for 700,000 dirhams, and bequeathed 4.4 million dirhams or, according to another narration, 30 million dirhams.[84] According to Mas'ūdī he also had a house in Madina.[85] 'Abd ar-Raḥmān b. 'Awf also built a house and extended it. He had 100 horses in his stable, 1,000 camels and 10,000 sheep. The value of a quarter of his wealth was 84,000 dīnārs.[86] Zayd b. Thābit bequeathed property of which the value of gold and silver alone amounted to 100,000 dīnārs in addition to properties and estates.[87] Ya'lā b. Munabbih bequeathed 500,000 dīnārs in addition to loans outstanding on others. The value of his property amounted to 300,000 dīnārs.[88] Zayd b. Thābit is stated to have spent 30,000 dīnārs on the construction of his house.[89] Sa'd paid 5,000 dirhams as *Zakāt* on his cash holdings alone. He bequeathed 250,000 dirhams.[90] Ḥakīm b. Ḥizām sold one of his houses for 60,000 to Mu'āwiya. He had the resources to volunteer the payment of half the amount of Zubayr's debt of 2,200,000 dirhams.[91] Mu'āwiya had lands in Ḥijāz which employed 4,000 workers.[92] Maslama b. 'Abd al-Malik was so resourceful as to have financed the construction of the canals which cost him 3 million from his personal resources.[93] The Governor of Iraq once wrote to 'Umar II that the people of Baṣra had acquired so much wealth as to make them arrogant.[94] At about the same time the officials of Egypt reported that their treasuries were so full that they could hold no more.[95]

The holding of large fortunes by any number of persons in any society does not necessarily represent the general condition of the society unless these fortunes are made to create their 'multiplier effect'. Hoarding of large treasures does not change the fate of even the owner. Investment in activities like housing has a very limited and temporary impact. But investment in productive activities like agriculture, industry, or trade effects a far-reaching change in the economic condition of the whole society. The bringing of new lands under cultivation would involve widespread mobilization in the different sectors of the economy: more employment, extension in the means of transport and communication, expansion of the market, increased demand and production of producer and consumer goods, increase in investment opportunities and in government revenues – all have direct and indirect impacts on the overall economic condition of the society. The institution of *Zakāt* had been effecting this change quite imperceptibly.[96] The later developments could not but accelerate that effect in a more pronounced way. And these activities must have brought a change in the general level of income of the common man too. As regards the price structure some reports suggest the situation in relation to general purchasing power.

Egypt, which some time before was the richest and the most valuable province of the Byzantine empire,[97] now formed part of the Muslim empire. But because of the difference in fertility the prices of food-grain also varied. Egypt had so far been supplying free bread to the Romans and then to the Byzantines.[98] But the Muslim conquest mitigated this burden of the whole empire to a few thousand conquerors who were stationed in Egypt. Grain was still exported from Egypt to Arabia, but reports suggest that it was not supplied free. For example, Ṭabarī gives an account of the digging of the old canal linking the Nile to the Red Sea in these words:

"Amr b. al-'Āṣ wrote to 'Umar: "If you wish that the prices in Madina may become like the prices in Egypt I shall get the old canal dug up again and the bridges reconstructed." 'Umar advised him to expedite. The people of Egypt tried to dissuade 'Amr from it and said: "Your *Kharāj* (land-tax) is sufficient *(zāj),* your Caliph is satisfied and if you complete the work it will break *Kharāj* (land-tax)." When 'Umar knew this he said: "Expedite it! If God deserts Egypt for the prosperity of Madina, let it be so." As a result, the prices in Madina also became like the prices in Egypt, and Egypt also became prosperous and such a situation never recurred until the blockade during 'Uthmān's time.'[99]

The above report suggests that the supply of grain was on trade terms, that is why it exercised a healthy effect on market prices in Madina and on general prosperity in Egypt. While increase in demand for grain in Egypt should have increased its prices and brought more income to the Egyptian peasant and hence his prosperity, the increase in supply in Madina should have brought down the food prices there and thus cut down the cost of living. That is why the report suggests that the prices in Madina became like those in Egypt and Egypt also became prosperous. Due to blockade, the regions which imported wheat from Egypt must have faced a shortage in supply, hence a rise in prices, as has been reported by al-Kindī.[100] But the reports about rising prices in Egypt first appear in A.H. 86–88 during the governorship of 'Abd-Allāh b. 'Abd al-Malik.[101] The impact of this rise in prices can be gauged by the prices of wheat in Egypt during this and the subsequent period.[102] The figures indicate that a man needed about seven dīnārs to buy his annual requirement of grain, although in a purely agricultural society a village man's needs for food and clothing are supplied from the farm.

Reports about the cost of living at some other centres also give a satisfactory picture. Ibn al-Faqīh reports about a man who went to Baṣra and on his return to Madina observed: 'It is the best place for the hungry, the traveller, and the destitute. A hungry man can eat rice bread with curry for two dirhams for a month . . . '[103] This is said to have been the situation during Ziyād's governorship of Iraq. It was an ideal situation of prosperity which could hardly continue for ever. 'Umar II's change in taxation policy, by allowing the farmers again to pay taxes in terms of commodity caused some increase in agricultural prices.[104] The trend seems to have continued later also but then the reason seems to have been different. According to Ṭabarī, Hishām's governor of Iraq, Khālid al-Qiṣrī used to say: 'You think I cause a rise in prices? Hell be upon the one who does it!' The fact was (Ṭabarī continues) that Hishām wrote to Khālid not to allow the sale of anybody else's grain unless his own commodities were sold out. As a result prices soared to such an extent that a *kaylaja* of grain was sold as high as a dirham.[105] It means that even in this period of expensive grain a man could get his grain requirements for about three dirhams a month – if grain was his principal diet. In spite of this level of prices Iṣṭakhrī insists that Armenia was the most prosperous and inexpensive region.[106] This might apply to his own period (third century) but anyhow helps us in assuming that in the early period the situation would not have been to the other extreme.

The above discussion gives some idea of the level of prices, level of incomes, the rate of investment, and the cost of living at certain places in Arabia, Iraq and Egypt. The data are supposed to be valid for towns but should not be applied to rural areas where the standard of living is different from that in the cities; prices of locally produced goods – necessities – are at a lower level, and the farmer's requirements of food and clothing are met from his own farm. As a result the rate of wages in these rural areas is also low.

D. POPULATION

The validity of examining the relationship of prices, incomes, and cost of living, to prosperity or the standard of living can be ascertained only when a study of the data of an important factor of change – population – is considered. A stationary population or a small population with a slow rate of growth and a fast rate of conquests would not affect the economic indicators nor would it disturb the routine functioning of the old institutions. It would simply enjoy the fruits of the labour of the previous owners and relish in their efforts crediting to itself its predecessors' achievements. It is, therefore, necessary to have some idea of the trends in population too.

The first century of expansion was the result of unceasing wars. As a result the rate of deaths on either side must have been high. It was quite a unique situation in Arabia that the fate of the entire Peninsula was decided with the loss of only a few hundred persons, although it involved some pitched battles too. But the situation outside Arabia was different. Over and above the loss of lives through wars was the toll of Muslim lives which civil war inflicted on them. Epidemics in and migrations from Muslim territories were also responsible for changes in the population pattern. It is said that the plague of 'Amawās took a toll of 25,000 lives.[107] Jabala b. Ayham is reported to have crossed into Byzantine territory along with his 30,000 tribesmen.[108] Many of the Jews and Christians who were expelled from Ḥijāz to prosper in Iraq and Syria might have crossed into other lands although their number should have been negligible. The flight of the Persians from their lands conquered by the Muslims must have been temporary but the Byzantines in Egypt took permanent shelter in Syria and a large number vacated Egypt.

In spite of these visible factors the overall situation presents an entirely different picture. While the dislocation of non-Muslim subjects in the conquered lands was a temporary phase, as soon as they reconciled to the new situation they engaged themselves in the normal routine of life. Polygamy, growing prosperity, increasing affluence, intoxication of conquests, and, above all, the social values of Islam were conducive to a rapid increase in the Muslim population. The more there were loses in the initial stages, the faster they multiplied which more than off-set their losses. It is interesting to have a rough idea about the rate of growth in respect of those persons whose number of children are recorded in books of history. The following table gives the names of such persons, and the number of their sons plus daughters. Single entries mean the number of sons only because the number of daughters is not recorded. Single entries in parenthesis mean a total of both or the gender not given. All the figures except three are taken from Ibn S'ad. For the remaining three, *cf.* Yaq., 3, 26; Mas'ūdī, 3, 290 and Kath., 8, 236–7.

Among these distinguished persons, the per-head average reproduction is about 18 or 12 + 6. In these figures the male population is not as significant as the female population which represents the Net Reproduction Rate. In this way the trend of productivity from the beginning to the end of the period is surely very promising.

(Continued on page 365)

Table 17. Reproduction Rate of Selected Persons

	Sons + Daughters
ʻAbd al-Muṭṭalib	12 + 6
ʻAlī	14 + 9
Zubayr	11 + 9
ʻAbd ar-Raḥmān b. ʻAwf	18 + 8
Saʻd b. Waqqāṣ	16 + 18
Ṭalḥa b. ʻAbd-Allāh	9 + 4
ʻUmar b. al-Khaṭṭāb	8 + 5
Saʻīd b. Zayd	13 + 14
Ḥakam (Marwān's father)	20 + 8
Saʻīd b. al-ʻĀs	20 + 21
Marwān b. al-Ḥakam	(13)
ʻAbd-Allāh b. ʻĀmir	12 + 6
ʻAbd ar-Raḥmān b. Zayd	10 + 6
Ibrāhīm b. ʻAbd ar-Raḥmān	10 + 9
Walīd b. ʻUbāda	10 + 2
Saʻid b. Saʻd b. ʻUbāda	10 + 5
Muḥammad b. Ḥanafiyya	12 + 2
ʻUmar b. Saʻd b. Waqqāṣ	11 + 10
ʻUrwa b. Zubayr	9 + 9
Mundhir b. Zubayr	11 + 2
Muṣʻab b. Zubayr	12 + 2
Jaʻfar b. Zubayr	9 + 15
Khālid b. Zubayr	8 + 6
ʻAmr b. Zubayr	2 + 3
ʻUbayda b. Zubayr	1 + 1
Ḥamza b. Zubayr	(1)
ʻUbayd Allāh b. ʻAbd-Allāh b. ʻUmar	11 + 5
ʻAbd al-Malik b. Marwān	16 + 2
ʻAlī b. ʻĀbd-Allāh b. ʻAbbās	21 + 15
Yazīd b. Muʻāwiya	15 + 5
ʻUmar b. Saʻd b. Muʻādh	9 + 3
Walīd	16
Sulaymān	10
ʻUmar II	9
Yazīd b. ʻAbd al-Malik	10
Hishām	10
Walīd b. Yazīd	14
Total 37	442 + 211 + (14)

or per-head average 12 + 6.

The first census of the Muslims was perhaps conducted when the Prophet (peace be upon him) was still at Makka. According to Ḥudhayfa, the number of Muslims at that time was about 1,500 while Bukhārī puts the figure at 500 and Abū Mu'āwiya between six and seven hundred.[109] The number of Muslims, when the Prophet (peace be upon him) migrated to Madina, cannot definitely be ascertained because the number of persons who really embraced Islam is unknown. A general remark that most of the *Anṣār* (Helpers) had come into the fold of Islam does not help us because the total number of *Anṣār* is also not known. But if we suppose that the number of *Anṣār* in the expedition against Makka was two-thirds of their total fighting strength, this would put the total number of fighters at about 6,500 because the expedition included 4,000 *Anṣār*.[110] Thus even without allowing for the very old, invalid, and the hypocrites who backed out, the total number of males and females of all ages comes to about 18,000 persons.[111] This is over and above the number of the Jewish population whose strength might be as follows:

1.	Banū Qaynuqā'	700[112]	exiled
2.	Banū Naḍīr between 1,000–1,500 or	1,200[113]	exiled
3.	Banū Qurayẓa	1,600–1,750[114]	(killed, 600–700) (enslaved 1,000)
	Total about	3,500	

The number of Emigrants *(Muhājirūn)* may also be worked out like those of the *Anṣār* but allowing for a lesser number of sitters. This would put the total number of Emigrants at about 2,500, because their number in the Makkan expedition was 700.[115] Thus the figures of the Madinan population come to a little more than 20,000 without the Jewish population. The rate of increase in population can be conjectured in view of the report that the population of Najrānites which was 25–30,000 in A.H. 8 rose to 40,000 within ten years.[116]

Khaybar, according to Wāqidī's sources, had 10,000[117] fighters. But if the report that under the terms of surrender the Muslims took over 100 coats-of-mail, 400 swords, 1,000 lances and 500 bows, is correct and represents the entire belongings of the Jewish fighters at Khaybar and does not pertain to some particular fortress or group, the figure of 10,000 is doubtful. The terms of the treaty with the people of Khaybar included surrender of all their arms. Would the 10,000 fighters possess only 400 swords? Even if lances and bows are calculated at one to each the total number comes to 2,000 fighters. With what arms did the other fighters take part in the war? It may be said that the agreement to surrender their arms was made with those Jews who took part in the war, but not with those who surrendered without confrontation. But even that would not cover up the fallacy of the figure because the strength of those who thought it safe to come to terms without a fight must have been less than the strength of those who dashed out for confrontation. Thus if the number of the latter was at the most 1,900, that of the former could not have been more than 1,500 or so. It seems that Wāqidī perhaps based his report on the statement of a disgusted Jew from Banū Naḍīr who, during their exile, proudly exaggerated the strength of the Khaybarites[118] and became vindictive. There is a possibility that the total population of Khaybar might have been 10,000, out of which about 1,900 + 1,500 or so might have been fighters, while the disgusted Jew perhaps used his eloquence but not mathematics.

As regards the number of Jews and Christians in other parts of Arabia some incomplete information can be had with reference to the amount of poll-tax levied on them. For example, the people of Najrān, mostly Christians, were communally required to pay their poll-tax in terms of gowns *(ḥulla)* but there are reasons to believe that their number was also kept in mind while assessing poll-tax. Two thousand gowns were required annually, each valued at one *ūqiyya* which equalled 4 dīnārs. Generally the Prophet (peace be upon him) levied one dīnār per head. With this hypothesis the poll-tax might have been calculated on 8,000 heads. Thus the total tax-paying community can be conjectured[119] at between 25,000 and 30,000. This seems to be a plausible figure in view of the reports that at the time Caliph 'Umar expelled them from Arabia about ten years after this agreement their total strength was 40,000.[120] The tax-paying population of Ayla, Adhruḥ, and Jarba' was 300, 100 and 100 respectively.[121] Thus the total population of each community, according to the same formula, comes to about 1,000, 300 and 300 respectively. The Christians, Jews and Magians in Yemen, Ḥimyar, Hajar, Baḥrayn, 'Umān, Maqnā', Duma al-Jandal, Taymā', Tabāla, and Jurash were also subjected to tax, but the figures of total levy on them are not given, thus making it impossible to conjecture.[122] It can, however, be observed that Yemen, Ḥimyar, Hajar, 'Umān, and Baḥrayn had a substantial number of these non-Muslims in the total population. Other places were probably just like villages, with a population not exceeding three figures.

At the time of the conquest of Ḥīra (A.H. 12) in Iraq the population of the town was about 20,000[123] while the total taxable population of Iraq west of Madā'in was 550,000 and across Madā'in about 35,000.[124] Thus the total population was around 1,800,000 persons. Kūfa, Baṣra, and Wāṣit were founded by Muslims after the conquest of Iraq. In the beginning Kūfa had a population of 20,000 persons; 12,000 from Yemen and 8,000 from Nazār.[125] Baṣra was originally founded by 'Utba and Muslims from different parts of Arabia inhabited seven different localities,[126] each marked for a tribe. But by the time of governor Ziyād the population of Kūfa had swelled to 60,000 and that of Baṣra to 80,000 fighters while the number of their family members stood at 80,000 and 120,000 respectively.[127] The number of civil servants, traders and craftsmen is not included. By the time of governor 'Ubayd-Allāh b. Ziyād the fighting strength of Kūfa had increased to 80,000.[128] This was over and above the large number of 140,000 civil servants.[129] These figures also do not account for those who were not working under the government.

In the early stages the increase in the Muslim population outside Arabia was the result of migration and mobilization, but later on one of the factors responsible was the birth rate. The rulers perhaps wanted to maintain a politically expedient balance between different political and tribal groups. Absolute increase in population was also not treated as desirable socially and economically. The rapid increase in population was more pronounced in Kūfa and Baṣra which resulted in the mobilization of a large number of fighters from these centres. Mu'āwiya shifted Sabātija and Zaṭ from Baṣra to Syria[130] while Sulaymān shifted 40,000 fighters from Baṣra and 7,000 from Kūfa to Khurāsān.[131] Earlier mobilization was also effected on strategic and political grounds. Caliph 'Alī, for example, despatched a number of pensioner Muslims to Azdabīl.[132]

The tendency to mobilize the whole or a part of the population for strategic or political reasons is mainly discernible in Syria throughout the period. Abū 'Ubayda had the Muslims in Syria transferred to Bālis (Polis).[133] Mu'āwiya, during 'Uthmān's reign, sent to Cyprus 12,000 pension receivers *(ahl-ad-dīwān)* and the people of Ba'labak to rehabilitate a city.[134] It is said that Caliph 'Uthmān encouraged Muslims to dwell in the border areas of Syria.[135] In A.H. 42 Mu'āwiya transferred the Persians of Antioch, Ba'labak and Emessa to the border areas of Jordan, Ṣūr and 'Akkā[136] while the cavalries at Kūfa, Baṣra, Ba'labak and Emessa were transferred to Antioch.[137] Emessa during Marwān's time had 20,000 Muslims, in addition to non-Muslims.[138] In A.H. 49 Mu'āwiya called for the craftsmen and carpenters and settled them in border areas.[139] 'Abd al-Malik also sent people to dwell in 'Asqalān.[140] While Caliph 'Umar transferred 4,000 persons of Banū Ayād from the Byzantine borders to Syria and Mesopotamia,[141] Hishām transferred 24,000 Syrians to the newly-founded city of Madīnat al-Bāb.[142] When the Muslims occupied Ṭarinda in A.H. 83, they began to settle there, but 'Umar II, due to a threat of enemy attack got it vacated.[143]

It will be seen that much of this mobilization was effected by a large number of Muslims. Such a large-scale exodus of Muslims should have left Arabia with a sparse population and almost deserted, but there are no indications to suggest such a situation. It is reported by some historians that most of the Helpers *(Anṣār)* had already moved out of Madina and settled in different Muslim cities outside Arabia, but along with it the population of Madina was also increasing. A general increase in the price of landed properties and estates in Ḥijāz also confirms the theory that the region was not relieved of the pressure of population which, in Madina, is reported to have begun in Caliph 'Umar's reign.[144]

Egypt was perhaps the country where the Arabs did not rush to settle as they did in the north and the east. One reason might be that it was already densely populated. The figures of the population of Egypt as given by historians are appalling. There is no doubt that constant wars between the Byzantine and Persian empires forced the people to leave Iraq, Syria and Palestine – the battlefield of the two powers – and to move towards a safer place like Egypt. Throughout the whole of the sixth century in particular the pressure of the Persians on the eastern frontiers of the Roman empire had been steadily increasing and it was beginning to be seriously felt in Egypt when Hiraclius was recognized as Emperor. As the Persian armies advanced, numerous fugitives from Syria and Palestine took refuge in Egypt; and when the enemy invaded the Delta, the refugees were driven into Alexandria. The city was thus crowded with a great multitude of people.[145]

In spite of this growth of population in Egypt generally and in Alexandria in particular, the figures given by historians are intriguing. It has already been argued that between 4 and 5 million would be a reasonable estimate of the population for the whole of Egypt[146] at the time of the Arab conquest.

The number of Muslims in Egypt at the time of the conquest was about 12,300.[147] By Mu'āwiya's time the number of Muslim fighters rose to about 27,000[148] while there are stated to be 40,000 names in pension registers.[149] It suggests that by this time the Muslims were settling permanently in Egypt along with their families. At the same time the number of Muslim soldiers in Ifrīqiyya who were deployed in Caliph 'Uthmān's time stood at 20,000.[150] In the later period every newly-appointed governor brought with him a large contingent of his clan and rehabilitated them. In A.H. 100 the police chief Ḥārith arrived with 5,000 persons.[151] In A.H. 109 during Hishām's reign governor Walīd called for 3,000 Qisrites[152] and rehabilitated them permanently. When Ḥawthara was made governor of Egypt in A.H. 128 he arrived with a company of 7,000 persons.[153]

These large-scale mobilizations of population from one inhabited place to a less inhabited place, without any sign of relief in the pressure of the total number, reflects the trend of abnormal increase in the population and provides a retrospect for the relative study of the trends in prices, cost of living and the standard of living of the people.

Notes and References

1. For a full discussion on exemption limits, etc., see Chapter 1.

2. For weights and measures, etc., see Appendix.

3. Tab., 1, 2413; Kh., 26. For a full discussion refer to Chapter 10 A.

4. Qut., 292.

5. I.A.H. (U), 58. This comes to five dīnārs per family per month or 600 dirhams per annum.

6. I.F., 90.

7. Kh., 92.

8. Waq., 635.

9. *Ibid.*

10. See p. 231

11. Balādhurī: *Ansāb al-Ashrāf,* ed. Ahlwardt, p. 34. *Cf.* S.A.E., 126 n.

12. Bal., 446.

13. Waq., 635.

14. The evidence of Pap. IV, 315 n. 128 suggests that even in Egypt the price of barley was half the price of wheat.

15. See Table 5, p. 216.

16. Ṣaḥīḥ Muslim, 7, 62.

17. Kh., 92.

18. Ibn Ḥabān; *cf.* Yūsuf al-Qarḍāwī, *al-Ḥalāl wa'l-Ḥarām, fi'l-Islām,* Beirut, 1967, p. 120. This is in contrast with ten dirhams for a chicken in Makka in A.H. 73 when local prices shot up due to floods. (Ahmad b. 'Alī al-Fāsī: *Shifā' al-gharām bi Akhbār balad al-ḥarām,* Makka, 1956), p. 269.

19. Waq., 635.

20. *Ibid.*

21. Jahs., 19.

22. Kath., 8, 3.

23. See above.

24. Kh. 17 (in Iraq); Kath., 8, 3 (perhaps in Iraq); Waq., 635; Sad., III, 1, 18; for 6 1/2 dirham see Bal., Ansab, Mss. 438a, *cf.* S.A.E., 129.

25. Waq., 635; Sad., III, 1, 132; Waq., 6, 35; Sad., 5, 39, III, 1, 92; IV, 1, 127; V, 161; Dh. (Tar), 2, 190.

26. Kath., 8, 3 (perhaps in Iraq)

27. Kh., 92; Sad., IV, 1, 45.

28. Jahs., 19.

29. See *supra*, ref. 17, 18.

30. Waq., 36, 400, 687; Tir., 6, 157, 162; Sad., 1, 1, 153.

31. Bukh. (Buyū'), 52.

32. Bukh. (Ḥudūd), 26.

33. Waq., 909.

34. Sad., 4, 2, 80.

35. Waq., 688 (calculated average), Sad., III, 1, 132 (with 15 *wasqs* of yield per crop), Bukh. (Khums), 37 (a plot of Zubayr's land was sold for 1,600,000 after his death. *Ibid.*

36. Bukh. (Buyū'), 52.

37. Sad., IV, 1, 49.

38. Mus., 7, 83; Bukh. (Buyū'), 116; Sad., III, 1, 27; Tab., 2, 1470; Bukh. (Kaffārat al-Aymān), 8; Kath., 9, 4.

39. Waq., 523–4 (calculated average: 2 female slaves and 6 children sold for 1,500 dirhams; one female slave and 2 children for 450 dirhams); I.A.H. (M), 58, 193; I.A.H., 80.

40. Pap. IV., Introduction, p. XXXVIII.

41. According to al-Kindī, the period of 'Abd-Allāh's governorship (A.H. 86 onwards) witnessed for the first time an unprecedented rise in prices. People alleged him to be corrupt and called him *mukayyis;* Kindi, p. 59.

42. Bukh. (Khums), 37.

43. Dh. (Tar), 2, 289.

44. Bal., 347.

45. Kath., 9, 4.

46. A.U., 651.

47. Sira, 2, 325.

48. Sti., 79.

49. *Ibid.*

50. Sad., III, 1, 197.

51. M.B.Y., 98–9.

52. A.U., 668–9.

53. I.A.H., 46.

54. Yaq., 2, 223.

55. Yaq., 2, 141.

56. Sad., III, 1, 220–1.

57. *Cf.* A.N., 141.

58. Bal., 338; Tab., 1, 2388.

59. Yaq., 2, 223.

60. Kath., 9, 22; Mas., 3, 283.

61. Kindi, 317. *Cf.* S.A.E., 118–19.

62. I.A.H. (M), 241.

63. Jahs., 42.

64. Qut., 35.

65. Kindi, 317.

66. *Ibid.,* also Dh. (Ibar), 97.

67. Bal., Ansāb, *op. cit.,* 5, 177; *cf.* S.A.E., 118.

68. Kath., 9, 51. *Ibid.,* S.A.E.

69. Pap. IV., Introduction, p. XXXVIII.

70. I.A.H. (U), 46.

71. For a full discussion see Chapter 10 A, Note on Pensions.

72. Waq., 957; Tab., 1, 1684.

73. Sad., II, 1, 7.

74. Sad., II, 1, 27.

75. Bukh. (Ṣalāt), 4.

76. IV, 1, 127.

77. Kath., 8, 306.

78. Bukh. (Zakāt), 21.

79. Yaq., 2, 139.

80. It is stated that he bequeathed a loan of 80,000 dirhams but this amount was also paid by his sons without borrowing. Sad., III, 1, 260.

81. M.B.Y., 65.

82. Mas., 3, 76.

83. III, 1, 76.

84. III, 1, 157, 158.

85. Mas., 3, 77.

86. *Ibid.* But according to Sad., III, 1, 96, he had 3,000 sheep and also bequeathed the estate in al-Juraf which had an irrigation system worked by 20 camels. The one-eighth portion of his wealth came to 80,000 dirhams.

87. *Ibid.*

88. *Ibid.*

89. I.F., 109.

90. Sad., III, 1, 105.

91. Dh. (Ibar), 60.

92. *Cf.* Abu 'n-Naṣr, *op. cit.,* 147.

93. Qud., 241.

94. Sad., 5, 282.

95. I.A.H. (M), 132.

96. See Chapter 6.

97. Ostro., 103.

98. J.M.H., 4, II, 86.

99. Tab., 1, 2577.

100. Kindi, 14.

101. Kindi, 59.

102. See Table 16.

103. I.F., 90.

104. Kh., 76.

105. Tab., 2, 1658. Kaylajā = gallon or 1 1/2 Sā'. For weights see Appendix.

106. Ist., 181. On p. 191 he has cited the price of goats as 2 dirhams each and honey sometimes at 2 to 3 *munn* per dirham.

107. Bal., 140.

108. Bal., 142; Yaq., 2, 137.

109. Bukh. (al-Khurūj fī Ramaḍān), 96.

110. Waq., 800.

111. For the formula of calculation see note 119 below.

112. Tab., 1, 1361; A.U., 348 puts the figure at 400, Ibn Hisham (Sira, 2, 171) between 600–900.

113. According to Sad., II, 1, 41, they rode 600 camels. The average load per camel has been supposed at 2 persons including children.

114. Sad., II, 1, 34 (gives the figure perhaps of those killed). Waq., 517, 518, 523; Sira, 2, 171.

115. Waq., 800.

116. Tab., 1, 1987.

117. Waq., 671.

118. Waq., 373.

119. The figures are computed from the following data: one twelfth of mankind above sixty, one third below 16, the proportion of men to women = 17:16 (*Recherches sur la population de la France,* pp. 71–2. *Cf.* Gibbons, 5, 458 fn. 152). (The same formula has been applied in conjectures, everywhere.)

120. Bal., 78.

121. For details see Table 4, pp. 205–6.

122. Collections from Baḥrayn also include the amount of *Zakāt* and thus it has become impossible to conjecture the relative strength of the different communities.

123. Refer to Chapter 7, p. 210. Six thousand assessees multiplied by three to compute the total number of heads.

124. Tab., 1, 2467.

125. Bal., 276.

126. Bal., 337.

127. Bal., 344–5.

128. Tab., 2, 433. It would perhaps be due to this total number of fighters that some people from Kūfa are stated to have written to Ḥusayn b. ʻAlī that 100,000 persons were ready to take an oath of allegiance to him (I.F., 173).

129. *Ibid.*

130. Bal., 166.

131. *Ibid.*

132. Bal., 324.

133. Bal., 155.

134. Bal., 158.

135. Bal., 124, 153.

136. Bal., 153.

137. *Ibid.*

138. Agh., 6, 50.

139. Bal., 124.

140. Bal., 150.

141. Khal., 2, 108 supp.

142. Bal., 209.

143. Bal., 189.

144. Sad., IV, 1, 13.

145. J.G.M., 113–14.

146. See p. 244.

147. Kindi, 9. The remainder, out of a total of 15,500, are reported killed in wars.

148. I.A.H. (M), 192.

149. Maq. (Kh.), 1, 79.

150. I.A.H. (M), 184.

151. Kindi, 68.

152. Kindi, 76–7.

153. *Ibid.*, 88.

Appendix

Weights and Measures

Ardabb (Artaba)	= 24 Ṣā‘s
Dīnār	= 4.25 Grams of gold
Dirham	= 3.98 Grams of silver
Farsakh	= 3 miles
Jarīb	= Artaba = 4 Qafīzs, also 60 yards
Mithqāl	= 22 carats (Egypt, 24 carats)
Mudd (Modius)	= 1 1/3 Riṭls
Modi (Mudī)	= 40 Riṭls (1/3 artaba)
Qafīz	= 1/4 Artaba = 6 Ṣā‘s
Qīrāṭ	= carat (1/22 Mithqāl)
Qisṭ	= 8 Riṭls = 1/2 Sā‘
Riṭl (Litre)	= 12 Ūqiyyas = 90 Mithqāl
Ṣā‘	= 5 1/3 Riṭls (Iraq, 8 Riṭls)
Ūqiyya	= 40 dirhams
Wasq	= 60 Ṣā‘s; 190 kilogram

Bibliography

For the purposes of alphabetical order of the Bibliography the word 'al-' in its different forms is disregarded:

Abū Dā'ūd, Sulaymān b. al-Ash'ath: *Sunan,* Cairo, 1950.

——: With Urdu translation, pub. Muhammad Said & Sons, Karachi, n.d.

Abu'l-Faraj Qudāma b. Jā'far al-Kātib al-Baghdādī: *Kitāb al-Kharāj wa Ṣan'at al-Kitāba,* Scripts, Book V. ed. De Goeje, Brill, 1889, appended with Ibn Khurdādhbih's *K-al-Masālik.*

Abū Ṣāliḥ: *Churches and Monasteries of Egypt,* ed. Evetts and Butler, Oxford, 1895.

Abū 'Ubayd Qāsim b. Sallām al-Harawī: *Kitāb al-Amwāl,* Cairo, 1935.

Abū Yūsuf Ya'qūb b. Ibrāhīm: *Kitāb al-Kharāj,* Cairo, 1302.

Aftīshiūs (Eutychii) called Sa'īd b. Biṭrīq: *Kitāb-at-Ta'rīkh* (Scriptores Arabici Seria Tertia-Tomus VI–VII) ed. L. Cheikho, etc., Beirut, 1905, 1909.

Agapius (Mahboub) de Menbidg: *Kitāb al-'Unwān,* Histoire Universelle, ed. and tr. Alexendre Vasiliev, Part II, (Patrologia Orientalis, Vol. 8), Paris, 1912.

Aghnides, Nicholas P.: *Mohammedan Theories of Finance,* New York, 1916.

Aḥmad Shalabī: *as-Siyāsa wa 'l-Iqtiṣād fi't-Tafkīr al-Islāmī,* Cairo, 1964.

al-Aṣbahānī, Abu'l-Faraj 'Alī b. Ḥusayn: *Kitāb al-Aghānī,* n.p., n.d.

al-Balạdhurī, Abu'l-Ḥasan: *Futūḥ al-Buldān,* al-Azhar Press, 1932.

al-Bayḍāwī, Nāṣiruddīn Abū Sa'īd 'Abd-Allāh ibn 'Umar: *Anwār at-Tanzīl wa asrār at-Ta'wīl,* ed. H.O. Fleicher, Lipsiae, 1846–48.

al-Bukhārī, Muḥammad b. Ismā'īl: *Ṣaḥīḥ* (with Urdu trans.), Lahore, 1962.

——: With Urdu translation, pub. Muḥammad Sa'īd & Sons, Karachi, n.d.

Butler, Alfred J.: *The Arab Conquest of Egypt and the Last Thirty Years of the Roman Dominion,* Oxford, 1902.

Dennett, Daniel C. Jr.: *Conversion and the Poll-Tax in Early Islam,* Cambridge, 1950.

Adh-Dhahabī, Shams-ad-Dīn Muḥammad b. Aḥmad b. ʻUthmān: *Ta'rīkh al-Islām wa Ṭabaqāt al-Mashāhīr wa'l-A'lām,* Cairo, 1368 A.H.

——: *al-ʻIbar fī Khabari man Ghabar,* Kuwait, 1960.

Ḍiyā' ad-Dīn ar-Ra'īs: *al-Kharāj wa'n-Nuẓum al-Māliyya li'd-Dawlat al-Islāmiyya,* Cairo, 1969.

ad-Dīnawarī, Abū Muḥammad ʻAbd-Allāh b. Muslim b. Qutayba: *Kitāb ʻUyūn al-Akhbār,* Berlin, 1900.

Elali, Saleh Ahmad: *Early History of Basrah,* An abstract of a Thesis for the Degree of Ph.D., (Typescript), Oxford University, 1948.

Encyclopaedia of Islam, New edition.

Eutychius, Patriarch Saʻīd, *see* Aftishius.

Fischel, Walter J.: *Jews in the Economic and Political Life of Medieval Islam,* New York, 1969.

Gibbon, Edward: *The History of the Decline and Fall of the Roman Empire,* Pts. I–VII, London, 1920–1925.

Greek Papyri in the British Museum, Vol. IV. The Aphrodito Papyri, ed. H.I. Bell, London, 1910.

Histoire Nestoriennie (Chronique de Seert), Pt. II. tr. Mgr. Addai Scher, (Patrologia Orientalis, Vol. 13), Paris, 1918.

Ibn ʻAbd al-Ḥakam, Abū Muḥammad ʻAbd-Allāh: *Sīra ʻUmar b. ʻAbd al-ʻAzīz,* Damascus, 1966.

Ibn ʻAbd al-Ḥakam, Abu'l-Qāsim ʻAbd ar-Raḥm.in: *Futūḥ Miṣr wa Akhbāruhā,* Baghdad, 1920.

Ibn ʻAbd al-Ḥakam: *Conquete de l'Afrique du North et de l'Espangne* (futūḥ Ifrīqiyya wa'l-Andalus) Texte Arabe et traduction Fradcaise Par Albert Gateau, Alger, 1947.

Ibn al-ʻArabī, Abū Bakr Muḥammad b. ʻAbd-Allāh: *Aḥkām al-Qur'ān,* ed. Alī Muḥammad al-Bajāwī, n.p., 1958–59.

Ibn al-Athīr: *Kitāb al-Kāmil fi't-Ta'rīkh,* Leiden, Vol. III, 1868, Vol. IV, 1869.

Ibn al-Balkhī: *The Farsnama,* ed. G. Le Strange and R.A. Nicholson, Cambridge, 1921.

Ibn al-Faqīh, Abū Bakr Aḥmad b. Muḥammad al-Hamadhānī: *Kitāb al-Buldān,* Leiden, 1885.

Ibn Ḥawqal, Abu'l-Qāsim: *Kitāb al-Masālik wa'l-Mamālik,* Leiden, 1873.

Ibn Hishām, Abū Muḥammad 'Abd al-Malik: *Sīraṭ an-Nabī,* Cairo, 1346, A.H.

Ibn Kathīr, Abu'l-Fidā' al-Ḥāfiẓ: *al-Bidāya wa'n-Nihāya,* Beirut, 1966.

Ibn Khaldūn, 'Abd ar-Raḥmān b. Muḥammad: *al-'Ibar wa dīwān al-Mubtada' wa'l-Khabar,* pts. 2 and 3 with supplements, Cairo, 1384.

——: *Muqaddima* (Prolegomena), Cairo, A.H. 1322 (1904).

Ibn Khurdādhbih, Abu'l-Qāsim 'Ubaidullāh b. 'Abd-Allāh: *Kitāb al-Masālik wa'l-Mamālik,* pt. VI, ed. M.J. De Goeje, Leiden, 1889.

Ibn Māja Abū 'Abd-Allāh Muḥammad b. Yazīd al-Qazwīnī: *Sunan,* Cairo, 1952.

——: With Urdu translation, pub. Muhammad Said & Sons, Karachi, 1380 A.H.

Ibn Rustah, Abū 'Alī Aḥmad b. 'Umar: *Kitāb al-A'lāq an-Nafīsa,* Leiden, 1891.

Ibn Sa'd, az-Zuhrī, *aṭ-Ṭabaqāt al-Kubrā,* ed. Sachau, Leiden.

Ibn Ṭayfūr, Abu'l-Faḍl Aḥmad b. Ṭāhir al-Kātib: *Kitāb Baghdād,* n.p., 1949.

al-Iṣṭakhrī, Abū Isḥāq Ibrāhīm b. Muḥammad al-Fārisī: *Masālik al-Mamālik,* ed. M.J. De Goeje, Leiden, 1870.

al-Jahshiyārī, Abū 'Abd-Allāh Muḥammad b. 'Abdūs: *Kitāb al-Wuzarā' wa'l-Kuttāb,* Cairo, 1938.

Al-Jaṣṣāṣ, Abū Bakr Aḥmad b. 'Alī ar-Rāzī: *Aḥkām al-Qur'ān,* Vols. I to III, Cairo, 1347 A.H., 1928 A.D.

Johnson, A.C. and West, L.C.: *Byzantine Egypt, Economic Studies,* Princeton, 1949.

Johnson, Allen Chester: *Egypt and the Roman Empire,* University of Michigan Press, 1951.

Khalīfa b. Khayyāṭ al-'Usfurī: *Ta'rīkh,* Part I, ed. Suhayl Zakkār, Irshād al-Qawmī, 1967. Part II, ed. Akram Ḍiyā' al-'Umrī, Najaf, 1967.

al-Kharbūṭlī, Alī Ḥasanī: *Ta'rīkh al-'Irāq fī ẓill al-Ḥukm al-Umawī,* Cairo, 1959.

al-Kindī, Abū 'Umar Muḥammad b. Yūsuf al-Miṣrī: *Kitāb al-Wulāt wa Kitāb al-Quḍāt,* Beirut, 1908.

Lane-Poole, Stanley, ed.: *Coins and Medals,* London, 1892.

———: *A History of Egypt,* Part VI, London, 1901.

Le Strange, Guy: *Palestine under the Muslims,* Beirut, 1965.

Løkkegaard, Frede: *Islamic Taxation in the Classic Period (with special reference to the circumstances in Iraq),* Copenhagen, 1950.

al-Maqrīzī, Aḥmad b. 'Alī: *Kitāb al-Mawā'iẓ wa'l-I'tibār bi Dhikr al-Khiṭaṭ wa'l-Āthār,* n.p., n.d.

———: *an-Nuqūd al-Islāmiyya al-Musammā bi Shudhūr al-'Uqūd fī dhikr an-Nuqūd,* Najaf, 1967.

———: *Imtā' al-Asmā',* Cairo, 1941.

Ma'rūf, Nājī: *'Uruba al-Mudun al-Islāmiyya,* Baghdad, 1964.

al-Mas'ūdī, 'Alī b. al-Ḥusayn: *Murūj adh-Dhahab wa Ma'ādin al-Jawhar,* Beirut, 1966.

Milne, J. Grafton: *A History of Egypt,* Vol. V, London, 1898.

Muḥammad b. Yaḥyā b. Abī Bakr: *at-Tamhīd wa'l-Bayān fī maqtal ash-Shahīd 'Uthmān,* Beirut, 1964.

al-Muqaddasī, Shams ad-Dīn Abū 'Abd-Allāh Muḥammad b. Aḥmad b. Abī Bakr, al-Bishārī: *Aḥsan at-Taqaāsīm fī Ma'rifat-al-Aqalīm,* Leiden, 1877.

Muslim b. Ḥajjāj: *Ṣaḥīḥ,* with commentary by an-Nawawī, al-Azhar, 1929.

———: With Urdu translation, pub. Maktaba Saudia, Karachi, n.d.

an-Naqshabandī, Naṣīr as-Sāyyid Maḥmūd: *ad-Dīnār al-Islāmī fi'l-Mutḥaf al-'Irāqī,* Baghdad, 1953.

Nasā'ī: *Sunan,* with commentary by Jalāl ad-Dīn as-Suyūṭī and marginal notes by as-Sindī, al-Azhar, Cairo, n.d.

———: With Urdu translation, pub. Hamid & Co., Lahore, n.d.

Ostrogorsky, George: *History of Byzantine State,* Eng. Tr., Joan Hussey, Oxford, 1956.

Qurṭubī, Muḥammad b. Aḥmad al-Anṣārī: *al-Jami' li-aḥkām al-Qur'ān,* Cairo, 1935–1947.

ar-Rāwī, Thābit Ismā'īl: *al-'Irāq fi'l-'Aṣr al-Umawī,* Baghdad, 1965.

Severus Ben el-Moqaffa': *Historia Patiarcharum Alexandrinorum* (Scriptores Arabici Textus Series Tertia, Tomus IX), ed. Chr. Fred. Seybold, Paris, 1904.

ash-Shāfi'ī, Muḥammad b. Idrīs: *Musnad,* ed. Zāhid al-Kawtharī, Cairo, 1951.

ash-Shayyāl Jamāl ad-Dīn: *Ta'rīkh Miṣr al-Islāmiyya,* Alexandria, 1968.

as-Suyūṭī, Jalāl ad-Dīn: *History of the Caliphs,* Eng. tr., H.S. Jarrett, Amsterdam Oriental Press, 1970.

Sykes, Sir Percy: *A History of Persia,* London, 1921.

Ṭabarī Abū Ja'far Muḥammad b. Jarīr: *Ta'rīkh ar-Rusul wa'l-Mulūk,* Leiden, 1893.

——: *Tafsīr,* Cairo, 1954–60.

at-Tirmidhī, Muḥammad b. 'Īsā: *Ṣaḥīḥ* (with commentary by Ibn al-'Arabī), Cairo, 1931–34.

——: With Urdu translation, pub. Lucknow, Vol.I 1891 A.H., Vol.II 1894 A.D.

'Umar Abū'n-Naṣr: *'Umar b. al-Khaṭṭāb,* Beirut, 1935.

al-Wāqidī, Muḥammad b. 'Umar b. Wāqid: *Kitāb al-Maghāzī,* ed. Marsden Jones, London, 1966.

Watt, W. Montgomery: *Muhammad at Medina,* Oxford, 1956.

——: *Muhammad, Prophet and Statesman,* Oxford University Press, 1961.

Wellhausen, J.: *The Arab Kingdom and its Fall,* tr. Margaret Graham Weir, Beirut, 1963.

Yaḥyā b. Ādam al-Qurashī: *Kitāb al-Kharāj,* ed. and tr. A. Ben Shemesh, Leiden, 1958.

al-Ya'qūbī, Aḥmad b. Abī Ya'qūb b. Wāḍiḥ al-Kātib: *Ta'rīkh,* Najaf, 1964.

——: *Kitāb al-Buldān,* Leiden, 1891.

al-Yasū'ī, Louis Cheikho: *Shu'arā' an-Naṣrāniyya qabl al-Islām,* Beirut, 1967.

——: *an-Naṣrāniyya wa Adabuhā baina 'Arab al-Jāhiliyya,* Vol. I, Beirut, 1912, Vol. II, Beirut, 1923.

Index

GENERAL

Index

PERSONS AND PLACES

306, 309, 311, 312, 313, 314, 315, 317, 319, 321, 332, 334, 335, 343, 344, 353, 354, 356, 360, 361, 362, 363, 368
Emessa, 107, 222, 224, 225, 367
Euphrates, 185, 211, 226, 227, 331

Fadak, 112, 121, 123, 124, 126, 141, 142, 143, 149, 152, 199, 205, 311
Faḍl b. 'Abbās, 175
Faḥl, 222
Faqīrayn, 120
Al-Faramā' (see Pelusium), 231
Fārs, 258, 261, 267, 292
Fazāra, 170
Fūrāt b. Ḥayyān, 120

Gharāba, 120
Ghassān, 185, 210
Ghaṭafān, 153, 170
Ghifār, 170
Ghūra, 120
Ghūrak, 263, 264, 265
Al-Ghūṭa, 123

Ḥabal, 120
Ḥaḍramawt, 120, 170, 180, 190
Hajar, 206, 366
Ḥajjāj, 113, 127, 139, 184, 185, 203, 208, 212, 218, 219, 220, 260, 261, 262, 294, 304, 305, 306, 313, 314, 317, 319, 320, 334, 343, 344, 356
Ḥakam b. 'Iwāna, 149, 317
Hamadhān, 267
Ḥamza b. Nu'mān, 120, 173
Ḥamza b. Zubayr, 296, 364
Hamzīr, 258
Hānī b. Hānī, 264
Ḥarashī, 162
Ḥarrān, 227, 228
Hārūn ar-Rashīd, 218, 237, 240
Al-Ḥasan b. Abu'l-Amarraṭa al-Kindī, 263, 264, 265
Ḥassān b. Thābit, 120
Hawāzin, 126, 128, 143, 155, 157, 170, 178, 336
Ḥawthara, 368
Heraclius, 227, 231, 233, 236, 238, 368
Herat, 203
Herodotus, 180
Ḥijāz, 121, 122, 200, 218, 342, 354, 360, 363, 368
Ḥimyar, 171, 183, 206, 366
Ḥīra, 108, 209, 210, 213, 221, 245, 255, 318, 366
Hishām, 113, 114, 185, 218, 225, 238, 240, 253, 292, 295, 301, 304, 305, 306, 309, 318, 319, 344, 362, 364, 367, 368
Ḥudaybiyya, 141, 303
Ḥudhayfa, 109, 214, 365
Ḥudhayma, 356
Al-Ḥuḍḍān, 172
Ḥulwān, 257, 267, 317
Ḥunayn, 120, 121, 143, 151, 152, 154, 158, 358
Hurmuzān, 257
Ḥuwayṭab, 143

Ibn 'Abbās, 52, 160, 184, 294, 295, 359
Ibn 'Āmir, 310, 318
Ibn al-Ash'ath, 113, 114, 260, 305, 315
Ibn Fūqā, 123
Ibn Hubayra, 233
Ibn Ḥujayra, 356
Ibn al-Lutbiyya, 84, 177, 191
Ibn Rabī'a, 143
Ibn Rafā'a, 240
Ibn Sīrīn, 293, 305
Ibn 'Umar (see 'Abd-Allāh b. 'Umar)
Ibn Zubayr, 139, 218, 293, 295, 342, 353
Ibrāhīm b. 'Abd ar-Raḥmān, 364
Ifrīqiyya, 159, 160, 208, 227, 231, 243, 246, 248, 249, 254, 368
'Ikrima, 318
Imrān, 258
Indus, 315, 335
Iṣfahān, 255, 257, 302
Ishbadād b. Jarījūr, 265
'Iyāḍ b. Ghanam, 227, 228
Iyās b. Mu'āwiya, 356

Jabala, 185
Jābir, 137
Ja'da, 260
Jadhīma, 143, 144
Ja'far b. Zubayr, 364
Ja'irrāna, 157
Jalūla, 149, 213
Jarbā', 206, 366
Jarīr, 160, 162, 320
Al-Jarjūma, 225, 301
Jarmūk, 159
Jashm, 170
Al-Jazīra (see Mesopotamia), 225, 226, 227, 228, 229, 230, 255, 309, 313, 317
Jerusalem, 107, 189, 223
Jews, 105, 121, 140, 141, 152, 175, 199, 200, 201, 205, 238, 262, 312, 363, 365, 366
Al-Jibāl, 255, 257, 267
Al-Jīza, 317
Jordan, 221, 222, 224, 225, 226, 231, 309, 367
Joseph, 77
Juhayna, 120
Al-Jurf , 122
Jurash, 201, 206, 366
Jurdamān, 258
Jurjān, 258, 261

Ka'b, 170
Kābul, 260, 293
Kafarbīs, 258
Kalb, 170, 171, 178, 188
Kaskar, 306
Kasāl, 258
Khadm, 179
Khālid al-Qisrī, 218, 362